*International African Library 21*
General Editors: J. D. Y. Peel, David Parkin and Colin Murray

# TRANSLATING THE DEVIL

D1615493

The *International African Library* is a major monograph series from the International African Institute and complements its quarterly periodical *Africa,* the premier journal in the field of African studies. Theoretically informed ethnographies, studies of social relations 'on the ground' which are sensitive to local cultural forms, have long been central to the Institute's publications programme. The *IAL* maintains this strength but extends it into new areas of contemporary concern, both practical and intellectual. It includes works focused on problems of development, especially on the linkages between the local and national levels of society; studies along the interface between the social and environmental sciences; and historical studies, especially those of a social, cultural or interdisciplinary character.

# International African Library

## General Editors

### J. D. Y. Peel, David Parkin *and* Colin Murray

To Jojada and Sybren

*Judgement Day* (artist unknown): a Ghanaian contemporary depiction of the delights of heaven and the terrors of hell. (Photograph: Janine Verrips)

# TRANSLATING THE DEVIL

## RELIGION AND MODERNITY
## AMONG THE EWE IN GHANA

BIRGIT MEYER

EDINBURGH UNIVERSITY PRESS
for the International African Institute, London

© Birgit Meyer, 1999

Transferred to Digital Print 2010

Edinburgh University Press Ltd
22 George Square, Edinburgh

Typeset in Plantin
by Koinonia, Bury
Printed and bound in Great Britain by
CPI Antony Rowe, Chippenham and Eastbourne

Publication was made possible in part by
a grant from the Netherlands Organisation
for Scientific Research (NWO)

A CIP record for this book is available
from the British Library

ISBN 0 7486 1303 X (paperback)

# CONTENTS

# LIST OF MAPS AND TABLES

# PREFACE

*Nunya adidoe asi metu ne o*, 'Knowledge is like a Baobab-tree, no single person can embrace it.' This Ewe proverb certainly holds true with regard to this study. During all the phases of working on this thesis my experience was a tremendously social one. Many people contributed to the project with their particular knowledge; and without it this study would not have been possible.

Financial assistance for the project was provided by the Netherlands Foundation for the Advancement of Tropical Research (WOTRO) and the Amsterdam School for Social Science Research (University of Amsterdam). The latter institution also provided an academic infrastructure which made working on this dissertation a less lonesome and trying adventure than it would have otherwise been.

Conducting historical research in Bremen was made possible through the support of Reverend Dieter Lenz of the Norddeutsche Mission and Mrs Breitenfeld from the *Staatsarchiv Bremen*. I also owe much to the late Reverend Paul Wiegräbe who related his own missionary experiences to me, and to my friends Waltraud Hummerich-Diezun and Irmgard Kirsch-Kortmann who helped me find appropriate information regarding theological questions.

For permission to carry out fieldwork in a congregation of the Evangelical Presbyterian Church (EPC) in Peki (Ghana) I wish to thank Professor Noah K. Dzobo, Moderator of the EPC until 1993. Reverend Edmund Y. Tawia and his wife Salome Tawia kindly let me stay and feel at home in their house in Peki Tsame during my research. The local historian and artist Gilbert K. Ananga, catechist Lawrence Adzanu, Mrs Pearl Kaklaku, Reverend Emmanuel Brempong and Reverend Stanley Amedzro supported and assisted me in many ways. All of them, but particularly Gilbert, led me to 'the ways between the houses', in the words of an Ewe proverb, and made sure that I was not merely a 'stranger with a big eye' who only observes without understanding (*Amedzro ŋku lolo menya xɔdome o*, 'The stranger with the big eye does not know the ways between the houses'). At the University of Ghana (Legon) I received a great deal of help from Misonu Amu (Department of African Studies) and Kodjo Senah (Department of Sociology). Thomas and Alexina Nyaku and Jill Flanders-Crosby kindly provided me with lodgings during my trips to Accra. Jill also taught me a great deal about Ghanaian dance.

In the process of writing I gained much from the critical remarks of friends and colleagues and the many discussions I had with them. My supervisors Johannes Fabian and Bonno Thoden van Velzen inspired me, each in his own particular way, from the project's conception until its eventual completion. I am most grateful to them for their intellectual inspiration and their critical reading. I would also like to thank Pauline Boogaard, Gerard Roelofs, Mattijs van de Port and Milena Veenis for their comments on various chapters, and John Peel for his overall encouragement and his useful suggestions of how to transform a dissertation into a book. In this process I also profited much from the inspiration and suggestions by my colleagues in the Research Centre Religion and Society and in the WOTRO research programme 'Globalization and the Construction of Communal Identities': Gerd Baumann, Peter Geschiere, Patricia Spyer, Peter van der Veer, Peter van Rooden and, especially, Peter Pels. I also thank Felix Ameka for correcting the Ewe transcriptions, and Jonathan Fletcher and Caroline Tingay for carefully correcting my English.

I am also grateful to my parents Hans-Jürgen and Else Meyer for supporting me in various ways. And last but not least I have to thank Jojada Verrips, who accompanied me through all stages of the project. He traced many important books and articles, went with me to Ghana, read my field notes, commented on all the chapters and, above all, encouraged me with his confidence that this book would eventually be realised. Therefore I would like to dedicate this book to him and to our son Sybren who was born in the course of this project.

# LIST OF ABBREVIATIONS

| | |
|---|---|
| BM | Basler Mission |
| BSPF | Bible Study and Prayer Fellowship |
| BSPG | Bible Study and Prayer Group |
| CO | Colonial Office (London) |
| EPC | Evangelical Presbyterian Church |
| EPC 'of Ghana' | Evangelical Presbyterian Church 'of Ghana' |
| MB | *Monatsblatt* |
| MT | *Mittheilungen* |
| NMG | Norddeutsche Missionsgesellschaft |
| Stab | Staatsarchiv Bremen |

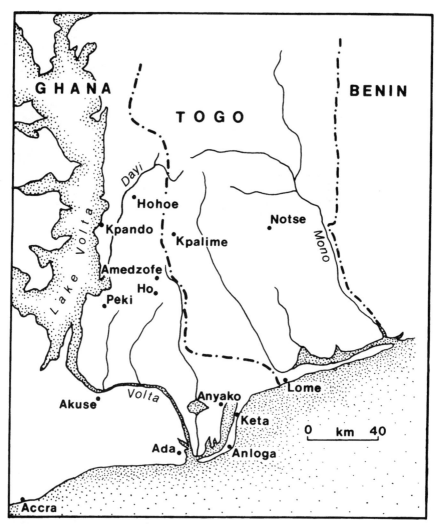

Map 1: The Ewe area between the rivers Volta and Mono

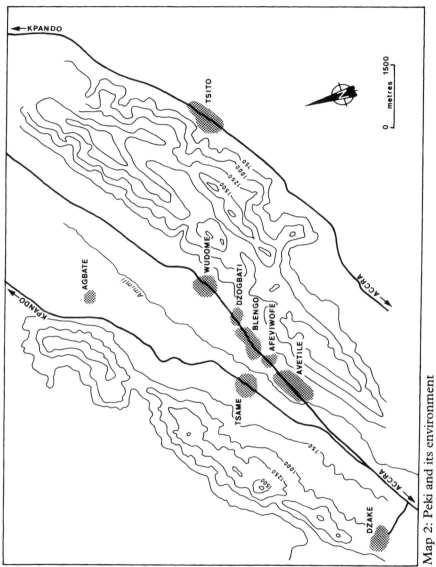

Map 2: Peki and its environment

# INTRODUCTION

In 1989 I started fieldwork among the Peki Ewe in Ghana to gain an understanding of Christianity at the grassroots level. Soon after I began, I visited a prayer service attended by virtually all the Christian churches represented in the area. It was held in the chapel of the Evangelical Presbyterian Church (EPC), a mission church which was established as a result of the activities of nineteenth-century German Pietist missionaries from the Norddeutsche Missionsgesellschaft (NMG), in Peki Blengo. This All Churches Prayer brought together various denominations such as Catholics, Methodists and Presbyterians, as well as a great number of African independent and Pentecostal churches. I was struck by the fact that these various and competing churches appeared to be united by a common enemy: the Devil. A huge part of the service was focused on his evil manifestations. One pastor preached on how to do away with 'pagan' gods which he described as Satan's demons. In the middle of the service there were attempts to exorcise a schoolboy who appeared to be possessed by a local god worshipped in his family, and there were numerous songs and prayers to ward off the Devil.

In the All Churches Prayer I began to realise the immense importance of the image of the Devil in local appropriations of Christianity among the Ewe. The Devil was called upon to draw a boundary between Christianity and 'heathendom' – in other words Ewe religion from a Christian perspective – thus demonising Ewe gods and spirits. Yet, as I came to understand in the course of my stay, demonisation by no means implies that the former gods and spirits will disappear out of people's lives. As servants of Satan they are still regarded as real powers that have to be dealt with in a concrete way – rather than as outmoded 'superstitions', as modern Protestant theology would have it. Thus, through the image of the Devil, 'old' Ewe spiritual powers continue to exist. Put differently, the image of Satan offers a discourse with which to approach these powers as 'Christian' demons.

As a matter of fact, people alluded to evil spirits and the Devil so frequently that I was drawn to deal with this apparently pivotal topic in the lives of many Christians as a main focus of my research. Interestingly, talk about demons and the Devil occurred most often and openly in Pentecostal churches. These churches, which have become increasingly popular in Ghana since the mid-1980s,[1] also shape the religious arena in Peki to a large extent.

Indeed, those people who left the EPC for another church mostly attributed their move – or better still, their conversion, which transformed them from 'nominal' church members into 'born-again' Christians – to the fact that the EPC failed to deal with demons satisfactorily because its leaders would take neither the Holy Spirit nor the Devil and his demons seriously. Therefore, this church would be unable to ward off or cast out evil spirits in the name of God and achieve protection and healing. This critique also played a major role in the secession of two prayer groups from the EPC in 1961 and 1991 respectively, which gave rise to two new churches under the name of Agbelengor – The Lord's Pentecostal Church, and the EPC 'of Ghana'. These churches have developed an elaborate discourse on demons as well as a number of rituals to deal with them. Along with the EPC, these two churches came to form my main field of investigation, and this study is about these three organisations and the relationships among them. I propose that by examining the images of the Devil held in these churches, it is possible to gain insight into the intricate process of the appropriation of Christianity at the grassroots level, as well as the widespread desertion of the mission-derived churches for Pentecostalism.

Yet all this is not enough to account for the evolution of Ewe appropriations of Christianity. Despite the fact that by referring to the image of the Devil a boundary is drawn between Christianity and Ewe religion, both share essential features. The point is that in order to be communicated, the Christian message had to be translated into the local language. Christian Ewe discourse thus contains many 'heathen' terms which also account for the peculiarity of local Christian interpretations. Both the image of Satan and Christian Ewe vocabulary in general have a special relationship with Ewe religion. Whereas through diabolisation spiritual beings are represented as demons, translation necessarily involves a positive integration of non-Christian terms. Therefore, it is important to investigate how these paradoxical strategies of both vernacularisation and diabolisation have contributed to local appropriations of Christianity on the borderline of the old and the new religions.

In this study I attempt to go beyond the still current, artificial compartmentalisation of research on religion in Africa, which not only entails a research praxis in which the study of African Christianity and 'traditional religion' appear as two distinct fields, but also an exclusive focus within the former on either African independent churches [2] or, to a much lesser extent, mission churches. [3] Although I agree fully with the call of Beidelman (1974, 1982) and others (e.g. Bowie 1993; Fabian 1971a) to devote more attention to the study of missions, a plea which has resulted in a range of studies concentrating on the relationship between missionaries and anthropologists, [4] and on the interactions of missionaries and non-Western peoples, [5]

I feel that the scope of the research has to be extended. The intricate and often conflicting relationships between mission churches and independent churches at the local level, as well as Christians' attitudes towards practitioners of what came to be reified as 'traditional religion' and vice versa also have to be taken into account. Indeed, the 'real story', which should form the main focus of anthropological investigation, is the 'concealed and mysterious' manner in which local Christianity evolves (Ranger 1987: 182). Gray has also noted the lack of knowledge about the 'myriad small, local Christian communities' and placed the examination of African local Christianity firmly on the research agenda (1990: 66). The focus on local communities does not of course imply any denial of the fact that these communities form part of a wider system. Peki is not approached as an isolated community, but rather as an arena where it becomes visible how people appropriate an initially foreign religion, such as Christianity, and how this appropriation speaks to concerns arising from their incorporation into wider political and socioeconomic processes.

This study refuses to take the accomplished domination of the colonised as a point of departure, and to focus merely on the suppression and alienation brought about by Western influences in general and Christianity in particular. It concentrates on the local appropriation of this religion in an African context by looking at the whole spectrum of Peki Ewe religious ideas and practices at the grassroots level. By doing so, I wish to unravel the ways in which African Christians have come to terms with, and possibly eluded or even subverted Western domination (see also Comaroff and Comaroff 1991). I hasten to add that it is of course not my intention to exonerate missionary Christianity from bringing about alienation and sustaining Western domination in Africa. The point I wish to make is that Christianity at the grassroots level cannot be reduced to the intentions and actions of Western colonial missionaries. African Christianity is not merely an extension of the missionary impact, but a continuously developing product which is shaped by a great number of experiences. Although the main focus is the situation as I experienced it during my fieldwork, in the course of fifteen months in three periods between 1988 and 1992, attention will also be devoted to the Peki Ewe's encounter with the missionaries of the German Pietist Norddeutsche Missionsgesellschaft (NMG) between 1847 and 1914, a seminal period in which the preconditions evolved for what occurs today.

## CONVERSION AND THE TRANSLATED DEVIL

The investigation of local appropriations of Christianity leads directly to the debates on conversion. While Christian discourses of conversion focus on an intra-personal shift of religious allegiance and conviction, social scientists have for some time conceptualised conversion in terms of increasing rationalisation and disenchantment (*Entzauberung*). This view of

conversion draws upon Max Weber's (1978 [1922]) work on religious
change and on the conditions and implications surrounding a turning away
from 'traditional religions' in favour of 'world religions'. Weber's understanding of religious rationalisation has recently been succinctly summarised
by Hefner. 'World religions' differ from 'traditional religions' by: '1) the
creation and clarification of doctrines by intellectual systematizers, 2) the
canonization and institutionalization of these doctrines by certain social
carriers, and 3) the effective socialization of these cultural principles into the
ideas and actions of believers' (1993: 18). These points refer to 'world
religions' in general. A fourth point of importance in the context of this
study relates to Weber's work on Protestantism (1984 [1920]) where he
suggested that the internalisation of this variant of Christianity would
eventually lead to a disenchanted, modern society.

Weber himself of course was aware that this is an ideal type description.
One can sense a tension in his work between the ideal type course of
religious development and the practical historical manifestation of religion
in everyday life. Yet many students inspired by Weber, especially those
introduced to Weber through Parsons, still fail to note this tension, and
understand his work merely in terms of his ideal type abstraction (see, for
instance, Hefner 1993). In this vein, Comaroff critically remarks that 'much
of his [Weber's] contribution to mainstream sociology bore heavy evolu-
tionary freight' (Comaroff 1994: 303). The following quotation dealing
with Christianity is of particular interest in relation to this problem, because
it reveals that Weber certainly noted that there was a gulf between the ideal
type and actual reality of Protestantism:

> The path to monotheism has been traversed with varying degrees of
> consistency, but nowhere – not even during the Reformation – was the
> existence of spirits and demons permanently eliminated; rather, they
> were simply subordinated unconditionally to the one god, at least in
> theory. The decisive consideration was and remains: who is deemed to
> exert the stronger influence on the interests of the individual in his
> everyday life, the theoretically supreme god or the lower spirits and
> demons? If the spirits, then the religion of everyday life is decisively
> determined by them, regardless of the official god-concept of the
> ostensibly rationalized religion. (1978 [1922]: 415–16)

In this fascinating passage Weber points to the gap between official
theological doctrine, with its monotheistic orientation, and people's actual
religious praxis[6] with its emphasis on demons. Thus, the rationalisation
implied in world religions on the level of doctrine does not necessarily imply
the closure of the doctrine and the disenchantment of the world in the praxis
of lay believers. It is exactly this tension – a tension which Weber only hinted
at but did not work out – that I wish to explore in this study. It may be

located between the ideal type description of Protestantism, on the one hand, in terms of a belief in God that is professed by professional modern theologians and taken for granted by many social scientists, and on the other, the popular praxis of demonology or diabology which focuses on the works of Satan and his agents. Thus, rather than inferring the characteristics of Protestantism from the claims of its theologically trained proponents, this study investigates how a historical encounter between missionaries and Africans, which involved both the diabolisation of the indigenous religion and the translation of the Pietist message into its language, gave rise to a peculiar African version of missionary Pietism. I wish to emphasise that although I take the emergence of new meanings from the encounter between the Ewe and the missionaries as a point of departure, this is not a mere hermeneutic enterprise. As Pietist Protestantism is part and parcel of colonialism, the relationship between conversion to Christianity and, simultaneously, to modern forms of life stands central to this study. It is not about ideas surrounding demons as such, but about how these ideas relate to Christians' changing social and economic circumstances.

The popularity of images of the Devil and demons evokes the question of why it is that, in terms of Weber's remark quoted above, demons exert a stronger influence than God on people's interests in their daily lives? What do people need diabology for? Which factors are responsible for the obsession with evil and demons? How does it relate to changes in people's conception of self? Or, more generally, how is people's emphasis on demons related to changes brought about by colonialism and missionisation? In order to answer these questions I examine the relationship between conversion, modernity, (dis)enchantment and the image of Satan.

In this context special attention will be given to the ambivalences stemming from the mission's introduction of the modern conception of the individual person. As Weber noted, this modern conception is essential to both capitalism and Protestantism (see also Van der Veer 1996; Van Rooden 1996). For its Western protagonists, conversion to Christianity was to entail a new definition of personhood in terms of a moral individualism. This went beyond, and represented as old-fashioned, collective forms of identity based on lineage or clan, in favour of new identities centred on nationhood and the nuclear family. However, as this study will amply show, the introduction of the notion of the modern individual self was not taken for granted, but rather gave rise to struggles both within and between people, and in their course much reference was made to the Devil.

Through colonialisation and missionisation the Ewe became involved in global processes which had severe and wide-reaching implications for their economic, political, social, religious and personal circumstances. Both colonial agents and a great number of Africans represented these changes in terms of an increasing 'civilisation' and 'progress' that was to replace 'primitive society'. In terms of a more recent, but no less value-laden, discourse the changes accompanying Africa's incorporation into world economics, politics and culture were identified as 'modernising' forces. But against the expectations of the modernisation theorists that dominated social science discourse in the 1960s and 1970s, these modernising forces did not lead to a uniform culture following the model of Western society, but instead gave rise to plurality. Western society itself did not conform to the secularised image of it created by social scientists; even in the cradle of modernity one can discern a reversal of disenchantment (for example, Kepel 1994; Verrips 1993).

The current globalisation discourse has demonstrated the highly ideological content of the assumption that modernisation would bring about replicas of Western modernity all over the world. In practice, globalisation involves the comparative interaction of different forms of life (Robertson 1992) which results in creative processes that have been described as 'creolization' (Hannerz 1987) or 'pidginization' (Fabian 1986). Modernity cannot be defined solely from a Western point of view, since local encounters with harbingers of Western modernity such as colonial traders, administrators and missionaries gave rise to different developments. Therefore, I fully agree with Appiah's remark that 'the question what it is to *be* modern is one that Africans and Westerners may ask together. And … neither of us will understand what modernity is until we understand each other' (1992: 107).[7] Rather than taking a well-defined concept of modernity as a point of departure, what has to be explored is how people have dealt and still deal locally with 'civilising', 'modernising' or 'globalising' forces, that is, forces entailing an increase in supra-local relations, societal differentiation, rationalisation and new notions of personhood. This study seeks to contribute to this project by investigating the relationhip between enchantment and modernity among Ewe Christians.

The notion that people's encounter with modernity and the rise of demonic beliefs are interrelated is of course not entirely new. In recent years anthropologists have shown how political, social and economic changes often give rise to beliefs and practices centred on new occult forces (for example, Behrend 1993; Crain 1991; Edelman 1994; Geschiere 1994, 1997; Lan 1985; Lattas 1993; Luig, 1994; Pels 1992; Shaw 1996; Thoden van Velzen and Van Wetering 1988, 1989; Thoden van Velzen 1990; Van Wetering 1992; White 1993). Through the study of such beliefs and practices, anthropologists are able to assess social tensions as well as individual intra-psychical conflicts resulting from them. Yet up until now, students of conversion in Africa and elsewhere have paid scant attention to this phenomenon and have neglected Christian imaginations of the Devil (Gray 1990: 104; but see Cervantes 1994; Ingham 1986; and Taussig 1980 on Southern America; and Stewart 1991 on Greece). Those participating in

the discussion on conversion in Africa basically understand conversion as a
turn towards the High God and, as a consequence, to a modern way of life
(for example, Horton 1971, 1975). Although the centrality of God in the
Christian doctrine cannot be denied, it is important to realise that the turn
to the Christian God simultaneously implies acceptance of his dark
counterpart as the head of the realm of darkness, that is, of deities associated
with local traditions.

I propose that the image of the Devil, which the Pietist missionaries
exported to the Ewe through translation and which currently receives so
much attention in the Pentecostal churches, played and continues to play a
central role in the process of conversion to Christianity and the
appropriation of it. In contrast to Horton, according to whom 'lesser gods'
lose their importance at the expense of the High God, and inspired by the
authors studying the rise of demonology in the context of change mentioned
above, this study will show that the involvement with globalising forces and
modernity may even stimulate an emphasis on demons, and will go on to
assess why this is the case.

Of course, I realise that an attempt to understand African appropriations
of Christianity through a focus on the occult may be found problematic
because it threatens to confirm existing stereotypes and to exoticise
Africans. Yet the point is that the image of the Devil and demons is a
product of the encounter between Africans and Western missionaries, a
hybrid form which helped to constitute the reality in which both parties
came to terms with each other. It is an image which, in ways similar to that
of the witch, embodies 'all the contradictions of the experience of modernity
itself, of its inescapable enticements, its self-consuming passions, its discrim-
inatory tactics, its devastating social costs' (Comaroff and Comaroff 1993:
xxix). This image lies at the base of the development of a particular
imaginary language through which people constitute their world and are
able to express concerns about what it means 'to be modern' (see also
Geschiere 1997; Mbembe 1992). As this study will show, the images of the
Devil and demons are means by which to address the attractive and
destructive aspects of the Ewe's encounter with global economics, politics
and culture. It therefore forms a link between the study of Christianity and
of African religions, as well as between the 'anthropology of evil' (Parkin
1989) and colonial studies.

## THE RESEARCH

In order to assemble the material for this study I carried out historical
research in the archives of the NMG in Bremen (Germany)[8] and of the British
Colonial Office in London, as well as conducting fieldwork among the Peki
Ewe[9] in Ghana. The historical documents of the NMG form the basis for the
first three chapters of this book. As well as the study of handwritten sources,

I read through the NMG's monthly magazine, the *Mittheilungen* (MT, 1840ff)
or the *Monatsblatt* (MB, 1851ff), from 1847 until 1922, and the yearbooks of
this period. All quotes from the MT and MB presented in this book were
originally in German and are translated by myself. Letters and reports by
native mission workers were originally written in either English, Ewe or
German. Whenever I quote statements that were originally made in German
or Ewe I indicate this; translations of German texts are mine, translations of
Ewe texts are by Misonu Amu, or Gilbert K. Ananga and myself.
Quotations from books by the missionaries Jacob Spieth and Diedrich
Westermann were originally in German and are translated by myself.

During fieldwork, I spoke to a large number of members of the three
churches as well as to representatives of Ewe religion, and attended a great
number of services, prayer meetings and 'traditional' celebrations. I tape-
recorded most of the sermons and interviews. The recordings in Ewe were
transcribed by the native speaker and EPC catechist Manfred Adzah, and
later translated by Gilbert Ananga and myself. In this way, despite my
difficulty in understanding what was being said at the time, I could still gain
insight into the discourses of Christianity and Ewe religion. To a large
extent, my experience of doing fieldwork was one of learning the language of
another discourse.

Working in this way led to the production of a large number of texts
which formed the basis of the present study. Although I take full responsibility for the interpretation I present in this study, I think it is important to
represent the voices of those to whom I spoke. By quoting recorded texts, I
want to emphasise that this study is the product of an intersubjective
encounter between myself and others (Fabian 1971b). By quoting extensively from texts produced in this encounter, readers are also invited to
participate in the encounter and to judge whether they find my interpretations acceptable. If not stated otherwise, all statements quoted were
originally made in English. Most short statements quoted were recorded
during my main fieldwork in 1992; if a statement quoted was recorded in
1989 I indicate this.

Recently, Nukunya (1994), himself a native Ewe, has stressed the virtues
of ethnography produced by native researchers. During colonialism, power
relations between white and black were such that Western ethnographers
could not expect to hear how things really were from informants. In the
same way, postcolonial ethnographers could never be sure whether what
they learned from their informants was true. In his view, despite being
personally involved in his or her culture, the 'anthropologist at home' could
not easily be misled by informants and could thereby produce more
representative accounts. I agree with Nukunya that writing about a foreign
culture is problematic. Perfect knowledge of, and personal experience with,
the culture one studies is certainly a great advantage. However, I think that

the problem amounts to more than the production of a true account. In recent years a great deal of critical work has appeared which problematises the representation of the Other (for example, Clifford and Marcus 1986; Fabian 1983, 1991). There is a growing awareness among anthropologists that ethnographic accounts are products of an intercultural encounter between anthropologists and the people they study and are not simply mirror images of the Other. From this perspective, insider and outsider anthropologists face the same problem. Both have to be aware of the fact that their own bias and the concepts employed by them permeate their accounts.

I understand this study as the product of an intercultural encounter between me, a foreign anthropologist originating from the same country as the missionaries of the NMG, and the descendants of the people evangelised by them. This encounter boiled down to a praxis of translation. I agree with Asad (1986) that the metaphor of translation may blur the fact that in practice cultural translation implies the submission of the culture studied to the dominant discourse of academic anthropology. Translation has to be examined as 'a process of power' (ibid.: 148). But whereas Asad concludes that the translation metaphor is inappropriate for an understanding of what anthropology does and is, I would like to argue that this metaphor can still be fruitful. In fact, Asad's critique is directed towards translation under-stood in a positivist way, which assumes that the transmission of meaning across cultural boundaries is quite unproblematic, thereby reducing the Other to Western categories. I want to advocate an understanding of translation – and hence anthropology – as a creative process, which does not aim for the correct representation of the Other, but which instead is a product of intersubjective and intercultural dialogue (Fabian 1971b). Understood in this way, the translation metaphor is fruitful because it implies a turning away from a positivist anthropology which pretends to represent the Other as he or she 'really' is. I understand my own fieldwork, which included a lot of practical translation, as an encounter with people of another culture that changed my understanding of established terms (such as religion, the body and emotions, the family). The point is that, rather than taking translation for granted and subsuming new experiences under established categories (which, as will become clear below, is basically what the missionaries did), one should realise the creative meaning-transforming process which is at work whenever people of different cultures meet. This is why I still deem it fruitful to conceptualise anthropology as translation, but in the creative – I might even say 'syncretising' – sense.

This study is structured as follows. Chapter 1 provides a historical overview of political, socioeconomic and religious developments in Peki which forms the background to the chapters to follow. Chapter 2 is devoted to the socioeconomic origins and the religious ideas and aspirations of the missionaries in their home base in nineteenth-century Württemberg. In order to determine which message they exported to the Ewe, special emphasis is given to their world view and their conceptualisation of the Devil and popular religion. In Chapter 3 the vernacularisation of the missionary message stands central. I try to show how the missionaries aspired to gain full control over the Ewe language and culture through linguistics and ethnography. Yet through vernacularisation, converts understood the missionary message in their own ways. Chapter 4 focuses on diabolisation and examines ideas about evil in the context of Ewe religion, how Ewe converts took over the image of the Devil communicated to them by the missionaries, how they used this image to draw a boundary between themselves and 'heathendom', and why some of them 'slid back' to Ewe religion. The remaining chapters concentrate on Christianity in Peki between the first secession in the EPC in Blengo in 1960 until the situation I encountered in the period of my fieldwork. Chapter 5 deals with the secessions of Agbelengor and the new EPC, and the old EPC's attempts to keep members within the church. Conflicts between proponents of Africanisation and Pentecostalisation are discussed in the light of the popularity of the image of the Devil and demonology. A detailed description of the doctrines and rituals which the three churches offer their members is provided in Chapter 6. In this context I discuss differences between the independent churches studied by anthropologists in the 1960s and 1970s and the more recent Pentecostal churches. Chapter 7 focuses on how church members experience human-spirit relationships. I present a number of cases of people possessed by 'evil spirits' and try to assess the attraction of Pentecostalism by focusing on the sequence of possession by demons, exorcism and possession by the Holy Spirit. The study is concluded by a brief reflection on the relationship between modernity, time and the image of the Devil.

In writing this ethnography I have made use of passages from articles written earlier (Meyer 1992, 1994, 1995b, 1996).

# 1

# SETTING THE SCENE: PEKI PAST AND PRESENT

PRE-MISSIONARY TIMES UNTIL 1918
## Political and Socioeconomic History

According to oral tradition, the Peki, like all other Ewe *dukɔwo* (states),[1] settled in their present area by the mid-seventeenth century (see Ananga n.d.; Amenumey 1986: 1ff; Mamattah 1976). In the course of a migration movement over several centuries, the Ewe and other peoples were pushed away from Ketu, a town in present Benin, by the expanding Yoruba. They moved westwards and founded the town of Notse (probably before 1600) between the rivers Mono and Haho. Because of the tyrannical rule of the King Agokoli and demographic pressures they formed three migration groups and left Notse (see Spieth 1906: 53*ff, 1ff; Gayibor 1984). They spread across the land between the river Volta to the west and the Mono to the east and founded several small states. An area stretching from the coast to 7°6' latitude north in the west and to 7°2' in the east (see Map 1), it consists of a coastal string with beaches and lagoons in the south, a fertile plain with the Adaklu and Agu mountains in the centre, and a wooded and hilly region with many streams taking their source in the north. The ancestors of the Peki, who belonged to an Ewe group called Gbi, settled northwest of Notse in the northern part of Ewe land; there they founded Gbidzigbe, or Hohoe as it is known today. The Peki, a part of the Gbi, moved southwestwards and finally settled near the Amimli river, a few miles from the Volta in an area covered with thick rain-forest. There they lived by hunting, farming and cattle-breeding, and eventually established the seven Peki towns of Wudome, Dzogbati, Blengo (the capital), Afeviwofe, Tsame, Avetile (the place of the state god Wuve) and Dzake.

Like other inland Ewe, the Peki were organised into various patrilineal and patrilocal clans (*xlɔme*). Several clans together formed one town (*du*) with a *fia* (chief), and several towns would make up the state (*dukɔ*) headed by the *fiagã* ('king' or 'head chief'). One may only speculate about the political organisation and economy of the Ewe states in those days; however, it would appear they did not form one united kingdom, but rather separate, autonomous states allying themselves with others whenever the political need arose.

The inland area, vaguely referred to as Krepe by eighteenth-century Europeans, contained several inland states, the majority of which were Ewe (such as Peki, Anfoe, Tsito, Kpando, Taviefe, Ho, Hohoe and Agotime, see Amenumey 1986: 66), while others were Guan and Kyerepon. Little information is available about the relationships between these states before 1734 when Peki came under the suzerainty of the Akwamu, an expanding Akan state which also controlled some coastal states. The Akwamu developed a lucrative business in slaves and ivory, the most important trade 'goods' of the eighteenth century. Krepe was rich in both elephants and human beings[2] and, in addition, the trade roads linking the coast with the important markets of Kratschi and Salaga in the north led through Krepe. Peki became the advance guard (*tuafo*) of the Krepe wing of the Akwamu army. This implied that Peki contributed to the military subjection of the states resisting Akwamu's hegemony, and collected tributes in the form of human beings, money and ivory from the other inland states for the Akwamu king.[3] The Akwamu and, at their command, the Peki both engaged in slave hunting within the Krepe states, a practice that became increasingly brutal with rising European demand. During the eighteenth century the majority of the inhabitants of Krepe lived in fear: slave raids were common, trade roads were insecure and travelling was perilous.

The political situation was complex: on the coast between Keta and Christiansborg were the Danish forts, the hinterland west of the Volta belonged to the Asante, the area to the east of the river was controlled by the Akwamu who had to pay tribute to the Asante, and the small states of Krepe were either subordinate to Peki or directly ruled by the Akwamu. Both the Akwamu and the Peki were economic and political brokers guaranteeing the continuity of the slave trade and upholding social order even in areas where Danish soldiers were not present. Through loyalty towards the Akwamu, Peki became rich, powerful and also unpopular among other Krepe states: 'Traditions of many Krepe states relate how harsh Peki was in carrying out orders from Akwamu in Krepe land' (Asare 1973: 62).

This power balance lasted until the third decade of the nineteenth century.[4] In 1833, under the leadership of Kwadzo Dei I, Peki, together with many other Krepe states, rose up against the Akwamu (Wilks 1975: 211). Views on the nature of this alliance diverge. Despite the views of many Krepe states that it was merely a wartime alliance, Peki maintained that this alliance resulted in the constitution of a more permanent union and that the *fiagã* became the king of all Krepe. Certainly, following victory, the allied states in its neighbourhood submitted to Peki's leadership. Kwadzo Dei I organised them according to the military-political principles of the Akwamu; that is, he formed a centre (*Adonten*) with a left (*Benkum*) and right (*Nifa*) wing. He controlled Peki itself directly, and the Krepe states to the left and right he controlled indirectly through the *Benkumhene*, the chief of Awudome, and the *Nifahene*, the chief of Boso. The states in the left and right wings paid tribute to Kwadzo Dei, who also held jurisdiction, through the *Benkumhene* and *Nifahene* respectively.

Both tributes and the court represented important sources of income. The military alliance of states thus resulted in a regional confederation with Kwadzo Dei as leader and supreme judge and Blengo as capital. However, due to linguistic and cultural heterogeneity and each state's striving for autonomy, this confederation remained fragile, 'fraught with tension and divisive factors' (ibid.: 137), and there were conflicts with other Krepe states that had been part of the alliance against Akwamu but refused to recognise Peki's leadership. Krepe being primarily an alliance against a common enemy, it was bound to crumble with the disappearance of this threat. Akwamu, however, refused to acknowledge the independence of Krepe, and this gave rise to mutual hostilities including hold-ups, kidnappings and the murder of traders. In 1845, Akwamu made a vain attempt to bring Krepe back under its rule; from then on, conflicts and hostilities between Peki and Akwamu were the order of the day.

Apart from military-political organisation, Peki took over some other elements from the Akwamu: cultural institutions such as the worship of ancestor and chief stools,[5] swearing of oaths, 'talking drums' and drum language (ibid.: 148ff). The number of Akan family names (ibid.: 151ff) as well as the names of weekdays and birthdays and other Akan loan words used in Peki all point to the influence of the Akwamu (ibid.: 153ff). These elements spread through Peki to the entire Krepe area. The existence of this Akan influence indicates that it is inappropriate to conceptualise traditional Ewe culture as a fixed, static and closed system.

Without written historical sources, it is difficult to reconstruct the pre-missionary social economy of the Peki. Yet it is possible to generate a tentative picture from, on the one hand, present-day informants' narratives about the past, and, on the other, from missionary ethnography (especially Spieth's *Die Ewe Stämme* (1906), in which he presented Ewe transcriptions of his informants' statements).[6] These earlier informants came from Ho and the surrounding area and since these places were geographically and politically close to Peki, I assume that their descriptions also apply to Peki.

In the inland area, every *du* ('town') consisted of several patrilineal and patrilocal *xɔmewo* (clans, in some areas also known as *sãmewo*). In every *du*, there was only one clan entitled to provide the *fia*, whereas the other clans held other offices such as the *tsiame* ('chief's linguist'[7]) and the *amankrado* ('regent'). All the *duwo* forming one *dukɔ* were, as we have already seen, headed by a great chief, the *fiagã*. Each *xɔme* was subdivided into several *fomewo* (families or lineages).[8] The family and clan heads, who maintained contact with the ancestors through libation prayers, were considered authorities by the younger people who were bound to accept their elders' verdicts. Though the Ewe counted descent along the male line (*tɔgbuinu*, or 'father's thing'), they also acknowledged the matrilineal link (*nyurianu*, or 'maternal uncle's thing') with the brothers of the mother. This is reflected in inheritance regulations. Whereas the sisters' children inherited their maternal uncle's (*nyuria*) personal movable properties, except his gun, the brothers (if still alive) and children received the deceased's palm tree plantations, as well as his gun. Land was owned by families tracing themselves to one common ancestor who had appropriated the land in the process of hunting. If this ancestor's name had been, for example, Hati, these families called themselves *Hativiawo*, 'the children of Hati'. Each member of the various *fomewo* was entitled to farm on the land, which was plentiful.

To obtain a wife, the groom had to work for his parents-in-law and present them and his bride with customarily fixed amounts of money, yam and palm wine.[9] Before a wife could reside with her husband he had to build, near his male relatives, a compound of his own, consisting of a house for himself, one for his wife and one to receive visitors. During menstruation, women had to leave the compound and stay in a hut on the outskirts of town. Menstruating wives were not allowed to cook for their husbands. If a man wanted to marry several wives, he had to build a separate house for each of them within his compound. Though men and women both contributed to the production of food consumed in the household, they did not eat together. Instead, the husband shared one dish with his brothers and grown-up sons, while the wife ate together with her female friends, small children and grown-up daughters. In order to run the household smoothly, each partner had to perform his or her duties and avoid disputes and troubles. Until the children were about six years old, both boys and girls stayed near their mother. Once boys reached that age, they accompanied their father who taught them the work of a man. Girls, in contrast, remained close to their mothers who trained them in various tasks assigned to women.

For inland Ewe, land was the basis of production. In principle, they were farmers, though the men also engaged in hunting and, to a much lesser extent, river-fishing. Work on the land was divided between men and women: men were responsible for clearing the bush and preparing the farms. Their main task was the cultivation of yams, which formed the basis of the inland Ewe's diet, being boiled and pounded into *fufu* by the women. While the men had to contribute yams or corn and meat to the household kitchen, the women, on farms of their own, grew vegetables to accompany the soup which went with the *fufu*.

The fact that the Ewe year was organised according to the cycle of yam cultivation reflects the tremendous material and ideal centrality of this crop. The Ewe year began with the planting of yams in February and ended with the yam harvest in December and January. The most important religious celebration was the yam festival held in the middle of the year when the first young yams could be harvested in order to obtain seed-yam. As well as yams, men cultivated maize (which formed the basis of a less popular staple dish, *akple*); palm trees for palm oil and palm wine; and cotton for the production of clothes.

In pre-missionary Ewe society considerable differences in wealth existed, usually achieved through the exploitation of palm plantations and the sale of palm wine or trade. Rich people were expected to assist needy members of their wider family. By lending money to others in need, the rich could greatly increase their wealth: the Ewe practised the giving of family members as security to such wealthy persons in return for loans. The family member given in bondage (*kluvi*), had to work for the money-lender until his relatives were able to buy him back, or until he had worked for an agreed period of time. Wealthy people who took poor people as *kluviwo* and treated them well were held in high esteem; they were called *amegãwo*. Such people usually had several wives and many children. They were also the first to buy European goods, such as gunpowder, rum and cotton thread, from the European traders who gradually replaced the slave traders from the beginning of the nineteenth century onwards.

When the first missionaries of the Norddeutsche Missionsgesellschaft (NMG) arrived in the Gold Coast – today's Ghana – in 1847, they settled in Peki Blengo, the capital of Krepe. Unaware that the Ewe, unlike the integrated kingdom of Asante or Dahomey, consisted of more or less independent small states, the missionaries, in order to Christianise the Ewe, considered it appropriate to take the capital as a point of departure. Only later did they realise that Krepe was in no way comparable to the two neighbouring kingdoms and that mission work could have started anywhere in the area. Missionaries represented the Ewe as people living in fear of their cruel and mighty neighbours, whom they depicted as wild barbarians (see Meyer 1989). This notion was strengthened by the Asante war (1869–74), during which many Ewe were killed or caused to flee and the mission had to give up one of its inland stations. The Krepe states, again obliged to pool their forces, defeated the Asante and Akwamu with the help of the British, the Accra and Akim. Peki, the leader of the Krepe forces, emerged from this war with new political strength and with greater authority over the Krepe confederacy than before.

In 1886, in the aftermath of the Berlin conference, Krepe became part of the British Protectorate of the Gold Coast. In order to prevent German expansion to Krepe, the British, though not eager then to colonise for the sake of gaining control over particular areas, decided to incorporate Krepe into the colony: Krepe had great commercial value because the trade routes between the coast and the north ran through the area. In 1890 the exact border between German Togo and the British Gold Coast was drawn, thereby separating Peki from a great number of *dukɔwo* over which it claimed suzerainty. In this way Peki was reduced to a small state with Awudome proper as *Benkum* and Boso/Anum proper as *Nifa*. Peki, as well as part of the coastal Anlo Ewe, became a definitive part of the Gold Coast, while most other Ewe *dukɔwo*, who wanted to escape from Peki rule and expected more autonomy under the Germans, became part of Togo. In 1890, Peki became part of the Volta River District (Eastern Province) and was administered by the District Commissioner (DC) at Akuse.[10]

In 1898, British rule over the Peki state was officially recognised. Though in theory this weakened the *fiagã*'s position, in practice he was fairly independent because the DC hardly ever visited Peki. As late as 1910, a district report lamented '[H]itherto Kwadzo Dei has been an absolutely independent chief, he was not under German rule and not ruled by the English'.[11] The British 'administration' actually consisted of a deal between the DC and the *fiagã*. The latter agreed to carry out administrative orders that suited British colonial interests, such as implementation of native labour ordinances and suppression of new religious cults, which were thought to disturb the colonial order. Most importantly, he agreed to make sure that his subjects, as well as traders passing through his area, would bring their cotton and other goods to British, rather than German, ports, though the roads to the latter were much shorter. In this way, he sustained British commercial interests. In turn, the DC promised to support the *fiagã*'s political position. When conflict arose between the *fiagã* and Awudome in 1896, and troubles with Boso/Anum began in 1906 (Welman 1925: 21–3), the British administration supported the Peki *fiagã* in his claims over Awudome and Boso/Anum and refused both wings' request for independence.[12] Throughout the colonial period, the British prevented them from breaking away and supported the Peki *fiagã* in the continuous series of conflicts with his disobedient suzerains. Of course, this support of the Peki *fiagã* suited British administrative interests: 'It was far easier and less expensive to organise indirect rule through a single chief who ruled over an extensive chiefdom than through a host of petty ones independent of one another' (Amenumey 1964: 194). Through the policy of 'indirect rule' – though this expression only came into use early in the twentieth century (see Pels 1993: 29ff) – the political relations in Peki were 'frozen'.

With the definitive integration of Peki into the colony and the improvement of the infrastructure, more and more Peki temporarily left their homes to work in the coastal ports of Keta and Accra, the gold mines in Asante, or on the cocoa plantations at Akropong. Through these contacts and the money brought home by the migrants, Peki developed quickly. In the first decade of the twentieth century particularly, many young men spent time in the more developed areas. In Peki there was constant coming and going. Many Peki migrants returned home with cocoa seeds and started cocoa farms.

Cocoa farming then became an attractive source of income, which prevented people from migrating to other areas and quickly became Peki's central cash crop. Acres of virgin forest were burned in order to extend these cocoa plantations. People started to value land as an important source of income and became interested in purchasing private land for themselves. The only people entitled to sell land were clan and lineage heads who had vast areas at their disposal and were in need of money. Gradually, land became a scarce commodity. Rather than applying shifting cultivation, as had previously been the case, almost all available land was now under cultivation. Another result of the extension of cocoa farms was frequent conflicts over land between and within families and clans. These conflicts were also due to the fact that the population of Peki increased – between 1901 and 1921 it grew from 2,889 to 5,686 – whereas land was relatively scarce in the Peki valley (see Appendix, Table 7).

The cultivation of cocoa was popular because once a field was prepared and seeds planted, it did not require much labour, since traders did not differentiate between high or low quality cocoa. At harvest, farmers cut the pods and sold them to trading firms that had established themselves in Peki towns. Virtually everybody, both the 'educated' and non-Christians, became involved in cocoa farming. In Peki, cocoa cultivation was organised on a small scale within the framework of the nuclear family, which replaced the extended family as the basic unit of production. Women and children earned their own money by carrying loads of cocoa on their heads to Labolabo on the banks of the Volta and this remained their source of income until a road was built from Accra to Peki (and beyond), and the first lorry reached Peki in 1927.

The Peki invested money earned through cocoa farming in the construction of new houses, in new furniture, Western clothes and luxury goods, and their children's education. Peki became the most 'modern', 'civilised' dukɔ of all inland Ewe dukɔwo. Some people even ceased cultivating food crops and turned completely to cocoa farming. They bought what they needed on the market.[13]

Some of the old people interviewed complained that cocoa farming had made men 'lazy'. Since money virtually 'grew' on cocoa trees, there was no need for them to engage in the tiring cultivation of yam and other crops. In line with the traditional sexual division of labour, many women, however, continued producing vegetables, both for personal use and for sale. As is often the case in similar circumstances, men profited more from the introduction of cash crops than women.[14] Whereas, in the case of cocoa, the former were able to make a great deal of money without working hard for it, the latter could only earn considerably smaller sums by transporting loads on their heads. Buying jewellery and European materials in return, many women began to invest the money earned by transporting cocoa in petty

trade. Though this was a new source of income, their economic situation
was not as good as that of the men, since women were more burdened with
the production of food for their family than had formerly been the case.

Until the end of the first decade of the twentieth century, the economic
situation was extraordinarily good. But in 1914 cocoa diseases began to
develop in Peki[15] and they remained an enduring feature of the cocoa
plantations in this area. Moreover, with the beginning of the First World
War, cocoa prices fell, and sank even further during the war years. Local
producers became pessimistic about international trade: many neglected
their cocoa plantations, revived oil palm plantations and food crop
production, and bought fewer European products.

## Pietist Protestantism and Colonialism

When the first missionaries started work among the Ewe in 1847, the NMG
did not limit itself to purely religious activities. Though, at home, the
missionaries belonged to a conservative movement (see Chapter 2), in the
African context they paradoxically became the first agents of 'civilisation'
and modernity among the inland Ewe. The same missionising strategy was
always followed: propagating 'civilisation' through evangelisation, they
instigated the establishment of Christian villages (called *Kpodzi*, i.e. 'on the
hill')[16] with a school, church, and small houses for nuclear families. People
were taught basic literacy in the Ewe language and hitherto unknown skills
such as carpentry, masonry and teaching. The NMG also propagated the
cultivation of cash crops such as cotton, coffee, and, most importantly,
cocoa. To the Ewe the mission appeared as a route towards 'progress' and
'civilisation', or as local terminology had it *'ŋku vu'* ('opened eyes') (Meyer
1997b). In striving for *ŋku vu*, the Ewe took up the central term in colonial
discourse, thereby opening themselves up to the civilising offensive of
Western agents aiming at the domination of the colonised. It was the Ewe's
first step into the 'long conversation' (Comaroff and Comaroff 1991) with
Western agents. As we shall see, it was a conversation entailing a continuous
dialectical process of appropriation and alienation in the course of which Ewe
Christians were neither totally free nor fully dominated by colonial agents.

Following the establishment of British and German colonial rule in the
Gold Coast and Togo, the group of converts among the Ewe, who lived in
both colonies, grew steadily. In 1890 the church had 717 members (MB
1891: 17), and in 1914 11,682 (MB 1915: 47). When, as a result of Germany's
involvement in the First World War, the NMG was forced to withdraw from
the field in 1916, it left behind an institutionalised mission church, the Ewe
(Presbyterian) Church, that was organised into a number of districts. It
became formally independent from the mother society in 1922 and from
then on, church affairs were run by native workers.

In 1892, the first year for which the mission drew up statistics, the Peki congregation accounted for 35 per cent of all Ewe Christians (MB 1893: 14). Most teachers and evangelists active on other posts in Ewe-land came from Peki. After the station at Blengo, in existence since 1847, others were opened in the Peki villages of Dzake (1883), Wudome (1889), Avetile (1893) and Tsame (1910), as well as in various places in Awudome. As a result of this explosive growth, *Kpodzi* became too small to contain all Christians; from the turn of the century onwards many built houses or stayed on family compounds in the 'heathen' villages, a development which made control over converts' way of life much more difficult. In 1888 the Reverend Rudolf Mallet, the first ordained Ewe minister (in 1882),[17] was posted to Blengo, a sub-station of the Ho district. The Peki congregation was visited by missionaries on a regular basis and from various accounts of these visits it can be deduced that they were not very satisfied with the work of the indigenous pastor and teachers – according to the missionaries their faith was too 'superficial' – and they found it necessary to bring the young congregation under better control. This was especially important against the background of economic developments which drew Peki fully into the colonial economy – a process during which the NMG ceased to be the sole mediator of 'civilisation' and started to complain about the supposedly loose morals of Ewe converts. In 1906, Blengo became the main station of the newly established Peki district. Two years later the station was again headed by a white missionary, for the first time since 1853.

The missionaries set down new rules of conduct for Christians which matched the Pietist lifestyle, but differed considerably from the Ewe's previous way of life. The first congregational order (*Gemeindeordnung*) was formulated by the missionaries and Ewe mission workers in 1876 and revised in 1909.[18] Submission to the congregational order was equated with obedience to God; Christian life boiled down to the observance of rules which, ideally, should be internalised.[19] Membership of the Christian congregation was confined to the one 'who is baptised in the name of the Trinity, who lives according to the Gospel, and who obeys the order valid in our congregations'. Baptism implied that a person had to choose a new Christian – preferably biblical – name, to reject any 'connection with idol-worship', to refrain from participation in 'heathen ceremonies', and to take off all *dzo* ('medicine/magic') strings and amulets; that is, objects extremely popular as means of personal protection against evil forces (see Chapter 4). Those baptised as children of Christian parents were confirmed as members of the Christian congregation once they had reached adolescence and knew by heart the Ten Commandments, the Creed and the Lord's Prayer.

Every Sunday congregations had to attend church punctually and neatly dressed. Before taking Holy Communion, Christians had to see the head of the congregation, who could disallow their participation if their behaviour had been inappropriate for a Christian. Christian marriages were performed

after having been announced twice during church services. If a previously
'heathen' couple converted, their marriage was confirmed. Noisy marriage
celebrations and the firing of guns on the occasion of funerals[20] were
absolutely forbidden. The mission prohibited childhood betrothals and polygamous marriage, but accepted the marriage of a Christian and a 'heathen'
partner. Divorce was only possible in the case of adultery. The mission
expected Christian couples to share table and bed and disapproved of wives
leaving their husbands alone for a long period of time because this would
encourage adultery. A Christian's property was to be inherited by the close
relatives, i.e. the partner and children. Christian children should 'not go
naked according to the heathen ways, rather a feeling of sense of shame and
discipline should be awakened in and demanded from them' (ibid.). In the
case of death Christians had to make sure that 'clothes, jewelry, objects,
cowries ... were not put into the deceased's grave'. 'Heathen lamentations'
and noise were to be prevented and after the burial in the congregational
cemetery there should be no funeral meal. The sick should never be treated
with 'heathen' medicines, but 'trust in the Lord' instead.

   In 'outward life' Christian behaviour should be honourable, virtuous,
simple, ordered and sober. They were to learn a profession, owe no debts,
and abstain from spending money on rum. Earthly goods were a 'blessing
from the Lord' which should neither be squandered nor kept avariciously.
The Christians' true home (*Heimat*) was heaven. Among the 'heathens' they
should walk with care, without, however, neglecting their obligation to
submit themselves to the political authorities. In line with Romans 13 they
had to obey the government, i.e. the colonial administration as well as the
*fiagã*.

   The whole Christian congregation was to monitor the 'purity of behaviour
and doctrine'. A person who violated this repeatedly, despite being
admonished, should eventually be punished. The most severe punishment
was the publicly announced, definitive exclusion from the congregation.
This implied exclusion from Holy Communion and, if a person lived in a
*Kpodzi*, expulsion from the Christian village. The excommunicated were
considered 'heathens' again. A person expelled was not to receive a Christian
burial. The decision to admonish and excommunicate members was taken
by the presbytery. This organ consisted of the (male) church elders chosen
by the congregation, the catechist, and the native pastor and/or missionary
in charge of the congregation. The order was read to the congregation once
or twice a year.

   Apart from this institutionalised repetition of rules, indigenous teachers
were supposed to provide practical examples of true Christian life. Missionaries devoted much energy to their training. Between 1871 and 1900 twenty
of these students were sent to the missionaries' home base in Westheim
(Württemberg) (Schreiber 1936: 249ff), where they had to learn the virtues

of Pietist family life (see Meyer 1995c). To missionaries, this was a prerequisite for the development of Christianity among the Ewe, and these
German-trained teachers became the central exponents of a Pietist lifestyle.
They met regularly at conferences and discussed topics such as the
improvement of Christian family life. Their material culture – the arch-
itecture of their houses as well as their furniture, household utensils and
clothes – and the way they organised family matters, provided the model for
a Western way of life. Commanding a high status in the new colonial
hierarchy, these teachers were much admired and copied by 'ordinary'
Christians. Although mission work would have been impossible without
these native intermediaries who proclaimed the Christian message in the
most remote villages, missionaries denied the teachers an equal status. Even
after ordaining some of the teachers as pastors, missionaries still adopted a
paternalistic stance towards them and regarded them as not fully mature.
This frequently led to conflicts between missionaries and native workers.
After the missionaries left the mission field in 1916, these teachers became
the leaders of the independent Ewe church.

At the beginning, only a few Ewe were inclined to convert. With the
establishment of colonial rule and the political and economic ramifications
it entailed, however, more and more people were attracted to the new way of
life. It was evident that Christians were the group able to profit most in
colonial society. An answer to the question as to why so many Ewe converted can be found in an essay by the native mission teacher Hermann
Nyalemegbe. According to him, people turned to Christianity for the
following reasons: healing through the medical care of Christians; sorrow
about the death of a child, assumed to be the work of local gods (tr̃wo, sing.
tr̃, see Chapter 3); a marginal position in Ewe society; comparatively cheap
Christian burial and the fact that Christians feared the dead less than
heathens did; Christian clothes and the white marriage; the conversion of a
partner; the fact that Christians neglected taboos and did not die from it; the
work of Christians; and their wealth.[21] Though this essay was described as
superficial by Ernst Bürgi (a missionary in charge of the mission teachers,
who was allowed to stay on in his post after 1916 because of his Swiss
nationality), in my view it leads straight to the heart of the matter: Christian
religion was attractive because it offered the material means to achieve a
prosperous and relatively high position in colonial society.

Though the mission's relationship with both the German and British
colonial administration was not free from tension, missionaries themselves
were proud of their important contribution to the colonial project of
bringing 'civilisation' to the Ewe.[22] For instance, Spieth emphasised the
mission's achievements: 'The civilization which was brought by the mission
and which also enters the country from other sides is best maintained in the

Christian congregations' (1903a: 15). He praised the missionaries for teaching crafts and the cultivation of cotton, cocoa, coffee and rubber, and thus contributing not only to the development of the colony, but also to the evolution of new individual needs. Through their work, be it as craftsmen, teachers, clerks and/or cocoa-farmers, the Ewe Christians had sufficient means to satisfy their want for European goods, thereby supporting colonial trade (ibid.: 16).

The mission did not only provide opportunities to achieve wealth; it also set new directives for its distribution. In an essay on the question of whether the greater part of Ewe Christians understood 'the real meaning of Christian life', Emmanuel Buama, a teacher, wrote of the Peki Dzake congregation: 'Many heathens have many things, and their families are troubling them [so] that they cannot keep what they save. This caused some to be Christians; thinking that being Christians all of their properties will be saved'.[23] The mission's emphasis on the Christian family thus implied that for a wealthy Christian there was no need to share his property with his wider family.[24] Pietism contributed to an undermining of the moral obligation of the rich to assist needy members of the wider family, underpinned by the threat of witchcraft: rich people failing to share risked falling victim to life-destroying witchcraft assaults from their jealous, poor relatives (see Chapter 4). Clearly Christianity not only offered the rich a new ethics allowing them to keep their wealth for themselves, but also a place where they felt emotionally free and secure.

Though they were proud of their contribution to 'civilisation', in line with their belief, missionaries considered material achievements to be 'outward' things that had to be paralleled by an inner individual development. Their stance towards 'civilisation' was paradoxical: whereas they considered it a prerequisite for Christianisation, they detested it at the same time because it made the Ewe focus on the outward rather than on the inward aspects of the Pietist message (Meyer 1997b). Missionaries' accounts abound with complaints about the inner state of the Ewe Christians who had eagerly taken up the material aspects of the mission but failed to supplement this with the Pietist worldview. From a Pietist point of view, all the reasons for conversion given by Nyalemegbe, although implying a rejection of non-Christian religious practices, were outward and materialistic. For missionaries it was not sufficient to leave the old religion because Christian rites were 'nicer' and cheaper, or Christians were free to violate taboos, or the medical treatment provided by missionaries happened to be more successful than local medicines.[25] However, the main attraction of Christianity did lie in these very material advantages. Therefore Nyalemegbe's essay is not 'superficial' at all, but rather an adequate assessment of the situation. In fact, contrary to the missionaries' perspective, it shows that, for the Ewe, religion could not be reduced to a state of mind, but was closely connected with everyday life. To them, it was not just a matter of belief but a praxis linking the ideal and the practical.

Unfortunately, church statistics do not tell us anything about the numerical relationship between men and women, and the age of their members; there has been no study of the NMG's impact on women. However, from missionaries' written accounts and my own investigations, I conclude that the mission began as a predominantly male enterprise and remained as such for a considerable time, at least in Peki.[26] Very much in line with widely shared ideas about the role of women in Western society, the NMG found that a good wife took care of the house and worked on the farm, rather than engaging in trade or similar lucrative occupations. Therefore young women were offered some training with regard to household duties and childcare, but this was in no way comparable to the professional training the mission provided for men expected to become the breadwinners. In line with this view, the mission also tried to intervene in the performance of marriage rites. Whereas traditionally, a bride received certain gifts from her groom, Christian marriage, seen to be a link between individual partners, did not include this practice, thereby depriving the wife of personal property.

In 1892, Spieth complained about the generally low standards of the teachers' wives: in his view they prevented their husbands from leading a Christian family life (MB 1892: 11). It would seem that young men were usually open to change, but women generally remained attached to Ewe religion and the established way of life for much longer. This posed problems for young Christian males, who found it difficult to find a Christian spouse and often had to marry a non-Christian girl who might later convert to her husband's religion. Although it is not surprising that initially the mission was much less attractive to women than to men, it has to be noted that under certain conditions, the mission's emphasis on the nuclear family also implied benefits for women. If a husband was indeed responsible for feeding his wife and children, the woman was relieved of the task of taking care of her children alone. In this way, Christianity countered the increased pressure laid upon women as a result of the men's shift to cocoa cultivation. Another benefit lay in the inheritance rules, which decreed that women and children would inherit everything from the husband and father (MB 1907: 34ff). And if a man married only one wife instead of several, he was able to take better care of her and the children. If a Christian husband did indeed live up to these expectations, it may have proved beneficial for a woman to convert. But if he did not, from an economic point of view, it was better for women to stick to the local ways. It is thus impossible to judge unequivocally whether the mission was beneficial for women. This depended on her familial situation.

In more narrowly religious respects, Christianity was less attractive for

women. Only men were allowed to be pastors, teachers and evangelists. In
Ewe religion, by contrast, women played an important role: inland, only
women were possessed by the gods and functioned as their mouthpieces
(see Chapter 3). In turning to Christianity, women lost this spiritual function,
and so had much to lose and were therefore less open to conversion.[27]
Another reason for women not to convert was their children's health.
Despite occasional successes, the mission could not offer remedies for many
sicknesses which were as good as, or better than, those of the Ewe priests.
Since the mission forbade Christians to resort to such medicines, many
women hesitated to convert. On the other hand, the failure of priests to cure
a child could also provide a reason for women to become Christian.
Compared to men – especially young men who could still undergo training
– women could thus gain far less material and spiritual advantage by turning
to Christianity.

In short, the congregation consisted mainly of people willing to participate
in the economic opportunities occurring as a result of the concerted
economic impulses of the missions, traders and administrators, and to limit
to the nuclear family the distribution of the riches earned through this
participation. They were a new social class of people attempting to
'progress' and profit in colonial society. But this was not reason enough to
be accepted into the Christian congregation. The decision to convert cannot
be reduced to purely economic considerations. Indeed, as we shall see in
Chapter 4, disappointment with the efficacy of Ewe religious practices also
played an important role.

## 1918 UNTIL 1989
## Political and Socioeconomic History

The political situation sketched above changed in 1918, when Germany
lost its African colonies as a result of its defeat in the First World War.
While the eastern part of the Ewe area in former German Togo then
became French, the western part was made a mandated territory under the
auspices of Britain; *de facto* it became part of the Gold Coast colony. The
Peki king petitioned in vain for the return of parts of Krepe that had been
German territory, but the various *dukɔwo* preferred to keep the independence
that had been granted them by the Germans. Thus the disappearance of
German colonial rule did not have direct consequences for Peki's political
situation and, after 1918, the Peki state remained the same size: the eastern
part of the area that had belonged to Krepe prior to the determination of
the border between German Togo and the Gold Coast in 1890 was placed
under British mandate, but not again under the suzerainty of Peki. Again in
1930 the Peki *fiaga* petitioned for unification,[28] but in line with the policy of
indirect rule, the colonial government sought to maintain the boundaries of

the 'native state of Peki' as described by Welman (1925), a British colonial administrator, and law and order within it. Welman represented this state and its history as much more fixed and inert than it actually was. The usual dynamics of traditional politics were not just neglected in theory, but also restrained in practice by the colonial administration, making it difficult for people to, for example, destool a chief.[29] Furthermore, the government was suspicious of self-conscious, educated subjects. In the colonial yearbooks, there are recurrent complaints about the decline of respect for traditional authorities as a result of education. The policy of indirect rule was trapped in a contradiction: the government (together with, and in the same way as, the mission churches) stimulated the creation of a new social class of educated people but, at the same time, denied them a political say. Throughout the entire colonial period, the government was unable to solve this contradiction, and eventually this gave rise to the formation of an intellectual, anti-colonial opposition and the fight for political independence.

After 1918, cocoa cultivation steadily increased, but as suitable cocoa land became a scarce commodity, this increase led to more land conflicts within and between families or lineages. After the first negative experiences of the dependence of cocoa prices on the world market, the farmers' situation improved. Prices rose until the world economic crisis of the late 1920s and early 1930s again turned cocoa cultivation into a barely profitable enterprise. As during the war, people bought fewer imported European products and devoted more energy to the cultivation of subsistence food crops.[30] As a result of this crisis, farmers organised themselves into associations to further the profitable marketing of their products and the situation improved once again until the outbreak of the Second World War.

Many people remember the period between 1920 and the beginning of the Second World War as Peki's golden age. Most houses standing in Peki today were constructed in this period. Virtually everybody made at least some cash through cocoa cultivation. The town was busy, with many European companies buying cocoa from the whole Peki area and offering building materials and European luxury commodities such as tinned food, biscuits, clothes and chinaware. Apart from these firms there were Hausa butchers selling meat as well as traders from Kwahu and Nigeria offering all sorts of desirable goods. An infrastructure developed, connecting Peki more closely with the rest of the colony, and it was possible to travel to Accra within a few hours. Many Peki inhabitants set up as small traders.

In Peki, unlike other regions in the colony where cocoa cultivation was organised on a grand scale involving the employment of migrant labour (Hill 1963), cocoa was to a large extent grown within the framework of the nuclear family and paid labour was hardly used. Women assisted their husbands and received some cash in return, which they could invest in petty trade. Many parents pressured their children to work on the cocoa farms during their holidays in order to earn school fees for the next school year.[31] These children were not supposed to go into agriculture and take over their fathers' cocoa farms, but to pursue their education in order to get well-paid jobs in colonial administration, trading firms, or the church (though the latter's salaries were relatively low). Thus, after building projects, the cash gained through cocoa farming was invested in further education which, in turn, resulted in the (at least temporary) migration of young people to Accra and other commercial and/or administrative centres in the colony.

Both the Second World War and the outbreak of 'swollen shoot' cocoa disease put an end to Peki's prosperity. During the war, which caused almost total decline in the cocoa business, many trading firms left Peki and after 1945 only a few returned. 'Swollen shoot', which had probably been spreading since the 1920s, but was only detected in the late 1930s, devastated the cocoa farms in the Peki area. Moreover, it became evident that in the long run the greater part of the soil around Peki – with the exception of the area around the *Ewetɔ*, the mountain chain separating Peki from Awudome – was not suitable for cocoa cultivation. Gradually, cocoa cultivation in Peki died out until it disappeared completely in the 1950s. By then, not only European firms but also African traders had left. People's scarce financial resources no longer allowed for the purchase of luxury goods and meat, and since a newly built road leading to the northern cocoa-growing areas passed through Tsito rather than Peki, travellers and traders stayed away. In this way, Peki lost its importance as a commercial centre on the trade route connecting north and south, the only testament to Peki's past glory as a bulwark of 'civilisation' being the abundance of schools and teachers, which kept up Peki's reputation as an educational centre (Tawia 1947: 16).

The consequences of this development were serious.[32] All those who had been able to make some cash through small-scale cocoa farming relapsed into relative poverty, relying on subsistence production and being deprived of earning money to satisfy needs that went beyond mere nutrition. As a result both of population growth (see Appendix, Table 7) and cocoa planting, land under cultivation increased. Since fallow periods were short or even absent, soil became more and more infertile and it was increasingly hard to grow sufficient amounts of food. Many young people decided to leave Peki in the hope of succeeding elsewhere. From the 1940s on, not only the educated young migrated, leaving Peki for further studies or well-paid jobs, but also others, including a growing number of women. Some went to Accra and elsewhere on the coast to take up administrative or commercial jobs. Others followed the trade firms up north to the areas around Ahamansu and Jasikan where they turned to cocoa farming once again. Many men left their wives and children in Peki and only returned home for special occasions.

Thus, with the decline of cocoa cultivation in Peki, migration became the only way to make money. Those who stayed were comparatively poor; they had enough to eat, but were more or less dependent on richer relatives for cash. While wives, children and old people mainly remained in Peki, the young and middle-aged men worked outside. Apart from a handful of educated unmarried women who could take up teaching and nursing,[33] women were deprived of a cash income and depended on their husbands' financial fortune and generosity. Some women traded in cloth, small goods and surplus foodstuffs, but since cash was scarce in Peki, this did not yield much profit. Thus, in the course of time, agricultural subsistence production largely came to depend on women, and the burden of feeding their children was placed on their shoulders. In short, this development can be described as the feminisation of agriculture.

Migrants remained attached to their home area. In Accra and commercial towns they could attend meetings of the 'Peki Improvement and Protection Society' that had been founded by educated young people. Members not only helped each other to find jobs, but also tried to further education in the home area. Migrants returned home for festive occasions such as Easter and Christmas, and supported family members' funerals which, I was told, became more and more 'societal': a costly funeral with many guests was considered a prestigious affair, expressing a family's social status. Such funerals emerged during the 1920s. Rather than burying a dead person immediately, as had formerly been the case, the body was kept for two days, during which a grand wake and burial service were performed. But not only the investment in funerals shows that migrants' ties with their extended families were still maintained: many of them also assisted needy relatives by paying for their education or helping them to start a career outside the area. Moreover, the better-off erected large houses at home and offered funds to build schools and chapels, thereby gaining the status of amegãwo ('great people'). Money was now indispensable to attaining high status in local society.

In 1948, Nkrumah visited Peki for the first time in order to campaign for Independence. Sections of the UGCP (United Gold Coast Convention Party) and, after Nkrumah's secession from it in 1949, the CPP (Convention People's Party) were set up in Peki. But whereas many young and educated but not (yet) prosperous people supported the CPP, the 'traditional' authorities as well as the old Christian elites at the core of the mission church were much less in favour of Nkrumah and the end of colonial rule. The CPP's cry of 'power to the people' pushed for more power for the young and the commoners, i.e. groups that held a low position and status in local society, at the expense of the old elites. Both mission church authorities and chiefs, who had worked out an arrangement of mutual acceptance, feared to lose rather than gain through Independence. The *fiagã* thought the departure of the British and the coming of a democratically elected president would reduce his power. In the same way, the old Christian elites feared that the CPP's emphasis on Africa's cultural and religious equality would undermine their influence on church members.

The pre- and early post-Independence period saw a rise in interest in national party politics among the people of Peki, but this political enthusiasm declined in the 1960s. In the long run, both disillusionment with national party politics and the recurrent interdiction of oppositional activities by various post-Independence governments led to the relative neglect of modern political activities. Even in 1991, when the Rawlings government, in power since 1981, lifted the ban on political parties, most inhabitants were reluctant to join any; they trusted neither the process of national politics nor the state.

Those active in political parties had deliberately turned away from 'traditional' politics: it could not fill the gap created by this disillusionment. Moreover, 'traditional' power was not what it had been under British colonial rule. Since Independence, the Peki *fiagã* had to accommodate to the governments of Nkrumah and the presidents following him. In one way or another, all post-Independence governments have been struggling to determine the relationship between the authority of chiefs and the state, which has remained problematic until the present. Though traditional authority was not abolished, it was much more limited in scope (i.e. confined to local politics) in comparison with the period of indirect rule (though the Rawlings government attributed more power to traditional authorities in the District Assemblies from the late 1980s onwards; see also Nugent 1996).

After Ghana's Independence, Peki lost two groups which had formed part of the Peki state. To the dismay of Peki people, the state was reduced in size, consisting of the seven Peki villages of Wudome, Dzogbati, Blengo, Afeviwofe, Avetile, Tsame, Dzake and a few other places in the area. According to the 1984 population census 40,000 people lived in Peki state, and about 15,500 in the seven Peki villages (see Appendix, Table 7). During the reign of Kwadzo Dei XI (installed in 1961), the *fiagã*'s authority has frequently been contested both by other Peki subchiefs and, more recently, by Blengo royal clans. Also, in the 1970s a major conflict with one of the groups which had left the Peki state arose. Peki and Tsito, an Awudome town on the northern side of the *Eweto*, became involved in serious conflict involving violence and deaths over scarce land. The conflict concerned a fertile stretch of land between Tsito and Avetile, which had been fallow for several years. In order to avoid more violent outbursts, the area was placed under the control of government soldiers. A case was brought before the High Court in Accra but remained unsettled. To most inhabitants of Peki, this local land conflict has been the most important political event in the last twenty years. People were deeply disappointed about the national government's failure to take sides and even suspected it of secretly supporting the enemy. This disappointment gave rise to a feeling of 'the whole country is against us' and a subsequent disinterest in the state and national politics.

After the decline of cocoa cultivation in Peki no other profitable sources of income emerged. In the 1970s, German development agencies set up a large maize farm in Agbateh, a newly constructed settlement near Wudome. The project attracted many people from different Peki villages, but after some initial years of good harvests, the fertility of the ground declined rapidly and the machines broke down. Apart from this unsuccessful attempt, no other significant income-generating development projects were instigated. Migration of the enterprising young and the relative poverty of those remaining were enduring features of the area.

## Mission Church Christianity

Following deportation of the NMG missionaries (except the Swiss Ernst Bürgi) in 1916, the Ewe Evangelical Church was formed, comprising all NMG congregations in Togo and the Gold Coast. The church became formally autonomous in 1922 when its first synod was held in Kpalime (Togo). Having almost collapsed in 1914, the church's work was reorganised after the war. The relatively wealthy Peki congregation was itself able to fund the salaries of its own clergy (Grau 1964: 38), and high church taxes were imposed on members. From 1923 onwards, though independent of the NMG, the church was supervised by missionaries of the United Free Church of Scotland, which was also Reformed. This was at the instigation of the colonial administration which, having supervised the church since 1917, wished to ensure the continuation of the church's educational work (Grau 1964: 64ff; 1968: 74ff; Oman 1927). But if in school matters the Scottish Mission could intervene, the Ewe Evangelical Church operated more or less independently as far as church affairs proper were concerned.

In 1923, the NMG was allowed to resume activities in the Gold Coast. The Scottish missionaries stipulated that their German colleagues should respect the young church's autonomy, should not interfere with its organisation, nor challenge its African leaders. Under these conditions some old NMG missionaries returned to the mission field. Yet the NMG had great difficulty in abandoning its paternalism and accepting the young church's independence. Missionaries of the old generation especially could not adapt to the new situation and became involved in authority conflicts with native pastors (see Grau 1964: 121ff; 1968: 74ff). New missionaries arrived in 1926.[34] Unlike earlier, missionaries no longer received half-yearly reports on all stations, and thereby lost one of the main means of control of church life. Being mostly involved in matters of school administration, teacher training and training of pastors, as well as in the church press, they were now even further removed from what happened in congregations.

When the Second World War began in 1939, the NMG missionaries were again expelled from the Gold Coast. After the war, the United Church Board for World Ministries of America (later called the United Church of Christ) sent out the first missionaries, some of whom were of German origin or even related to old NMG missionaries, and they supported the training of teachers and catechists. In 1947, the church celebrated its centenary in Peki, free from German interference. In 1948, an appeal by the NMG to be permitted to return to the mission field was turned down by the Ewe Evangelical Church; its leaders preferred not to work under German domination again (Parsons 1963: 44). When, in 1951, the Scottish Mission voluntarily withdrew, not only the church proper but also school management was completely left in African hands. Meantime, people from other ethnic groups had become members, and so the church's name was changed in 1954 to the Evangelical Presbyterian Church (EPC) (in the Gold Coast) and Église Évangelique du Togo (in Togo). Since then both churches, which hold a common synod every two years, have been supported by partner churches in Germany, Scotland and the United States, and the EPC has been organised into regional presbyteries with several districts, each in turn comprising a number of congregations. Synod is the ruling body, supervises all church affairs and elects the church leader, the Moderator. The EPC's headquarters were installed in Ho.

Well into the 1960s, mission church organisation followed the model developed before 1914. Though more converts now lived outside the Christian village, *Kpodzi* remained the ultimate model for Christian life. There was a core of strict believers who more or less followed church rules. The elders, both male (*hamemegãwo*, 'great men in church') and female (*hamedadawo*, 'church mothers'), were elected from this group. Like non-Christians, Christians used to perform the 'outdooring' of a new-born baby on the eighth day after its birth, but rather than praying to the ancestors, they asked the Christian God to protect the child. Confirmation replaced girls' puberty rites, or *gbelelewɔwɔ* (only after this was a girl considered marriageable).[35] Christian marriage usually encompassed the traditional presentation of gifts to the bride's father as well as a ceremony in church. Well-to-do people, such as teachers, clerks, traders and big cocoa farmers, would marry in European style, while poorer couples would just ask the pastor to bless their union. After the death of her husband, a Christian widow would wear black. Christian funerals were devoid of special rites. The funeral of someone regarded as a 'good' Christian was performed by the pastor, and such a burial was considered to be a gateway to heaven. However, 'if your life was too rough and you didn't care for the church, they would not bury you,' one old lady (the late Mrs Felicia Ansre) asserted. In such a case, the funeral was performed solely by the deceased's relatives. For many people the fear of not being buried by the pastor because of failure to live according to church rules was an effective threat against 'un-Christian' behaviour.

On weekdays, the congregation assembled as early as 5a.m. for a short morning devotion. On Sunday mornings, a sober church service was conducted according to the missionaries' practice. The congregation remained seated, listening to prayers and the sermon from the pastor, and sang Ewe hymns in Western style (written both by missionaries and Ewe Christians) from the Ewe hymn book. Apart from attempts to introduce tunes composed by African musicians – see Chapter 5 – nothing changed. On Sunday afternoons there were Bible lessons, in the course of which texts like the Ewe translation of Bunyan's *The Pilgrim's Progress* (see Chapter 2) were read and explained to the congregation. There was also a prayer service on Wednesday evenings.

Every three months, on a Sunday afternoon, the communicants met to partake of the Lord's Supper. Gilbert K. Ananga related how impressed he was when as a small boy (he was born in 1923) he saw his grandparents attend this event. They would be dressed in black and walk to church without saying a word. To Ananga, and probably to all those excluded from attendance, the performance of this ritual, which symbolised full membership and was considered a prerequisite for heaven, was surrounded by secrecy. The pattern of distribution of the bread and wine mirrored that of the church hierarchy: first came the pastors and pastors' wives, followed by catechists and teachers, as well as their wives, then church elders, and the couples whose union had been blessed in church. The last to receive the sacred food were all unmarried people among whom were counted all those merely married traditionally. Thus, the most important church ritual not only separated the full members from the 'less perfect', it also differentiated the communicants in terms of status, thereby reinforcing the church hierarchy. The church's strongest punishment for bad behaviour was exclusion from Communion. If an excluded person failed to repent, he or she would not be buried by the pastor.

For a considerable number of Christians it was difficult to maintain the strict boundary between Christianity and 'heathendom'. There were cases of 'back-sliding', both with regard to violation of strict sexual morals and so-called 'relapses into heathendom'; for example young unmarried teachers were prone to 'fornication' while other church members became involved in 'pagan' customs. The church diary of 1935 reports the excommunication of Christians participating in the stool-cleansing ceremonies performed by the Peki *fiagã* in the context of the yam festival, still the most important annual celebration. The pastor and presbyters made clear to both the members and the *fiagã* that Christians were not to take part in any such rituals. Other 'relapses' occurred on the occasion of the funerals of non-Christian relatives. The fact that Christians found it difficult to abstain fully from participation in rites performed by their families and clans shows how important these bonds remained, despite Christian emphasis on the nuclear family.

Though there are no church membership statistics available for the period under discussion, I gathered from interviews with older church members that the congregation continued to grow. According to Parsons, in 1955 as many as 90 per cent of people living in Peki were baptised (1963: 203). Though this estimate seems rather high, it indicates that church membership grew considerably. The worship of *trɔwo* was on the decline (Tawia 1947: 7). Yet, as will become clear below, this reported neglect of the *trɔwo* did not imply the complete decline of 'heathendom' or, as it came to be called more neutrally, 'traditional' religion; the individual, secret use of *dzo* continued to increase.

The growth in membership was mainly a result of the baptism of children of Christian parents and pupils. Since, as stated above, an ever increasing number of parents realised the importance of education and saw school and church as almost identical, school attendance, and thereby church membership, grew. The fact that the terms *Kristotɔwo* (Christians) and *sukutɔwo* ('school people') were used as synonyms also reveals how deeply intertwined church and school were. The church-school complex was considered the ultimate symbol of, and road towards, 'civilisation'.

In school, pupils had to submit to a strict discipline, which included attending church services. Those failing to attend without excuse were punished (which often meant a beating). People assured me that after leaving school they were happy they were no longer forced to go to church and many stopped attending: 'There was so much compulsion in it, that your determination was, when I finish, I am finishing with this church. You won't see me again' (Dr Seth Bansa on his feelings as a schoolboy). Obviously, it is not easy to obtain faithful believers by brute force. Therefore, one may conclude that the church somehow became a victim of its own success. Whereas it attracted many people, at the same time it lost a large number of them through the implementation of a harsh discipline. For many, Christianity was an outward sign of 'civilisation', whose ultimate demands were difficult to live up to. Therefore, they secretly sought to enjoy life, and to solve their spiritual and material problems by behaviour qualified as 'heathen'.

In the course of time more churches were represented in Peki. After Methodists and Catholics, came the Salvation Army (established in 1935), Jehovah's Witnesses (established in 1937) and the Apostolic Church (established in 1947). They were introduced into Peki by migrants who had previously been members of the Ewe Evangelical Church but for various reasons were disappointed with it. However, not only branches of already existing Western churches were opened in Peki. As early as 1911 the former cook of the Basel Mission Station at Anum had opened the Church of the Second Adam, or Yota Mission, the first independent church active in the area. However, this church disappeared after about twenty years. The time was probably not yet ripe for such independent movements in Peki. Yet, the fact that its members went about almost naked and refused to work, own private property, or have children no doubt also contributed to its decline.[36] The next independent church to be established in Peki, the Apostle's Revelation Society (Baëta 1962), proved more successful. Founded by a former catechist of the Ewe Evangelical Church in the Keta District, it was established in Peki in 1949. But it was only from the 1960s onwards that independent churches entered into serious competition with the EPC.

These developments have to be seen along with the Ewe Evangelical Church's refusal to allow NMG missionaries to return after the war.[37] After 1945 the time of European domination was definitely over. Now the church was to be truly independent from the mission. This quest for autonomy not only had consequences for church leadership as such, but also led an increasing number of lay members to request more African forms of worship. The story of this begins in Chapter 5.

## PEKI AT THE TIME OF THE RESEARCH

At the time of my fieldwork Peki was not (and probably never has been) an isolated locality. Each day, mini-buses conveyed travellers to and from the capital Accra where they underwent new experiences and were confronted with new information before being brought back home. Through these links and contacts with returning migrants, people were well aware of what was going on in the country, especially in the capital. During my stay, there were no direct, regular bus connections with other places in the Volta Region, including the regional capital Ho, but cars came to transport passengers to markets in the area and to bring traders and customers to the Peki market on Wednesdays.

Despite the proximity of the Akosombo Dam, where electricity had been produced since the 1970s, electricity only reached Peki in the mid-1980s. Now there are street lights on the main roads, and those who can afford it (only a small minority) can use electricity to run lights, cassette players, television sets, refrigerators and freezers. Bars also have electricity and this attracts many people who come to listen to music and watch television or videos. Water can be collected from pipes at particular times and at certain places, but due to irregularity of water provision, most people still fetch it from wells. Some prosperous people have water reservoirs on their roofs, which are filled whenever the waterworks open the pipes. There is a post office at Blengo, and a mail van delivers and collects mail weekly. But since the lines collapsed about fifteen years ago it has been impossible to use the telephone kiosk which, like deserted trade stores, stands as a symbol of better days.

The court is presided over by a magistrate judging regional, civil and criminal cases and is situated at Dzogbati. Apart from bars, where tinned food, soap, sweets, batteries and other smaller items are sold, there are no significant shops in the area. In each village there is at least one pharmacy offering drugs against common illnesses. A branch of the Ghana Commercial Bank can be found in Afeviwofe, in front of which the Ghanaian newspapers are sold. Until 1992, an office of the Committee of the Defence of the Revolution (CDR), whose representatives made sure that men and women participated in communal labour, was still situated in each Peki village, but shortly afterwards various political parties opened their own offices. Between Avetile and Afeviwofe there is a communal centre, which is mainly used for film shows and weekend dances.

There are several primary schools in each village as well as one secondary school (in Tsame) and one technical school (in Wudome) which serve the whole of Peki. A teacher training college, attended by students from within and outside of Peki, is on the main road between Tsame and Dzake. There are also several privately organised vocational institutes. Each school requires their students to wear uniform, and one can therefore always discern which institution the pupils attend. Although the main language of communication is the Peki variant of Ewe, most people speak and understand English, the language of school instruction. Many old people complain that education was on a qualitatively higher level when it was still fully in the hands of the churches (i.e. before Independence), but whether this is true or not is difficult to assess.

Apart from church activities there is little entertainment. There are a few drumming and dancing groups (see also Agawu 1995), but attendance of them is frowned upon by Christians who denounce these activities as potentially or actually amoral. In their leisure time women visit their mothers, sisters and friends, while during the day time, many men frequent the little palm wine bars by the roadside where they enjoy a calabash of the cool sparkling liquid and discuss family and village matters with other customers. In the evenings, most prefer to drink Akpeteshi, a strong spirit distilled from palm wine, which is sold in bars found in each Peki village. Most men lack the money to buy bottled beer or lemonade. At weekends, many people attend funerals, which usually involve a wake on Friday evening, a burial on Saturday and attendance at church on Sunday. Since people usually marry within the Peki area, most inhabitants are connected by various kinship ties and there is almost always a funeral of a distant or close relative or friend to attend. Despite economic decline, funerals are still grand, expensive occasions which may involve up to 1,000 guests.[38] In order to meet these expenses, many people become members of a funeral society, which involves the payment of certain fees at each funeral they attend. Once their own time has come, their family can draw on this fund for assistance.

Each village is divided into particular clan areas. For instance in Blengo, where I conducted most of my fieldwork, there are the Adivieyi, Adivieyi Dome, Dzama and Atsiadome clans. Each clan area is further subdivided into family quarters, and each contains the family's male descendants' home. Usually, the wife and children stay in the husband's own building or, if he does not own one, in his family house (a house inhabited by a man's various sons and their families). However, if a husband is permanently away and cannot provide sufficient space, or if a couple divorced, the wife and children can remain in her family house, sometimes to the dismay of her brothers. Polygamous marriages are no longer the rule, but the prevalence of monogamy does not mean that couples stay together all their life. Divorces are common and there are many women with children from different husbands. Teenage pregnancies occur frequently, often resulting from affairs with married elderly men who attract girls because they pay their school fees or present them with small highly sought-after luxury items. But pregnancies may also result from a girl's relationship with a young man who is unable to obtain sufficient funds to marry her. In this situation, even if a man admits he is the father, the child will usually grow up in the mother's family.

Most houses are constructed from a mixture of earth and cement and the walls are plastered and painted. Window shutters and doors are made of wood. Most houses are rectangular and the rooms can be reached from a veranda. Family houses usually have an inner courtyard where each wife has her own fireplace. Since the 1930s only a few, mainly prosperous migrants, have been able to construct new houses. If there is enough space, these modern houses, designed for the nuclear family, are still built within the family quarters; if not, they are situated a short distance from the home village. Modern houses are built from cement blocks, have glass windows and contain a kitchen and a bathroom. Owning such a house is a matter of high prestige and for many men this is a lifelong project. But even middle-aged and older men find it hard to achieve this. Though many prefer to live in a house surrounded by their immediate nuclear family, they frequently have to remain within the extended family network. Since in most families not all are Christians (or at least, do not attend church regularly), those who belong to a Christian church and seek to dissociate themselves from Ewe religion still encounter it in their daily lives. In this way, knowledge about ancestors, gods and their worship is passed on.

Those staying at home in Peki are mainly children and youngsters, women of all ages, and some middle-aged and older men, with women forming the majority. Apart from some elderly *amegãwo* who built modern houses as migrants and came to retire at home, most men engage in subsistence farming on the family and clan land or on privately owned plots.

But farming does not often yield much surplus and little cash can be earned. The few working as artisans, tailors, bar owners or teachers are also involved in farming, as are most of the women. As well as this, some people trade on a small scale, either selling agricultural products or goods like sugar, spices, cigarettes, sweets, candles and milk powder in the street or in the Wednesday market. Small traders buy goods in the capital, subdivide them into affordable bits, and sell them to people who are too poor to purchase the product as a whole. A few women bake and sell bread, type letters or make dresses, while an even smaller number work as teachers, daycare centre attendants, midwives and nurses. Salaries are so low that these women also usually grow the food they need and carry out some additional trading. For young people in Peki life is difficult. After leaving school, there are few possibilities of finding a job. If they are unable to migrate and stay with relatives in Accra or other large Ghanaian towns (their ideal), young people often have no choice but to turn to small-scale farming. But this is not very lucrative and it is difficult for young men to earn enough money to get married. If, however, they get a girl pregnant, the burden of caring for the child remains with her and her family. Apart from elderly migrants and a handful of prosperous people, most live on the edge of poverty and, as a result, many suffer from various health problems, above all malaria.

When I asked people in Peki about their situation, their general complaint was that things had steadily worsened. Before, the ground was more fertile and farming was easier, but nowadays people's basic food is cassava rather than yams (whose cultivation would require much better soil and much more traditionally male labour). There were also complaints about the absence of migrant family members working in Accra and other Ghanaian towns as well as in various African and European countries. Whereas formerly they had helped needy members of the extended family, there was now a tendency to limit assistance to one's closest relatives and the funding of prestigious funerals (see also Lentz 1994). Some migrants were even reluctant to return home and share anything at all. This also applied to quite a few husbands working outside the Peki area. Many wives complained that the men failed to send home sufficient money to feed their offspring and pay the school fees. So women had to work harder than ever before in order to care for their children.

I do not think these complaints express mere nostalgia. After 1961 economic decline set in in Ghana as a whole, due to very low world market prices for cocoa on the one hand, and an almost complete dependency on this sector which has continuously been squeezed for money by the 'vampire state' on the other (Frimpong-Ansah 1992). The severity of the situation increased after 1983 when the generally difficult economic situation worsened due to continuous drought and heavy bush fires, resulting in the almost total destruction of food crops. Ever since, poverty has been a continuous feature of Ghanaian people's lives. The World Bank's 'Structural Adjustment Program', which the Rawlings government had to accept because of the disastrous economic situation, resulted in some economic consolidation, but the situation of ordinary people did not improve significantly. Indeed, this programme resulted in more unemployment among state workers and pushed still more people into petty trade and other 'informal' activities. In contrast with some years ago, it is now possible to buy luxury Western goods in Accra, but they are only available to a small minority. For the rest, Western glitter and glamour only generates desires which cannot be satisfied.

The economic decline had severe consequences for all those working in government administration, commercial enterprises or firms. It was not only more difficult to find jobs, but inflation also reduced people's purchasing power. Many people with whom I spoke recalled that, whereas in the 1960s and early 1970s they had been able to spend money on beer, cigarettes and other luxury items, they could no longer afford to do so. With the rising cost of living it became more and more difficult for migrants to take care of their relatives at home, and input of migrant resources into the home area decreased. Thus, because of the bad state of the Ghanaian economy as a whole, migrant labour could no longer alleviate the situation at home as had happened during the 1950s and early 1960s. Both migrants and those remaining at home have barely been able to provide for basic needs such as food, shelter, clothes, education and medical treatment for themselves and their spouses and children, not to mention extended family. Chronic lack of money characterises their lives and, as we shall see, this clearly has repercussions on the religious life of the community.

# 2

# THE HOME BASE OF THE MISSIONARIES

The nineteenth century has been called the century of the missions. Indeed, within the framework of the Awakening, many mission societies aiming to convert all non-Christians within and outside their own society were founded in Europe, (Gray 1981; Neill 1975: 251ff). One such society, founded by Lutheran and Reformed Protestants in Hamburg in 1836, was the Norddeutsche Missionsgesellschaft (NMG). Due to confessional conflicts between the two denominations (the Lutherans contested the ecumenical orientation) the society was reorganised in 1851 as a Reformed Protestant mission society operating out of Bremen (Strümpfel 1902: 51; Wiarda 1936).

Since 1847, when the first four missionaries had been sent to the coast of West Africa in order to find an appropriate mission field, the society had been active among the Ewe.[1] As accounts of colonial history are incomplete without analysis of its Western agents (see Beidelman 1974, 1982; Comaroff and Comaroff 1991: 54), this chapter is devoted to detailed investigation of the background of these missionaries active among the Ewe. In this way, the production of new meanings and practices in the process of the interaction between the Pietist missionaries and the Ewe and local Ewe appropriations of Christianity will be investigated, particularly with regard to divergences from the missionaries' versions of this religion.

## THE NORDDEUTSCHE MISSIONSGESELLSCHAFT: BOARD AND MISSIONARIES

Nineteenth-century Germany was characterised by substantial changes: the gradual transition of traditional corporative and agrarian forms of life to increasingly modern, democratic and industrial ones, which ultimately integrated the German states into the evolving capitalist world economy; the political changes eventually resulting in a German nation state; general suffrage for all adult males; and the cultural and religious transitions following the Enlightenment. The nineteenth-century Christian Awakening, which was inspired by seventeenth- and eighteenth-century Pietism, dealt with the field of tensions that resulted from these changes in its own specific way.

The NMG leaders, the members of the mission board (the so-called Committee), consisted of influential traders and pastors from the upper classes of Bremen. Apart from common conservative political ideas and anti-rational theological opinions, they also shared family ties (Ustorf 1986a: 8–14; 1986b: 124ff). Despite disapproval of empirical-rational thought and modern science, they did not oppose the latest economic and technological developments and the resulting possibilities for the expansion of trade – a paradox characterising not only the NMG, but many other mission societies. Their motivation for organising and partly financing the mission resulted from the conviction that the expansion of the kingdom of God was the task of every true Christian. In their view, mission and world trade belonged together (Tell and Heinrich 1986: 272; MB 1857: 339).

Ustorf (1986b: 160ff) has shown that the NMG board members interpreted political and socioeconomic problems associated with the rise of capitalism from a religious standpoint: poverty as well as political protest resulted from a lack of faith. Consequently, both 'problems' would only vanish through conversion to Christianity. In the same way as evangelisation played a key role in solving problems at home, missionisation was considered to be the appropriate way to 'lift' Africans to 'civilised' standards (including involving them in trade), as the mission terminology put it. Moreover, it was hoped that the conversion of Africans would serve as an example for the destitute and the unbelievers at home, so that they would then return to the church, and peace and order in society would return.

Unlike members of the board, the missionaries recruited did not belong to the upper classes. Most had only basic education and had trained as farmers, craftsmen or petty traders. Most candidates originated from southern Germany, especially Württemberg, which was known for the vitality of its Pietist tradition. After 1850, the NMG missionaries were trained for five years at the school of the Basler Mission (BM), a society which, though much larger and wealthier than the NMG, was based on the same theological and ideological premises.[2] Candidates had to be between eighteen and twenty-four years old, unmarried, healthy males of 'unimpeachable conduct', and willing to obey orders in the mission school as well as later in the mission field.[3] Once accepted into the mission school, they had to put themselves at the disposal of the Society, though the latter had no legal obligation to support them.

To understand the missionaries' background it is necessary to place them in the context of their homebase. Since the Pietist Awakening was heavily influenced by its Württemberg variant and developed its most characteristic form in that area (Scharfe 1980: 25), Württemberg Pietism can serve as a paradigmatic case.[4] Within Württemberg, industrialisation and urbanisation, which brought about new patterns of (mass) production and (mass) consumption, gradually got under way by the mid-nineteenth century,[5] though Württemberg was not fully industrialised until the beginning of the First World War. Meantime, many features of pre-industrial society remained (Jenkins 1978: 7). Though engaged in manufacture and, later, factory production, many people commuted from rural villages to their workplace each day by bicycle or train. Many factories, according to Jenkins (ibid.), would have differed little from traditional craft shops. In their spare time, people worked for themselves, keeping a few animals and cultivating their land.[6] Thus traditional farming, including small-scale agriculture and viniculture, crafts and trades that could be practised in the framework of either traditional or modern production, as well as modern industrial production, existed side by side. Even those employed within the latter two categories alone still possessed some basic agricultural knowledge.

Pietism had a long tradition in Württemberg, reaching back to the seventeenth century.[7] Popular among the *petite bourgeoisie* who made a living by agriculture, viniculture or crafts in the framework of a household economy, the nineteenth-century Pietist Awakening combined a focus on the inner life with an extremely strict and sober way of life. Pietists were part of the orthodox Protestant church,[8] and not only attended the official church service but also a weekly meeting, the so-called *Stunde*, which was conducted in private houses. (The *Stunde*, however, was attended by only a minority of Christians who were often mocked by other villagers.) Pietists took a keen interest in the work of the mission societies, visited the yearly mission feasts, read mission pamphlets and listened to guest speakers trying to win young men for the service of the mission. And through the mission, Pietists became comparatively well informed about other parts of the world.

Pietism was popular among people whose economic and social position was threatened by industrialisation and urbanisation (Scharfe 1980: 135). The mid-nineteenth-century Pietists were not among the poorest but, in order to survive, their lifestyle had to be sober and ascetic. To them, Pietism accounted for the fact that one was still getting along despite all difficulties (ibid.; Medick 1992: 324ff). Moreover, Pietism offered a means of orientation that was of great help in supporting their attitudes towards the modernising world. One of these perspectives that amply illustrates the traditional and conservative character of the Pietist way of solving problems was the idealisation of rural life. Indeed, the villages of Korntal and Wilhelmsdorf, which had been founded by royal charter in 1819 and 1824 respectively, formed the Pietist model of a Christian community (Jenkins 1978: 4; Kottje and Moeller 1974: 131). In these villages craftsmen and farmers lived and worked within the framework of the traditional rural way of life: the extended family was the main unit of production and consumption, and the symbiosis of farming and traditional crafts made for a considerable degree of family autarchy. These model villages continued to uphold the Pietist ideal even after industrialisation and urbanisation had long progressed in Württemberg. Fear that this idealised way of life was threatened by modern developments – a concern enhanced by the fact that the lives of many people no longer corresponded with this ideal – was an important factor in the candidates' wish to become missionaries among 'heathens' who were still unaffected by modern life (Jenkins ibid.). It is ironic that, as we shall see later, in Africa the missionaries were involved in bringing about exactly those developments from which they sought to escape at home.

## PIETISTS AND THE WORLD: THE LANGUAGE OF IMAGES
### The Broad and the Narrow Path

A picture entitled *The Broad and the Narrow Path*, based on Matthew 7: 13–14, was immensely popular in Pietist circles and was alluded to in many other missionaries' life histories. In Württemberg, this lithograph decorated the walls of many homes.[9] This image belonged to the popular culture of the Awakening and allowed religious imagination to link the dualist conception of God and the Devil to the experience of everyday life. In this picture things not explicitly and systematically defined in the Scriptures, and hence open to religious imagination, were defined (Scharfe 1980: 77ff). Since the picture taught Pietists how to look at the world, examining it can aid our understanding of the Pietist worldview (*Weltanschauung*).

At the top of the picture there is an eye in a triangle looking at a hilly landscape through which the broad and the narrow path each run towards their separate goals. A biblical text says that God will look after the just, but not after the 'wrong-doers' (1 Peter 3: 12). The lithograph's first message to the observer is that he is seen. Indeed, Awakened Pietists believed that God was able to look into everybody's heart. The idea of being always observed by God and fear of being rejected by him went hand in hand with the meticulous self-observation of one's 'inner' life. This focus on the 'inner' was and still is a typical trait of Protestantism in general and of Pietism in particular. To be accepted by God, it was not considered sufficient to perform particular rituals as, for example, Catholics did, or to behave well (i.e. to attend church, obey the authorities, follow the Ten Commandments, and love one's neighbour). What really mattered was the individual's state of mind and this was only known to God and the believer. Pietism thus implied an individualistic concept of the self, a self that was always observed by God, whose all-seeing eye had to be paralleled by continual personal introspection.

At the bottom of the picture there is a wall with a small door to the narrow path on the right and a wide gate to the broad path on the left. A signpost points out that one finds death and damnation on the left, and life and salvation on the right. In front of these entrances are many biblical texts discouraging people from taking the broad path and telling them to convert. The two paths stand for the possible course of a person's life. By representing a lifespan as a journey through space, a clear-cut imaginary world is constructed. In contrast to life in the real world, which one cannot overview from birth to death, it is possible to survey life in the imaginary world from beginning to end. By transforming time into space, life thus becomes predictable and, as a consequence, determinable in advance.

The picture suggests that people have to choose the path along which they walk, putting the observer in a position to consider the implications of both ways of life, just as the eye of God does from the opposite end. By representing life as an imaginary world with clear limits, observers are provided with an eye similar to God's, capable of surveying what is really going on beneath the surface of the evidence. The bird's-eye position, which empowers observers to travel through time and see the final consequences of a choice made much earlier on, transcends the chronological order of things. It is a position beyond time, where the truth of the biblical text announcing how one's life will end in either salvation or damnation is illustrated by the images of heavenly Jerusalem on the one hand, and hellfire on the other. In the framework of the imaginary world, biblical text and life event match. This was meant to illustrate the literal truth of the biblical text and how in daily life one had to rely on this truth, rather than analysing it as enlightened theologians did. Being set in front of the imaginary world, the observer is put in the extraordinary position of seeing the truth of the Bible which is not evident in ordinary life. This is exactly the perspective from which the lithograph 'asks' to be viewed, and, in doing so, teaches how Pietists should see the world.

Moreover, the observer is placed on the neutral ground of the outside observer, whereas, according to the Pietist dualist conception of God and the Devil, in real life, people were always on either the broad or the narrow path. In the framework of the picture, future damnation or salvation is thus presented as a result of one's own will to follow one or the other road. As many Protestants found themselves in a state of permanent uncertainty as to whether they would be saved, the emphasis on personal choice was a spectacular message. For, in the framework of the imaginary world, certainty was given with regard to a problem about which many Protestants (Pietists included) were concerned.

This certainty over things unknown in daily life made the imaginary world depicted in *The Broad and the Narrow Path* very attractive. By looking at this image, observers were granted God's perspective, revealing things invisible, uncertain and unknown in everyday life. The Pietists' urge to look behind the manifestation of life in this world and the need for permanent self-observation points to the emphasis on the eye in this variant of Protestantism. However, it was important not in the scientific-positivistic sense, but in a figurative sense: Pietism enabled believers to share the perspective of the all-seeing God, thereby providing them with the consoling idea of maintaining control in a seemingly chaotic world. According to Pietists, true knowledge about the world could not be achieved by science, but could only be revealed by God.

To return to the lithograph, the broad path depicts a number of scenes showing people engaged in worldly pleasures such as eating, drinking, gambling and having sex, and showing reprehensible attitudes such as greed, treason and selfishness; all these depictions are accompanied by references to biblical texts. The path ends in an inferno. The accompanying text notes that this fire stems from the anger of God, and that it will finally destroy the whole earth (Deuteronomy 32: 22; 2 Peter 3: 10). Above the flames there is a pair of scales surrounded by flashes of lightening, which weighs the travellers of the broad path and finds them to be too light (Daniel 5: 27). In the flashes black devils with wings force people back into the fire. Here is the realisation of the vision that the children of the world will eventually be thrown into outer darkness where there will be weeping and gnashing of teeth (Matthew 8: 12). Awakened Pietism was chiliastic in outlook, relying heavily on a Pietist tradition which expected the second coming of Jesus Christ in the near future (Groth 1983). This coming would culminate in the end of this world and the binding of the Devil. Then, on Judgement Day, the damned would be sent to hell and the saved to heaven (Groth 1983: 56ff). The picture represents this in an unambiguous way, thereby producing a certainty which the Bible itself could not provide.

The narrow path forms at many points an opposition to its broad counterpart. No entertainment can be enjoyed here, and though in front of the Sunday School an old man provides two travellers with food, the image merely illustrates care for the hungry and thirsty (Matthew 25: 35), not the pleasure of eating. The picture makes clear that Pietists were not supposed to indulge in bodily pleasures. This echoes Scharfe's account (1980: 80) that Pietists considered such basic needs as sexuality and food to be sinful. Satisfying these needs thus became a moral problem that could only be solved by the systematic distinction between necessity and lust. As far as food was concerned, they developed techniques of asceticism and self-denial. After all, the Devil had overcome Adam and Eve through food. Hence eating was understood as one of the ways through which temptation came, and the course of the broad path depicted clearly what would happen to those who gave in. Pietists also abhorred the pleasure of luxury goods, which, due to the rise in mass production and consumption since the 1870s, had become available to more of the population. Although their sober lifestyle can be described in Weber's terms as inner-worldly asceticism (1984 [1920]), in contrast to the well-to-do seventeenth-century Calvinists examined by Weber, most nineteenth-century Pietists were balancing on the edge of poverty. Rather than having funds for economic investments, their soberness was functional in their fight to survive, and the Pietist ethic provided them with the consolation that there was no need to have more money to spend, since any surplus might result in devilish temptations. Any extra funds should be offered to Pietist welfare institutions.

Pilgrims on the narrow path have to climb a steep staircase and cross a small bridge. Around the landscape there are biblical texts promising salvation. Having passed the old man providing food, the observer sees a man carrying a cross, symbolising that he denies himself and would rather follow Jesus (Luke 9: 23). There is a second text emphasising that people will not be saved because of their deeds, but only by God's grace (Ephesians 2: 8, 9). According to Pietists, salvation could not be achieved through good works as such, though a Christian was nevertheless supposed to behave as well as possible. By granting a look at the world from God's perspective, the image resolved the classical Protestant paradox of the urge to do good on the one hand, and the irrelevance of deeds for salvation on the other, by showing that the eventual reward for good behaviour was eternal life. Those who did good were assumed to be able to do so because God had already chosen them. Choosing to follow the narrow path was a sign that one belonged to the elected. Pietists were therefore encouraged to lead Christian lives all the time. To them, religion was not a matter of attending rituals at particular times, but of dedicating their whole lives to God. They believed that, in contrast to Catholic doctrine, the performance of rituals such as baptism, marriage and burial would not alter a person and not bring him or her closer to salvation. In their view, the performance of rituals as such could not bring about anything, but merely symbolised something done by God already.

Where the path becomes more and more steep, there is a lion threatening three pilgrims. What they cannot see from their perspective – but is revealed to the all-seeing observer – is that the lion is chained. They ward him off with the cross. According to the text the lion is the Devil. The text warns Christians to be on the alert because the enemy is roaming about like a lion, searching for victims to devour (1 Peter 5: 8). There is thus no guarantee that the pilgrim on the narrow path will be undisturbed by the Devil. Though chained, he is trying to tempt even those who have decided to take the path of the cross. The Christian's only remedy against his malicious attempts is prayer, the armour of God (Ezekiel 6: 11). The Devil was an important figure in the Pietist worldview. Later on we shall examine the Pietist image of the Devil in more detail. Here it is enough to remark that even Christians were called on to be permanently on guard against falling for one or other worldly temptation. The only assurance the image provided was that the Devil did not have the power to destroy the pilgrims on the narrow path because God was stronger (Romans 8: 31–4).

The narrow path eventually ends in the heavenly city with the lamb of God in its centre, surrounded by white angels blowing trumpets. The texts around the city leave no doubt that here John's vision from the Book of Revelations has come true (Revelations 2: 10; 5: 11–14; 7: 9; 14: 1; 21; Hebrews 12: 22). The picture thus assures Christians that in the end they will be rewarded for their denial of worldly, bodily pleasures. In contrast to those following the easy, broad path, sober Christians will enjoy everlasting life in heaven, whereas worldly people will perish in flames.

The lithograph not only grants a perspective on the world from God's point of view, but also teaches that this perspective is the right way to view the world. It thus represents the Pietist worldview, and approaches this worldview through the image of the two paths. To achieve a deeper understanding of the Pietist perspective, it is necessary to become aware of what happens in the process of looking at the picture. The point here is not an analysis which aims to look 'behind' the picture, but an awareness of the how the picture 'works' on the viewer.

The lithograph is made up of a series of images which illustrate the Scriptures, and invites observers to understand them by relating them to the world. Its constitutive element is the relationship between the biblical texts, images, and their meaning. This relationship, of course, also stands central to a classic of Christian literature, which has much in common with *The Broad and the Narrow Path*: John Bunyan's (1628–88) allegory, *The Pilgrim's Progress* (1902 [1678]). Published for the first time in 1678, in the 300 years of its existence this allegory has been translated into more than 200 languages (Hill 1989: 375). This classic of Protestant devotional literature, which casts a Christian's lifespan in a dream journey towards Jerusalem, has become part of popular world culture. In the nineteenth century, it belonged to the standard literature read in Pietist circles, the BM and NMG missionaries included, and translations of the book followed the missionaries all over the world. In 1906 the first translation into the Ewe language appeared.[10]

## Words, Images, the Bible and the World

*The Broad and the Narrow Path* and *The Pilgrim's Progress* have virtually the same plot. Being based upon, as well as exemplifying, a strict dualism between God, who is associated with soberness, and the Devil, who stands for the pleasures and values of this world, they depict life as a journey towards a goal: heaven for good Christians and hell for the worldly-minded. And although picture and allegory are different mediums, they tell their story in a very similar way. Both make use of images to convey their message, and link these images and the biblical text in a particular manner. But whereas Bunyan used metaphor to evoke images before the mind's eye of his readers, in the lithograph the images are presented directly to the observers, thereby liberating them from the task of transforming words into images. The picture is an externalisation of the stream of images evoked by the words in the allegory. It visualises the imagination brought about in the mind by reading the allegory, just as in reading the latter, it is up to the observer to realise that, for example, 'way' stands for 'life'. Both picture and word-image entice the observers and readers to find its signification. This similarity implies that literary theories on allegory can be of help in understanding the relationship between image and language, not only in *The Pilgrim's Progress*, but also in *The Broad and the Narrow Path*, and, subsequently, the Pietist worldview itself.

In the examination of figurative speech, anthropologists have focused on metaphors (for example, Fernandez 1974, 1986) and, more recently, other tropes (Fernandez 1991). The study of allegory, however, has been comparatively neglected (but see Fabian 1977). This is regrettable because allegory, though consisting of metaphors and other tropes, is a particular literary genre involving more than a juxtaposition of tropes. There is a characteristic difference between the 'work' of metaphors within and outside the framework of allegory. Metaphors consist of two dimensions: the 'word said' and the 'meaning referred to'. Due to the coexistence of the literal and the figurative, metaphors have a creative potential: by linking one term with another a new meaning emerges. This is at least the case so long as the users of a metaphor are aware of the coexistence of both dimensions – if they are not, the metaphor is dead. By contrast, allegory is defined by the fact that it provides rules for the interpretation of the metaphors and other tropes of which it consists (Fabian 1977). In the framework of allegory, metaphors are restricted and bound to reproduce meanings that are fixed.

But how does this semantic closure actually come about? Or, put more concretely, how does the Pietist worldview emerge from reading Bunyan's allegory and looking at the lithograph? An answer to these questions can be found through Maureen Quilligan's brilliant definition of the genre of allegory, in the course of which she also discusses *The Pilgrim's Progress*. She points out that an allegorical text always implies a pretext, the 'source that always stands outside the narrative' (1979: 97). The relation between pretext and allegory is of central importance because the status of the pretext's language is extended to the allegorical narrative. Christian allegory, whose original pretext was the Bible, can therefore claim to represent biblical truth – a claim acceptable to all those who consider the Bible to be authoritative. Indeed, both *The Pilgrim's Progress* and *The Broad and the Narrow Path* can function as powerful revelations because they profit from the authority of the pretext they claim to illustrate. However, this claim does not imply that they truly represent the biblical text. By embedding images which are not mentioned in the Bible in the biblical image of the 'way', it is suggested that the former derive from the Scriptures as well. Moreover, by presenting images derived from texts scattered all over the Bible – some of them even from unclear passages such as the book of Revelation – within the framework of an orderly imaginary world, picture and allegory provide a clarity and certainty the biblical text itself lacks. This, of course, is interpretation, not mere illustration; both picture and allegory thus clearly profit from the authority attributed to the Bible which they claim merely to expose. They reduce the complexity of the Bible by fixing it into a crude dualistic scheme which is presented as the essence of the Bible.

At the same time, both confirm the authority of the Bible. Quilligan has observed that in Bunyan's classic the language of the pretext is so dominant that his narrative hardly has any autonomy. Bunyan not only remains close to, and often quotes from, the biblical text, but he also lets his main character, Christian, frequently make use of the Bible during his journey. Thus, the pretext is present in the allegory. Bunyan's speaking in terms of the Bible implies a statement regarding human language: he lacks trust in the human capacity to express truth and reveal essential things by its own means (ibid.: 121–31). *The Broad and the Narrow Path* echoes this low opinion of human language and the emphasis on the biblical text. Refraining from the use of human language at all, it abounds in biblical references without which certain images would remain obscure (such as the image of the lion which stands for the Devil). By making observers understand images through the lecture of the pretext, the picture tells its observers that the Bible is the key to understanding what remains unclear at first sight. In presenting the Bible as the only way to reveal truth and understand what is unclear, both allegory and picture (re)produce effectively a central feature of Awakened Protestants' worldview: meaning can only be found through the Bible.

Yet, although I agree with Quilligan's proposition that the meaning of allegory is realised by the reader, I wonder how much freedom Awakened Protestants had in this process. After all, the choices they were to make in their interpretation were based on the pretext. Was not reading *The Pilgrim's Progress* and looking at *The Broad and the Narrow Path* rather a didactic device which tricked them into the Pietist worldview? In my view, one should not overemphasise the freedom of individuals to produce meaning, or underestimate the power of the language of allegory to lure readers into the imaginary world they themselves are expected to produce. In this way, too much emphasis is given to the solitary reader, whereas the ideological function of allegory is neglected. At any rate, Christian allegory, which exposes the biblical pretext, does not simply leave it to its readers to realise its meaning; it also provides rules for its interpretation which limit their freedom (Fabian 1977: 327). They are invited to reproduce the worldview of the social group expressed by the allegory; those who follow identify with that group and distance themselves from others who do not share their worldview.

I therefore conclude that both allegory and picture exercised power to involve their readers and observers in their imaginary worlds and let them reproduce the Pietist worldview by understanding images through the authoritative pretext. Allegory and picture thereby provided exercises through which the Pietist worldview could actively be reiterated and appropriated. Those who did so were confirmed as members of the Pietist group. Providing the didactics of Pietism, allegory and picture taught this worldview as a *practice* applicable in daily life; their worldview was thus not a mere picture of the world fixed in their minds, not a static religious system, but a way of linking the visible and the invisible.

## 'Transgression auf das Himmlische' or the Link between World and Word

In Pietist circles, the idea that only the Bible could make things transparent was applied over and over again in everyday life. Pietists therefore devoted much of their time to reading the Bible, either alone or in the *Stunde*. This reading, however, contrasted deeply with the textual analysis of liberal and rational Protestant theologians which Pietists abhorred. For the latter, reading the Bible was not a question of analysis, but of confirming their faith. Each passage contained divine truth and could be linked to their daily life. In this context it is worth mentioning that the anti-ritualist attitude that goes with the Protestant emphasis on the Word alone did not prevent the evolution of divination rituals in the framework of Pietism (Narr 1957/58: 20ff; Scharfe 1980: 92–7). These, however, were based on the revelatory capacity of the Bible. Both *Bibellose* (a lottery with Bible verses) and *Däumeln* (opening the Scriptures and pointing to a verse arbitrarily) were very popular practices which employed the magic of the Word to understand what had hitherto been unclear and difficult to overlook. This magic was based on the notion that words, albeit biblical ones, were able to act. Whereas this notion contradicted the modern conceptualisation of language as a system of arbitrary signs in which words were separated from the things they describe, it was very similar to the Ewe idea of language which also attributed to words the power to influence things.

The Bible was not only used to understand things that were unclear, but also to transcend daily life in general. In fact, all experiences were considered to be possible vehicles of the divine. Anything that a Pietist experienced could express biblical truth. The fragility of a water glass could remind a Pietist of his own finiteness, dirty dishes or burned pots could evoke the notion of personal pollution through sin, protecting oneself against rain with an umbrella could bring to mind that the only true umbrella was God, a growing vine could be likened to a person's life, etc. This endeavour to find divine meanings behind daily experiences was a typical trait of the Pietist worldview. This activity was called *Transgression auf das Himmlische* or *Geistliche* ('stepping towards the divine' or 'the spiritual'). It was conceptualised as a practice of speaking bringing about a link between ordinary, daily experience and the divine, and it was applied by pastors, popular evangelical writers as well as ordinary believers (Narr 1957/58: 25ff; Scharfe 1980: 97ff). In the framework of Pietism it was thus possible for individual believers to become linked with God. In Awakened

Pietism, a layman could be in contact with the divine as much as a professional pastor.

*Transgression* also provided a treasury of metaphors that could be employed to speak of the world. Indeed, Pietist language abounded in images. Pietists frequently cast experiences in terms of metaphors, be it established biblical images such as 'the way', 'the harvest', 'the war between the Devil and God' or newly created products of *Transgression* which assumed a quasi-biblical status. Pietists considered metaphors the only suitable medium for relating daily life to the divine. Daily experience could thus be rendered meaningful through the capacity of metaphor to let concrete experience 'transform' into an image that linked experience with the divine. This conclusion can be used to criticise the widespread notion of metaphor as a figure of speech concretising abstract experiences, which is analysed without taking into account its embeddedness in practices of speaking (see for example, Lakoff and Johnson 1980: 25). At least in the Pietist religion the task of metaphor was not to concretise experiences which were difficult to grasp, but to connect daily experiences (often not at all difficult to grasp) with the divine. The metaphors used by Pietists were embedded in their allegorical worldview and this limited the creative potential of these tropes to produce new meaning by free association (see also Roelofs 1994). Whenever Pietists spoke in metaphors, the link between the world and God that was brought about with the help of allegory was implied. For that reason it would be inappropriate to approach these metaphors as separate figures of speech. Instead it would be fruitful to introduce the notion of allegory into the anthropological discussion on metaphors and other tropes. In the case of figurative religious language especially, it is worthwhile to focus on this genre, because allegory provides a very special context for metaphorical speech without which the same metaphors would achieve something else.

*Transgression*, which was operative in the appeal to the magic of the Word, as well as in the attempt to discover the divine in daily life and the use of metaphorical speech, was the systematic application of the allegory's and the picture's lesson of how they should be understood. Analogous to these two paradigms, Pietists saw the world as a field for the revelation of biblical truth. In providing the means to detect God's finger in daily experience, *Transgression* inseparably linked the Word with the world. *Transgression* was thus a cluster of practices that confirmed the basic idea of the Pietist worldview and at the same time provided the means with which to relate human beings to God. Though Pietists denied the power of ritual action to link human beings with God, their religion was not devoid of a practical dimension. Rather than through ritual drama, which was central to Catholicism and many other religions, the link with God, in whose light life became meaningful, was achieved by individuals through speaking (and reading, which provided believers with religious images). For Pietists, the visible world became transparent and transcendent through their allegorical language. Speaking in images was the main practice of their religion.

### The Christian Tradition of Diabology

Whereas liberal and rational Protestant theologians tried to sort out contradictions and reconcile the Bible with scientific knowledge through a critical analysis of the biblical text, Awakened Pietists vehemently resisted such an analysis. However, they too – though unconscious of the fact – interpreted the Bible from a particular point of view. The image of *The Broad and the Narrow Path*, which claimed to represent the Bible, actually presented the Book in terms of a crude dualism, reducing its complexity and ignoring uncertainties. The dualistic conception of God and the Devil formed the basis of Awakened Pietists' approach to the Word, and, subsequently, their understanding of the world.

By basing themselves on this dualism, Awakened Pietists relied on a Christian tradition of diabology[11] that speculated about the origins of Satan and the existence of evil in the world and tried to synthesise the scattered biblical fragments concerning these issues. In doing so, this tradition thus went beyond the Scriptures as such. Its diabology was based on information on the Devil and evil provided by the Old and New Testaments, as well as on further speculations that were nourished by the Apocrypha as well as Manichaean and Gnostic thinking.

The diabology of the church fathers provided a myth that went beyond the biblical story of the creation of the world and the Fall and integrated this story into a much more complex cosmological scheme. Though there is some variation, this myth, which was later also communicated to the Ewe, basically runs as follows: God created the cosmos, and thereby the dimensions of space and time. The first creatures he made were the angels, powerful beings with a free will to choose either for or against God. A group of angels, led by Satan, revolted against God and was subsequently cast out of heaven to the lowest place in the universe. The higher an agent had been in the hierarchy of heaven, the deeper he would fall. Then God created the material world, including human beings, who were also given free will. Satan, envying the happiness of Adam and Eve, changed himself into a snake and tempted Eve to eat the apple from the tree of knowledge. As a result they were expelled from paradise, and from then on humanity was under the domination of the Devil and his demons, alienated from God. These demons comprised the gods of the 'heathens' as well as other spiritual beings residing in the cosmos, which could take the form of animals and monsters and attack people with sickness and death. They had to be warded off through baptism, which was thought to achieve the separation of the baptised person from the 'heathen' demons exercising power over all non-Christians (see Kelly 1985), or, if evil should still befall a Christian, another form of exorcism ritual. But eventually God sent Jesus down to earth to open the way for human beings' reconciliation with Him. From then on a cosmic war between God and the Devil with his demons occurred on earth. In this phase, both God and Satan were trying to gain followers. With the end approaching, the Antichrist would appear and it would seem as if Satan would be on the winning side. But the power of the Devil would finally be broken with the Second Coming of Jesus Christ. After Judgement Day, some would enter the heavenly Kingdom of God, whereas others would burn in Satan's everlasting hellfire. Finally, however, the cosmos would be in harmony again. There was disagreement as to whether in the end Satan would be destroyed in hell or finally be forgiven and taken up into the harmony of the cosmos.

The fact that this diabology was not a closed logical system made for its longevity. It could not solve what became known as the theodicy problem, that is, the question of how to reconcile the supposed omnipotence and goodness of God with the existence of evil in the world. This problem brought about a 'creative tension' (Russell 1989: 110) that challenged thinkers to focus on developing new solutions to the problem of evil. But it did not just entice theologians to think again and again about the theodicy problem; its mythological cosmology with the emphasis on the Devil and demons was also popular. The dialectics of theology and folklore triggered a rich imagery around the figure of the Devil. He was imagined to be present on earth in the shape of animals such as black goats, dogs, snakes or dragons, as a misshapen monster with a second face on his belly and bat-like wings, as a person with a lame foot, or as an elegant fellow offering human beings his assistance in exchange for their souls (Russell 1988b: 62ff; 1989: 111ff). The existence of sickness and death, but also anti-social, immoral habits and behaviour such as greediness, were explained by reference to Satan. The iconography of the Devil was enriched by the idea that he was the Lord of 'pagan' gods and ghosts, who thereby became integrated into the Christian diabology as demons. At the same time, this perception of non-Christian religions as the domain of Satan justified the often cruel persecution of people not professing Christianity, such as Jews, Muslims and exponents of 'pagan' cults. In the course of the diabolisation of non-Christian religions, witchcraft, too, came to be considered and persecuted as a satanic activity. Thus, it appears that the figure of the Devil, being ill-defined by the Bible itself, provided much room for continuous speculations about the origins and nature of evil in the world. The prince of darkness is the shady side of both theology and Christian popular religion, which allows for the unrestricted imagination of evil as well as the diabolisation and subsequent persecution of people perceived to be on the side of evil.

Traditional diabology remained popular food for thought throughout the Middle Ages and well beyond the Reformation. The Protestantism of Luther and Calvin, despite their eagerness to sort out ideas that were not strictly scriptural, accepted virtually all aspects of medieval diabology, including the idea that witches were agents of the Devil, and the practice of witch hunting. It has to be noted that, contrary to the still current prejudice that the Reformers had broken with medieval tradition, Protestantism emphasised the Devil's powers even more than medieval Catholicism (Brückner and Alsheimer 1974: 408; Russell 1986: 30; Vogt 1913: 1,155), and saw him at work not only in witchcraft, but in popular religion – 'ordinary' people's religious ideas and practices – in general (Clark 1990). This emphasis on the Devil was above all worked out by Luther[12] who devoted more theological and personal attention to the Devil than anyone else since the desert fathers (Brückner and Alsheimer 1974; Roskoff 1987 [1869]: 365ff; Russell 1986: 34ff; Selge 1993). According to him, the Devil could not only take possession of a human being's heart and entice bad thoughts and behaviour, but also be physically present and confront a person. Consequently, he spoke about the Devil both as an external reality and in terms of a metaphorical personification of bad behaviour (Brückner and Alsheimer 1974: 408). Despite his renunciation of the Catholic practice of ritual forms of protection, Luther kept the practice of exorcism, both through baptism and as a means of driving out evil spirits. His appropriate prophylaxis against Satan was prayer, preaching, Bible lecture, baptism and, last but not least, song. Protestants were held individually responsible for preventing the Devil from entering their hearts through these means. They could never get rid of him because, according to Luther, the more they grew in faith the more Satan attacked them. Luther's ideas about the Devil were popularised and distributed through a range of catechisms, sermons and songs. His best-known contribution to popular diabology was his song 'Ein feste Burg ist unser Gott' which dramatises the opposition between God and Satan and asserts that the latter, despite his attempts, would not be able to get hold of the singers. This hymn, which became *the* song of the Reformation, kept awake the omnipresence of the Devil. It has been included in Protestant hymn books until the present day and has been translated into many other languages, including Ewe, in the course of missionisation. Luther's emphasis on the Evil One also stimulated the growth of Protestant stories about him that were transmitted both orally and in writing (Brückner and Alsheimer 1974: 408; Röhrich 1970; Roskoff 1987 [1869]: 378ff). The popularity of these stories points to the fact that Protestants, following Luther, have always been extremely fascinated by evil. Whereas they had to refrain from the satanic in their lives, it still kept them busy in their minds.

Traditional Christian diabology, which came to be emphasised so much in the sixteenth and seventeenth century by both Catholics and Protestants and culminated in the European witch craze, was heavily attacked by thinkers of the Enlightenment.[13] From the second half of the eighteenth century onwards, scepticism about the existence of Satan gained momentum. The traditional diabology became considered a dangerous 'superstition', responsible for the deaths of thousands of supposed witches and other presumed agents of Satan. At the same time, non-Christian popular religion, based on belief in the existence of spirits, was also denounced as 'superstition'.[14] Thus, from an enlightened perspective, both traditional Christian diabology and 'pagan' folklore were alike in their belief in the reality of demons, while, from a Christian angle, Christianity and 'paganism' formed a radical opposition.

Whereas this criticism in the name of the disenchantment of the world proved unable to abolish either popular beliefs and practices or the traditional Christian diabology, it still had considerable impact on the Protestant churches. By emphasising rational thought, limits were set on the capacity of religion to explain the world. Protestant theologians, following Kant's concept of rational religion (*Vernunftreligion*), which submitted divine revelation to the human ratio, attempted to adjust Christianity to modern rational thinking. Theologians now tried to explain miraculous biblical passages in the Bible scientifically, thereby depriving them of their wonderful character, and discarded the belief in the Devil and demons as folk 'superstition'. Also, liberal Protestant theologians who opposed the rationalistic reduction of religion to morality and strove to recapture the specificity of Christian faith in the post-Enlightenment era,[15] denounced traditional ideas about Satan. In particular, the German liberal Protestant theologian Schleiermacher, the most influential representative of liberal theology, contributed to the destruction of traditional Christian diabology in Protestant theology with his work, *Der christliche Glaube* (first published in 1830).[16] He considered the biblical texts dealing with the Devil and demons as purely culturally determined. Satan and the evil spirits were not demonic realities, but mere images personifying the abstract force of evil. Therefore, Christianity should go beyond the dualistic conception of God and the Devil, which attributed too much power to the latter, and concentrate on God and Jesus instead. Schleiermacher's position came to be accepted by many modern Protestant theologians, who were eager to demythologise concepts of the Devil and demons and who spoke about evil not in terms of a person (*der Böse*), but an abstract force (*das Böse*). This became the position of mainstream Protestant theology up until the present day (Tavard 1981: 298ff).

In the beginning of the nineteenth century, many pastors were inspired by the Enlightenment and subscribed to the premises of rationalism and critical biblical interpretation or were at least in favour of liberal theology. At the same time, Pietists, both theologians and 'ordinary' believers, still upheld the traditional diabology and the dualistic conception of God and the Devil. Whereas both views had until then coexisted and only given rise to theological disputes, from the second decade of the nineteenth century onwards, rational and liberal theology in particular and secularisation in general were heavily criticised by the Protestant (and partly Catholic) Awakening. The Awakening protested against the results of secularisation that increasingly determined all domains of everyday life. The movement was characterised by conservatism, not only in the religious, but also in the political arena. By identifying the ideas of the Enlightenment with the French Revolution, the terror regime of the Jacobins, and Napoleon's struggle for power, the Awakening represented the Enlightenment as a 'French' phenomenon that should be resisted by every good German patriot. In the same vein, the Awakening protested against the democratic and socialist ideas held by members of the middle and working classes who became increasingly non-church in the late nineteenth century. The aim of the Awakening was the restoration and maintenance of the old order (Müller-Salget 1984: 18ff; Lehmann 1989),[17] though, somewhat paradoxically, at the same time modern inventions improving the possibilities of trade and mission were praised. With regard to the Christian religion, the Awakening sought to restore belief in the reality of the Devil, the Last Ordeal and life after death; the ability of God to reveal himself through signs and to observe individuals and to punish or reward them accordingly; and the necessity for Christians to engage themselves in the spread of the Kingdom of God (Lehmann 1989: 45–6). As we have seen, all these points were condensed in the image of *The Broad and the Narrow Path*.

## The Devil Inside and Outside

The image of the Devil and traditional diabology were of central importance to Awakened Pietists. *The Pilgrim's Progress* as well as *The Broad and the Narrow Path* represent the Devil, in good Lutheran tradition, both as a separate agent and as an evil force causing bad attitudes and behaviour. The images of the Devil as a separate person are in line with medieval diabology: in the lithograph he is depicted as a dark creature with horns and batwings, flying around hellfire, or, in consonance with the biblical image, as a lion, whereas he appears as a dark, winged dragon in the allegory. Thus, in the imaginary world evoked by both allegory and lithograph, the Devil still figures as a being. Certain authors have claimed that since the sixteenth century the Devil has been conceptualised less and less frequently as a separate, external being and has gradually come to be understood in psychological terms (see, for example, Russell 1986: 76). It may be true that the Devil was no longer thought to encounter people directly in the external, objective world, but he undoubtedly became omnipresent in the imaginary realm that was so vital for Protestants, albeit before enlightened theology started to deconstruct traditional images of evil. Pietists, who reverted to traditional diabology, considered the imaginary world evoked by the image of the two paths, which granted a glimpse of the world from God's perspective, to be truer than the evidence of this world produced by the human eye. Rather than disappearing completely, the personified Devil was thus transposed into the realm of the imaginary, which Pietists considered the source for the revelation of truth.

At the same time, the allegory and the lithograph define bad and worldly attitudes and depict them as satanic temptations. The Devil was held responsible for all sorts of sexual, culinary, material, anti-social and egotistic desires that enticed people to forgo the heavenly kingdom and finally face Satan in hell. Though Satan, not the individual person as such, was considered the cause of the bad desires, it was up to the individual to fight against them and allow for God's good influence. Rather than protecting themselves against these devilish attacks through rituals, Protestants had to cope with them privately, by relying on the weapon of the Word. Thus, the fight against Satan was basically a permanent inner struggle. According to Pietists, Christians could never be sure of getting rid of the Devil's machinations in this life. Indeed, he was even trying to attack people on the narrow path, an idea that is very much in line with Luther's suggestion that the more believers grew in faith the more they were likely to be attacked by Satan.

Pietists, unlike (academic) mainstream Protestants, did not simply internalise the Devil and come to understand him in psychological terms. The point here is not the internalisation of evil at the expense of its external personification, but the development of the notion that the inner state of a person was the main area of satanic action. Pietists depicted this inner state as an imaginary space where Satan appeared as an external power. Under the condition of internalisation, the Devil kept his old external iconographic form. In the case of Pietists, the internalisation of the Devil thus gave rise to an inner imaginary space within which he still figured as an external being.

However, the notion that the Devil was active in one's own heart did not only encourage careful introspection. At the same time, other people, whose behaviour did not conform to Pietist standards, could be assumed to have Satan ruling their hearts, though only God and the person concerned could know this for sure. Pietists were not wary of representing others as people ruled by, or working for, Satan. In this sense, to them the Devil was still an outward reality present in the world. This conceptualisation of people who did not behave according to certain Christian standards in satanic terms has been common practice in the history of Christianity. It used to be applied to Christian heretics as well as non-Christians. This diabolisation of others is evident in the Pietist attitude towards what they called 'paganism', at home as well as abroad. Before turning to their conceptualisation of those abroad who were to be missionised, it is illuminating to situate the Pietists in the context of nineteenth-century popular religion, by focusing briefly on the work of the Pietist pastor and theologian Johann Christoph Blumhardt (1805–80), who exorcised evil spirits in nineteenth-century Württemberg.

## Exorcising Demons

Blumhardt[18] had a typical Pietist background. He was born into a Pietist family and since his youth had frequently visited the Pietist model village of Korntal (Groth 1983: 70). In 1830, his uncle Christian Gottlieb Blumhardt, who was the first mission inspector of the Basel Mission, invited him to teach at the mission school where the BM and NMG candidates were prepared for their service overseas. After leaving the school in 1837, he remained closely attached to the mission: he was a frequent speaker at mission feasts, held *Missionsstunden* in which he informed the congregations of the work of the mission, wrote a handbook about its history, and had close contacts with missionaries throughout his life. In short, he was an influential man in mission circles.

Blumhardt had been the pastor in Möttlingen (Württemberg) for some years before, in 1842, he was confronted with the sickness of a female member of his congregation. This woman, Gottliebin Dittus, seemed to be possessed by evil spirits. Blumhardt, who had never before dealt with demons and had no experience with their exorcism, devoted the following two years to a struggle with these spirits and finally succeeded in healing the woman. In its aftermath, a Christian Awakening occurred in Möttlingen, during which many people were healed from sickness and demonic possession. Gradually, numerous people from other villages came to seek deliverance through Blumhardt, who would lay his hands on them and pray for them. In 1852 Blumhardt bought the former sulphur bath Bad Boll, where he institutionalised the practice of prayer healing and exorcism. After his death in 1880 the work was taken over by his son Christoph. The practice of prayer healing and exorcism, however, was not confined to Bad Boll. Other men and women, both pastors and lay people, in other parts of southern Germany also engaged in this practice.[19] Thus, Blumhardt's activity was not an isolated phenomenon, but embedded in a wider Pietist practice of healing and deliverance, of which he was its best-known protagonist. This practice, which took place outside the church at the time of Blumhardt, was eventually institutionalised by a faction of the *Gemeinschaftsbewegung* which emerged from the Pietist Awakening. At the beginning of the twentieth century, this faction gradually took the course of Pentecostalism. Thus, there is a direct line from nineteenth-century Awakened Pietism to twentieth-century Pentecostalism (Lange 1979; Maccia 1989; Ruhbach 1989).

Whereas Blumhardt was popular among the people, the church officials, who at that time were not in favour of Pietism, opposed his work, which they considered the domain of medicine, not theology. Even some of his Pietist colleagues were sceptical about his practical exorcisms and ideas about demons. Though the Devil was an omnipresent reality to them, Pietist theologians considered it wrong to talk about him too much, especially if not only Satan himself, but also demons were concerned. To them, the realm of darkness was a hidden reality that should not be touched upon too frequently in Pietist discourse. By contrast, ordinary Pietist Christians were keen to gain deeper insight into this realm. Thus, in Pietism there existed a paradoxical stance towards the Devil: whereas he was considered to be active in people's hearts at all times, or at least threatened to be, it was considered inappropriate to focus too closely on his machinations. A tension existed between his presumed omnipresence and importance on the one hand, and the taboo to speak about the realm of darkness on the other. This tension is a reflection of the fact that, for Pietists, the Devil was horrible but at the same time fascinating; he stood for desires that had to be repressed. Talking about the evil work of the Devil and his demons made it possible for Pietists to somehow confront these desires by viewing them voyeuristically. Hence the popularity of the theme of the realm of darkness. Blumhardt himself did not talk about demonic things in public, but he considered it sinful to simply negate and keep quiet about the work of evil spirits. In order to defend himself he wrote a history of the exorcism of Gottliebin Dittus and some other pamphlets explaining his praxis. His description of the exorcism, which he wrote in the first instance for church officials, was copied illegally many times and finally reprinted as an authorised version in 1850.

It is worthwhile having a closer look at his description. In his account of the struggle against the demons possessing Gottliebin Dittus, Blumhardt not only described an exorcism lasting over two years, but also developed his perspective on demons in the process. In many respects, his account of the exorcism resembles the exorcisms undertaken in the context of Ewe Pentecostalism that we shall encounter later. Blumhardt discovered that spiritual powers had tried to exchange Gottliebin for a changeling when she still was a baby and that she had only been saved because her mother sought the help of Jesus just in time. When she was a little older, she had stayed with a paternal aunt who was known to be an evil woman involved in sorcery. This aunt, who had wanted to teach her certain things when she was ten, fortunately died before Gottliebin reached that age. Other, more friendly relatives tried to protect her by magic. In her childhood and youth she experienced several temptations through devilish money appearing suddenly in her pockets. Though she resisted, because she preferred being poor to being bound to the Devil through riches, she once unknowingly accepted the miraculous appearance of this money because it was accompanied by a biblical text. According to Blumhardt, Gottliebin became linked to Satan through these experiences in childhood and youth, and, as a result, his agents had been able to possess her. But since her spirit resisted being bound to the Devil, the evil spirits had manifested themselves, thereby exposing her latent possession. At times she was possessed by more than 400 demons consisting of fallen angels and spirits of dead people who had failed to break away from Satan because of their sinful lives. Blumhardt prayed feverishly in order to free these spirits from the Devil. In doing so he encountered much resistance from the demonic possessors who scolded him because of his attacks on their power. The more he prayed, the more serious the possession became. Gottliebin developed severe bleedings, and objects of glass, stone and iron, which had once been placed in her body by sorcery, reappeared. She also told him about nightly tours where she witnessed natural disasters which did indeed take place elsewhere in the world. For Blumhardt, this was proof that Satan and his evil spirits were responsible for the catastrophes distressing the world.

Before his involvement with Gottliebin, Blumhardt did not know much about popular beliefs and practices pertaining to demons. He had dismissed the few stories he had heard as fairytales. However, in accordance with the Pietist religion, he had not denied the existence of Satan and shared the traditional Christian diabology sketched above. But in the process of the exorcism he came to realise 'that everything that had hitherto been reckoned under the most ridiculous popular superstition, stepped over from the world of fairytales into reality' (1978 [1850]: 58; original in German, my translation). To him, the case of Gottliebin was thus not an extraordinary, individual sickness, but a revelation of the state of humanity in general. In the course of his confrontation with demons, which he experienced as a revelation of what was going on in the realm of Satan, Blumhardt became aware that the evil of his time, an evil that had affected almost all Christians, Protestants included, was the sin of idolatry, which had gradually developed into sorcery and black magic. He defined idolatry as belief in an other divine, supernatural and invisible power by which a person could obtain health, honour, wealth or other pleasures. But the common practice of using the name of God in the framework of sympathetic magic was also idolatrous. Through the practice of idolatry, people became bound to dark satanic powers. The influence of demons on people could be either physical, causing sicknesses which doctors were unable to heal, or psychical, evoking melancholy or triggering rude desires such as lust, drunkenness, avarice, jealousy, anger and similar desires represented in *The Broad and the Narrow Path*. If people did not become aware of the sinfulness of their idolatrous practices which invited demons to enter their bodies, they would not be able to go to heaven, but remain bound to serve Satan after death. Blumhardt distinguished between being consciously and unconsciously 'bound' to Satan. Whereas black magicians and sorcerers had consciously made a pact with the Devil, many other people, even those accused of witchcraft, were linked to Satan without being aware of the fact through their idolatrous practices and bad behaviour. According to Blumhardt, it was Satan's ambition to obtain numerous followers and it became Blumhardt's declared task to throw light on all powers which operated in the hidden realm of darkness. As soon as both living and dead people became aware of the Devil's influence, they could decide against the evil power. Blumhardt therefore tried to make people aware of what was happening inside them, to drive out demons from the people in whom they were manifest, and to reconcile those demons, who were the spirits of dead people unconsciously bound to Satan, with God. The dualistic conception of God and the Devil was thus the core of his theology, and he found that those 'who did not understand Satan, also did not understand Christ' (Blumhardt, quoted in Schulz 1984: 142; original in German, my translation).

## The Devil and Popular Religion

The case of Gottliebin Dittus, on the basis of which Blumhardt developed his general demonology, has been discussed by several psychologists, physicians and theologians (for example, Barth 1947: 588–97; Bovet 1978; Michaëlis 1949; Schulz 1984). However, I have not come across any serious analysis of Blumhardt's relationship to popular religion, although this is of crucial importance to an adequate understanding of Awakened Pietism. After all, this movement developed not only in response to, and as part and parcel of, modern changes such as industrialisation, urbanisation and rationalisation, but also in the context of popular peasant religion, a religion that, as we can deduce from Blumhardt's account, comprised 'Christians' as well as 'pagans' who were united in their belief in the existence of spirits and the application of certain magical practices. Indeed, in nineteenth-century Württemberg, spirits were still a reality to many people. So-called superstitious beliefs and practices were common among the peasant population. There were people accused of witchcraft, as well as others known as black magicians or sorcerers who could bring about wealth or health for some, and harm others through their magic (see Bohnenberger 1961).[20] Many were members of the Catholic or Protestant church, and would consult these sorcerers at the same time. The Pietists, though they resisted involvement in these popular practices, still lived within this context and had to define their position against these practices. As will be seen, in this respect the missionaries' position at home did not differ much from their position among the Ewe in Africa, and the comparison of conversion and exorcism in the context of Württemberg popular religion on the one hand, and Ewe traditional religion on the other, will be illuminating.

    In the discussion of Blumhardt's exorcism summarised by the theologian Schulz (1984), there are only some few scattered remarks about Blumhardt's relationship to popular religion. Whereas the psychologist Michaëlis found that Blumhardt had surrendered himself to the 'animistic trains of thought of the superstitious environment' (1949: 101; original in German, my translation), Schulz maintained that he had not done so, because he dealt with magic and sorcery *theologically* by considering them as sins separating human beings from God (1984: 164). According to him, Blumhardt did not indulge in animism and 'superstition', but approached these popular phenomena from a distance. These two positions, however, do not seem contradictory to me. Indeed, in contrast to enlightened Protestant theologians who considered popular beliefs in the existence of the Devil and demons as unchristian 'superstitions', Blumhardt came to take these beliefs seriously.

He could do this because, as a Pietist, he believed in the existence of Satan. The point is that the Devil provided a link between Pietism and popular religion. Thus, Blumhardt did not simply surrender himself to popular religion, nor did he merely deal with it theologically in terms of sin. By considering Satan to be the force behind the popular beliefs and practices dealing with spirits, Blumhardt subordinated popular religion to Pietism without dismissing the former as irrational 'superstition'. The spirits of popular religion were thus integrated into the Pietist religion by denouncing them as agents of Satan who could be either dead human beings involved with popular religion in their lives, or angels who had fallen with the Evil One as a result of their rebellion against God. This integration into Pietist discourse, however, occurred at the cost of the diabolisation of popular religion and the exclusion of popular practices of calling spirits and performing magic. From the Pietist point of view, the popular practices which sought to bring about health and wealth bound people to Satan and had to be replaced by the Pietist way of looking at the world, prayer, and allegorical language bringing about *Transgression*.

Of course, this was not new in the history of Christianity. Its protagonists had always been able to diabolise non-Christian religions in consonance with Psalm 96: 5 which states that the gods of the gentiles are demons (see Pfister 1924: 54ff; Pina-Cabral 1992; Schneider 1990; Stewart 1991; Wagner 1930). This viewpoint was re-emphasised by sixteenth- and seventeenth-century Protestant pastors. In contrast to their Catholic colleagues, who confined themselves to condemning witchcraft as satanic, they laid much emphasis on the diabolisation of popular religion in general, thereby launching a total attack on it (Clark 1990). But after the enlightened Protestant critique on traditional Christian diabology, Blumhardt was the first Protestant theologian and author to reiterate explicitly this old way of dealing with other religions, both at home and abroad. Although, as we have noted above, not all Pietists were in favour of practical exorcisms and talk about demons, Blumhardt's stance towards other religions was commonplace among Awakened Pietists. In any case, the missionaries, whether they were in favour of practical exorcism or not, shared this stance in their approach to the Ewe. Indeed, both the NMG mission board and missionaries understood Africa to be a realm of darkness, where the power of Satan was manifest. They considered the Ewe to be servants of Satan, though not yet conscious of the fact. It became the declared task of the mission to open the Ewe's eyes about their condition and fight Satan, just as Blumhardt wanted to fight the Devil by making people aware of his influence on them. At the same time, the Ewe religion was fascinating to the missionaries, because it could provide them with more insight into the realm of darkness that obsessed Awakened Pietists. A sermon by the Pietist pastor Mallet from Bremen, held on the occasion of the departure of two NMG missionaries for Africa on 12 November 1854, pointedly expresses the mission's image of the 'heathens' in Africa:

> Yes, if the heathens were merely unknowing, weak and frail people, if they felt their poverty and misery and longed for salvation; however, among them the Devil has had his unlimited kingdom for such a long time that they have become his slaves and have sunk into bestial and demonic conditions. One has to break chains to free them, one has to overcome Satan's bulwarks to save them from the government of darkness and transfer them into the realm of God's dear son. (MB 1854: 3)

In the chapters that follow we shall examine how the Ewe dealt with the diabolisation of their religion by the missionaries and explore the consequences of this diabolisation for their appropriation of Christianity. This will enable us to analyse in detail the integration of popular beliefs into Christianity under the condition of their subordination.

## THE PIETIST RELIGION

Though anti-modern in outlook, the Pietist Awakening was a phenomenon of its time (see Van Rooden 1990). Its emphasis on individual self-control and its sober ascetic ethics even fitted in perfectly with the evolving capitalist economy that required from workers many of the virtues propagated by Awakened Pietists. Moreover, the denial of 'worldly' pleasures made it easier for people to accept their lack of prosperity and poor working conditions. Nevertheless, although their ethics were adequate for modern conditions, on a conscious level the missionaries defined themselves as opposing the modernity and rationality professed by rational and liberal theologians, liberal philosophers, democrats and socialists.[21] In this definition of themselves as resisting the mainstream ideas of their day, they had to adopt current themes and adapt them in their own way. The Awakened Pietists can thus be described as 'modern conservatives' (see Nipperdey 1983: 452). Later it will be evident that their somewhat paradoxical modern conservatism evoked contradictions in the African context which they were unable to resolve.

Though they went to church and practised baptism, marriage and burial rituals, their religion was anti-ritualist in outlook. This stance implied that rituals were not thought to link human beings and God. Basically, their individual lives as a whole had to please God, and it depended on their total behaviour as to whether they would be saved in the end. However, this alleged neglect of established religious practices does not mean that their religion was devoid of any practice. On the contrary, their religious practice consisted of allegorical speech aiming to achieve a permanent link between the individual and God, transcend the boundary between the visible and invisible, and make daily experiences transparent. This allegorical way of speaking was not confined to particular hours; rather, it took place all the time, since Awakened Pietists were supposed to devote their whole lives to the Lord. In this sense, the main practical activity of their religion was the permanent control of their worldly, bodily desires. This control was achieved by linking all their experiences to God through allegorical and 'transgressive' speech.

The Pietist worldview was a shared way of looking at the world that could be practised in any situation, and one that would nevertheless always reproduce the same message. The reproduction of the same message is based on the fact that the Pietist perspective on the world took a particular definition of the true state of affairs as a point of departure. This definition was represented in the imagery provided by *The Broad and the Narrow Path* and *The Pilgrim's Progress*. Both acquired the authority to reveal truth through the fact that Awakened Pietists accepted the picture's and allegory's claim to provide a glimpse of the real nature of life from God's perspective. This assumption implied a fixed perspective that predetermined how Awakened Pietists should view the world and deal with experiences. All experiences were perceived and described in terms of the dualistic conception of God and the Devil, and explained in the allegorical or 'transgressive' mode by reference to the Bible. No experience could change the basic structure of their approach to the world. This dualism was also at the basis of Pietist ethics, which strictly distinguished between attitudes linking people to 'this' world or the Kingdom of God, and cautioned that joy and pleasure in this world implied suffering in the hereafter, thereby calling for a strict control of Christian bodies and minds.

Through diabolisation, Awakened Pietists could draw a boundary between themselves and others, but at the same time integrate others into their world as representatives of evil. The missionaries could thus already export to Africa a model of how to conceptualise and treat the 'pagans' in the framework of their Pietist worldview, according to which the Ewe were servants of Satan. The Ewe, though still unencountered, were *signifiants* of a predetermined *signifié*.

However, the fixity and closure of doctrine implied in the perception of the daily experiences in terms of the dualistic conception of God and the

Devil were compensated for by the freedom of imagination in the framework of the imaginary space. As we have seen, this space contained a world full of personified attitudes and even certain medieval images of the Devil, hell and heaven. By imagination I mean the process of turning words into images which figure in the framework of an imaginary world, and vice versa. Pietists themselves, however, did not talk about imagination, but instead about the revelation of divine truth offered to them, because they considered images to be given by God, not made by themselves. Though Awakened Pietism was sober in ritual action and strict in representation of divine truth, it was extremely rich and open at the level of imagery. At this level, Awakened Pietists were free to acquire new revelations about the disasters of hell and the sweetness of heaven through dreams, confessions, and accounts of exorcisms. They considered these stories, which they related to biblical passages, as additional revelations of divine truth. The revelations concerning the realm of darkness, however, were much more attractive than those pertaining to the heavenly kingdom. Especially fascinating to Awakened Pietists were confessions by sinners formulated after their conversion, and the accounts of the exorcism of demons, such as Blumhardt's, which provided a glimpse into the realm of God's dark counterpart. Hence we may conclude that the message the missionaries exported to the Ewe was not fully rationalised in the sense of Weber (see the Introduction above). Laying much emphasis on the image of the Devil, missionary Pietism saw the world as enchanted.

But why this fascination with evil? What did the Devil stand for? What was considered 'satanic' in these cases was above all the desire for bodily pleasures, money and personal power to fulfil certain wishes. Awakened Pietists could confront these forbidden desires by way of a detour through the realm of darkness, the ever present dark side in their conception of the world. At the level of imagery, in the position of voyeurs, Awakened Pietists could thus fantasise about 'worldly' desires for food, sex and consumption which they were expected to suppress and control in their lives for fear of ending up in hell. Although even Pietist theologians, not to mention their mainstream colleagues, did not appreciate too much talk of the Devil and his evil machinations, many lay believers were fascinated by revelations about the whereabouts of Satan. This voyeuristic fascination with the satanic was pointedly expressed by Christoph Blumhardt (1842–1919) who, though he continued the work of his father in Bad Boll, was critical of this fascination: 'What stupid people the Christians often are: When they are to talk of heaven, they do not know of anything to say, and when they are to talk of the Devil, they all know something' (1972: 115–16; original in German, my translation). This fascination with the 'satanic' continued to intrigue the missionaries in Africa as well as the readers of their accounts published in the mission journals at home.

# 3

# VERNACULARISATION

Although the missionaries actually devoted a good deal of time to setting up and running mission posts and schools, their main aim, in consonance with Pietism, was to spread the Christian message in order to make converts. Immediately upon his arrival in Peki in 1847, the missionary Lorenz Wolf, who was the first to communicate the Gospel to the Ewe, began preaching. As soon as they had found some suitable interpreters, the missionaries held sermons in any Ewe town they could reach. In this way they gradually involved the Ewe, who were not only interested in the 'outward' aspects of the mission but also in the message proclaimed, in a conversation. In order to understand this process, it is instructive to read of an early discussion between Wolf, a so-called 'fetish priest' and the Peki king (*fiagã*). This conversation contains the characteristic features of the interaction between missionaries and Africans.

> A fetish priest, a well-built man more than seven feet tall, with fetish signs hanging everywhere on his body, visited me together with his entourage, posted himself boastfully in front of me and started bragging: 'God and I are one; he tells me everything.' I [Wolf] asked him what that should mean, and how he knew something about God. 'I go to God in heaven,' he said. I: 'By what means?' He: 'I know it.' I: 'Show it to me.' He: 'No, God and I are one.' I: 'I am afraid you are a liar and you just talk like this to deceive the people, because if you had been to God or if you had really heard about him you would know that God hates the fetishes you claim to have received from him. God is angry with the idols.' Then the King said that all the fetishes came from God. 'No,' I said, 'they are from the Devil.' The fetish priest stood there silently. Then I said, pointing to my Bible, 'Here is God's word, here God talks to us through his dear son, Jesus Christ, and that is why I have come so that you will hear the word of God.' 'Yes,' the fetish priest said, 'that is true. You know about God.' I: 'Do you believe that?' He: 'Yes.' 'Well,' I said, 'then give me the fetishes you wear on your chest, then I shall believe that you believe my word.' He, however, refused and I said: 'Look, how you are a deceiver and a liar.' (MT 1848: 64)

The first point to be made is that this conversation does not represent the actual communicative event, since it is the author's translation of Wolf's German text, which in turn is his translation of his discussion with the two Peki men in Ewe. Things are probably even more complicated: since he largely depended on an interpreter, it is likely that Wolf's German text is a translation of his interpreter's translation of Wolf's statements from English into Ewe, and the priest's and *fiagã*'s statements from Ewe into English. Thus it is a translation of a translation of a translation. But what did the speakers actually say? Or, to put it more generally, what happens to the meanings of words once these meanings cross linguistic boundaries? Regarding the translation of Wolf's German text into English, it can be assumed that it more or less conveys the meaning of the source text. For there is a long, established praxis of translation from German into English and vice versa; people involved in it can make use of dictionaries providing generally agreed upon equivalent terms in the two languages. Here lies a crucial difference between the translation from German into English on the one hand, and that from Ewe into English or German, and vice versa, on the other. At the time of Wolf's stay in Peki there was no information on the Ewe language to which he could refer. The praxis of translation still had to develop.

Nevertheless, it is a fragment of an ongoing communication preceded by Wolf's preaching. It is easy to guess the gist of his sermons: he told people that he knew the way to the one and only God, who was the God of the Christians, and that they should abandon their old ways of worshipping and believe in Him, otherwise they would perish in hell, and so forth. Much more difficult to assess, however, is how he communicated this message to his listeners. And this is the crux of the matter: in order to be able to preach, the missionary had to find appropriate Ewe terms to convey his message. Those terms had to be familiar to his listeners, and, at the same time, able to convey something new. For the sake of communication, the discourses of Pietism and Ewe religion had to be made comparable and compatible – they had to make use of a common language.

The reported exchange reveals that the priest and the missionary did indeed come to terms. Having heard Wolf preach, the priest came to inform him that he, too, worshipped God. Since the conversation was originally written down in German, we cannot know for sure which term Wolf (or his interpreter) used for God in this conversation. But what we do know is that Wolf was not yet aware of the term *Mawu*, which the missionaries later used for 'God', but instead referred to 'Jümbö' (later transcribed as *dziŋgbe*), or heaven. This deity was worshipped in Peki by a priest from Avetile (Spieth 1911: 47). Therefore, it is most probable that it was this priest who came to see Wolf and told him that they were colleagues. He thus took the proclaimed comparability of the missionary's and his own God as a point of departure. This assessment of the analogy of Ewe and English or German terms was an important step in the communication of the missionaries and the Ewe that, as we shall see further on, was not confined to this particular conversation. Many Ewe noticed similarities between their own religion and that of the missionaries, and, as a next step, insisted on the equality of both. Hence they saw no need to give up their own ways.

Of course, this claim went completely against the mission's view. Here there is another important difference between the translation of Wolf's German text into English and the missionaries' translation of the Pietist message into Ewe. The missionaries wanted more than merely exchanging viewpoints with the Ewe and representing the latter's ideas in a European language. Rather, they strove to make the Ewe acknowledge the superiority of the Christian religion and convert. Like Wolf, they claimed the superiority of Christianity by referring to the fact that this religion possessed a book containing God's word. Once converted, the Ewe were to be in touch with the supernatural through reading the Bible, rather than through the intermediation of a priest, as was hitherto the case. The Bible was thus both a symbol of Christianity's superiority and the medium through which its message was to be communicated. In order to maintain this superiority, the missionaries had to make sure that the Ewe understood the message in the way intended by the mission. Thus, although for the sake of communication and translation the missionaries had to link the two religions, they could not accept the equality of both and discuss religious matters with native priests as if they were colleagues. They wanted the Ewe to abandon those forms of worship that came to be reified as 'Ewe religion' or 'heathendom' (and later as 'traditional religion') for Pietism and to accept the authority of the Bible.

As was usual in Christians' encounters with other religions (see Chapter 2), Wolf claimed the inferiority of the priest's religion by denouncing it as Devil worship. It will soon become clear that his statement that the 'fetishes' were from the Devil amounted to more than a mere insult. For the diabolisation of Ewe religion remained a characteristic feature of mission work. The mission's preaching was thus characterised by the following paradox: on the one hand, terms from the non-Christian religious framework had to be integrated into the Christian Ewe discourse through translation, while on the other hand, a strict boundary was drawn between the two religions by diabolisation. Thus, once the Ewe had come to terms with the missionaries and talked about 'God', the latter expected the former to acknowledge the superiority of Christianity and reject their old ways as Devil worship. This paradox will concern us in this and the following chapter. The translation process bringing about the comparability and compatibility of Ewe and English or German terms, and the mission's strategies for establishing the superiority of their own religion, as well as Ewe responses to these endeavours, is examined next.

## MISSIONARY LINGUISTICS

In line with Protestant tradition, the NMG missionaries saw it as their main task to provide non-Christian peoples with the Bible in their mother tongue. Although anthropologists have dealt with Protestant missions' linguistic work (see for example, Clifford 1982: 74–91; Comaroff and Comaroff 1991: 198–251; Ranger 1989: 125–34), the motives of these missions in translating the Bible have not yet received much attention. This is a regrettable omission, for the investigation of these motives is essential to grasp the very fundamental of Protestant missions' representation of non-Christian peoples, which in turn had a great deal of influence on new converts.

Protestant missions legitimised the objective of translating the Bible and making it available to a large number of peoples by reference to a myth connecting the Old Testament narrative about the building of the Tower of Babel and the New Testament account of the outpouring of the Holy Spirit at Pentecost. One version of this myth was formulated by the inspector of the Rheinische Mission, F. Fabri, in his book on the origins of 'heathendom' (1859: 39ff). The myth connects passages in the Old and New Testament and rules out flaws and uncertainties in the biblical text. It can be summarised as follows: once upon a time, when human beings were still one people speaking one language, they attempted to reach heaven through the construction of a huge tower, thereby contesting God's power. God, however, destroyed the building, and punished the human beings by dividing them into various peoples speaking different languages. Since then, a confusion of tongues has prevailed on earth. Because of their pioneering role in the tower building project, the descendants of Noah's cursed son Ham were severely punished. Therefore, Ham's children were situated at a greater distance from God than all others and, according to nineteenth-century Protestant missionary discourse, the African peoples were descended from them. This situation endured until Pentecost when God sent his Holy Spirit to the disciples Jesus had gathered around him. This spirit enabled them to communicate in all languages once only. It was intended by God as a sign to encourage the learning of all languages of all peoples on earth and to preach the Gospel to them in order to reunite them in the worship of the Christian God. According to Protestant missionary discourse, the Catholic missions had failed to achieve this objective because they did not consider it important to translate the Bible into the languages of the world and place it at the disposal of ordinary believers. Placing themselves in the tradition of Luther, Protestant missions claimed to strive for these aims, thereby leading people back to Christianity.

The NMG endorsed this myth (for example, MB 1875: 373ff). While many missionaries' accounts allude to it, a report by Bernhard Schlegel, the first NMG missionary involved in the linguistic study of the Ewe language, clearly put the Ewe within its frame of reference. He agreed with the then current view that Africa was in a low state of development, but argued that it was the responsibility of Christians to uplift its inhabitants, the descendants of Ham. Approaching the Ewe from this perspective, he represented their religious ideas and practices as a typical instance of 'heathendom'. In his view, 'heathendom' in general, and Ewe religion in particular, were defined by the fact that:

> it is Satan and his angels who let themselves be adored in the heathenland. He is the prince of this world, and a divine hour of their salvation first has to be prepared and has to come, before they can be free from his power. (MB 1857: 319–20; see also Schlegel 1857: XIIff)

Thus, the Ewe were classified as belonging to the general category of 'heathens' and assigned a place in the history of mankind: separated from the God they had originally worshipped and serving the Devil in the meantime, their customs and language had degenerated in the course of time. It was the task of the mission to lead them away from Satan and back to the Christian God, which had become unknown to them. Thus, the Ewe were to go forward in order to be led back to God. In this way, the mission constructed Ewe religion in a paradoxical fashion. On the one hand, the Ewe's ancestors were considered worshippers of God, whereas on the other hand, they had been serving Satan. Later it will be obvious that this paradoxical stance towards Ewe religion recurs in current Ewe Christians' evaluations of non-Christian worship.

Since the myth mentioned above states that the time when humanity had shared one language and ethnicity was over, the Christian message was to be translated into as many languages and related to as many peoples as possible, in order to reunite humanity in the worship of the Christian God (Zahn 1895). According to Protestant missions, each language was considered an equally appropriate medium for its expression. Thus, Protestantism, unlike Islam for instance,[1] did not have an untranslatable holy language: a language in which, to use semiotic terms, *signifiant* and *signifié* converged. These semiotic concepts are useful to clarify the Protestant missions' definition of translation, which held that, in principle, each language could provide the word forms (or the *signifiants*) to express the Christian content (or the *signifié*), and that it was possible to separate the former from their previous *signifié*. Thus, in theory, the translatability of Christianity was considered unproblematic.

According to this view, the NMG, like many other Protestant mission societies, saw language studies as a prerequisite for what it took to be its proper work: the preaching of the Gospel to the 'heathens' worshipping Satan. Mastery of the Ewe language was considered the most important tool of the missionary. It was the 'weapon' in the 'war' the mission waged against 'heathendom', as the mission's metaphorical terminology put it. From the outset, NMG missionaries attempted to learn the Ewe language. In the history of the NMG among the Ewe, a handful of missionaries was fully devoted to the study of the Ewe language and the translation of the Bible. All other NMG missionaries took this linguistic work as a point of departure in their private language studies, in the course of which they reproduced the linguistic experts' findings. In 1857, Schlegel finished his *Schlüssel zur Ewe-Sprache* (Key to the Ewe Language), a book containing a grammar and a list of 2,400 Ewe terms and their translations.[2] This word list was supplemented by other missionaries' collections[3] and culminated in the publication in 1905 and 1906 of Westermann's Ewe-German and German-Ewe dictionary, which contained about 20,000 entries. Westermann, who eventually became professor of African linguistics at the University of Berlin and one of the founders of the International African Institute, and editor (until 1940) of *Africa* (see also Forde 1956), also wrote a new grammar in 1907. The missionaries regarded the Ewe spoken by the Anlo as the purest form and their standardisation of the Ewe language, which was to be the basis of the Ewe written and spoken in NMG congregations, relied heavily on the Anlo Ewe (Ansre 1971). The missionaries argued that this standardisation would play a vital role in the reunification of the scattered Ewe 'tribes' speaking various 'dialects' as one 'people' with one 'language' (e.g. Westermann 1936; see also Meyer 1995c).

Linguistic studies were carried out along with ethnographic research and translation of the whole Bible. Although from the outset the missionaries had devoted themselves to translating the Bible into Ewe, it was the missionary Jacob Spieth who fulfilled this task in cooperation with native employees. These were old, experienced men, who knew the 'heathen' religion well, but were at the same time staunch church members convinced of the superiority of Protestantism. In this way, they could advise Spieth on which terms to choose and which to avoid in the translation (MB 1897: 67ff; MB 1909: 34ff). When the missionaries had to leave the field due to the First World War, the first fully translated Ewe Bible, which they saw as 'the greatest missionary of all times' (MB 1915: 68), arrived to replace them. In the course of time, in addition to the Bible a whole range of Christian literature appeared, among them the very popular Ewe version of Bunyan's *The Pilgrim's Progress* (1906).[4]

Despite increasing knowledge of the Ewe language and belief in the translatability of Christianity, in practice, the transfer of meanings across the linguistic boundary separating missionaries and the Ewe was a tricky affair. For missionaries, it involved a high grade of uncertainty about the actual meaning of the translation of the Pietist message into Ewe. Particularly at the beginning of mission work, when missionaries depended on native interpreters who were employed because they happened to speak English, it was difficult for the former to assess how their sermons were translated, let alone how the Ewe apprehended them. At the time, the interlocutors' translations were totally beyond the mission's control. Gradually these people were replaced by native Christian mission workers who had been educated in mission schools and accepted the superiority of the Pietist religion. Still, however, the missionaries could not be certain that these translations really mirrored their statements, or in the case of Bible and hymn translation, the original text. Thus, in retrospect, Spieth noticed that the mistakes in early attempts to translate the Bible were due to missionaries' linguistic incompetence on the one hand, and their employees' insufficient understanding of the Gospel on the other: 'They [the employees] frequently only half understood the biblical term explained or misunderstood it completely and subsequently suggested an Ewe term derived from a truly heathen view [*Anschauungskreis*]. By integrating the term, this view was then biblically confirmed' (MB 1909: 35). Missionaries tried to reduce the possibility of such mistakes by achieving control over the people acting as their interpreters and by investigating the Ewe language and religion.

## MISSIONARY ETHNOGRAPHY

To investigate the Ewe's own understanding of how they appropriated the Christian Ewe discourse established by the NMG, it is necessary to have some idea of their point of departure: Ewe religion has to be understood. This is important for two reasons: Ewe religion was not only what Ewe converts left behind in favour of Christianity, but also the reservoir of terms from which the missionaries selected appropriate *signifiants* to translate the Pietist *signifiés* (and excluded others). Since the only way to assess what the missionaries meant (and what the Ewe understood) by the Christian Ewe discourse is to compare it with Ewe religion, an overview of the latter's basic features is needed.

The fact that the first written documents about this religion were produced by those intending to replace and to destroy it certainly constitutes a handicap for its reconstruction.[5] Rather than mirroring actual Ewe religious deeds and practices, the descriptions echo the missionary bias which not only influenced the missionaries' perception of this religion, but also their actual communication with the Ewe. This being the case, it still seems possible to infer, albeit tentatively, some of its distinctive traits from missionary ethnographies (above all Spieth 1906, 1911) and linguistic studies (above all Westermann 1905a, 1906), because they contain detailed descriptions of religious phenomena and terms, as well as transcriptions and/or translations of statements made by elderly non-Christians.

Spieth was not only the NMG's main Bible translator, but also its chief ethnographer. Like all ethnography, his is based on particular suppositions guiding his description and echoing his point of view: he thought about the Ewe and their religion in terms of the construction of the Tower of Babel. Though Spieth did not mention this myth in his ethnographies, it is clear he considered the Ewe to have originally believed in one high God, and in the course of time, to have degenerated into 'tribes' with 'dialects' and 'local gods'. Making use of horticultural metaphors he stated that their original state was overgrown (*überwuchert*) and overwhelmed (*erdrückt*) by other beliefs (1911: 5–6). He thus distinguished between the Ewe's original state, which had been close to the divine, and their further development which he and his colleagues considered to be dominated by the Devil.[6]

This premise was worked out in a range of assumptions guiding Spieth's ethnographic work. One assumption directly following from the degeneration thesis is that of the Ewe's presumed original monotheism. Concomitantly, Spieth began his book with a chapter on *Mawu*, the High God, although his informants actually hardly spoke about *Mawu* and his ethnographies abound with descriptions of the worship of various *trɔwo*.[7] Thus, it is clear that the worship of the *trɔwo* was a much more vital element of Ewe religion than Spieth acknowledged. And it seems that he not only played down the centrality of the *trɔwo*, but also the importance of worship.

Thus there is another assumption informing Spieth's ethnography: in line with the Pietist worldview, he underplayed the importance of religious practices and emphasised 'belief' (*Glaube*) instead. He even went so far as to interpret the lack of concrete forms of *Mawu* worship as an indication of the Ewe's original monotheism and the High God's central importance. However, his chapters on the *trɔwo* and *dzo* (magic, medicine) reveal that the performance of individual and collective rituals were the pivot of Ewe religious life. Whereas for him religion was essentially a matter of the mind, it seems that for the Ewe it was also a matter of bodily action. It is probable that his contempt and subsequent neglect of practical forms of worship prevented him from delving further into the details of ritual performances. Therefore his ethnography fails to throw sufficient light on the actual religious practices of the Ewe.

Another assumption becomes evident through Spieth's distinction between native (*einheimisch*) and foreign (*fremd*) beliefs. He not only distinguished the class of *trɔwo* according to these categories, but also considered the belief in the existence of witchcraft (*adze*) and magic (*dzo*) as being more recent, foreign phenomena (1911: 11). Spieth excluded new cults such as *Yewe* (a secret society that was popular among the Anlo, cf Spieth 1911: 172–88), and phenomena such as witchcraft, magic and divination as being distinct from what he defined as authentic Ewe religion. Thereby, he represented Ewe religion as consisting of an inert local basis that had been supplemented with some new, more superficial phenomena, some of which had gained regional importance. According to him, the latter deserved much less attention. However, being aware of this bias, his representation of the 'authentic' part of the Ewe religion as local, fixed and stable has to be questioned. That he did not take into account the development of Ewe worship should not blind us to the fact that actually Ewe religion was, and probably had always been, dynamic and open to going beyond the local.

Moreover, in his whole ethnographic work, priestesses received much less attention than the prayers and sacrifices of male priests. However, the role of female priests can be assessed from numerous accounts in the MB where missionaries complain about the so-called 'fetish whores' (*Fetisch-dirnen*), that is, bare-breasted women disturbing their sermons with singing and dancing (see Meyer 1989: 97–8). These women clearly inverted the Pietist definitions of both religion and womanhood. The missionaries were unable to see the sexual division of labour in the worship of *trɔwo* and could not help but dismiss them as oversexed, immoral people.

In sum, although abstaining from overtly missionary statements, Spieth's description of Ewe religion echoes the Pietist point of view. He presented Ewe religion according to his understanding of the essential features of religion: a system of representations with regard to God that was shared by believers. He had comparatively little interest in people's actual religious praxis and the power relations involved, which he considered to be the domain of the Devil. This representation of religion was typical of the Protestant missions' approach to non-Christian forms of worship, which they constructed as exponents of the broad category of 'heathendom' (see Warneck 1913). This view of religion in terms of belief, however, is not confined merely to Protestant missions, but is part of a general and dominant Western tradition in the study of religion. As Asad has shown (1993: 27–54), this tradition is based on a post-Enlightenment Christian definition of religion as 'belief' at the expense of religious practices, and is falsely taken to be universal.

## EWE RELIGION: A TENTATIVE RECONSTRUCTION

Spieth's informants did not talk about Ewe religion in general – there is not even an Ewe term to express 'religion'. Rather, they talked about service (*subɔsubɔ*) to particular gods with particular names. Indeed, in contrast with Pietism and similar written religious traditions, Ewe religion did not form a fixed system of representations and practices to be shared by everyone. In every Ewe state, town, clan and family, people worshipped different gods, and there was much variation in the extent of individuals' involvement in worship. This must be borne in mind in any attempt to get an idea of what Ewe religion was about in general, and the situation in Peki in particular. In the framework of this study it is impossible to represent the colour of religious life. What follows should be read as a vocabulary of the semantic field concerning the links between the invisible and the visible realm, rather than as a description of Ewe's actual religious practices. Another point to be made here is that, since Spieth gained his information about Ewe religion mainly from informants from the Anlo area on the coast, and inland from the area around Ho, the reconstruction developed on the basis of his ethnographies is confined to western Ewe groups. It does not describe the religious situation of the Ewe groups in coastal Togo where the NMG only became active much later on.

## Ideas about the World and the Person

Spieth did not provide specific information about the concept of the person and the cosmology held in Peki, but described that of the Ewe in general (1911: 243ff). He developed this general image mainly on the basis of his research at Ho (1906: 502ff). Since there is no reason to assume that its basic ingredients were not shared in Peki, his description of the Ho will serve as a guide. There is a juxtaposition of stories, some of which contradict each other, but rather than arranging these stories into a consistent whole, as Spieth did in his work of 1911, the contradictions, inconsistencies and open ends will be indicated.

According to Spieth, the Ho did not see the world as a divine creation, but found that at a certain point in time the visible, material world (*kodzogbe*) appeared out of the darkness of the invisible. The realm where human beings (*amewo*) stayed before they came into the world (called *bome*, *bofe*, *amedzofe* [a human being's place of origin] or *ŋɔlime* ['among spirits', i.e. 'land of spirits']) was thought to be in the sky (*dziŋgbe*). This realm was a mirror image of the known world. Before being born into the world, spirits had to determine when they would return home again. The promise to return at a certain point in time and in a certain way was called *gbetsi*. If a human being failed to return in time, the *gbetsi* was sent after the person to call him or her back. In that case the person would die through a snakebite, an accident, or suicide. In the world of human beings, such a death was known as *ametsiava* ('a person remaining in war', i.e. a person dying through a [bloody] accident – see below). Human beings termed such a promise *gbetsi vɔ̃*, i.e. 'evil promise' or 'evil fate'. *Kodzogbe* and *ŋɔlime* were thus mirror images of each other: whereas the human beings mourned the death of one of their fellows, this departure was considered positive in the spirit world (ibid.: 502–6).

Once a person (*ame*) was born into life (*agbe*), he or she was made up (according to some informants by *Mawu*) of a body (*ŋutila*), thought to consist of mud and the cheekbone of an ancestor, and three invisible, spiritual entities: *aklama* (also *kla*, *kra*) or *dzɔgbe*,[8] *luvɔ*, and *gbɔgbɔ*. When they had all left the body, the person was dead (*ku*). The stories dealing with this phase in human life are silent on the origin of these entities. Of the three, *gbɔgbɔ* is the easiest to describe: it simply designates breath. It was not considered to determine the course of people's lives, but just to keep them alive (ibid.: 563). It was their vital power.

A person's *luvɔ* is his or her shadow. Spieth translated *luvɔ* as soul (*Seele*) (ibid.: 563–4). Some of his informants distinguished between a *luvɔagbetɔ* (soul of life), and a *luvɔkutɔ* (soul of death). But it was also common to talk about *luvɔ* in general. There is no indication that a person's *luvɔ* had any direct influence on the course of his or her life. But it was the entity that left people whilst they slept to walk around in *drɔ̃efe*, the land of dreams. Dreaming (*drɔ̃ekuku*, i.e. 'being half dead'), was understood as an activity of *luvɔ*. It provided insight to the invisible realm that was inaccessible for human beings while awake. In the case of death, *luvɔ* definitely left the person; and whereas the soul of life turned into a spirit (*ŋɔli*) walking around restlessly among the living, the soul of death joined the ancestors (*adefiewo*) in the realm of the dead.

It is impossible to find an English equivalent for *aklama* (ibid.: 510–12). *Aklama* was held to determine a person's character (*dzɔdzɔme*), i.e. his or her peculiarity. It came into the world with individuals on their birthdays[9] and saw to their well-being, but could also punish them with sickness or madness, if they acted against their character. *Aklama* was symbolised by a statue to which a person made sacrifices as a sign of gratefulness for its protection or, if the need arose, as a sign of pacification. At the moment of death, *aklama* left the person. It is not clear what then happened with a person's *aklama*. Spieth mentioned that it went back to God with the intention of returning later in another human being. However, since there are no further stories dealing with reincarnation, it seems to be an open end.

Though one might expect that the Ewe imagined death as a return to *amedzofe*, this is not the case. Whereas Spieth's informants were vague about the lot of *aklama* and kept silent about *gbɔgbɔ*, they said that the person's *luvɔ* turned into a spirit (*ŋɔli*) and went to *tsiefe* ('staying place'), the place of the ancestors (*tɔgbuiwo*) imagined to be located under the earth (ibid.: 563; Spieth 1911: 241ff). However, not all dead souls reached or stayed in *tsiefe*; we have already noted above that some spirits of the dead (*ŋɔliwo*) remained on earth to frighten and trouble the living. Those who died prematurely, and the *ametsiavawo* in particular, were thought of as continuing to haunt the living. Other *ŋɔliwo* were supposed to do so because they were dissatisfied with the funeral rites performed for them. In order to make sure that these *ŋɔliwo* reached *tsiefe*, the living had to consult *trɔ̃*-priests or special callers of *ŋɔliwo* (*dzevusi*) to contact the spirits (*ŋɔliyɔyɔ*, that is, 'calling a spirit') and finally perform rites according to the latter's wishes. Ideally, once arrived in *tsiefe*, a dead person's spirit would turn into an ancestor (*tɔgbui*).

To reach *tsiefe*, a dead person's soul had to make a long journey eastwards, in the direction from which the Ewe had migrated into their present area. It had to cross the river separating the realm of the living from the dead. The dead were given money to pay *Kutsiame* ('spokesman of death'), the greedy ferryman, in order to be able to get to the other side. A soul unable to do so would return to the living and trouble them until he or she succeeded in reaching *tsiefe*. *Tsiefe* was a mirror image of the world, it consisted of the same towns, clans and families which the dead souls joined. However, in contrast with the visible world, the ancestors did not grow food themselves, but depended on food and drink from the living. The latter therefore placed these things on the ground for their dead ancestors and prayed to them that they would receive protection in return. People who died a violent death (*ametsiavawo*) were sent to stay in a separate place. This mirrors the special death rites performed with respect to such people: their bodies were laid in state at the outskirts of the town, they were buried in a special cemetery and their property was not inherited by relatives, but thrown away. Spieth also mentions a selection of the dead in moral terms: witches (*adzetɔwo*) and evil sorcerers (*dzoɖuametɔwo*) were sent to live apart from the rest. It is possible that this idea developed in the course of the Ewe's encounter with Christianity. After all, in the visible world, whose mirror image *tsiefe* was said to be, good and bad people also mixed.

The stories concerning the spirits' place before birth (*amedzofe*) and after death (*tsiefe*) are thus inconsistent, and even contradictory. In both cases the spiritual entity is termed *ŋɔli*, but the two realms seem to be separated, or better, the stories pertaining to them exist independently of each other. There were no religious specialists attempting to formulate a clear-cut worldview marrying the various stories. The non-Christian Ewe evidently felt no need for a consistent cosmology. This suggests that in order to understand Ewe religion we have to go beyond Spieth's conceptualisation of religion as a coherent philosophical system shared by believers, a conceptualisation that is still held by other students of Ewe religion following in his footsteps.[10] But before attempting to reconstruct the individual Ewe's concerns and needs, as well as the religious practices by which they dealt with them, another area in their religious vocabulary has to be charted: the gods and spirits, their priests and their service.

## Mawu and Trɔwo

Originally *Mawu* was not a generic term for 'God', but the personal name of a distant deity already known in pre-Christian times.[11] Ewe groups did not share a set of unified ideas about him. Many considered *Mawu* to be the maker of human beings who was unconcerned with their further well-being in life (Spieth 1906: 419). Most informants did not have much to say about *Mawu* at all, and instead talked about the female caring earth God *Mawu Sodza*,[12] the male aggressive thunder God *Mawu Sogble*,[13] and the money-giving God *Mawu Sowlui*. No generally shared image of *Mawu* can be discerned from the statements of Spieth's informants. It seems that *Mawu* was considered to be far away, and if people wanted to achieve something,

they addressed the various *trɔwo* (gods with specific domains and responsibilities) through their priests, and brought them sacrifices if requested.

Spieth's ethnography does not make clear whether the Peki knew *Mawu*.
When Wolf investigated Peki ideas about God, he did after all have to find
the appropriate Ewe term to refer to the Christian God and came across the
name of a certain 'Jümbö', later transcribed as *dziŋgbe*. However, according
to Spieth, *dziŋgbe* (sky) was not God, but rather a *trɔ* (1911: 5). When
confronted with this passage, informants retorted that since time
immemorial, prayers began with the calling of *Mawu Sodza*. Be that as it
may, it is clear that, in practice, the *trɔwo* were much more important than
*Mawu*, for they were accessible through priests.

Wuve was the state *trɔ* of the Peki (ibid.: 105–8). There were two places
where he could receive sacrifices – a small forest between Avetile and
Afeviwofe near a stream named after the *trɔ*, and a large forest near Dzogbati.
On Fridays, the common rest day of all Peki, nobody was allowed to fetch
water from the Wuve stream, nor to work on or bury somebody in Peki land.
Wuve was the only deity served by the whole group. Its worship played an
essential role in the yam festival (*teɖuɖu*), the most important collective
ritual that was attended by all inhabitants, involving the cooperation of the
*fiagã* and the Wuve priest. It was a politico-religious ritual aimed at the
future well-being of Peki as a whole. The yam festival, which took place in
September when the first yam could be harvested, marked the end of the
old, and the beginning of the new year.[14] It started with the ritual sweeping
of the town and of each house and hearth. With this purification ritual, all
evil (*vɔ*) was removed from the town (see Chapter 4). Afterwards, people
were allowed to bring the new yams from their farms to the outskirts of the
town. The next day the Wuve priest presented the new yams and other
sacrifices to the *trɔ*. At the same time, people brought the new yams into the
house, killed a goat or a chicken and started to cook. Each family head
mixed part of the boiled yams with oil and offered it to the ancestors, the
*trɔwo* in the compound, his *aklama*, and his working materials, such as his
loom or his gun. Then the family ate the *fufu* that had been prepared from
the new yams, with meat soup. As the families cooked their new yams, the
Wuve priest, the chiefs and the elders offered a sacrifice to Wuve in the small
forest. From then on, people were allowed to eat the new yams or to use
them as seed yam for growing more.

Another *trɔ* important for all Peki was the stream Amimli, who was
considered the linguist of all the Peki *trɔwo* and through whom all *trɔ* priests
called their *trɔwo*. Amimli was served by one priest in Blengo, another in
Avetile, and also had priestesses in both towns (something Spieth typically
failed to mention). On Wednesdays, his day of worship, he received food
from his priests and could be consulted by people in need of, or thankful for,
his assistance. On that day people were not allowed to work on his land and

fetch his water. Amimli was held responsible for rain which he could provide or withold. If the latter was the case, women would offer him sacrifices of corn flour to make it rain (1911: 93).

Besides Wuve and Amimli, who were important to all Peki, there was a great range of other *trɔwo* that were peculiar to towns, clans, families and individuals (in the case of new *trɔwo*). Some of them were famous for their capacity to heal or bring about riches and were therefore visited by a great number of people. Thus, on the one hand, the worship of the *trɔwo* integrated people on varying scales, from local to state level. On the other hand, individuals were free to consult any *trɔ* they deemed capable of helping them achieve their ends.

How was the worship of a *trɔ* organised? What were the key terms used for the various practices? Unfortunately, as a result of Spieth's relative neglect of actual forms of worship, his ethnographies are incomplete in this regard. In most cases, he only provided information about a *trɔ*'s name, the place he inhabited, and some fragmentary particulars about his service. Only occasionally do we come across some scattered additional information. Combining these passages with the results of interviews with current *trɔ* priests and priestesses, the following general picture of *trɔ* worship emerges.

*Trɔ* worship was a dynamic affair; new *trɔwo* spread and their worship was taken up by local people.[15] *Ametsiavawo* who manifested themselves after their bloody death could become installed as *trɔwo* in the same way as powerful *dzo*, which would then be called *dzozutrɔ* (*dzo* that became *trɔ*). Thus, there was no fixed pantheon. With the exception of female *ametsiavawo* worshipped as gods, the *trɔwo* were considered male. Each *trɔ* inhabited a particular natural phenomenon or artificial object and was held responsible for it. For instance, a *trɔ* inhabiting a stream was considered to provide drinking water. Each *trɔ* was served by a priest (*trɔnua* or *Osofo* [Akan]) of the family or clan to whom the *trɔ* belonged. This priest was either chosen by the *trɔ* through possession or appointed by the clan elders. He had to serve his god on a particular day. His task was to pray to the *trɔ* (*do gbe na trɔ*, that is, 'to raise the voice towards the *trɔ*'), through pouring drinks (either strong liquor, palm wine, or water mixed with cornflour) for him on the ground. As well as a priest, each *trɔ* had a couple of priestesses who were imagined to be the *trɔ*'s wife, a notion reflected in the term '*si*' (spouse) in the Ewe expressions for priestess (*hɔnusi* or *trɔsi*). These women mainly came from the same clan as the *trɔ*, but it was also possible for a married woman to become a priestess of a *trɔ* in her husband's clan. Whereas a priest was at best possessed by his *trɔ* in the course of his selection and initiation and gradually achieved control over his god, the priestesses were possessed regularly. In a state of possession, they were in trance and no longer conscious of their own personality. The process of possession was expressed by the following sayings: *eva lé ame* ('it comes to catch a person' [in order to let him or her become a priest or priestess]) *ele ame dzi* or *eɖe ame dzi* ('it is or comes upon a person'), *ele trɔ fom* ('he or she is "beaten" by the *trɔ*,' i.e. a person who is moved by the *trɔ* and dances), and *egli* (he or she is out of his/her mind, in a rage). When possessed, the priestesses danced in the way the *trɔ* was supposed to move and articulated the *trɔ*'s wishes; this state was called '*ele trɔ fom*'. Thus, the sexual division of labour in the *trɔ*-worship was such that the priest communicated with the *trɔ* through libation prayers whereas the priestesses got moved by the *trɔ* and danced, thereby lending their body and voice to the *trɔ*'s manifestation. Possession and dance were indispensable elements of Ewe religion, by which the gods were present in the visible world. The female body was thus an instrument of divine expression.

Each *trɔ* had a particular day on which he was served. On that day, nobody was allowed to enter the particular *trɔ*'s land (if it was a piece of land) or fetch his water (if he was a stream). Such interdictions (*nukikli*) were the law (*se*) of the *trɔ*. If they were violated, the *trɔ* had to be pacified with drinks and the sacrifice of a goat (*vɔsasa*). Many *trɔwo* were conservative, they 'disliked' contact with new materials such as brass pans and restricted the unlimited cultivation of land. As well as general laws, the priest and priestesses had to observe particular food taboos. On the *trɔ*'s day they dressed in the *trɔ*'s attire, a dress made from black cotton (*blusi*) if it concerned local(ised) *trɔwo*, and white if it concerned *trɔwo* from elsewhere; cleaned the *trɔ*'s place (*trɔkpɔ*, the '*trɔ*'s fence', i.e. the area of the *trɔ* delineated by a fence), which was usually in the priest's compound; and provided it with food and drinks. The corpus of rites performed in the service (*subɔsubɔ*) of the *trɔ* was called *wɔ trɔ nu*, 'to make the *trɔ*'s thing' – an expression emphasising the importance of human activities with regard to the gods. On the *trɔ*'s day people could request various things of him, such as health, fertility, protection, success in life, or help to win a court case. If people wanted a *trɔ* to achieve one of these things, they had to offer him drinks, which the priest used as a prayer offering, and promise to bring a more substantial gift in return for the accomplished favour. The *trɔ* priests and priestesses were also consulted in order to find out the reasons for a person's suffering: was the person's own *gbetsi vɔ* or bad *aklama* the source of the trouble, or rather *adze* or a *dzoɖuametɔ*? Or was it the person who had behaved badly? It was up to the *trɔ* priest or priestess to consult the *trɔ* about the cause and find the appropriate remedy. If the person's problem resulted from his or her own bad deeds, he or she would have to confess before the situation could improve. A person could also call a *trɔ* upon somebody (*yɔ trɔ*) in order to let the *trɔ* punish someone harming him or her unjustly. In such a case the priest or priestess would call both parties to the *trɔ*'s place and judge the case. If somebody had cursed a person unjustly, the former had to pacify the *trɔ* with sacrifices, but if the cursed person was judged to be wrong, he or she had to pay.

Once a year, after the yam harvest, priest and priestesses had to perform their *trɔ*'s particular yam festival – offer him drinks, yams, and sacrifice a goat. The priests and priestesses of all other *trɔwo* attended the festival and shared the *trɔ*'s meal – cooked goat's meat and corn flour mixed with red palm oil (*akpledze*). On such occasions, the priestesses were possessed by their *trɔwo* in the course of dancing to the rhythm of the drums. These meetings were attended by the clan or family to which the *trɔ* belonged. There they purified their faces (*klɔ ŋkume*) with *amãtsi*, water mixed with herbs kept in an earthen pot on a three-branched fork of a tree (*zɔze*), that was held to have protective power.

## Other Powers and their Representatives

The spiritual powers mentioned in the previous section were worshipped by groups on varying scales to ensure these groups' well-being in life. This shared praxis of worship brought about and confirmed the coherence of the group involved. However, Ewe religion cannot be reduced to this collective dimension. I have stated already that individuals used to consult a *trɔ* priest of their own choice whom they deemed especially capable to help them achieve their ends. Next to these priests, a person could also see other experts.

Apart from the *trɔwo*, the Ewe also had the category of 'little people' (*adziakpewo* [inland] or *azizawo* [Anlo]), whose realm of operation was the bush (*gbeme*). Spieth mentioned that people believed in their existence – he translated them as 'forest devils' (*Waldteufel*) – but he failed to say how they were thought to act or how they were worshipped. From my own interviews with *adziakpe* priests, it seemed that the 'little people' were three feet tall and had bushy brown hair. Living in the bush, they were able to confuse human beings returning from their bush farms so that they could no longer find their way home (*gbɔme*). Such a person would then be lost for several days. When the *adziakpewo* selected a priest to serve them, they kept the person of their choice in the bush for some days where they provided their captive with knowledge about herbs and informed him where to find game to shoot. Therefore, the *adziakpe* priests were good hunters and medicine men. Like the *trɔ* priests, they would be consulted by people in order to be cured of disease, as well as for other purposes. *Adziakpe* worship seemed to be organised in a similar fashion to that of the *trɔwo*, the only difference being that their priests and priestess were dressed in white rather than black.

Another group of specialists were the *dzotɔwo* ('those owning *dzo*', i.e. native healers or magicians) (Spieth 1906: 515ff; 1911: 250ff). In order to become a *dzotɔ*, a man – apparently there were no female *dzotɔwo* – had to acquire various *dzo* from other *dzotɔwo*. The various types of *dzo* were not confined to particular local settings, but rather a matter of regional distribution. Having bought a couple of *dzo* – an expensive investment that had to be repaid – a *dzotɔ* could treat others with his medicines.[16] Like the *trɔ* priests, the *dzotɔwo* had to make sacrifices to their *dzo* regularly.[17] *Dzo* consisted of natural materials such as feathers, bones, eggshells, cords, bark and herbs. In order to endow these ingredients with power, the *dzotɔ* had to sprinkle his saliva over them, which the Ewe held to be a powerful fluid. Since much *dzo* had the shape of a string (*dzoka*) worn as a chain or tied around a person's arm, leg, or waist, the *dzotɔ*'s praxis was described as *dzokasasa* ('binding a *dzo* string'). However, there was also *dzo* in the form of powder, or a liquid consisting of water and herbs. For the Ewe, binding was a powerful image. It was also employed in the case of the ritual purification of the town, in the course of which evil was bound.

*Dzo* was applied in fields of (potential) affliction such as war, health, pregnancy and birth, hunting and agriculture, trade, play, love affairs, family conflicts and dead persons' spirits. There was an uncountable number of different *dzo*. *Dzo* was an ambivalent power that was employed individually (often in secret) and that could not only provide protection against certain evils, but also bring them about. According to Spieth, *dzo* was extremely popular all over Ewe land. Virtually every person, both men and women, consulted the *dzotɔwo* in order to get *dzo*. They often did so for the same reasons that Europeans saw doctors, i.e. to get medicine (*atike*) against sickness. But people used *dzo* not only to cure bodily ills, but also to improve their trade or the growth of their plants, to become invulnerable in war and win fights, to be protected against evils inflicted upon them by others (for example, the evil eye or mouth, witchcraft, spirits of the dead), or to harm others. A person who was thought to make *dzo* against others in secrecy was called *dzoɖuametɔ*, 'somebody eating a person with *dzo*'. Many people feared these evil sorcerers as much as witches and sought to protect themselves against their possible attacks with all sorts of *dzo*.

Another group of experts was the *akatɔwo*, people in charge of an ordeal (*aka*) (Spieth 1906: 535ff; 1911: 288ff). There were various forms of *aka*, but they all shared the aim of detecting the guilty. Many *dzotɔwo* also owned *aka*. It was acquired in the same way as *dzo*. The *akatɔwo* were not present in every town, but called upon in times of need. The *aka* was used in court trials between individuals to determine who was guilty, as well as in the case of collectively experienced affliction, when a whole town could be asked to undergo the *aka* in order to sift out the person causing it (Spieth 1906: 542). It was also used to detect *dzoɖuametɔwo*, and, according to my informants in Peki, witches. A person found guilty through the *aka* had to pay the *akatɔ* as well as the people claiming to have been harmed by him or her. As well as *aka* forms merely detecting a guilty person, there were also poisonous ordeals resulting in the immediate death of the supposed evil doer.

The last group of specialists to be mentioned here are the *afakalawo* or *bokɔwo* (or *bokɔnɔwo*), who practised the art of divination (*afakaka*, i.e. 'saying the *afa*') (Spieth 1911: 189–225). The literal meaning of *afa*, 'cool', reveals its purpose: the *afa* was to 'cool' a person down, i.e. to restore his or her peace (ibid.: 189). For the Ewe distinguished between 'coolness', their favourite state of body and mind which implied perfect peace and the absence of troubles, and 'heat' (*dzo*), a state which could only be accepted temporarily and often implied sickness and other problems. Much religious activity was aimed at restoring people's cool state and bringing them peace (*ŋutifafa*, 'a cool body'). Spieth's informants attributed the art of divination to the Yoruba, who called it *ifa* (for a concise description of *ifa* see Peel 1990: 339–45). It had spread from there through Dahomey (presently called Benin) to the Anlo. A man could become a *bokɔ* by initiation and every *bokɔ* disposed of a number of different *trɔwo* and other spirits considered to assist the *afa*. Like all priests, he had to observe certain taboos. Diviners also had representatives in many Ewe towns. Like *dzo* and *aka*, *afa* was thus a phenomenon of regional distribution. People would consult a *bokɔ* in order to find out the reasons for particular troubles in all the fields of potential affliction mentioned above.

## Religion in Individual Praxis

It is now time to exchange the bird's eye perspective of the all-seeing observer (which resembles the Pietist perspective on the image of the broad and the narrow path) for a more modest sketch of how the Ewe coped practically with their concerns and needs. This can be understood by regarding the *rites de passage* in the course of a person's life. Since Spieth failed to give a complete description of such rituals due to his bias for collective represent-ations, other sources have been examined.

On the eighth day after birth, a child underwent the 'outdooring' ceremony (*viɖeɖeɖego*), when it was taken outside for the first time. In the course of this celebration the child received its name and was integrated into the father's family. The head of the family poured a libation to the ancestors and prayed for the child's life and well-being. Initiation was the next important stage marked by ritual. For a boy this was circumcision (*avatsotso*, 'cutting a penis'). According to some of Spieth's informants, boys were circumcised at the age of three, whereas others gave a much higher age. In any case, circumcision symbolised the boy's transformation into manhood (Spieth 1906: 227, 627). A girl's initiation into womanhood (*gbelelewɔwɔ*) was performed after her first menstruation. After a period of seclusion spent together with her female friends, the girl was dressed in gorgeous pieces of cloth and decorated with the family beads. Together with her friends she enjoyed a feast and then visited the market to parade her beauty. After this ceremony had been performed, a girl was considered marriageable. Marriage involved a whole complex of rituals (*srɔ̃ɖeɖe*) which it is unneces-sary to describe in this context. But as on all family occasions, the ancestors of the families of the groom and the bride were called upon to bless the marriage. A person's death was a great occasion for the deceased's family and involved high costs. When a person died, a number of rituals (*kunuwɔwɔ*) was performed in the course of his or her burial (*kutefe*), the main purpose being to make sure that the deceased's soul was able to join the ancestors in *tsiefe* rather than remaining in the world as a *ŋɔli* to trouble the living. One year after the burial, a funeral feast was held. If everything had gone well, the deceased had by then reached *tsiefe* and turned into an ancestor. For the deceased's spouse there were a number of rites (*ahɔwɔwɔ*) aimed at ensuring the widower's or widow's separation from the dead spouse's spirit and enabling him or her to remarry after this period of one year.

On the occasion of all these *rites de passage*, the family elders undertook libation prayers to the ancestors. Worship of the ancestors was the most common feature of people's religious life. It formed the basis of people's identification with their family and was thought of as a means by which to ensure the family's well-being, and as a prophylaxis against all sorts of evil. Prayers of libation to the ancestors were supplemented with participation in the yearly yam festival, in the course of which the whole town was purified and the ancestors and all other spiritual guardians present in the house were worshipped. Moreover, if there was a *trɔ̃* in the family, people would participate in his particular yam festival and clean their faces with *amãtsi*. All these rituals marked people's group membership and were designed to ward off evil. Next to these rituals, people had to comply with certain behavioural rules. In the compound, husbands and wives had to avoid certain forms of offensive behaviour and in town people had to comply with set interdictions, such as the common rule of not entering the town with a whole, uncut bunch of bananas. Neglect of these regulations threatened to put at risk the well-being of household and town members.

As long as things went well, people would confine themselves to these practices and hardly ever consult *trɔ̃* priests outside their family, or other ritual experts. In the case of sickness and troubles, however, people had to go beyond these prophylactic forms of ritual behaviour. In order to find a suitable remedy, the afflicted person had to know the cause of the trouble. Depending on the nature of the problem, the person would see the most appropriate specialist. If the procedure did not yield the desired result, he or she might proceed to other specialists until either the problem was solved or hope for a cure was lost.

## CHRISTIAN EWE DISCOURSE

Recently, anthropologists have started to examine how a Christian vocabulary developed in the process of communication between European missionaries and non-Western peoples. Whereas Comaroff and Comaroff (1991) have concentrated on the dialectics of this communicative process in more general terms and paid little attention to the meanings attributed to particular terms by each side involved, Jolly (1996), Peel (1990), Tanner (1978) and above all Rafael (1988), have examined in detail new converts' appropriations of Christian terms. Since the assessment of the peculiarity of local understandings of Christianity depends on knowledge of people's interpretation of vernacular Christian discourse, a detailed study of the latter is, in my view, indispensable.

Since it is impossible to investigate Christian Ewe vocabulary as a whole, this section is confined to some crucial key terms without which Pietism could not be expressed, and which were used in almost every sermon: the three personages of God, the Devil, and ideas about the world (life, death, heaven and hell) and the person. Each of these terms belongs to one of the four linguistic frames of reference from which Ewe Christian vocabulary originates. *Mawu* (God), *luvɔ* (soul), and *tsiefe* (underworld or hell) belong to the terms taken from pre-Christian religious vocabulary. *Yesu Kristo* is a loanword from the Bible. *Dziŋgbe* (heaven), *dzomavɔ* (everlasting fire) and the two words making up the phrase *Gbɔgbɔ Kɔkɔe* (Holy Spirit) originate from secular Ewe language. The last two expressions, like so many others, are new linguistic creations that did not exist in pre-mission times. The Devil *Abosam* is referred to by a word from Akan and thus represents the fourth linguistic frame of reference.

## The Three Personages of God: *Mawu, Yesu Kristo, Gbɔgbɔ Kɔkɔe*

Missionaries and their native mission workers continuously talked about the necessity of believing in God, though as we already noted, the different Ewe groups shared no unified set of ideas about *Mawu*. Since he did not intervene in daily affairs, *Mawu* played only a limited role. Yet once involved in a conversation by the mission, the Ewe responded in terms set by the latter. Thus, they also talked about *Mawu*. The following argument put forward by a non-Christian inhabitant of Taviefe reacting to an evangelist's sermon (most probably William Lemgo), and which the latter reported to the mission in 1893, forms a case in point:

> One day I [William Lemgo] went into a town called Taviefe, and they had heard the good news of Jesus Christ before, but it did not please them. And one of them stood up and said that *Mawu*'s first creation was the *trɔwo*, and the second was human beings, and *Mawu* appointed the *trɔwo* to be the head of the human beings in order to look after them. And *Mawu* divided the spirit (*gbɔgbɔ*) within a person into two, and he kept half with himself and he gave half into the hands of the *trɔwo* to be used in looking after people. And half of everybody's spirit is in the hands of *Mawu* himself and half is in the hands of the *trɔwo*. And when the part of a person's spirit which is in the hands of

the *trɔwo* is finished, then the *trɔ* goes to *Mawu* to receive the person's spirit again, the other part which is in *Mawu*'s hands. And *Mawu* refuses and does not want a person to receive the second part of the spirit again. Then the person dies. Therefore, in their eyes the *trɔwo* have become more merciful than *Mawu*, but since he is the one who made everything and yet he does not want them to lead a long life, he is guilty. [...] And there are some who say that *Mawu* did not send the *trɔwo*. He sent Jesus so that they would worship Jesus. Their Jesus, the Tafi people's, is an *ameklu* (a Tafi *trɔ*); he, the great *Mawu* who made the human beings, sent a guardian to them, the Tafi people, to look after them. For this reason they would not know any Jesus. (Stab 7, 1025–56/8: 82ff; original in Ewe)

Such discussions between Ewe evangelists and people who had not (yet) become Christians do not reflect the non-Christians' original ideas in a straightforward way – after all, normally they would not compare Christianity and their own religion. But in order to defend that religion against Christianity they had to compare it with Christianity and describe it in terms of Christianity. Rather than representing an established concept of God, the conversation thus echoes a symbolical struggle over the meaning of terms. Therefore, the opponent's emphasis on *Mawu* cannot be taken as an indication of the High God's centrality in the pre-Christian religion. His argument is already influenced by the Christian religion which concentrated much more on *Mawu* than people would have done otherwise.[18] Indeed, Ewe mission workers noted that some people combined local and Christian ideas, thereby 'messing up the word of *Mawu* with the *trɔ*'.[19] The term *Mawu* even came to be used as a generic term for 'god'; and as a consequence, the *trɔwo* and the *aklama* were sometimes referred to as *mawuwo* (gods), although missionaries saw them as agents of *Abosam*.

Nevertheless, sources like the one quoted reveal the difficulty the Ewe had in understanding *Mawu* as a positive, caring power. One might say that listening to the Christian message triggered a reflection about the old religion on a new comparative level, and that statements on this level provide valuable insights into both the nature of the old religion and the way new influences were dealt with. As a result of such comparison, the opponent quoted insisted that there was no need for him to turn to Christianity. By stating that the *trɔwo* were more merciful and effective than *Mawu*, he criticised the missionaries' reliance on a God he considered to be too far away.

But he did not leave it at that. He was probably well acquainted with the Christians' argument. The latter would retort that indeed *Mawu*, being far away, was to be approached through an intermediary, but that this was his son *Yesu Kristo*, rather than the *trɔwo*. Thus, although the mission set the terms of the conversation with the Ewe and started to talk about *Mawu*, in the course of this conversation an inversion occurred. Whereas non-Christians talked in terms of *Mawu* in response to the mission's emphasis on God, the latter introduced Jesus as analogous to the *trɔwo*. Anticipating this, the evangelist's opponent continued that they would not need Jesus. Thus, he took the structural similarity of the *trɔwo* and *Yesu Kristo* postulated by the mission as a point of departure, but, in contrast to the Christian message, he used it to defend the superiority of these local intermediaries over the Christian one.

Whether they accepted the idea of replacing the *trɔwo* by Jesus or not, people perceived him as analogous to them. This was certainly enhanced by the fact that Jesus died the bloody death of an *ametsiava*. As has been seen, when the spirit of such a dead person manifested itself through a living human being, it was considered a powerful *trɔ*. At the same time, however, the mission could not leave it at the level of analogy. Although they had to tie their message onto existing concepts in order to make it intelligible to the Ewe, the missionaries also had to make sure that the worship of Jesus was different from that of the *trɔwo*. This was made clear by emphasising that Christians were not supposed to make any sacrifice (*vɔsasa*). Ewe sacrifices to the *trɔwo* were conceptualised as a relation of gift exchange in Mauss's sense (1990 [1925]), which entailed the obligation to accept a gift and return it later. Missionaries took this reciprocal relationship between human beings and gods as a point of departure, but inverted the direction of the gift exchange:

> Since my boy soon arrived, Brother Schlegel preached on the One Sacrifice, which alone is fully valid and irreplaceable by any other. The attention was quite split, and when the interpreter told them what Brother Schlegel had said, they laughed. Finally Brother Schlegel explained to them that all their sacrifices made to the fetish were made to the Devil and that thereby they surrendered themselves into the hands of Satan, and that before God none of our sacrifices was agreeable, except a humble repentant heart and a beaten spirit (MB 1854: 192).

The practice of sacrifice was thus depicted as devilish. According to missionaries, the one and only sacrifice was Jesus. Because of him, human beings had an eternal obligation towards God. In contrast with the *trɔwo*, he could not be placed under obligation by human beings through a sacrificial gift. Instead, human beings were to abstain from the practice of influencing the *trɔwo* through gifts, and submit themselves completely to the Christian God. Comparing Ewe and Pietist understanding of *vɔsasa*, many people refused to convert because they understood that in doing so they would lose the means with which to influence spiritual beings.

What is so interesting in these fragments of communication is not only that the analogy between Jesus and the *trɔwo* was proclaimed by both the mission and the Ewe, but above all that the analogies were at the same time denied by the mission. Through this, a crucial difference between the Pietist and the Ewe approach towards a deity becomes apparent. Whereas the latter provided people with rituals to serve, and thereby influence, the gods, missionary Pietism did not do so and merely emphasised belief.

To be sure, Pietism's neglect of religious practices and its confinement to allegorical speech was claimed, rather than real. Actually, despite the doctrinal emphasis on mere belief, Pietism offered a whole range of practices that an outside observer would identify as rites. Next to the attendance of the morning and evening devotion and the Sunday Service, and the observance of the Church Order, there were explicit rites for baptism (*Mawutsiɖeta*, 'God's water placed on the head', thus *Mawutsi* came to replace *amãtsi*), confirmation (*konfirmatio*) and the Lord's Supper (*Afetɔ fe kplɔ nu*, 'the Lord's table'). Among the rites mentioned, the performance of the Holy Supper was the most dramatic. In fact, it was a secret ritual which took place after public church service, behind closed doors and windows. The sacred meal joined a select number of people who were all dressed in black and had come to church without speaking.[20] Those taking the holy food without being worthy (because they did not have a clean conscience) would call down the anger of God upon them. In order to be accepted as participants, people had to see the native pastor or missionary and confess their sins. As a result of the mission's threat that God would punish those taking his food unworthily, people saw the Lord's Supper as a powerful ritual strengthening the good and destroying the bad. Although according to the Pietist understanding such ceremonies merely symbolised an inward relationship between a person and God, they went beyond that in the view of Ewe converts and were held to actually change a person's state. The Ewe certainly did not share the mission's emphasis on belief and its insistence that practices were a mere outward thing unable to entice God to do anything, but rather took the practices that missionary Pietism offered at face value.

The Holy Spirit, *Gbɔgbɔ Kɔkɔe* in Ewe, is a new phrase consisting of two terms which previously did not belong to religious discourse. Westermann wrote that the Christianised term *gbɔgbɔ* only reshapes or increases the original sense 'breathing', 'breeze' (1905b: 8). In the use of *gbɔgbɔ* lies a very interesting phenomenon: through translation a hitherto secular word is vested with a new meaning which expresses an idea that did not exist in that form before. At the same time the importance of the term in its new meaning is supported by its original meaning. 'Spirit', by implying 'breath', becomes a matter of vital importance. In contrast to *Gbɔgbɔ Kɔkɔe*, evil spirits were termed *gbɔgbɔ makɔmakɔwo* (*ma* negates *kɔ*, thus 'unclean breaths') or *gbɔgbɔ vɔ̃wo* (*vɔ̃* 'evil', thus 'evil breaths'). These terms, too, were new creations to designate the *trɔwo* and other powers conceptualised as evil. Whereas, in the first instance, evil spirits and demons had been translated as *gbetsi vɔwo* ('evil fates'), the mission later exchanged this very specific term for the more general expression *gbɔgbɔ vɔwo*, which encompassed all former gods, ancestors' spirits, *adziakpe*, witchcraft and *dzo*. In Spieth's ethnographies the word *gbɔgbɔ vɔ* does not appear; his informants referred to specific spiritual agents as either *vɔ* or *nyuie* (good), but they did not conceptualise a large class of 'evil spirits'.

It is interesting to note that no documents have been found in which the missionaries or their native mission workers discussed the Holy Spirit. This is not an accidental omission, but a reflection of the fact that missionaries shrank from talking about the Holy Spirit. The Christianity they preached in the mission field was very much centred on Christian behaviour and the observance of rules. They taught that God's word was revealed through the Bible, and there was no room for unpredictable manifestations of the Holy Spirit. In the same way, they refrained from introducing Blumhardt's practice of calling on the Holy Spirit in order to drive out evil spirits, although from a linguistic point of view the divine and satanic spirits belonged to the same class of beings. Missionaries confined themselves to prayer. I asked the old missionary Paul Wiegräbe why his predecessors, although they were familiar with the practice of exorcism, abstained from talking about and making use of the Holy Spirit in the way of Blumhardt. He asserted that they had been afraid to do so because they might not have been able to judge whether a person was possessed by the divine Spirit, or an agent of the Devil. It seems therefore that the missionaries did not fully introduce the Holy Spirit to the Ewe out of fear that the Ewe themselves might understand it as analogous to the possession cases familiar to them in Ewe religion. To avoid this analogy, they preferred not to turn the Holy Spirit into a subject for discussion. In doing this, they left out an important element of the Pietism they were acquainted with in their home area.

## The Devil: Abosam

The term *Abosam* is derived from the Akan language. Why the missionaries chose this term as a translation for 'Devil' is apparently not documented.[21] *Abosam* can refer to three concepts in the Akan language which all contribute to its present meaning. First, it is possible to trace *Abosam* back to (*ɔ*)*bonsam*, which designates a male witch or a wizard, or a sorcerer in Akan discourse,[22] and the Devil in the Christian vocabulary (see Christaller 1933: 38). Second, the term *Abosam* evokes the image of *Sasabonsam*, a bush monster, which was also known and feared by the western Ewe groups who were in contact with the Asante (in Ewe: *Sasabosam*). According to Christaller this monster was 'inimical to man, especially to the priests, ... but the friend and chief of the sorcerers and witches...' (1933: 429). Rattray

(1927: 28) also noted that *Sasabonsam* was in league with both the female and the male witch (*obayifo* and *bonsam*). The first and second connotation of *Abosam* both imply witchcraft. Westermann (1905a) noted in his Ewe-German dictionary under *Abosam*: '(... initially sorcerer, witch, syn. *adze*), Devil, Satan. To the Ewe, however, the word *abosam*, as well as the term Devil, is initially foreign.' There was thus a strong connection between witchcraft and the Devil. With the issue of diabolisation comes the third possible reference of the term *Abosam*, which is *ɔbosom* (pl. *abosom*), the Akan word for deity (see Christaller 1933: 43). In their attempt to evangelise, missionaries told people that through worship of the *trɔwo* they were serving the Devil (see next chapter).

## Ideas About the World and the Concept of the Person

In talking about heaven (*dziŋgbe*) and hell (*tsiefe* or *dzomavɔ*) missionaries and their native mission workers addressed the most loosely defined semantic field in Ewe religion. They referred to the two realms in terms of the image of the broad and narrow path. Although the Ewe worldview did not offer a clear-cut doctrine, the knowledge claimed by the Christians about the Hereafter evoked a good deal of mockery and protest. People found that since Christians were unable to prove the truth of their view, there was no need to assume that they were right. In the following document an evangelist complains about the Adaklu people, illustrating this line of reasoning:

> It is the idea of the Daklu people that they have to see things with their eyes and that they would have to see signs, too, before they believed. That is why they keep saying that the day they hear that we, wor-shippers of God, are about to die, they would see something descend from heaven to earth, and we would get all our things ready and they would see it, and we would walk quickly to heaven, then they would know that all our words were the truth. Because they also die and are buried in earth in the same way that we too die and are buried in earth and not buried in the air. And this makes them feel that all our words are deceiving. And other people also keep saying that if they heard the bell ringing one day and they saw that God himself descended from heaven and said that the people should come and that he told all of them how they should live in the world, only then they would believe. (n.d., probably around 1900. Stab 7, 1025–56/8: 1; original in Ewe)

Thus, in comparing the two religions, people came to the conclusion that every human being would die in any case. Since Christians, too, were unable to overcome death, there was no need for them to convert. This idea was confirmed by the fact that Christians also used the term *tsiefe* to describe the place where a person would go to after death. In this way the old religion's space of death was incorporated into Christianity, but it is not clear how the mission represented the events after a person's death. Was he or she to stay in *tsiefe* and wait there for Judgement Day and then be sent to hell fire (*dzomavɔ*) or heaven (*dziŋgbe*)? Or would each person be judged immediately after death? Was 'hell' confined to *dzomavɔ*, as some sources suggest, or was *tsiefe* also part of it? These ambiguities cannot be sorted out. Rather, they reflect the different ideas held in nineteenth-century Pietist circles about the time when God would judge human beings.[23] The mission was thus unable to provide people with a clearer idea of the Hereafter than the one they had previously held. Missionaries only added their view to the existing ambiguity with regard to the realm of death. This explains why many Ewe were not ready to change the non-Christian conception for the Christian one.

Yet there was a crucial difference between the Ewe and the mission's image of the Hereafter. *Tsiefe* was considered a mirror image of the world of the living. By contrast, the Christians emphasised that after death people would not stay in *tsiefe* forever, but would rather be selected at a certain point in time on the basis of the lives they had led. Documents revealing Ewe Christians' ideas about the Christian concept of the person are virtually confined to accounts of dreams and deathbed conversions. It seems that hope for salvation and fear of ending in *dzomavɔ* often developed in precarious situations, such as on the deathbed. There are many examples showing that in such a situation people wanted to be baptised in order to be certain of being accepted into heaven.

The dualism of heaven and hell is related to the mission's concept of the person, for it depended on the latter's own choice where he or she would end up. The mission retained the term *ŋutila* for a person's body, and *luvɔ* for 'soul'. The latter was said to have everlasting life; it was the part of the person that would go to either heaven or hell. Apart from the dualist conception concerning a soul's future after death, the Ewe and Christian concept of *luvɔ* were thus more or less identical. The term *gbɔgbɔ* was also retained and designated a person's spirit. However, in the Christian concept of the person there was no room for *aklama*, which, as we have seen, was imagined as a spiritual entity that was worshipped on the day of the week upon which a person was born. Missionaries, who systematically avoided making use of terms which originally implied a ritual praxis, discarded this term because according to them it would be impossible to free it from its previous meaning. Many historical documents of discussions between Ewe evangelists and non-Christians reveal how important the *aklama* was for the latter, who, taking up the Christian terminology, even called them their personal *mawu*.

By excluding *aklama* there was no room for a predetermined character defining a person's course of life in the Christian concept of the person. According to missionaries, it was up to a person to choose which life to lead.

Therefore, a good deal of emphasis was placed on conscience (*dzitsinya*, 'the word staying in the heart'). Though the term had previously existed, in the framework of Christianity it became much more important because missionaries expected Christians to feel responsible for their lives as individuals. They would not accept any explanation of bad behaviour with reference to other powers. However, Christians tended to excuse faults as temptations of the Devil. It was difficult for missionaries to introduce the concept of the individual person who was responsible for his or her faults. Also, the concept of sin (*nuvɔ̃*, 'evil thing') was not easy to transmit, since the Ewe had a very different idea of the causes of and remedies against evil. Ewe Christians did not leave this idea behind completely: mere exclusion of a term did not imply that converts endorsed the Pietist concept of the person.

## TRANSLATION

By developing a Christian Ewe discourse, the NMG intended to convert the orality of heathendom into the written fixity of Christianity. In this way missionaries attempted to gain hold on converts' ideas. However, they did not realise that the meanings of translated terms might not be identical with the original ones. Their view on translation was rather simple: according to Spieth, the content of a term could be separated from its form, and then be transferred into a word form in another language without being changed (1907: 9). To him, the relationship between form and content was thus arbitrary.[24]

This translation theory is still accepted today. The linguist missionary Eugene Nida is one of its best-known representatives. He was personally involved in the translation of the Bible and published various books (1961, 1982) on how to achieve the best transmission of the Christian text into other languages. Although he is aware of the fact that meaning might be changed through translation, his purpose is to achieve translations that mirror the original meaning as closely as possible. For him, transformation of meaning is a problem that should be reduced to a minimum, rather than an unavoidable given to be studied. This stance is shared by other theologians and anthropologists involved in (the study of) Bible translation (for example, Damman 1977; Doke 1958; Kassühlke 1969; Kumbirai 1979; Sanneh 1991; Stine 1990; and Weich 1977). These authors acknowledge the fact that the Christian message has to be expressed in a culture- and language-specific fashion and they conclude that therefore no expression can claim to be universalistic; but nevertheless, they assume that all expressions derive from and refer to the same divine source. This, of course, is a question of belief. Such a view stems from an essentialist notion of Christianity, which assumes that the transmission of content through translation is unproblematic (see Waldman's and Yai's critical review of Sanneh's book [1992]). It implies a theologically inspired perspective on language which is unable (or unwilling) to grasp the nature of intercultural communication.

In a significant study, the Catholic Ewe theologian and linguist Tossou (1988) has shown that Bible translation is much more problematic than theologians and missiologists are inclined to think. He discerns transformations of meanings occurring in the process of translation from the biblical languages into Ewe. He makes a powerful case against the simplistic assumption inherent in the above mentioned Christian translation theory which holds that the relationship between word and content is arbitrary. However, Tossou approached translation as a merely linguistic problem, not as a sociolinguistic process. Therefore, he did not consider how the Ewe appropriated Christian terms on the basis of their own ideas. The mere focus on translation defined as the replacement of one term by another is too narrow to understand the evolution of a local understanding of Christianity. In order to do so, the whole process of communication and appropriation has to be taken into account.

Thus, as has been seen, the meanings of translated Christian key terms were brought about in the process of communication between missionaries and the Ewe. For missionaries, the chosen Ewe terms denoted the content they put into them. For Ewe Christians the terms' old meanings did not totally disappear but continued to form part of the terms. One and the same term would thus have different meanings for missionaries and the Ewe Christians. We also saw that even although through translation old religious practices had been excluded by avoiding terms implying ritual action, people did not accept Pietism's claimed anti-ritualistic attitude towards religion, and endowed Christian terms with a ritual dimension. Leaving out terms in the process of translation does not therefore guarantee that the things they stand for are indeed excluded.

Each Ewe term referred to several *signifiés* which together comprised the *signifiant*'s space of meaning. In other words, each *signifiant* entailed the possibility of comparing its meaning in the framework of the Ewe and the mission's religion, and of evaluating the former in the light of the latter, and vice versa. To use an expression employed by Lienhardt (1982) in his study of Catholicism among the Dinka, each translated Ewe term was 'a kind of linguistic parallax', that is, a term viewed from both the non-Christian and the Christian 'point of observation'. There was no single clear meaning of translated Ewe terms. Rather, each of them called for religious comparison from two viewpoints. Although this religious comparison is best documented in the case of the non-Christian Ewe who insisted on the equality of both religions, Ewe Christians also engaged in it. Despite the fact that they had come to accept the superiority of Christianity, they continued to compare the former with Ewe religion. The fact that they took the practices offered by Pietism at face value illustrates this stance. Comparing the religion they had left behind with the one they adopted, they were not prepared to give up the idea that religious rituals could in fact achieve something. In other words, comparing the mission's representation of religion in terms of belief with their own more practical understanding of religion as worship, they were reluctant or even refused to adopt the former.

In the case of the transmission of missionary Pietism to the Ewe, translation for the Ewe was a matter of comparing religion. Translation, then, can be understood as interpreting and transforming the original statement, thereby creating something of a new quality (see Hallen and Sodipo 1986: 37; Hobart 1987; Overing 1987: 37ff; and Venuti 1992). This comparative practice is what actually occurs in the process of vernacular-isation, although the translators themselves might not be prepared to recognise this, and thereby neglect the creative potential of translation. Through translation, Christian key terms thus acquire a new quality which becomes an inalienable feature of these terms. This holds true despite the fact that missionaries would not have been willing to acknowledge this and instead preferred an objectivist perspective to translation. With their insistence on the superiority of Christianity and the desire to control Ewe converts, missionaries missed the creative potential implied in intercultural communication. This potential can only be realised if the participants in such a communication refrain from an objectivist perspective on translation and the imperialist desire to dominate the target language and its speakers.

Of course, the recognition of translation as a comparative, creative process would have led the missionaries' efforts to control the Ewe's minds through a Christian vocabulary *ad absurdum*. Yet Ewe Christians under-stood terms in other ways than the missionaries. This means that the power of the missionaries to know and control the ideas of Ewe Christians was limited. Thus, as a result of translation, a form of Christianity came into being which, albeit partly, evaded missionary control. This supports Rafael's finding that '[t]he necessity of employing the native vernaculars in spreading the Word of God constrained the universalising assumptions and totalising impulses of a colonial-Christian order' (1988: 21; see also Fabian 1986). By studying the indigenous interpretation of the vernacularised Christian message, 'alternative native responses to the dominant and dominating interpretation' can be discerned (Rafael ibid.).

# 4

# DIABOLISATION

## THE MISSIONARIES AND THE DEVIL

The NMG's activities among the Ewe were characterised by a paradox. On the one hand, existing Ewe concepts were integrated into the Christian Ewe discourse through translation, while on the other, a strict boundary between Christianity and Ewe religion was drawn through diabolisation. Missionaries based the claim that the gods and ghosts served by the Ewe were real agents of the Devil on their interpretation of the New Testament.

> The great Apostle Paul has said in 1 Corinthians 8, 4: Hence we know that an idol is nothing in the world, or in a better translation: that there is no idol in the world. He does not mean by this that what the heathens worship as gods has no existence, since according to 1 Corinthians 10, 20 he himself considered the gods of the heathens to be demonic realities. And in Ephesians 6, 12 he talks about lords and authorities, about the rulers of this world, who reign in the darkness of this world, and about evil spirits under heaven. There is an authority of darkness, an influence of diabolical powers. It is most pronounced among those who worship idols and who are thus subject to the direct control of darkness. *These are the heathens surrounding us, separated from God, but all the more bound to the Devil.*(MB 1864: 157; my emphasis)

The missionaries communicated this perspective to the Ewe, whom they called *Abosamtɔwo*, 'people belonging to the Devil', and assumed that *Abosam* and his agents were using diabolical powers to achieve real results; dark forces manifesting themselves through the 'heathen religion' in general and the activities of Ewe priests and priestesses in particular. In accordance with their calling, missionaries had to fight against Satan and his vassals and destroy the old Ewe religion. To achieve this, street sermons were held.

The Devil scored highly in the range of preaching topics. One missionary wrote the following about a street sermon at the market place of Anloga, a 'centre of fetishism, and linked to fetishism by the Devil himself as it were':

> I started with the mission order, Matthew 28, 10–20, and explained to the people that we had come to them because of this order and that we

had left our beautiful country, as well as our father, mother and family in order to work among them for the King of heaven, and that there were just two things: either the eternal glory through Jesus Christ, or, for the one who scorned and despised Jesus, there was no other thing than eternal damnation. I begged them to become reconciled with God through Christ, I depicted death to them with all its horrors and explained that death would lose its horrors as soon as one believed in Christ. *Then I finished with an attack on the fetish, contrasting the power of the Devil with the power of Christ, thereby comparing them.* (MB 1854: 193; my emphasis)

Many similar accounts show that representation of Ewe religion as satanic prevailed throughout the period of the NMG's activities among the Ewe. Ewe evangelists preached in the same way as their masters (see below) and thereby realised the mission's ideal of true distance from the old ways. Due to a lack of successful conversion stories, there are more texts dealing with the Devil in the first decades of mission activity. But also when conversion became more frequent, from 1884 onwards, the missionaries still wrote and preached in this way (though later, some missionaries became reluctant to talk about Satan too much). For instance, on his journey to Peki in 1887, the missionary Carl Oßwald related his conversation with an Ewe priest at Bakple who claimed that he, too, was a priest of God:

Thereupon I made him understand in unambiguous terms, for the whole meeting to hear, how great the difference was between me and him. I, I said, am a servant of God and have come to show you the unknown God to whom you make sacrifices. *You, however, are an agent of Satan, a liar and deceiver...* (MB 1887: 128; my emphasis)

These reports illustrate how important and meaningful the Devil was for the missionaries. The Devil was the link between the missionaries' and the Ewe's worldview: to state that Ewe religion was a work of Satan made it meaningful in the light of Christianity, and subordinate to it. It also legitimated the necessity to evangelise the Ewe. Moreover, the missionaries used the image of the Devil in order to frighten people: those refusing to convert would end up in hell. It seems that they considered the threat of hell a more appropriate means to bring about conversion than allusions to the sweetness of heaven. Sermons concerning the coming end of the world abound in the MB.

By diabolising Ewe religion, missionaries constructed Pietism and Ewe religion in terms of oppositions: while they served God, the Ewe worshipped the Devil and his demons; while they emphasised belief, the Ewe relied on rituals; while God revealed himself through the Bible, the Ewe communicated with Satan's agents through dance and possession; and while Pietism's agents were male, the Ewe relied on priestesses in addition to priests, and it was the former who expressed the voice of the gods. In the variant of Christianity advocated by them, there was no room for any of these things. The missionaries thus represented Ewe religion as Pietism's Other, thereby defining the two religions in terms of radical difference and denying Ewe Christians their previous expressive forms of worship.

The missionaries diabolised the Ewe's religious concepts and, above all, religious practices, and this resulted in the overall construction of Ewe religion as 'heathendom' and implied an undifferentiated attack on the Ewe's own ideas about good and evil and ways of dealing with them. By diabolising Ewe religion as a whole, the morals entailed by it were declared satanic and inappropriate for Christians. How did Ewe Christians deal with the overall diabolisation of their former religion, and how did they understand the new concept of 'sin' propagated by the mission, and how did Ewe and Pietist concepts of evil blend? To grasp in what ways Ewe Christians appropriated the Pietist concept of evil propagated by the NMG, an overview of non-Christian concepts of evil and practices of dealing with it need to be considered.

### EWE CONCEPTS AND PRACTICES REGARDING EVIL
## Sin versus Nuvɔ̃ and Busu

According to Pietism, evil manifested itself through the bad thoughts and actions depicted on the broad path. The ultimate reason for evil was the intrinsic sinfulness of human beings which made them give in to Satan's temptations. The link with Satan and the 'broad path' could only be broken by a deliberate change of one's state. In order to remain good after conversion, Pietists had to be in full control of their inward and outward life (see Chapter 2). Ewe concepts and practices with regard to evil differed considerably from this stance. The Ewe terms belonged to the complex, semantic domain 'evil', against which – but, due to the necessity of translation, also *with* which – the missionaries presented their point of view. Though there may be more adequate translations for these terms, it has to be acknowledged that Westermann's dictionary (1905a, 1906) is a tremendously important historical document, for it reveals those terms which the missionaries paired, i.e. how they tried to establish linguistic compatibility. Thus, though not defending the value of the dictionary in absolute terms, it is a document able to reveal how misunderstandings evolved by linking Ewe *signifiants*, which hitherto referred to particular Ewe *signifiés*, with new German *signifiés*. In the case of 'sin', things clearly did not work out according to the missionaries' ideas.

The Ewe term *vɔ̃* best approximates the meaning of the adjective 'evil'. Something qualified as *vɔ̃* was found to threaten or even destroy the continuation and good quality of life (*agbe*). Indeed, like many other African

peoples, the Ewe considered 'life' as the highest value.¹ Regarding good
health and offspring as the ultimate aim in peoples lives, they understood
sickness and infertility as an expression of 'evil'. The adjective *vɔ* could be
applied to all sorts of nouns perceived as 'evil' in this sense of causing the
destruction of health, fertility and wealth. *Vɔ* was also used in combination
with *nu* (thing), a term employed by the mission to translate 'sin'. This
translation was not unproblematic, for according to Westermann, *nuvɔ*
designated 'evil (*Übel*), something wicked (*Böses*), mishap (*Mißgeschick*),
accident (*Unfall*)' (1905a: 378). In contrast to the Pietist notion of sin as
bad behaviour resulting from a bad inner state, *nuvɔ* did not define evil in
terms of agency, but rather as something undergone. This is not to say that
the Ewe could not conceive of evil as committed by somebody – the
expression was *wɔ nuvɔ* (to do an evil thing). The point, however, is that
there was a crucial difference between the semantic fields covered by the
terms 'sin' and *nuvɔ*. While the mission conceptualised sin exclusively in
terms of agency (as evil committed), the Ewe term *nuvɔ* described evil above
all in terms of agony – people's suffering from and struggle against hostile,
anti-life forces. Thus, the Ewe concept of evil clearly went beyond personal
agency, while not denying it, and focused on the disastrous results of bad
actions.

As well as *nuvɔ* the Ewe employed the term *busu*. Overlapping with the
semantic field of *nuvɔ*, *busu* was broader in scope. For that reason the
mission probably found the term unfit to designate 'sin'. Westermann
rendered the following translations: '1. Evil, something wicked, mishap, fault,
offence, desecration, profanation. 2. something incredible, unbelievable,
completely extraordinary, miraculous, worthy of astonishment' (1905a:
32). To begin with the second set of possible translations, these terms
emphasise the extraordinary nature of the event and evoke the idea that *busu*
might not be exclusively bad. Indeed, as will be seen later, the Ewe, like
many other African peoples, did not oppose good and evil in dualistic terms,
but rather understood both *nyuie* (good) and *vɔ* as potentials of all things.

Looking at the first set of terms, it appears that the first three translations
correspond to the meaning of *nuvɔ*, and thus also stress 'evil' as something
endured rather than committed. The next four translations, however, go
beyond *nuvɔ* and provide reasons for the occurrence of evil: it could either
result from a fault or an offence, or from desecration or profanation.
Westermann did not specify which actions were implied by these terms. To
understand this, it is necessary to investigate how the term *busu* was
employed.

Though Spieth did not devote particular attention to Ewe concepts of
evil, it can be inferred from his work that *busu* was used in the case of both
collective and individual mishap. For instance, he described the case of an
*ametsiava* death (a death by accident) which was considered to bring *busu* to

the town (*du*). After the person had been buried in the bush, it was necessary to purify the whole *du*. This procedure, which was termed *busuyiyi*, basically implied the following actions: the priests tore up a frog (*akpɔplɔ*) and a fowl (*koklovi*), which were then both tied onto a palm branch, and walked from one end of the town to the other while ringing a bell and sprinkling *amãtsi* ('herb water' with healing power) on the ground; and finally the palm branch was left on the outskirts of the town. Through this ritual action they cleansed the town and chased away evil (1906: 296–7). Thus, a person's unnatural, bloody death was considered to have defiled the town and it was necessary to remove this pollution and restore life through a purification ritual. This is a *busu* resulting from desacralisation. My own informants also told me of *busu* caused by taboo breaches that had gone unnoticed, such as the pollution of a *fia*'s (chief's) stool by the touch of someone thought to be unclean, for example a menstruating woman or a six-fingered person. This is probably what Westermann's terms 'fault' and 'offence' refer to. Since breaking a deity's laws brought about desacralisation, we may conclude that 'fault' or 'offence' and 'desecration' were closely interrelated.

*Busuyiyi* could be organised for a particular clan, *du*, or even for a whole *dukɔ* (state). I learned from the Amimli and Abia priestesses that in the 'olden days', when *busu* afflicted the Peki towns in the form of smallpox and cholera, all Peki priests and priestesses of 'black' *trɔ̃wo* (gods) would do *busuyiyi*. Dressed only in their loincloths, they would silently perform the sweeping ritual in the dead of night, from Wudome throughout all other Peki towns to Dzake. The aim of this ritual purification was to counter evil and to restore order.

A similar procedure was conducted four days before the yearly yam festival. Spieth presented it as *nuvɔnyanya*, 'sacking evil', though his informant, whose statement he transcribed, also employed the term *busuyiyi*. According to my informants the name of this ritual was *gbɔmekpɔkplɔ*, 'sweeping the town'. They told me that the most important difference between this ritual and *busuyiyi* was that the latter was performed whenever an acute need arose, whereas the former took place on a regular basis. The procedure itself was a more complex purification ritual than the *busuyiyi* described above; however, *busuyiyi* itself was part of it. The *gbɔmekpɔkplɔ* ritual was performed as follows (Spieth 1906: 304–7): the *trɔ̃* priests tied creepers and leaves from the *Wɔ* and *Adzu* tree onto sticks from the *Adzu* tree. In the process of binding they called *ŋɔli vɔ̃* (evil spirit of a dead person), *gbetsi vɔ̃wo* ('evil fates'), *trɔ̃ vɔ̃* (evil god), *adze vɔ̃* (evil witch), and *nuvɔ̃siwo katã le dusia me* (all evil things in the town) to get into the sticks with the leaves tied round them (*nubabla*, 'tied thing') and be bound. Then they smeared ashes mixed with urine on each *nubabla*, saying that this would blind all those evil powers bound within them. The people then threw all the sticks on the ground and insulted them; the priests then carried the sticks through the town and eventually planted one on each of the paths leading into it. They said that in doing this they were chasing all evil things from the town and closing off the way back for them. Afterwards, all inhabitants of the town washed their faces with *amãtsi*. On their return, they swept their houses and compounds so the whole town would be clean. During the night, when the priests performed the *busuyiyi* ritual described above, nobody was allowed to light fires in their houses. The following morning women swept their fireplaces: dressed in rags or with creepers tied round their bodies, they would summon all sicknesses troubling their bodies to go away. Then they would run out of the town, again calling the causes of all evils to leave them. Two days later they celebrated the yam festival (see Chapter 3), marking the beginning of the new year.

Thus, by translating 'sin' as *nuvɔ̃*, two concepts were related that were not equivalent. In contrast to the Pietist concept of sin, which defined evil in terms of agency and requested individual repentance, *nuvɔ̃* and *busu* represented evil mainly as something undergone and to be countered by purifying rituals.

## Fears and Images of Evil

The occurrence of *busu* and the performance of purifying rituals was not confined to groups. Individuals could also suffer from *busu*. Unfortunately, Spieth did not document how individuals coped with the *busu* which befell them. However, it is clear from scattered passages (for example, ibid.: 486–7) that *busu* could be attributed to the following entities: an evil fate or destiny (*gbetsi vɔ̃* or *aklama vɔ̃* or *dzɔgbe vɔ̃*),[2] a dead person's malevolent spirit (*ŋɔli vɔ̃*), a malicious deity (*trɔ̃ vɔ̃*), black magic (*dzoɖuame*), or witchcraft (*adze*). People suffering from sickness or other problems would consult a diviner (*bokɔnɔ*) or *trɔ̃* priest in order to find out the cause and to perform a ritual known as *busuyiyi* or *nuvɔ̃ɖeɖe* to remove it. Although certain symptoms were associated with particular powers, there was no binding relationship between the two; practically, if one treatment failed, the trouble could be attributed to another cause and another ritual performed to counter the *busu*. It would be impossible to describe these rituals in detail. In each case, the *busu* afflicting a person was removed through a symbolic procedure (often including taking a herbal bath) which restored his or her spiritual and physical integrity so that life could continue.

On looking more closely at the different entities to which evil was attributed, they reveal what the Ewe considered to be life-threatening forces: the various entities can be considered as crystallisations of particular fears which, in turn, are centred around particular ethical values. Ewe ethics can be glimpsed through the analysis of these particular images of evil.

To begin with 'evil fate' or destiny. Before someone came into the world, he or she had promised their day of return to the spirit realm and this promise was thought of as a personified spiritual entity called *gbetsi*. If a young person was frequently sick or did not grow well – for a girl this might imply not developing breasts at puberty – this *busu* could be attributed to a *gbetsi vɔ̃*. In such a case the *gbetsi vɔ̃* was exchanged for a *gbetsi* that would guarantee a longer life and offspring. The trouble existing between someone and his or her *gbetsi vɔ̃* was the opposition between life and death. Expressing the wish to die early, the *gbetsi vɔ̃* was the absolute negation of the Ewe culture's highest value. It represented the fear of leaving this world too early to contribute to the prolongation of life by procreation. The ritual of exchanging the *gbetsi vɔ̃* for a life-affirming *gbetsi* was an attempt to cure the person affected in order to enable him or her to be a full human being – someone bringing forth offspring.

Another group of malevolent spirits able to inflict *busu* on people were the spirits of the deceased. As noted in the last chapter, these spirits were unable to join the ancestors (*adefíewo*). Thus, there were two types of dead people. True ancestors saw to the well-being of the living and received gifts of food and drink in return. By contrast, the *ŋɔli vɔ̃wo*, since they had not yet arrived in *tsiefe* (the hereafter), haunted human beings with sickness and other misfortune. What does the fear of the *ŋɔli vɔ̃wo* stand for? In order to find an answer to this question, one has to realise that the *ŋɔliwo* were a category in between *kodzogbe* (this world) and *tsiefe*, who troubled human beings because the latter still owed them something. The living were therefore punished for their failure to comply with their dues. This in turn made it impossible for the *ŋɔliwo* to turn into ancestors and engage in the proper exchange relationship between the living and the dead, which guaranteed the continuation of life. Fear of *ŋɔli vɔ̃wo* reveals that the deceased were still very much present in the memory of the living, and possibly reminded them of unsettled conflicts and problems. Often widows and widowers feared their deceased partner and were afraid that he or she would continue to visit the house. In order to avoid this, particular rites had to be observed. The image of the malevolent deceased relative bringing sickness and death instead of health and life represents the fear of the devastating consequences of unsolved family conflicts. The ritual pacifying of a *ŋɔli vɔ̃* settled the relationship between him or her and the afflicted human being, thereby restoring health and transforming the liminal *ŋɔli vɔ̃* into a benevolent ancestor.

Another cause of *busu* could be a *trɔ̃*. Ambivalent in nature, a *trɔ̃* supported his worshippers as long as they observed his rules and taboos. Anyone failing to do so would trigger the anger of the *trɔ̃* upon him or herself; sickness and other misfortune would result. People's fear of a malevolent *trɔ̃* shows how powerful these deities were considered to be. Just as they could restore health and wealth, they could also destroy it. If one failed to comply with their laws, it was necessary to pacify them with a sacrifice so that the relationship with the *trɔ̃* could be restored. It was also possible for a *trɔ̃* to inflict evil upon someone because he wanted him or her to be a *trɔ̃* priest. This could happen if a new *trɔ̃* manifested himself, perhaps through a family member having died as an *ametsiava* and then wanting to be served, or if a *trɔ̃*'s priest had died and the god selected a new one or wanted to possess more priestesses through whom he could speak. In each case the chosen person had to be initiated into the service of the *trɔ̃* in order for the sickness to disappear. Fear of the malevolent *trɔ̃* shows that the Ewe considered power (*ŋusẽ*) as ambivalent: power to heal and bring about life also implied the ability to cause the contrary.

The same ambivalence applied to *dzo vɔ̃* (bad magic, medicine), another potential source of *busu*. As noted already, each *dzo* could bring about sickness or health, life and death. Most people owned a couple of *dzo* strings as a prophylactic against all sorts of misfortune, or to improve their prospects and plans for the future. Others, however, performed *dzo* in order to destroy and possibly even kill their enemies. Such a person was called *dzoɖuametɔ* ('somebody eating a person with *dzo*'). Fear of such *dzo* was widespread. Spieth, for instance, mentioned that in Ho pregnant women used to consult a *trɔ̃* priest shortly before delivery in order to counteract evil charms preventing them from giving birth. The priest would then perform a ritual in order to deter the evil powers and 'open' the women so that they could deliver safely (ibid.: 433–4). Fear of *dzo vɔ̃* was fear of the destructive potential of human beings, who for one reason or another (often out of envy or greed) secretly wished to destroy. Such people, mainly men, were considered extremely bad morally.

Witchcraft was a destructive power used by both men and women, and while it was by and large confined to one's own blood relatives, *dzo* could also be directed against other people with whom one had had conflicts (for instance, over land). If such people, performing destructive *dzo*, were detected and found guilty in their lifetime, they had to pacify their victims. If anyone known as a *dzoɖuametɔ* died, the body was burned or buried in the bush, thereby excluding the evil doer from the human community.[3] Many tried to counter the possibility of being attacked by evil *dzo* or other bad powers by buying charms from *dzotɔwo* (native healers, magicians).

The last evil power to be considered here, which was able to bring about *busu*, also relates to inter-human conflicts: *adze*. Note that some of Spieth's informants talked about *adze vɔ̃*, whereas others simply used *adze*. The use of the adjective *vɔ̃* suggests that *adze*, like *dzo*, was not held to be evil *per se*. Indeed, there are indications that *adze* was considered a power able to achieve special, miraculous things.[4] However, the negative valuation of *adze* largely prevailed. In speaking about *adze*, it was unnecessary to add the epithet *vɔ̃* in order to express its malice. According to Spieth,[5] *adze* was one of the most feared powers in Ewe land: it was said to be active at night; it was a light, shining apparition; it could take possession of human beings with or without their consent. Such a person became *adzetɔ*, a witch.[6] At night, *adze* would pass through closed doors and suck blood from people while they slept. The victim would then fall sick after a couple of days and die, if the cause of the disease remained undetected (Spieth 1906: 544–5). It was the witches' 'dearest longing ... to make somebody poor. If he becomes rich, they destroy him. If he has children, they kill them all. Secretly they destroy everything he has' (ibid.: 300). Spieth did not specify which people were considered potential witches. However, *adzetɔwo*, who could be either male or female, normally directed their destructive power against members of their own family whom they envied. In particular, the paternal aunt, *tasi*, was considered a potential witch. If her brother's children fared better than her own or, worse still, if she herself did not even have offspring, she was suspected of harming them out of jealousy. Other potential *adzetɔwo* were old people. When young children in the family kept on dying while the old people continued to live, the latter were suspected of feeding on the blood of the young. Another category considered prone to deal in witchcraft were poor people envying rich family members who failed to share their wealth with them. Thus witchcraft suspicions are to be understood in the context of conflicting relationships. 'And those who long for things too much and those who hate people bitterly, black people used to regard these people as witches', an evangelist remarked pointedly (Stab 7, 1025–56/8: 239–40; original in Ewe).

Of course, all women with brothers could be considered witches, but a woman was only suspected of having *adze* when her brother's children suffered a mishap which they then attributed to her. In the same way, old people were only considered *adzetɔwo* if small children frequently died in the family, and poor people could only be suspected of harming others if there was reason for envy. *Adze* therefore expressed tensions in family relationships. Fear of *adze* represents the fear that the people with whom one is closely related secretly seek one's downfall. It expresses the fact that the family was not only functional for the reproduction of life, but also a potential source of destruction.[7] Secrecy was a central aspect of *adze*. People were reluctant to talk about it and kept their suspicions to themselves. As long as suspicions did not develop into accusations, there was no direct remedy against *adze*. One could try to protect oneself against it, but there was no ritual whereby conflicts between the two family members involved could be settled.[8] It was because of this impossibility that both *adze* and *dzo vɔ̃* were feared. They were seen as extremely destructive forces against which people tried to protect themselves as best they could. I was told, however, that occasionally people were openly accused of witchcraft and required to submit themselves to an ordeal. If found guilty, they had to pacify their victims and undergo a purification ritual in the course of which *adze* was taken away from them. The assumption must be that this did not happen very frequently, one would otherwise have found occasional descriptions of such ordeals in the mission journal. Since this is not so, *adze* was probably confined to an invisible, secret realm and hence it was almost impossible to restore the strained relations between an assumed witch and his or her victims.

Ewe ethics were centred on the reproduction and continuation of life. In order to achieve this aim it was considered necessary to ensure that relationships among human beings, as well as between them and spiritual entities, were kept in balance through the reciprocal exchange of gifts: sacrifices in the intercourse with spirits, and services and mutual assistance in interpersonal relationships. In all cases described, *busu* was a result of a relationship that was out of balance: with *gbetsi vɔ̃*, this imbalance occurred within a person; with *ŋɔli vɔwo*, between a living and a dead person; with *trɔ̃ vɔ̃*, between human beings and a deity; and with *dzo vɔ̃* and *adze*, between people. In the first three, the distorted relationship was restored through ritual, so that life could continue. In the case of *dzo vɔ̃* and *adze*, however, due to the secrecy of both offence and suspicion, it was much more difficult to settle the conflict. The only thing to be done against these aggressive evil powers was personal prophylactic protection measures.

## The Power of Dzo

From whom did people receive this protection? It seems that there was an ongoing rivalry between *trɔ̃* priests and *dzotɔwo* and that the latter became increasingly important. This can be inferred from an Ewe evangelist's report on people's fears written in 1909, in which he mentioned the same powers as described above. According to this document there was a rivalry for clients between *trɔ̃* priests and *dzotɔwo*. The evangelist stated that people turned to either *dzotɔwo* or *trɔ̃* priests in order to deal with these evils. The *trɔ̃* priests, however, not only relied on the power of their *trɔ̃wo*, but in addition they owned *dzo*, thereby acknowledging that *dzo* had more power than the gods. The evangelist emphasised that the *dzo* binders (*dzosalawo*, synonymous with *dzotɔwo*) actually presented themselves and were considered to be the most powerful people:

> People fear *dzosalawo* very much, because they regard *dzosalawo* as people who have a special kind of dark power. That is why *trɔ̃* priests, witches or ordinary people who do not have a *trɔ̃* with them and who do not have a lot of *dzo*, or those who do not make these things, are afraid of the one who carries out a lot of *dzo*. The *dzosalawo* rely on their *dzokawo* a great deal and they obey them as well. *Dzosalawo* are people who keep on scaring people who do not have any [*dzo*]. And they scare *trɔ̃siwo* and witches, too, saying that *dzoka* has a special

power which is such that it can destroy the power of *trɔ̃*. And it also has such power that it will catch witches, too, by using witchcraft power. Therefore great *dzosalawo* often brag about their *dzokawo*, praising the things the *dzokawo* do. The *dzosalawo* think that *dzo* has such power that it can bring sickness to a person for many years or many days or many months. (Stab 7, 1025-56/8: 233–5; original in Ewe)

Thus, *dzo* surpassed all other powers and was the best remedy against *adze*. The rivalry between *trɔ̃* priests and *dzotɔwo* was possibly a new development concerning the most effective remedies against witchcraft and other forms of spiritual destruction and was decided in favour of the *dzotɔwo*. Otherwise the evangelist would not have devoted so many words to the phenomenon and emphasised that even witches feared *dzo*. Other Ewe mission workers also noted the tremendous power attributed to *dzo*[9] and the widespread fear of *adze*[10] as if it was an important message to bring home to the missionaries who were to read their reports. Of course, Spieth also described the popularity of *dzo* and quoted informants who stated that there was a rivalry between *trɔ̃* priests and *dzotɔwo*. But he never said that the *dzotɔwo* were considered more powerful than the *trɔ̃* priests. During his research in the last two decades of the nineteenth century, rivalry between *dzotɔwo* and *trɔ̃* priests already existed, but presumably at that stage the *dzotɔwo* were not yet considered to be so powerful. This development may only have occurred in the course of the first decade of the twentieth century. The popularity of *dzo* may also be due to the fact that many *trɔ̃* priests were relatively conservative, while *dzo* was more flexible and allowed those using it to go along with the new developments as well as protect themselves against problems raised by them.

In my view, the relative weakening of the power of the *trɔ̃wo* in favour of *dzo* indicates a move from more collective to more individualist forms of religion. Although people could consult *trɔ̃* priests individually if need be, the worship of a *trɔ̃* was defined as a collective cult integrating a whole family, clan, or even town. *Dzo*, by contrast, was a purely individual matter. In order to be protected by *dzo* there was no need to participate in any organised worship. One just had to buy *dzo* strings from a specialist and have them tied around one's body. The predominant popularity of *dzo* suggests a need for individual forms of protection in addition to or even at the expense of participation in collective cults. Of course, this evokes the question as to why an increasing need for individual protection arose; the reason for this probably lies in increasing fear of *adze* and destructive *dzo*, two evil powers stemming from unresolvable, secret conflicts between human beings. Of course, conflicts between humans occur at any time and in any place. But there are indications that the Ewe's incorporation into the colonial political and economic system (especially through cocoa cultivation, but also other modern professions) resulted in a very unequal distribution of wealth, which in turn gave rise to envy. And envy, as we have seen, was considered the main motive of people employing *adze* and *dzo vɔ̃* against others. Those who profited were afraid that less prosperous, jealous family members would seek their downfall. Therefore they needed effective protection against *adze* and *dzo vɔ̃*. This not only explains the increasing importance of *dzo*, but also the popularity of anti-witchcraft movements such as the Dente cult (Maier 1983) and, last but not least, the growing popularity of Christianity.

### THE EWE AND ABOSAM

Ewe ideas about evil were completely different from those of Pietist missionaries. In their construction of the Ewe religion as 'heathendom', Pietists did not take into account Ewe ways of conceptualising and dealing with evil. Not realising that these ideas entailed central ethical concepts, the missionaries dismissed them as satanic. As a result, the differences between the mission's and Ewe dealings with evil made it difficult for many Ewe to convert, since in their view the Pietist concepts and practices, which were presented to them in terms of words from their own language, made little sense.

## The Theodicy Problem

Initially the missionaries' claim that God was good and that the Devil was responsible for all evil in the world made little sense to the Ewe who thought of the *trɔwo* as ambivalent beings. Hence, the bulk of discussions on *Abosam* deal with the theodicy problem. The following excerpt from a report of an evangelist's visit to Akrofu illustrates the matter:

> One day I [the evangelist] went into the town of Akrofu, and I explained to the people the downfall of human beings and the coming of their saviour. And they asked me whether this *Mawu* [God] who made the human beings and everything on earth was the same one who had made *Abosam* before *Abosam* became the killer of people. *Why did Mawu not kill Abosam once and for all as well so that the human beings would have peace?* And I replied by telling them that there was a certain father who had two children. The elder child did not respect the father and did not act according to his wishes, but the younger child respected his father and did act according to his wishes. One day the rough one took something and hit the good sibling and hurt him. Now what did the father do? They replied that he would take hold of the rough child and kill him. And I told them: 'No, he will not kill his rough child. However, what this father will do first is to lift his wounded son from the ground, wash the wound for him, put medicine onto it and dress it. Only afterwards, when the father sees whether the wounded son will survive or not, will he be ready to do what he wants to the rough child.' They replied that it was indeed so. I told them that now *Mawu* was the father, who brought forth the human beings, and

it was *Abosam* who turned to become *Mawu*'s rough child. By doing this, he hurt human beings. And if *Mawu* would leave us behind and would want to pay *Abosam* for his work, then those of us already hurt by *Abosam* would die. Therefore, *Mawu* sent his child so that he could make medicine for us, so that we would stay alive. Later on he would pay *Abosam* for his work. If he deserved a beating, he would be beaten, if he deserved to be tied up, he would be tied up, if he deserved to be killed, he would be killed. And I saw that it shook their heart when they heard these words, but longing for worldly things was deceiving them. Now, in this matter I indeed recognised that sin destroys us black people more than the *Ablotsi* people [people from abroad]. (Stab 7, 1025–56/8: 80ff; original in Ewe)

Such discussions occurred frequently. For instance, the evangelist Samuel Atakuma reported that his listeners asked him why Jesus had not killed the Devil before his word was preached to them: 'Therefore we should tell our God Jesus that he should kill the Devil for them, so that he could tempt them no longer' (MB 1897: 71–2). The evangelists always cast their reply in allegorical speech, thereby imposing their own images upon their listeners who were to accept the solution proposed.

However, it remains doubtful whether the listeners were satisfied with these allegorical explanations, even partially, because there was evidently so much misfortune in the world. For instance, a man from Wudome said after listening to a sermon: '*Mawu* is a deceiver because he has made my head hair red, but my beard is black' (Stab 7, 1025–56/8: 506; original in Ewe). Other people expressed their surprise that Christians also still suffered in the world. Like non-Christians, they endured all sorts of misfortune, fell sick, and died. The Ewe clearly grasped the crucial, unresolved tension in the Christian doctrine. Comparing the Christian image of God with their own ideas about the *trɔwo*, and looking at the state of the world, many Ewe found the Pietist message made little sense.

Others, however, appreciated the idea of a God who would not ask his followers to bring expensive sacrifices, and punish them if they failed to do so. For instance, having listened to a street sermon, an old man in one of the Agotime towns complained that they were worshipping a god – a *mawu* the mission would call *Abosam*, as he admitted – whose worship was expensive. Since they could not afford the worship of a second god, they were unable to serve the Christian one. This is how the report of the conversation continued. The evangelist went on:

I was not telling him that he should also accept the *Mawu*, whose word I was preaching, and add it to his; rather, that he should leave the one which he was worshipping and accept mine. And as for the *Mawu* in heaven, no other *Mawu* was worshipped in addition to him any longer.

In the same vein, in his worship, animals were not killed and no other things were used to sacrifice to him because he did not need anything like that. And when the preachers preach to them about *Mawu*, they do not want to take a drink or any other thing, nor go and collect money from them as the *trɔ* priests do. They said to me again: 'Their [the *trɔ* priests'] worship is not good, it is too difficult, if you commit a small mistake, he [the *trɔ*] kills you.' That is why they were afraid of him and they were worshipping him so that he would not kill them. And yet if they left him and came to *Mawu*, would he [the *trɔ*] then not be more angry and kill them? I said to him: 'No, it is not so.' If only they themselves really refused to serve under *Abosam* from deep down in their own heart, he would no longer persecute them to do anything for him. He would be hurt, however, as long as they were with *Mawu*, he [the *trɔ*] would no longer perpetrate evil against them. (Stab 7, 1025–56/8: 119–20, 1909; original in Ewe)

Thus, the evangelist grasped the chance to talk to dissatisfied *trɔ* worshippers and made it clear that Christian worship did not require sacrifices and any other expenses. By the performance of such rituals, they were actually serving *Abosam*. Therefore, they should convert, and if they did so, the Christian *Mawu* would protect them against *Abosam*'s anger, and he would be unable to kill them. Their lives would thus be safer if they turned to Christianity. Moreover, worship would be less costly. It is not clear what the listeners did after this particular conversation, but in general the comparative cheapness of Christian worship was attractive to many Ewe. Thus, though the theodicy problem was unsolved and evil remained in the world, the distancing from non-Christian practices through diabolisation was appealing to some people dissatisfied with Ewe religion because, among other things, Christianity seemed to provide salvation at a comparatively low cost.

## The shift to Christianity

Conversions mainly occurred from the 1890s onwards. While some were mainly attracted by the Christians' material possessions and the qualifications achievable in mission schools and usable in colonial institutions, others converted because of sickness, misfortune or social problems. The will to convert indicates that people were in one way or another dissatisfied with the state of things and wanted to improve their situation. Indeed, Christianity offered a way out of various existing constraints and promised upward social mobility. Spieth acknowledged that people rarely converted to Christianity because they were persuaded by the Gospel and started to reflect upon their lives, but rather because they were already dissatisfied and thought Christianity might improve their condition

A strong feeling of great desolation as a result of all sorts of needs, sickness, the death of relatives; greed of chiefs and priests; fear of death etc. create a strong longing for liberation in them. In this longing they painfully remember all the attempts, throughout their whole lives, to find help from the many gods of their country. (MB 1896: 11)

The majority of conversion candidates were people who had played no special role in the framework of Ewe religion and had merely sought a *trɔ*'s or *dzo*'s protection when required. Many converted because they were tired of serving a *trɔ* without profiting from it. For instance, a man from Peki Avetile complained:

When my first child was sick, I offered a goat to the family god Abia; however, the child died. For the second child I even bought three goats, but it also died. The god Abia has received no less than twenty-five goats from me. This, however, did not make my heart happy. Rather, it emptied my hands and made my heart poor. Now my eyes are open to recognise Christ; with him there are no goats and chickens. Salvation from sin and death is only with him; for he loves us, although we are in the dark. (MB 1902: 36)

Many people had similar problems and were disappointed by both the power of the *trɔwo* and *dzo*. Indeed, 'the main reason, ... which causes the heathens to start something new lies in the paltriness of their idols and fetish strings, as well as in the experience of the priests' fraud' (MB 1902: 36). Thus, the change of religion was basically a deliberate turning away from the old.

Occasionally, even priests turned to Christianity. In such cases, all paraphernalia related to *trɔ* worship were burned and the priest openly rejected this service. Spieth, for instance, described the case of a priestess of the *trɔ* Fofie in Peki, who had been possessed and turned into his priestess against her will. The service of Fofie, who demanded expensive food sacrifices and forbade her to work in the field and to leave her compound, was costly and tedious, though she did earn some money through consultations. Eventually she became a Christian. On the night after her decision to convert, she had a vision:

A big European had a book in his hand. The teacher was sitting to his right and a hideous male creature, dressed only in a loin-cloth, was sitting to his left. The European opened the book, read it, and at the end said 'No'. At this, the teacher shouted at the hideous creature, which as a result, got up and fled. Then she fell asleep. (1908: 12)

This vision casts the priestess's wish to leave her old god in a symbolic battle between Christianity, represented by the European and the Ewe teacher (certainly both dressed in jacket and tie), and the old religion, represented by the sparsely dressed creature. Her own decision is confirmed by the fact that the European finds her name in God's book of life (an image also used in *The Pilgrim's Progress*), so that the teacher can chase away the old god. Conversion was frequently cast in similar dream images which emphasised the superiority of the book-religion, whose followers adopted it by their own individual decision, as opposed to the possession cults, whose followers were chosen against their will by the *trɔwo*. The issue of sin and internal change, however, was virtually never raised in the framework of this imagery, an imagery which emphasised a turning away from the old, 'uncivilised' form of worship.

However, the will to escape from old constraints and to become 'civilised' was not sufficient for acceptance as a church member. There was a time-span between the initial willingness to be a Christian and a person's acceptance into the mission church. In order to become a member, a person had to follow baptismal lessons. After the course, which was given by a native mission worker teaching the basics of Protestant doctrine and morals, each candidate was interrogated by a missionary who then decided whether the person was to be accepted. In this context, the candidates had to confess their involvement with 'heathendom' and their moral trespasses, such as non- or extra-marital affairs.[11] The NMG did not strive to baptise as many people as possible (for example MB 1899: 8), but submitted each candidate to careful selection. In many cases, aspiring Christians were refused because they were not yet considered to be mature (for example, MB 1896: 11); that is, they did not sufficiently match the mission's ideal of conversion.

To the missionaries, the ideal conversion resulted from a feeling of total sinfulness and entailed a complete change in a person's inner state and, as a next step, also in their behaviour (see Chapter 2). Hardly any candidate met this ideal.[12] The missionaries continuously complained that many just repeated what they had heard in the lesson, without seeming to have internalised the message. Moreover, rather than having a notion of sinfulness, the candidates mainly complained about the priests' inability to bring about health and protection, and about the fact that in the framework of *trɔ* worship they could not be masters of their own, individual lives. The historical documents abound with missionaries' lamentations that most Ewe lacked the 'inner' dimension of conversion, that there was no real change of heart (as suggested by *dzimetɔtrɔ* – 'turn in the heart' – the Ewe term newly coined to designate conversions). However, the missionaries' uncertainties and complaints about the converts' inner state should not blind us to the fact that conversion was actually a radical step. It not only implied the complete neglect of Ewe religious practices, but also the separation from groups of which the converts had hitherto been part.

Since there was no way to look into people's minds, all those openly dissociating themselves from the old religion and adopting the Christian church order had to be accepted as members. Whatever reasons had initially driven people to the baptismal class, they could become church members if they took up the missionaries' discourse and renounced the Ewe religion as 'heathendom'. Indeed, rejection of Ewe religion as satanic and backward was considered the hallmark of conversion by both Ewe Christians and missionaries. Spieth summarised this succinctly in his essay on conversion: 'If we could ask the almost 6,000 Christians of Ewe-land where they come from, they would all reply: "We come out of the dark, where we stood under the power of Satan"' (1908: 1). Ewe Christians thus adopted the diabolisation of the Ewe religion continuously preached to them by the missionaries. But the missionaries were none too pleased with the popularity of this view. To them, conversion amounted to more than the mere turning away from old religious concepts and practices.

## Peki Converts and the Devil

In 1890 the missionary Gottlob Däuble questioned sixteen Peki men and women to find out whether they were ready for baptism. The examination had been preceded by baptismal lessons given by the native pastor Rudolf Mallet. Däuble asked each candidate separately for the reasons why they wished to convert and finally admitted five men and six women.

> Most of them gave the following reason: *The Devil, that is, the fetishes, evil spirits and fetish priests* had troubled, deceived and ruined them; they had killed their children or siblings or had failed to rescue them from death as they had promised. The required sacrifices had been made, but in vain. They had received the help they had asked for. That is why they now came to God, whom they had once left behind, in order to find redemption, peace, happiness and life; they also did not wish to die amid the worship of idols. Formerly, they had not known anything about God or sin, but now God had sent his Word to them and changed their minds, he had opened the door for them so that they could be saved. (MB 1890: 31; my emphasis)

These answers again reveal a dissatisfaction with the religion previously adhered to and with sacrifices vainly carried out. This religion was now associated with the Devil, *Abosam,* and was disapproved of. The Christian God was opposed to the Devil in a dualistic way, but although this dichotomy was in line with the missionaries' teachings, Däuble had certain objections:

> Many of them are more occupied with and driven by *the fear of the Devil* than by the anguish of conscience over their own sin, and in some cases it was difficult to make clear to them *that not only the Devil would ruin them*, but that everyone would be lost because of personal sin. Moreover, I told them *that they may not attribute misery and suffering to the Devil and evil spirits alone.* After all, they themselves referred to the fetish priests as liars and deceivers, and indeed, that is what they

were. Hence the things they made them believe were also lies. If, for instance, they said that they had to carry out sacrifices because otherwise the Devil would kill their child, this was a lie. If the child subsequently died, and they made them believe that the Devil had killed it, this was also a lie. But I believe that God had taken their children away in order to convince them of the deceit of the fetish worship and to draw them to himself. (ibid.: my emphasis)

Although the candidates adopted the missionaries' arguments, Däuble remained dissatisfied because their self-image was still too positive and lacked an awareness of sin. While the Ewe held all the powers under *Abosam* to be ultimately the cause of misfortune and misery, the missionaries explained that this was really due to inherent evil in human beings which drove them to the Devil or invoked God's anger and punishment. Däuble's examination aimed to discover the extent to which the Ewe realised this:

Moreover, I wanted to examine the extent of their awareness of sin, longing for salvation, confidence in God and awareness of our Saviour Jesus Christ and his redemption. I was not so interested in what they had learned by heart, but rather to discover whether their old heathen superstitious views had been transformed into Christian views by the things learned and heard; whether at least they had some under-standing of the Godly, whether there was a longing which had already taken and understood something of God's salvation through faith. And regrettably I found that several of them were still stuck in their old dark views ... (ibid.)

The candidates were thus not satisfactorily converted, but remained attached to the old religion: they continued talking about the old gods and ghosts and failed to adopt the Pietist concept of sin.

## The Remnants of 'Heathendom' and the Devil

For Ewe Christians the Devil was clearly the link between Christianity and the Ewe religion: as *Abosam*, he represented all *trɔ̃wo* and other spiritual beings, and as the Devil he was God's counterpart. He integrated into the Ewe's Christian worldview all the gods and ghosts previously known to them, and thereby the non-Christian religion became meaningful in the light of Christianity. It also became an integral part of it, though negatively defined and transformed. As the Devil played such a crucial role in the missionaries' worldview, it is not surprising that he figured even more prominently in the Ewe's worldview, and that through him the pre-Christian religion became a building block of their Christian understanding. The Ewe Christians seem to have grasped perfectly and applied to their own situation the central dichotomy of the Pietist worldview which was continu-ously communicated to them.

Thus Ewe Christians fully adopted Pietism's dualistic stance, which enabled them to dissociate themselves from the old religion which they considered 'pagan' and backward, was very attractive for those who strove for 'opened eyes', fitted perfectly with the spatial and social separation of the Christians from all other people and emphasised their own superiority and ability to look down upon them. In this sense, the diabolisation of non-Christian practices reified as 'heathendom' was a symbolic means with which the new elite could define itself as superior.

However, diabolisation not only entailed the possibility for people to dissociate themselves from 'heathendom', but at the same time confirmed it. The old gods and ghosts were actually present for the Ewe Christians in the same way as for the missionaries. But in contrast to the latter, most Ewe Christians had experienced their presence in their own lives and this had attracted them to Christianity. This even applied to many second and third generation Christians, many of whom still believed that the local powers were real. After all, though Christianity increased in popularity, non-Christians still far outnumbered Christians. Thus even after turning to the Christian God, non-Christian religious practices remained a reality from which converts had continually to dissociate themselves (and this, after all, was what the church order demanded). It was the basis against which, and hence also with which, Ewe Protestant identity was defined.

The missionaries were startled by the success of their own arguments. Although they themselves had diabolised Ewe religion, Däuble's reaction shows that for him, the Ewe Christians' understanding of *Abosam,* which he considered a product of 'heathen' backwardness, went too far. The missionaries diabolised the old religion in order to denounce it as backward 'heathendom'. They expected that once people had accepted the old religion as the work of Satan they would leave it behind and concentrate fully on the Christian God and realise their personal sinfulness. Christians should no longer think about the old gods. The mission even emphasised the paltriness of these powers in the form of a song which became the 'anthem' of Christianity. The song went as follows: 'There is no Fofie [any other *trɔ* name could be inserted here] / There is none in the world / Life is only with Jesus / Life is only with Jesus' (Spieth 1908: 12). However, to recall the first quotation in this chapter, it should be clear that the expression 'there is no idol' did not mean that the spiritual beings worshipped by the 'heathens' did not exist, but rather that they should not be taken too seriously because God's power surpassed that of Satan. (This, by the way, is also how contemporary Ewe Christians explained the meaning of this song to me.)

Ewe Christians continued to be afraid of the same powers as non-Christians. For instance, the evangelist who described the popularity of the *dzotɔwo* (see above) emphasised that both 'heathens' and Christians feared *gbetsi võwo, ŋɔli võwo, trɔ võwo, adze,* and *dzo* (Stab 7, 1025–56/8: 242).[13]

Like non-Christians, Ewe Christians understood sin (*nuvɔ̃*) primarily as something endured, rather than committed by themselves. Also, if they exhibited 'broad path' behaviour and violated the harsh sexual morals and Pietist ascetic lifestyle, they would then deny their personal responsibility and state that it was the Devil who had tempted them to commit these sins. In 1903 Spieth complained that besides the 'still not yet fully erased belief in the existence of gods ... the heathen conception of evil in particular often has a lasting effect' (1903b: 11). The 'heathen' concept of evil was manifest in the fact that 'sinners' withdrew from their personal responsibility by attributing their faults to the Devil. 'This heathen way of excusing oneself in the case of the Christians,' wrote Spieth, 'appears in the fact *that they foist everything on the Devil. A fall, for example, is preferably described as a deception by the Devil*' (ibid., my emphasis). It therefore appears that many Ewe Christians did not adopt the Pietist feeling of internal sinfulness, in no way conveyed through the term *nuvɔ̃* in any case, but partly clung to the old understanding of evil described above. They found that evil was expressed through sickness and other forms of life-destruction, and considered it the result of inappropriate behaviour in a relationship, not as an individual state.

However, in contrast with non-Christians, Ewe Christians also considered as evil attempts to deal with these powers by way of sacrifices offered through intermediating *trɔ̃* priests, and by way of protective or counter-*dzo*. These powers were no longer considered ambivalent, but solely as agents of Satan. This shift is probably not surprising because it was in line with existing ideas about relations between human beings and spirits. The fact that Ewe Christians refused to undertake sacrifices turned the ancestors, *trɔ̃wo*, and other spirits into powers threatening to bring about evil in order to recall their servants once again. For Ewe Christians the only escape from such powers was to claim that God was more powerful than Satan. This stance is illustrated in the critical remark of Theodor Sedode, an Ewe teacher, who referred to what he considered to be a 'superstitious' conceptualisation:

> When I once asserted in a baptismal lesson that there are no idols, one grey man looked at me astounded and replied: 'Surely there are idols, but the God of the Christians is more powerful than all of them.' *Likewise, the existence of sorcery, sorcery power, witches and all sorts of evil spirits is believed in firmly, which limits very much the Christian faith and makes superstition persist.* The best console themselves with the words: God is more powerful, and since I belong to God they cannot harm me. (Baeta and Sedode 1911: 16; original in German, my translation and emphasis)

It is not surprising that Sedode stressed the continued existence of witchcraft and sorcery, since, as noted in the previous chapter, *Abosam* not only referred to the old religion in general, but also designated witchcraft in particular. Indeed, the existence of *adze* was confirmed by the term *Abosam* itself. Through the claim to be more powerful, missionary Pietism seemed to offer protection against witchcraft by liberating Christians from old familial ties. This was one of the reasons why the mission church was so attractive. After all, some people were supposed to become church members because they did not want to share their riches with their families. While it is difficult to make any categoric statement with regard to the 'true' motivations of converts, it has to be realised that Christianity offered new patterns of distribution and consumptions and a new ethics which stressed individual personhood.

This confirmation of the widely held belief in the continued existence of witchcraft was an unintended and undesired result of vernacularisation and diabolisation. The missionaries did not like the existence of this belief which they considered to be a superstitious 'heathen' remnant. Although they themselves had turned all spiritual entities into demons by denouncing them as agents of Satan, in their opinion Ewe Christians' continued belief in the existence of witchcraft went too far. But for many Ewe Christians the old powers were still too alive and real to be neglected in their discourse. To the dismay of the missionaries and some enlightened Ewe mission workers, Ewe Christians continued to talk about them and believe in their existence. Thus, *Abosam* gave Ewe Christianity a particular new meaning which differed from that attributed to it by the missionaries. On the one hand the perspective propagated by the missionaries themselves was the cause, and on the other hand the peculiar position of the Devil in the Pietist doctrine triggered speculations and associations. Thus, Ewe Christians enthusiastically adopted the freedom to imagine the actions of the Devil in the framework of Pietist imagery offered them by the missionaries.

The missionaries clearly did not follow Blumhardt's strategy of thematising or exorcising specific occult powers. They were afraid of becoming too enmeshed in the old 'heathen' ways and did not appreciate the old powers being discussed too often. These powers were to be subsumed under the image of the Devil, functioning as a sort of sponge absorbing the old spiritual beings. If mentioned at all, they were to be discussed only in general terms as satanic powers. In other words, a centripetal movement occurred in the course of which all these powers were stored within the category of '*Abosam*' – a process of diabolisation. *Adze* and *dzo vɔ̃* in particular were tabooed subjects and were not referred to openly in sermons and prayers, although they were still feared by many Christians. Gradually, in public Christian discourse, an aura of silence developed around the old religion's spiritual beings, although as older people assured me, they remained alive in private talks. Because of this, only a few historical documents written by missionaries or Ewe evangelists deal with *adze*. According to my sources, *adze* was a secret topic and was not discussed in public in *Kpodzi*;

one could only talk about *Abosam*. Moreover, the mission did not offer ways of freeing people from evil spirits such as witchcraft, or provide special ritual protection against it. The Ewe Christians had to make do with the observance of the church order, prayers, participation in church services, and the Holy Communion.

## 'Back-sliding into Heathendom'

As long as no misfortune occurred, participation in church activities was enough, although Ewe Christians tended to read much more into the few rituals provided than the missionaries themselves. However, when Christians faced severe problems which they were unable to solve, they often considered insufficient the practices entailed by missionary Pietism. In such cases, 'back-sliding into heathendom' occurred – an expression emphasising the spatial and temporal difference constructed to distinguish Christianity and 'heathendom'. For example, in 1901 Mallet reported that he had excommunicated a Christian woman because she had become a 'fetish priestess'. Christian medicines had failed to cure her illness and when she was informed that her uncle's 'fetish' was angry with her and that she would not be healthy as long as she remained a Christian, her family took her to her uncle's 'fetish' to sacrifice an animal. The woman recovered, left the Christian quarter together with her husband, and herself became a *trɔsi*.[14] There were many similar cases, revealing that Ewe Christians' separation from their wider families was a critical affair. Especially in cases of sickness and other misfortune, Christians began to cast doubts on their new independence. As long as everything went well, Christians could feel independent and loosen ties connecting them with the members of their extended family; in times of trouble, however, many Christians rediscovered the importance of the family. For many of them, the wider family was still too important to be simply discarded. No doubt they were affected by the fact that farming land was still allocated by the lineage head, and Christians had to consult him in order to get access to the predominant means of production. Hence, it is not surprising that missionary Pietism, with its emphasis on individuality, gave rise to contradictions both between and within people.

But it was not only independence from their families that made some Ewe Christians feel insecure. Over and above this, in their experience missionary Pietism lacked effective means with which to counter evil. Christians not only fell sick as well, but also lacked the practical means with which to seek recovery. After having 'slid back' to the old ways, a former Christian woman from Tsibu stated:

> I had believed that, being a Christian, one would no longer fall sick; but I now see that the worship of God and idolatry is one and the same thing, for wherever one is, one falls sick and dies. Therefore I have gone back. (MB 1890: 10)

There are many similar cases which make clear that people conceived of the Christian God on the basis of existing concepts and still expected religion to *work*. In some households there was a sexual division of religious allegiance. The husband might be a Christian, but the wife and children, except for the first-born, might not be baptised. In this way they were able to make use of the local remedies against sicknesses which missionary Pietism lacked. Since women were certainly more reluctant to convert because they had comparatively more to lose, it is not surprising that in the period until 1918, 'back-sliding into heathendom' occurred much more frequently among women than men. Although some men, of course, also 'relapsed', their main offence was the violation of the Pietist sexual morals. The occurrence of 'back-sliding into heathendom' – and such cases are amply documented – shows that most Christians, especially women, did not share the missionaries' proclaimed rejection of ritual at the expense of belief, and retained an understanding of religion as a practical affair. They maintained this stance even when they turned to Christianity, since, as we have seen, they often did so for the very same reasons which made others return to the Ewe priests.

There was a clear paradox inherent in the Ewe mission. On the one hand, the mission intended to abolish the old religion; on the other, it was indispensable in demonstrating the meaning of Christianity. In this context *Abosam* was a key figure, because through him the *trɔwo* and other spiritual beings remained real powers. In this way, the 'old' religion was never abolished but only viewed from a distance and through a particular filter. Thus, once people faced trouble, they gave up the hegemonic view of looking down on Ewe religion from a Christian perspective and the strict Pietist dualism of God and Satan. In such a situation they were forced to evaluate which of the two could best provide a remedy against the *nuvɔ* that had befallen them. People affected by sickness or other problems had to conclude that missionary Pietism, with its claimed anti-ritualistic attitude, could not really satisfy their needs, for just like non-Christians they still felt that evil could be removed through ritual. Some people did this openly and returned to the old community and means of worship, thereby admitting the latter's superiority. Others consulted the priests in the dead of night and remained part of the Christian congregation until they were found out, thereby upholding and yet doubting Christianity's superiority at the same time. Even if they were detected and excommunicated, they often remained within the church until they were once again allowed to take communion, because they no longer felt at home in the framework of Ewe religion. These people were in a dilemma: on the one hand, they wanted to be Christians, on the other, they still needed the 'old' religion.

This need has persisted throughout the EPC's history. When I enquired about the period after 1918, I learned that there had been quite a few cases of people, among them even pastors and teachers, who secretly owned *dzo* and went to church at the same time. While it was impossible for a Christian to take part in the worship of a *trɔ* without being seen by the congregational authorities, it was much easier to possess *dzo*:

> *Trɔ* is a public thing. If you belong to it, then others would know. You would be excommunicated. But *dzo* is secret. So you can belong to that, and nobody knows it. And you can belong to the Christian church. (Dr Seth Bansa)

The attitude of Christians relying on magic in addition to church attendance was termed '*Yesu viɖe, dzo viɖe*' (*viɖe*: a little bit); i.e. 'a little bit of Jesus and a little bit of magic'.

In the church diaries, the real extent of this attitude is not revealed, since many people succeeded in 'relapsing' without being detected. Unless the congregational authorities found out, a person could both take communion at the Lord's Supper and participate in 'heathen' customs. Once Christians were no longer confined to *Kpodzi*, but lived anywhere in town, ultimate control was difficult, and if people were accused of owning *dzo*, they could defend themselves by stating that it was not 'magic', but merely 'medicine' (*atike*); thereby deceiving the church authorities that these materials had not been blessed by a *dzotɔ* (healer, diviner) but were just ordinary barks and medicinal plants. Although there was a core of staunch members respecting the church order, many members turned into more or less 'nominal' Christians, baptised because the church stood for 'civilisation', but at the same time failing to observe all the regulations.

Belief in *adze* continued to exist among congregations. Though this is difficult to prove, the impression is strong that fears of being bewitched increased with prosperity. Whereas Debrunner (1961), Field (1960) and Ward (1956) suggested that, due to modern economic changes, witchcraft accusations and suspicions were on the increase, Goody (1957) stated that they were also a feature of pre-colonial society. Although I agree with his argument that African pre-colonial societies and religions should not be conceptualised as static, I would nevertheless maintain that the incorporation of Ghana into a global economy brought about new problems which had to be dealt with in new ways. In pre-colonial times, the tension between individualism and family affiliation was never as marked as in colonial and post-colonial society (see McCaskie 1981: 136–7).

In any case, many people told me that, formerly, when people were living off the produce of their farms and had no extra cash income, witchcraft had been much less prevalent. An often heard complaint was that people became increasingly 'greedy' over time and that this individual accumulation of wealth gave rise to feelings of envy among others, who were jealous of the success of their relatives and secretly sought their downfall through *adze*. For instance, the car accident of a wealthy Peki trader, G.

Addo from Blengo, while he was returning home with some goods from Accra in 1928, was attributed to witchcraft. Clearly here fear of witchcraft did not work as a levelling mechanism, but rather enticed the wealthy to protect themselves as efficiently as possible, either through the purchase of protective *dzo*, participation in anti-witchcraft cults, or through Christianity.

That this subject was rarely mentioned in written documents only illustrates that witchcraft remained a taboo topic. For instance, Mrs Felicia Ansre, who grew up in *Kpodzi*, recounted that although she did not believe in the existence of witches herself, many fellow Christians were afraid of them. However, she asserted that this enlightened point of view was not generally shared. Alice Mallet, for instance, recalled that her father, the Reverend Barnabas Mallet (a son of the Reverend Rudolf Mallet), explained to her: 'If you don't believe in *adze*, you don't believe in God. In this world, there are two things: the good spirits and the evil spirits. What Jesus called Beelzebub is *adze*.' He prayed privately with members of his congregations (though a native of Peki, he was mainly posted in the Togo area) who were witches themselves or had fallen victim to witchcraft attacks. Miss Mallet's statement reveals that belief in the existence of witchcraft was not only held by less educated church members, but also by pastors. Whether witchcraft existed or not was a matter which separated the converts. In any case, however, witchcraft was not expanded upon or even treated in public, but only in private. Although spiritual beings of the non-Christian religion thus remained a reality to most Christians, these spirits were not spoken about explicitly in services, but bracketed within the category of '*Abosam*'. The church made no attempt to offer any public discourse dealing with fears represented by, for example, *adze*, nor did it provide any protective rituals apart from private prayer and sober public church services.

That many Christians were concerned about witchcraft is also confirmed by a report (1932) of the Christian Council of Gold Coast,[15] to which the Ewe Evangelical Church belonged. According to the council, such beliefs were very common throughout the colony. Though it did not deny the existence of witchcraft as such, it recommended exposing all 'charlatans' claiming falsely to be able to perform witchcraft, and discouraged consulting 'witch doctors' (a task undertaken by the *dzotowo*) (1932: 6). The latter advice was in line with the colonial government's view of witch-finding as a criminal offence, a view which probably led people to believe that the colonial state and the church protected witches (see also Geschiere 1997: 15).[16] Apart from asserting that for Christians there was no need to be afraid (ibid.: 7), no practical means of protection against witchcraft were recommended. Though this document only consists of a brief statement, it reveals that despite the fact that fears of witchcraft were a matter of great concern in Christian congregations, no special remedies to counter this threat were offered. In my view, the continuing (and probably even increasing) fear of witchcraft helps to explain the popularity of secret *dzo*, referred to above. Since there was no proper church discourse and ritual complex dealing with evil spirits such as *adze* (and also spiritual beings like *ametsiavawo*), church members who wanted to maintain their wealth, or receive any other protection, were virtually obliged to consult Ewe specialists in secret. As far as spiritual protection was concerned, missionary Christianity was thus still of little value.

There are indications that during the Second World War 'heathen' practices became much more popular among Christians than before. The Reverend Andreas Aku, a native minister, said of the church as a whole that many members were disappointed that European Christians were fighting each other. Disillusionment with Western 'civilisation' as well as the confused situation led to the increase of 'heathendom' and 'idolatry'. Moreover, in the church as a whole, school attendance declined and many congregations were unable to pay their pastors (Aku, quoted in Grau 1964: 38). Though I do not have access to detailed historical records documenting congregational life in Peki during the war,[17] I assume on the basis of Aku's remarks that not only the economic situation but also church life was disrupted during these years. An increasing number of educated young people sought their fortune elsewhere, thereby leaving the church to women, children and the old. I believe that in these years many church members, both migrants and those staying at home, began to cast serious doubts on the capacity of the church to improve their lives. Since Christianity and prosperity no longer formed a 'natural' combination, more and more members faced serious financial, medical and spiritual problems which the mission church was unable to solve. In line with the attitude of '*Yesu viḓe, dzo viḓe*', some of them continued to call themselves Christian but secretly consulted Ewe priests if the need arose.

An increasing number of converts, however, were not satisfied with this compromise and wished to address their problems in the framework of Christianity. Searching for a more adequate, African form of the Christian religion, they developed an increasing interest in the African independent churches which, in the 1950s, through visiting or returning migrants, gained increasing popularity within the colony (for example, see Parsons 1963: 205, Baëta 1962).

## CONVERSION AND THE DEVIL

Similar processes of diabolisation seem to have occurred not only all over the African continent, but also worldwide. It would require a separate study to examine which mission societies were more inclined than others to approach African religions in these terms, at what times this strategy prevailed, and how African mission church members dealt with it. Though diabolisation was certainly a decisive strategy of nineteenth-century Pietist mission societies formed in the framework of the European Awakening, this probably also applied to other societies at other times and places. Indeed, there are indications that missionaries of other denominations and nationalities, elsewhere on the African continent, also preached that the Devil was the power behind African religions (for example, Fernandez 1982: 227ff; Kirwen 1987: 37ff; Kuper 1947: 127; Lienhardt 1982; Peel 1990: 351ff; and Shorter 1973: 131).[18] It is worth pointing out that the Devil is indeed sometimes referred to in the index of publications dealing with the spread of Christianity in Africa (for example, Fasholé-Luke et al. 1978: 620), and is mentioned briefly, for example, in Sundkler (1961: 112, 189, 20–4). However, there is no analysis of the meaning of the concept of the Devil and people's appropriation of diabolisation. This omission cannot simply be taken as evidence that Satan was meaningless to the people described in these publications, but may well indicate that students of African religion by and large have failed to investigate how indigenous and Christian concepts of evil blended together in historical processes (Gray 1990: 106ff). The main reason for this neglect seems to be the relative separation of the anthropological discourses on African Christianity on the one hand, and African 'traditional religion' on the other. While the latter is concerned exclusively with non-Christian concepts of evil, the former does not usually concentrate on evil at all.

These findings are immediately relevant to a better understanding of the processes of conversion to Christianity. In his important work on conversion in Africa, which has dominated debates for years, Horton (1971, 1975) understood the replacement of old spirits by the High God as the most important feature of people's switch to Christianity. According to him, next to a feeling of community, African religions provided people above all with knowledge to explain, predict, and control the framework of the microcosm they lived in. However, once people became integrated into wider contexts, the local gods could no longer provide sufficient knowledge and people tended to turn to world religions. For Horton, the weakening of the microcosm thus went hand in hand with the attribution of less power to local gods, and enhanced the adoption of a High God considered to be in charge of the macrocosm as a whole – a process we could also discern among the Ewe.[19]

My main critique of his theory on conversion pertains to his undue emphasis on the High God. For the Ewe, conversion entailed a socioeconomic as well as a religious dimension, which, as we have seen, were interconnected. In this context it is important to realise that the adoption of belief in the High God went hand in hand with the adoption of the image of the Devil, considered to be the Lord of the old gods and spirits and defining the boundary between Christianity and Ewe religion, though at the same time integrating the latter into Christian discourse. While Horton occasionally remarked upon the fate of the previous gods in the framework of world religions – he stated that people came 'to regard the lesser spirits as irrelevant or downright evil' (1971: 102) – he did not realise the importance of these beings in the minds of African Christians. In his view, sooner or later, people would stop believing in their existence. However, as already noted, Ewe Christians eagerly took up the missionaries' dualism of God and Satan and the diabolisation of 'heathendom'. Thus, the image of the Devil played a central role as mediator between boundaries: not only mediating between Ewe and Christian religion in the narrow sense, but also between old and new ways of life, with people's integration into a global, political, economic and religious configuration.

When Horton wrote his articles on conversion, little research had been done on encounters between missionaries and Africans. Students of African Christianity took modern theologians' neglect of the Devil as representative and simply conceptualised conversion as a turn towards the High God,[20] and not at the same time as a turning from (and thus, on another level, *to*) Satan. Nevertheless, there are indications that all over the African continent, and even all over the world, conversion to Christianity coincided with the diabolisation of African religions. Thus it may be of fundamental importance to concentrate on the 'dark' side of the Christian religion which structured the worldview of both Western missionaries and African converts, and this seems crucial for a better understanding of the genesis of local variants of Christianity.[21]

These conclusions are relevant to one of the main concerns of this study: the relationship between conversion, modernity, (dis)enchantment and the image of the Devil. In the Ewe's encounter with Pietist missionaries, conversion did not bring about what professional theologians and social scientists tend to expect, namely rationalisation and disenchantment. And this is probably not confined to the case studied here. In the context of Pietist (and also Pentecostalist) missionaries who approach the world in terms of the dualism between God and Satan, new converts tend to adopt a variant of Protestantism, emphasising the image of the Devil and transforming gods and ghosts into 'Christian' demons. By directing people's attention to demons and by providing temptations, 'the Devil' continuously endangers the purity of the doctrine and Christian lifestyle. This gives rise to a popular, 'syncretistic' variant of Christianity centred on demonology and raises the question as to why, in Weber's terms, spirits and demons exert such a strong influence on the interests of the individual in his other everyday life? Ewe Christians' obsession with the Devil has to be explained against the background of politics and the economy of colonial society being partly out of tune with the new Christian religion. Though Christianity offered a route towards 'civilisation', it did not fully modernise society. In inland areas especially, people's relationship with modernity was largely mediated through the NMG, and Christian converts, though professing modern individualist notions of the person, were actually still involved in the 'old' way of life. Above all, they could not completely renounce their extended families: for economic reasons, they were unable to dissociate themselves fully, because land was still allocated by the lineage heads. And in times of need, there was no other agency than the family to turn to for help. In addition, Christianity could not always compete with the more practically oriented Ewe religion. Through the image of the Devil, Ewe converts were able to deal with the religion and way of life they wanted to leave behind, and from which they could not fully dissociate themselves at the same time. Satan was 'good to think with' about the ambivalence entailed by adopting the new ways and leaving the old. In talking about Satan and his demons they could even thematise hidden desires to return to the old, without actually doing so. The image of the Devil and his demons thus enabled them to reflect upon the problems they had with the 'civilised' state they strove for. And if things seemed insoluble in the framework of missionary Pietism, they could still, and perhaps temporarily, 'slide back'. For Christianity's Other was still there.

In short, Ewe Christians had an ambivalent stance towards modernity, which they found attractive and problematic at the same time. The vehicle to express this ambivalence was the image of the Devil and his demons, continually referred to, yet at the same time denounced. This image enabled Ewe Christians to reflect upon, and fantasise about, the problems and opportunities of their integration into a modern global political economy.

# 5

# THREE CHURCHES OUT OF ONE

Up until the late 1950s in Peki the EPC lost only a handful of dissatisfied members to new rival churches and there were no great attempts to transform the church from within. This situation changed when, very much in tune with the spirit of the time, hitherto nominal members established a 'prayer group'. This group eventually broke away from the mother church and became autonomous in 1961 under the name of The Lord's Church – Agbelengor (from *agbe le ŋgɔ*, 'there is life ahead'). Agbelengor was one of the first African independent churches to be established in Peki, and in the 1960s an increasing number of independent and Pentecostal churches appeared, to whom the orthodox mission churches (the Presbyterians, Methodists and Catholics) lost more and more members. Despite attempts to Africanise the EPC, this process continued and the new churches became a serious 'problem' to the church authorities. In 1990, almost thirty years after the secession of Agbelengor, the members of an intra-church prayer group decided to leave the mother church, causing another split (this time at national level). These secessions are part of a general trend towards Pentecostalism throughout Ghana (and indeed throughout Africa). How they occurred in Peki, and the main differences between the EPC and the new churches, are discussed in this chapter. In this way it will be revealed how this trend materialises at the local level.

## THE LORD'S (PENTECOSTAL) CHURCH – AGBELENGOR
### Conflict with the EPC[1]

The founder of Agbelengor was Samuel Yao Amedzro from Blengo (Atsiadome clan), son of a polygamous 'pagan' father and a mother who was a member of the Apostolic Church of Ghana. Although he was baptised in the EPC and had attended its school, according to the written church history 'he took to reckless living, indulging in all kinds of social vices' (*Brief History of the Lord's Pentecostal Church*, n.d.: 2). He smoked, drank and danced, had several wives and ridiculed his mother's loud prayers. When he suddenly fell ill in October 1958, he sought help from doctors, 'herbalists' and 'juju men', who were all unable to cure him. He threw 'the god which could not heal him and ... the rings and the accompanying talisman' into the latrine (ibid.)

and accompanied his mother to Tekrom (a village in the area) where a 'prayer group'[2] within the EPC was operating. The group leader, T. K. Borkuma, healed the sick by prayers and the laying on of hands. It was there that Amedzro was converted and recovered. In the fifth month of his stay in Tekrom he had a vision of an angel writing 'John' on his forehead; and in the eighth month a second vision followed, which he understood as the call 'to go and work for the Lord'. From then on he called himself John Sam Amedzro. By doing this he gave up his birth name Yao and placed a short form of his baptismal name second. Clearly this change of name symbolised a new identity as a full convert.

When he returned to Blengo in 1959, Amedzro organised prayer meetings in his own house which were attended by family members and other inhabitants of Peki. He healed sick people through prayer, exorcised evil spirits 'and the Lord was blessing him with miracles' (ibid.: 3). He joined forces with B. A. Y. Menka, an EPC member, and Emmanuel K. Wuaku, who had been a nominal member of the Methodist Church and who had also been healed in Tekrom. Their group, which called itself the Tekrom Prayer Group, quickly attracted many members who had either been 'heathens' or members of the Methodist Church and the EPC. Most were women who, if at all, had only a basic education. This fact contributed to the group's low reputation, which in turn put off more educated people from joining it. 'People have been looking at us so low, so mean, that you don't get intellectuals or learned people at all,' Menka recalled.

The group differed from the EPC and the Methodist Church not only with regard to prestige. In contrast to sober EPC services, the prayer group drummed, clapped hands and danced, and its members practised tithing, fasting, speaking in tongues and prayer healing. They took off their shoes before entering the prayer hall and fasted every Thursday morning at a prayer place in the bush. There were also taboos: menstruating women were not supposed to attend meetings and it was forbidden to have sexual intercourse on the night before the Sunday service. Sick people were not allowed to go to a hospital or take Western medicines, but were to rely on prayer alone. In order to heal or prevent sickness, as the Reverend S. Amedzro explained to me, use was made of 'Florida Water' (a sort of eau de Cologne – 'if you drink it, the evil spirit comes out'), oil ('then no evil spirit or witch can touch you'), candles ('they drive away evil spirits'), holy water ('it has healing power'), and a necklace with a big cross ('when the Devil sees the cross, he won't approach you'). The use of these remedies reveals that the prayer group took evil spirits very seriously. Indeed this was probably the most important difference with regard to the EPC. Whereas the latter did not deal with evil spirits discursively or ritually, the prayer group offered special means by which to counter the forces of evil. This, as it turned out, was the main source of its attraction.

Soon the prayer group came to be treated with hostility by some 'heathens' as well as pastors, presbyters and 'some highly educated people' in the EPC (ibid.: 4). The *dzotɔwo* (healers, magicians) and priests were afraid they might lose their customers to the prayer group. The EPC authorities, who disliked the group's peculiar practices, joined forces with the Methodists with whom until then they had had a troubled relationship. Uniting against a common enemy, the two mission churches adopted the same strategy vis-à-vis dissident members. Because most prayer group members came from the EPC, the conflict between it and the prayer group was more pronounced and problems with the EPC establishment escalated when Christian Sai Kwadzo, a 'heathen' who had converted to the EPC via the prayer group, lost his son in December 1959. Before his conversion, he drank and participated in the drumming sessions at 'fetish houses'. When the EPC refused to bury his son unless he left the prayer group, the dissidents conducted the burial themselves. Having thereby reached 'the point of no return' (ibid.), the group organised its first independent Sunday service on Christmas Day, 1959.

For the next two years, the group found itself in a betwixt and between position. Its members informed Borkuma in Tekrom that they wished to become part of an independent church under his leadership. Borkuma refused, preferring to keep his prayer group within the EPC (though twenty years later he founded the Peaceful Healing Church – Nutifafa Nami). During negotiations with Borkuma, which lasted until 1961, the Blengo prayer group members remained part of their original churches, conducted services by themselves but also occasionally attended those of the mother churches. But prayer group members were anxious for a solution: because the EPC refused to offer its services to group members, they could not undergo the Christian *rites de passage*, such as baptism, marriage and burial. It was the performance of these rituals which distinguished a mere prayer group from a church, and for this reason the EPC's refusal to provide prayer group members with these facilities brought powerful pressure to bear on the members, forcing them either to remain loyal or become fully independent.

In the EPC diary, the case of the Tekrom Prayer Group appears four times in 1960. The reports clearly document EPC reaction to the dissenters. According to Menka, excommunication of the prayer group members was publicly announced as early as Easter 1960. When I questioned Tawia (the EPC pastor at Blengo at that time) about this, he told me he had not excommunicated anyone, but had read a circular from the synod stating that 'all those whose practices clashed with the EPC should no longer consider themselves members'. Thus, for those failing to submit to the EPC's order there was no room in the church. It is striking that the whole matter was not discussed in terms of doctrinal content. Rather, the local EPC authorities accused the prayer group of violating church rules and neglecting the church's monopoly on the organisation of Christian life, especially by adopting 'unusual methods of prayer' and conducting church services by themselves (Blengo Evangelical Church Station Chronicle, 20 April 1960). Ordinary members, and certainly those lowest in the church hierarchy, had to submit to them and obey.

In discussion with the group, Tawia referred to the EPC's 'long tradition with set rules and certain modes of conduct' and urged its members not to interfere with the form of Sunday service; they should do as they liked apart from that (ibid., 29 April 1960). The EPC authorities claimed power over the prayer group and could not accept any critical self-reflection. The furthest they could go was to accept separate prayer meetings. This option being unacceptable, on 29 October 1961 the prayer group split decisively from the EPC when it baptised one of its members in the Amimli stream. From then on the church called itself The Lord's Church; the term Agbelengor, which enemies of the new church initially used as a nickname, was added later. Right from the start, the church attracted new people, both *trɔ̃* worshippers and EPC members. These people had common experience of suffering pains which were incurable by either local or Western medicine, and which they therefore attributed to the machination of 'evil spirits', i.e. the former gods, ancestors' spirits or witchcraft. In Agbelengor these spirits were driven out (for specific cases of people turning to Agbelengor see Chapter 7). Its leaders took the existence of these beings as seriously as that of the Holy Spirit and denounced Ewe religion as the realm of Satan.

## Further Developments until 1992

The young church continued to grow and opened branches in other areas of the Volta Region,[3] as well as in Accra. It adopted a constitution and organisational form similar to that of the mother church. A few years after its independence, the church lifted the taboos on attending church service during menstruation and having sexual intercourse on the night before the services, and abolished the interdiction of entering the church wearing shoes. It refrained from the use of candles, Florida Water, and the cross, and relied on the use of prayer alone. It was argued that 'if the Holy Spirit is within you, you need not rely on any object' (Reverend Stanley Amedzro, in an interview with me).

In order to cure the sick the church eventually opened a healing station in Tokokoe, a village close to the Togo border. This station was to be 'a mighty fortress to many afflicted and oppressed by the evil one' (*Brief History of the Lord's Pentecostal Church*: 6). Here, evil spirits were driven out by calling upon the Holy Spirit – a practice known as 'deliverance'. To this day, this healing centre is frequented by sick members of Agbelengor as well as of other churches. Many Agbelengor congregations have constructed a house in the station area to lodge their sick. Some people stay there for a long period, others only attend the healing and deliverance services for one or two weeks. Every year the church assembles in the healing centre.

Shortly after the celebration of the tenth anniversary of the church's foundation, John Sam Amedzro, who supervised the healing station, fell ill and died. Many church members remember this as a time of depression and despair. I assume it was also a period of severe doubt about the efficacy of the church's healing methods, as I learned that after Amedzro's death the interdiction of consulting trained physicians and taking Western drugs was abolished. Though the church still considered prayer the most powerful remedy against all troubles, members making use of Western medicine were no longer excommunicated, as had previously been the case. Some church members told me that they understood this change as a sign that the immense spiritual power, which in the beginning had enabled Amedzro to perform 'miracles', had gradually ceased.

However, although the death of the founder led members to conclude that the early spiritual power had declined, there is still much more room for the Holy Spirit in Agbelengor than in the EPC. Sermon texts are not prescribed and there is no written church order. In each congregation there are recognised prophets and prophetesses who communicate to the members their dreams and visions, which they consider as deriving from the Holy Spirit. Under the leadership of Reverend E. K. Wuaku (president) and Reverend B. A. Y. Menka (vice-president) the church spread and grew. In the 1980s, the church, which had started as a lay movement, began to employ young pastors who were trained at Pentecostal Bible colleges in Accra. However, the church did not find this theological training sufficient and demanded its young pastors undergo practical training in deliverance in Tokokoe. Thus, besides the new emphasis on 'the letter', expressed by the introduction of theological training for pastors, the church continued to attribute much importance to the work of 'the spirit' (see Probst 1989), which was to be experienced in the healing station.

In 1985 the church's name was changed to the Lord's Pentecostal Church. Dropping the name Agbelengor emphasised that the church was not an 'ethnic' but a national association, while the addition of 'Pentecostal' made a decisive theological statement: it marked a turning away from the use of objects employed to gain contact with God or to heal and protect people, as was the practice in African independent, so-called Spiritual churches. Reliance on things was replaced by full reliance on the biblical text, which was cited in order to invoke the Holy Spirit and to cast out evil ones. As noted above, Agbelengor had already done away with candles, Florida Water, crosses and incense in the 1960s, but until the early 1980s the church still employed large wooden crosses on its prayer grounds. In line with Pentecostalism, which was dominant in the Bible colleges where the church's young pastors were trained, the use of crosses was denounced as 'idolatrous' and 'occultistic', for Christians were not to believe in the power of objects, but in that of the biblical Word through which alone the Holy Spirit worked.

In Ghana this became the great dividing line between Pentecostal and Spiritual churches. The former accuse the latter of placing their trust in magic through the use of objects, thereby becoming 'occult groups' which can succumb to the Devil's machinations. True believers should not place their trust in any kind of magic. Thus, in the course of time, Agbelengor (as it is still called in Peki) underwent a transformation from an indigenous, local, Spiritual church to a Pentecostal church, part of a national, and even international movement. In 1992 it was about to become a member of the Christian Council of Ghana Pentecostal Churches, a Pentecostal organ-isation founded as an alternative to the Christian Council of Ghana which is dominated by former mission churches. This move signals the wish to attune the church to developments taking place beyond the local level and to be part of Pentecostalism as a(n inter)national movement.

## The Secession as Critique

The history of the secession and accounts of the prayer group members can be read both as a critique of the EPC and as an indication of an alternative.

The prayer group was founded by non-active, male EPC members who, once they were in a personal crisis, could not find the help and security they needed in either the EPC or Ewe religion. Other prayer group members, mostly women, joined for the same reasons. Above all, the prayer group articulated a critique of the EPC's understanding of Christian life. At the beginning of the 1960s there was no prayer healing and the services pro-ceeded according to the disciplined pattern introduced by the German Pietist missionaries. Whereas the EPC authorities focused on the observance of church rules, prayer group members sought for more spirituality, wanting to express their faith in a more moving way, to obtain more access to God through common prayer and receive the results of true faith promised in the Bible – miracles and healings. The prayer group offered nominal, dissatis-fied Christians experience of the work of the Holy Spirit and miraculous healings, aspects of the Christian religion that were virtually absent in the EPC where the Holy Spirit was discussed less frequently than church order. Thus, in contrast to the EPC, where closeness to God was to be achieved basically through the observance of rules, in Agbelengor this closeness was to be experienced by feeling the Holy Spirit.

Another interesting point is that Agbelengor leaders had no theological training, and furthermore most members were not educated beyond the elementary stage. In the EPC, trained pastors and intellectuals who based their authority on written texts determined church life. In Agbelengor, by contrast, prophets who saw themselves as vehicles of the Holy Spirit revealing itself through dreams and visions, took a central position. Therefore, the appearance of Agbelengor was a critique of the EPC's reduction of Christian religion to written texts explained by trained pastors, without any provision for contact with the Holy Spirit through dreams and visions. Moreover, as most Agbelengor members were relatively uneducated women, this was an expression of a rejection of a rigid, male-dominated church. It was also rigid in the literal sense, for in those days EPC members sat motionless for hours on hard church pews.

From a social point of view, foundation of an independent church enabled male prayer group leaders to attain a position in church hierarchy, much higher than the one they could reach in the EPC. As polygamists, they were not allowed to partake in communion and could not be buried by the pastor; hence, they were considered to be less close to God than communicants and could not be certain of eternal salvation. Foundation of an independent church enabled these people to participate in church rituals which until then had been denied them. It was thus no accident that the EPC's refusal to bury the child of a prayer group member was the defining step towards secession: the enhancement of status was not so much a reason for the secession, but rather a most welcome result. Of course, the rise in status did not apply to all prayer group members, which included EPC church mothers and communicants for whom participation in the prayer group actually meant a decline in status, but what they lost in terms of reputation, they gained in terms of access to the divine and healing possibilities.

Agbelengor defined the boundary between Christianity and 'heathendom' rigidly and took an uncompromising stance towards Ewe religion. Members of the prayer group (and later Agbelengor) refused to adopt the common, ambivalent *Yesu viɖe, dzo viɖe* stance. Rather than turning to healers outside Christianity, they wanted to solve their problems within Christianity. To them, the EPC's variant of Christianity had too many shortcomings and was unable to solve spiritual problems. Enabling people to tackle these problems implied lifting the ban on talking about evil spirits (the old gods and ghosts and witchcraft matters), and the recognition that these beings did indeed exist and were powerful. It was not enough to subsume them under the category of *Abosam* (Devil) and neglect their actions, as the EPC did. Many people, Christians and *trɔ̃* worshippers alike, still experienced their reality and power and could not feel at home in a church which simply banned these powers from its discourse.

Why did this happen so many years after the initial introduction of Christianity, and at a time when the EPC had already been independent for almost forty years? Of course, similar attempts had been made earlier, for instance, by the Yota Mission in the 1910s and 1920s, as well as the Apostle's Revelation Society and the Apostolic Church after 1945. All these churches had taken a similar uncompromising stance towards Ewe religion and offered prayer healing. But the point about the rise of Agbelengor is not that it was a novel phenomenon as such, but rather that it involved a great number of people and occurred within the mission church. By the late 1950s the need to overcome the *Yesu viɖe, dzo viɖe* stance had become so strong that a church like Agbelengor could secede from the mother church and develop independently. Perhaps the real question should be: why was there a massive interest in a church like Agbelengor on the eve of the 1960s? One answer must lie in Independence for Ghana. Though indigenous mission elites now ran church affairs without the interference of missionaries, congregations began to request a greater say in how Christianity was given form. And the economic situation also played an important role. The decline of Peki's economic situation after the Second World War resulted in more and more people facing physical and spiritual problems; this prompted an ever increasing number to search for ways to maintain or achieve the prosperity that they had up until then taken for granted. The practices Agbelengor and similar churches offer to the people in order to maintain or improve their economic position will be considered in later chapters, thereby deepening our understanding of the relationship between economy and religion.

Foundation of the prayer group preceding Agbelengor was not exceptional. In other EPC congregations similar prayer groups existed. As early as 1939, encouraged by an EPC pastor, Charles Kobla Wovenu began to organise healing prayers in his home town Tadzewu. However, since the practices of his group were similar to those described above, it is not surprising that the EPC had strong reservations which finally led to the secession of the group which became independent under the name of the Apostle's Revelation Society (see above, and also Baëta 1962: 76ff). Later, more prayer groups developed in various EPC congregations within the Volta Region. Besides the group at Tekrom, there was one at Etodome which practised fasting, speaking in tongues and prayer healing, observed the menstruation taboo, paid a great deal of attention to satanic forces and expelled evil spirits (ibid.: 94ff). Despite a latent conflict between the EPC and the Etodome prayer group because of this distinctive form of worship, the prayer group remained within the church. It seems the EPC was afraid of losing too many members if it simply forbade deviant practices, and therefore maintained a somewhat ambivalent attitude, letting the decision as to whether a prayer group was allowed to continue or not depend on local conditions. Nevertheless, the existence of such groups led to unrest within the mother church:

> From all over the Church, persistent and ever more insistent demands have been coming in to Synod for a clear statement as to whether the 'new customs' being practised at Etodome are Christian and good or not: if good, why are they not being taught and practised everywhere else in Church; if not, why does the Church allow this group to continue in them? (ibid.: 111)

In the 1960s this remained an enduring problem for the EPC leaders. And there was indeed a problem. The rise of churches like Agbelengor must be seen as a protest of the lower ranks of the church hierarchy and of women against the rule-centredness of the EPC and its neglect of the Holy Spirit. In the course of the twentieth century the EPC had been transformed from a minority movement to a *Volkskirche*, i.e. a church attended by the majority of the Peki population (for a similar process at the Akuropon BM station, see Middleton 1983). Its members could be divided into communicant members who more or less complied with church regulations; members who paid their dues but still performed libation prayers and similar customary rites, or adopted the *Yesu viɖe, dzo viɖe* stance; and a large group of people who had once been baptised into the EPC but had lost interest in it and occasionally participated in the performance of 'heathen' rites. Since these last no longer paid church fees, they were not regarded as real members.[4] Churches like Agbelengor brought about a 'second christianization' (Schoffeleers 1985: 18) which placed the Holy Spirit in the centre of the Christian message. In doing so, Agbelengor articulated wishes which many EPC members of all three categories shared, though not all sought openly to fulfil them.

## CONSEQUENCES IN THE EPC
### The Necessity for Change

Following the secession of Agbelengor, other independent Spiritual and Pentecostal churches appeared in Peki. This is illustrated by Table 1, constructed from personal observations and a questionnaire distributed to all churches participating in the monthly All Churches Prayer referred to in the Introduction.[5] This overview is possibly incomplete because churches established at a certain time may have vanished and been forgotten. Yet what it reveals, despite this, is the pronounced rise in the numbers of new churches which are Spiritual (in the sense described above) in the 1970s. It also shows that since the beginning of the 1980s the newly established churches were mainly Pentecostal, indicating a shift towards Pentecostal churches claiming to rely on the Word and the Spirit alone – a transform-ation also undergone by Agbelengor, as already described. In this section the reaction of EPC leaders to the establishment of the new churches, to which they lost an increasing number of members, is reconstructed.[6]

It has already been pointed out that in reacting to the prayer group that gave rise to Agbelengor, that EPC authorities in Peki referred in the first instance to the Church Order and showed no inclination for self-critique and reform. Well into the 1960s, the EPC services organisation followed the missionaries' model: the congregation sat along the hard church pews for about two hours; those who didn't fall asleep (I was informed that this happened frequently and it was the presbyters' task to wake such people) listened to the long prayers, the pastor's sermon and the catechist's endless

Table 1: Rise of churches in Peki between 1947 and 1992 (dates given indicate the year of establishment of a church's first branch in one of the Peki villages)

| Date | Church |
| --- | --- |
| before 1947 | EPC, Methodist Church, Roman Catholic Church, Salvation Army, Jehovah's Witnesses |
| 1947 | Apostolic Church of Ghana[a] |
| 1949 | Apostle's Revelation Society (split from EPC) |
| 1961 | The Lord's Church – Agbelengor (split from EPC) |
| 1964 | United Pentecostal Church (split from Apostolic Church)[a] |
| 1968 | A.M.E. Zion Church |
| 1972 | Christian Assembly |
| 1974 | African Evangelism |
| 1976 | New Covenant Apostolic Church (split from Apostolic Church)[a] |
| 1979 | Peaceful Healing Church (*Nutifafa Nami*, split from EPC), House of Israel |
| 1981 | Musama Disco Christo Church (split from Methodist Church) |
| 1984 | Apostolic Healing Church of Christ[a] |
| 1985 | NB: Agbelengor renamed as 'The Lord's Pentecostal Church'[a] |
| 1986 | The Lord's Mission Church[a] |
| 1991 | EPC 'of Ghana' (split from EPC)[a], Great Commission Church International[a], Christian Evangelical Ministry[a] |

Note: [a] Pentecostal or pentecostally oriented churches

announcements. The ponderous, devoutly intoned hymns which had been translated from German into Ewe by the missionaries and the first Ewe evangelists were the only relief. However, in the course of time a willingness to change developed both in Peki congregations and in the church as a whole. Evidently, by the 1960s the questions formulated by Baëta (see quotation above) were in the minds of many EPC pastors and members. The following critical contribution in the *E.P. Church News*[7] illustrates this:

> At present our standard of worship is pitifully low. The manner in which church services are conducted is very 'shallow'. Too much talking (other than reading the Bible and preaching) makes our services unspiritual. Spiritual meditation is poor. People are bored especially when lengthy announcements about money dominate the service. The proper regular use of our rich litanies should be drawn up immediately. The service should be planned in such a way that the people feel the presence of God. The present form of worship should take a new form consisting of saying of prayers either from Liturgy or from memory, with singing, dancing and clapping. We should stand to sing, and sit to listen to the sermon and kneel down while praying in consonance with African emotion and the Ghanaian way of worship. – Do you agree with these new ideas about worship? (1964: No. 2)

This statement has to be understood against the background of the need to understand, and possibly prevent, the exodus of members into the booming less formalistic rival churches. In the 1960s, this led to a great deal of discussion among theologians and intellectuals who criticised Christianity in Africa, saying that it had, until then, been too Westernised. They wondered 'how to be both Christians and Africans at the same time' (Baëta, quoted in Mobley 1970: 110), and they searched for a more appropriate synthesis. The debate also developed in the EPC as well as in other Ghanaian mission churches and led to the conclusion that members could only be retained if church services were fundamentally changed.

## Africanisation of Form and Content

In the 1970s the EPC synod decided to introduce liturgical changes resulting in the integration of African music. The church kept the old hymn book containing translations of European hymns,[8] but from then on all songs, even old hymns, were accompanied by drums and bells rather than a harmonium (an instrument which always caused problems because of high humidity). New songs with African tunes were added to the repertoire of the Christian Youth Builders (CYB), the first church group to use drums; the Women's Bible Class (WBC), which mainly made use of bells; and the Great Choir (Hadzihagã), an old people's choir that usually sang *a capella*. With regard to the introduction of new African songs, the EPC profited enormously from the work of Dr Ephraim Amu, a famous Ghanaian (church) musician and composer born in Peki Avetile (see Agyemang 1988). While teaching music in the 1920s at the Basel Mission seminary at Akropong, where the Ewe Church catechists also received their training, he had already begun to Africanise church music. But it was only thirty years later that his pioneering musical work was formally adopted into the church. Despite Amu's objections to the clergy's Western attire, his ideas about clothes were not fully adopted. Pastors still wear Western Presbyterian-style black gowns; only recently have some of them started to add colour to their attire by wearing a traditionally woven Kente shawl.[9] In the 1980s, dancing during the offertory was introduced (and may thus have enticed members to give more).

Thus, EPC authorities tried to solve the problem of membership loss and low spirituality through Africanising the form of worship. Some older, more conservative people who wished to keep everything 'as the missionaries had brought it' were against these changes and sceptical of attempts to Africanise Christianity. For instance, Mrs Felicia Ansre commented: 'If you want to be a Christian, be a Christian. If you want to be a heathen, be a heathen. We don't force anybody.' She clearly wanted to maintain the boundary between Christianity and Ewe religion as it had been drawn by the missionaries. For her, as well as for other older inhabitants of *Kpodzi*, there was no need to indigenise Christianity; what made the church distinctive was precisely the fact that it was different from and incompatible with non-Christian worship. She and others of her generation did not see any need to dance in church. But this refusal to adopt African elements was not shared by other communicants who, as well as more marginal members, enjoyed the incorporation of drumming and dancing into the service. However, it seems that most did not conceptualise such reforms as Africanisation, but rather as the realisation of biblical directives (after all, the psalms approve of making music to the glory of the Lord) or as an expression of the Holy Spirit.

The Moderator of the EPC, Professor Noah K. Dzobo (in charge from 1981 until 1993), went one step further towards the Africanisation of content. Trained in pedagogics, philosophy, psychology and theology, he went beyond the mere academic debate on African Christianity and formulated a new theology called *Meleagbe* ('I am alive'). Only fragments of it were known within the congregations. Dzobo formulated his new ideas in lectures given at international theological conferences (e.g.1988a, 1988b, 1992, n.d.). The following summary is based on these papers and on personal discussions I had with him in 1988 and 1989.

A tenet central to Dzobo's approach is the value of 'indigenous African religion and culture'. Contrary to the missionaries and their conservative followers, he does not understand Ewe culture and religion as a diabolical expression of 'heathendom', incompatible with Christianity, but rather as a realm in which God revealed himself long before nineteenth-century missionary activity. Thus, he states: 'However terrifying and bizarre Africa and its indigenous culture may look to the outsider, I believe it is the house of God, it is the gate that leads to heaven' (1988b: 2). For Dzobo, the 'indigenous culture' or 'tradition' of the Ewe, which he reconstructed on the basis of his own linguistic research and missionary and anthropological ethnographies, contains many positive elements. Earlier he had demonstrated that Ewe religious ideas and proverbs initiated morally positive behaviour (1971) and that their old ideas about God included positive values (1976). Instead of rejecting this culture as diabolical, he argues that the Christian religion has necessarily to be expressed in the cultural context into which it is introduced. Thus, Western Christianity being just one cultural expression of this religion among many others, its proponents cannot claim, as the nineteenth-century missionaries did, that it is the only true one. In order to implant the essence of Christianity in the African context without unnecessarily taking over typically Western features, Dzobo advocates a synthesis of Christianity and the pre-Christian Ewe religion. The two are similar in that they are both 'life-affirming': 'the common convergence of the indigenous African cultural tradition and the biblical tradition is the abundant life and its affirmation and importance' (n.d.: 2). By contrast, Western culture, which he considers a 'thing-affirming and having culture' (1992: 3), is much further removed from biblical essence than the 'life-affirming' African culture.

Affirmation of life is his criterion for the integration of African traditions
into his version of Christianity. The most telling expression of this synthesis
is his symbol of the cross incorporated into the form of the *Gye Nyame* sign.
This symbol is to show that 'this is a theology intended for people who are
Africans and Christians at the same time, and to conceptualise what it means
to be an African Christian' (1992: 2). The *Gye Nyame* is one of the Adinkra
symbols (Akan) that are stamped onto particular clothes. It represents the
statement 'Except God (I fear none)' (Rattray 1927: 267), refering to the
Akan supreme being *Nyame*, which also became the Akan name of the
Christian God. *Gye Nyame* is also the name of a perennial plant (known in
Ewe as *Gbenɔkunɔku*, 'herb that lives and dies, lives and dies'). By combining
the *Gye Nyame*, which refers to an African (in Dzobo's view *not* just Akan)
conception of confidence in God and everlasting life, [10] with the cross, which
stands for the death of Christ, Dzobo seeks to express the ultimate victory of
life over death:

> The *Meleagbe* symbol then is a strong affirmation of life in spite of its
> denials as we see in the Cross of Jesus and in the cutting down of the
> herb by the farmer. Indeed this is the symbol of the true life which is
> the subject of negation but is continuously being rejuvenated and
> renewed by the experience of its negation. (1992: 4)

Although Dzobo asserts (at least in 1992) that 'Africans are excessively
preoccupied with forces that negate and deny life, such forces as evil spirits
and people, witches and wizards, demons and tragic deaths' (1992: 5), he
emphasises that in the last instance these fears confirm Africans' preoccu-
pation with the protection of life. In his theology these evil, life-threatening
forces do not play a significant role. When I questioned him about these
matters he told me that, rather than confirming the existence of these
beings, he wants people to go beyond fearing them and leave behind such
'superstitions'.

Thus, in his view of African culture and religion he distinguishes life-
threatening elements which he considers as 'superstitions' to be overcome,
and life-affirming elements that form the 'metaphysical' foundation of his
approach, and on which he bases his synthesis. In other words, he
emphasises the moral good entailed in non-Christians' concepts and rituals,
but neglects belief in the existence of spirit possession, magic and witchcraft. In the same vein, he contests the existence of the Devil as a person,
which, in accord with modern Protestant theology, he understands as outdated. Thus, he clearly counters the diabolisation of Ewe religion which, as
we learned earlier, was crucial for the construction of Christianity's
superiority over 'heathendom'.

The new *Meleagbe* theology did not have direct significant, practical
consequences for church life. Though Dzobo himself experimented with

the introduction of adapted traditional rituals, libation prayers and drum rhythms in church service, this was not a common policy. Church members at the grassroots level had no clear idea of the content and implications of the new theology, the latter being much better known outside the country where Dzobo presented it to international theological audiences. One can safely conclude that most supporters of Dzobo's theology are found among Western critical theologians, while few EPC members approve(d) of it. For many believers at the grassroots level the positive integration of elements hitherto conceptualised as 'heathen' meant a threatening disturbance of their Christian worldview and so they were not open to his ideas and symbols. For instance, Mrs Agnes Binder, an old communicant member brought up in *Kpodzi*, who was in favour of dancing and drumming in the church, harshly criticised the new theology when I interviewed her in 1989. Though she had only heard of it through hearsay, like many others, she was especially concerned about the supposed introduction of libation prayers, which were traditionally used to address the ancestors and the *trɔwo*:

> *Meleagbe* theology is not good. Then we go back to our forefathers who didn't know anything about Jesus. We knew there is God. But not so clear as we do now. *Meleagbe* is an old thing. We cannot use it now. You cannot give drinks to a dead man or give food to a dead man. So *Meleagbe* is not good, it is bad.

Likewise, many others complained that one could not invite the Christian God 'to drink from the ground'. Binder's statement makes clear that she understood the introduction of *Meleagbe* theology as a return to the old ways, which Christianity was supposed to have left behind. Thus, the new theology threatened to dissolve the boundary separating 'heathendom' and Christianity, the basis for the latter's identity and superiority over the former ever since its introduction. This becomes even clearer from my conversation with Emmanuel Brempong on 12 February 1989:

> MEYER: Why are you against Dzobo?
> BREMPONG: His theology is some kind of heresy. He is teaching things that our fathers left behind. He is leading us back to paganism. His teachings are contrary to the Scriptures. But we don't want to go back to paganism, that is why there was an uprising against him last June [in 1988]. He is trying to bring in African tradition and customs, but they should not be integrated. We are against traditional worship.
> MEYER: But why is it so bad?
> BREMPONG: They are lesser gods. It is dangerous to go back to the fetish. People who have seen the light should not go back into darkness.

## A New Prayer Group

Brempong was a harsh critic of the Moderator and could no longer accept his authority. As the leader of the Bible Study and Prayer Fellowship (BSPF) (a prayer group within the EPC, see below), he expressed not only his personal opinion, but also that of his group, which organised systematic protests against the church leader and his new theology. The rise of this prayer group was another indicator of transformations within the EPC. The group was formed in the 1970s in the EPC congregation of Kumasi under the supervision of Reverend Edmund Y. Tawia who, as mentioned above, had severely criticised Agbelengor a few years before. However, by accepting a prayer group in his congregation, he hoped to prevent the exodus of members seeking healing and deliverance in other churches. He instructed the group to rely on prayer and the Bible alone, and to do away with taboos and objects such as candles and incense. Similar prayer groups sprang up throughout the EPC in the 1970s. Having drawn up a constitution, the Bible Study and Prayer Group (BSPG) was officially confirmed by the synod in 1978.[11] The celebration of this occasion in Peki was attended by Moderator C. K. Dovlo, the highest Church authority (until 1980), who also became a BSPG member.

Though not convinced of the necessity of more emphasis on prayer and healing, even sceptics hoped that through formal acceptance of the BSPG, the EPC would be able to supervise the otherwise uncontrollable prayer groups. In this vein, one year after the establishment of the BSPG, the synod decided to expel 'members who are connected with prayer groups whose faith, practice and procedure are not conformable to those of our church', especially with regard to the observance of taboos and the use of magical objects, and urged pastors to keep control over existing groups (Synod Report 1979: 119.) Thus, the BSPG was acceptable as long as it remained controllable and refrained from certain practices characteristic of the Spiritual churches.

Sceptics also existed in Peki. Some of the older, conservative inhabitants of *Kpodzi* saw no need to institutionalise prayer groups. However, many other EPC members saw the BSPG as the vehicle for spiritual renewal in the EPC, something that had been due for a long time. To them, the BSPG was a group capable of developing those aspects of Pietism which the missionaries themselves had failed to implement. By practising prayer healing and deliverance from evil spirits, the BSPG would transform the EPC into a more powerful church that would not have less 'spirit' than the new ones and that at long last would fully realise the Pietist heritage.

When I encountered the prayer group in 1989, it had changed its name to the Bible Study and Prayer Fellowship (BSPF). The group organised its own prayer meetings and healing sessions. It participated in the EPC Sunday service and dominated the usual Wednesday evening prayer service. Members consisted mainly of middle-aged women and young men. During their meetings, they read the Bible, which was interpreted literally, prayed together loudly, danced, clapped their hands, drummed and gave testimony to the Lord's great deeds. During healing sessions, members gifted with the power of healing – two nurses, Juliana Sunu and Joana Ayer, and the leader Emmanuel Brempong – laid hands on the sick and called for the Holy Spirit to drive out evil spirits. The members of this group believed in the existence of witches and other evil spirits and understood them to be Satan's servants – ideas shared by many EPC members. In many respects, the BSPF resembled the Pentecostal churches.[12] The BSPF criticised the routines of the EPC and strove for a transformation from within. Rather than joining a Pentecostal church, BSPF members remained in the EPC in order to bring about change. They felt satisfied that, thanks to the BSPF, they did not have to leave the church they had been born into. Nevertheless, there was a lively exchange of preachers between the Pentecostal churches and the BSPF. Contacts with Agbelengor, whose members greeted the rise of the BSPF and changes in the services with great satisfaction, were especially intense. After all, what they had been criticised and excluded for had now become accepted by many people in the mother church. Sharing basic ideas with the BSPF, Agbelengor members also radically rejected *Meleagbe* theology.

By admitting prayer groups into the congregations, the EPC came closer to the new churches from which it had distanced itself until the late 1970s. Loss of members was thereby avoided at the risk of deviating from the Presbyterian missionary heritage. In 1985 the synod praised the BSPF because (together with other groups) it supported 'the spiritual growth of the church'. On the other hand, however, it was criticised for its closeness to the Pentecostal movement:

> [S]ome of the units like the Bible Study and Prayer Groups have some few problems connected with Christian practices of the Evangelical Presbyterian Church. The members of the church are expected to avoid practices such as: a) clapping of hands while singing, and instead of this the groups should use local percussion instruments. b) Pentecostal prayer, whereby the whole group prays loudly at the same time and thereby misses the serenity when one communicates with God. c) In baptism immersion instead of infusion/sprinkling of water which is the accepted form of baptism of the E.P. Church. d) Bible Study and Prayer Groups be encouraged to use hymns from the 'Hadzigbale' [the old church hymn book] since these hymns contain great inspirational feelings. (Synod report 1985: 20)

In the same way as the EPC authorities had prevented spiritual practices in the prayer group's early beginnings, they now opposed Pentecostal practices which they also considered deviant from Presbyterian doctrine, but to no avail. Except for baptism through immersion, in 1989 the Blengo BSPF continued the practices mentioned above without the EPC pastor (Reverend C. K. Amegashie) taking any measures against it. Pentecostalisation of the mission church was thus in full swing. In this context, the first point of critique mentioned above is especially interesting, because here, African – and thus originally 'heathen' – drums are preferred to the clapping of hands among the Pentecostals. In this way 'Africanisation' and 'Pentecostalisation' were represented as incompatible. Indeed, as already seen, members of the BSPF were staunch opponents of Dzobo's attempts to Africanise church theology. Thus, the EPC's search for change resulted in two contradictory strategies. Whereas the Moderator and a few followers opted for a new African theology which incorporated African traditions, the BSPF and many other EPC members drew a clear boundary between 'heathendom' and Christianity. It is not surprising that these two radically different strategies of achieving the same aim – namely, preventing the migration of members to other churches – eventually clashed.

## The Second Secession: The EPC 'of Ghana'

While most local pastors simply ignored the new *Meleagbe* theology, the BSPG stood up to it. As its members strongly believed that Satan was operating through the old gods and ghosts, they could not accept a more positive valuation of Ewe religion. The group's opposition to the Moderator became vehement when, in 1988, he was re-elected for a third four-year term which, according to the prayer group, was against the church's constitution. During the meeting of the synod in that year, the BSPF organised a public demonstration against the Moderator. In turn, the church authorities forbade the celebration of the BSPF's tenth anniversary in Anloga. They did so in vain, for the majority of members – among them Dovlo, Dzobo's predecessor – attended the meeting.[13] This conflict led to a crisis within the church. In order to challenge Dzobo's re-election, the BSPF leaders brought the case to court. The conflict was thus cast in juridical rather than theological terms.

The majority of church members, though in general not in favour of the new theology, supported the prolongation of the Moderator's term because this had been decided by the highest church authority, the synod. For them it was sufficient that the Moderator agreed to stop propagating his own ideas as the new church theology; but for the prayer group this was not enough. During my fieldwork in 1989, the BSPF was still part of the EPC. However, there were already severe conflicts between the BSPF and national and local EPC authorities. Though not against prayer healing, the latter accused the BSPF of bringing unrest to the church and asked them to obey the decisions of the synod. But the BSPF could not accept the compromise of Dzobo staying on and just ceasing to propagate *Meleagbe* theology as the new church doctrine. Since the BSPF's request to elect a new Moderator was not honoured, it finally caused a split in the church.

Since 1991 there have been two EPCs, both claiming to be the rightful successor of the missionary heritage. The old EPC retained its former organisation, and its members can still be divided into the three categories distinguished above. The new EPC added 'of Ghana' to its name and its members are therefore often called 'of(f) people' by members of the old EPC. It adopted Pentecostal practices (with the exception of baptism by immersion and adult baptism) and claims to have a much higher rate of true Christians ('born agains') than the mother church. The split occurred both at the national and at the local level and divided not only lay church members, but also the clergy. The new EPC 'of Ghana' opened its headquarters in Accra. Despite attempts by the EPC's partner churches in America, Scotland and Germany (the latter even ceased financial support for the old EPC for some time) and by the Christian Council of Ghana to reconcile the two parties, the split became definitive. As a consequence, violent fights broke out in many local congregations over church properties.

This was not the case in Peki, where the old EPC's buildings were not contested. Many active female members, some of whom had been church mothers, and many young people, joined the new EPC which gathered its members from Dzogbati, Blengo, Afeviwofe, Tsame, Avetile and Dzake under a corrugated iron shed on the outskirts of Avetile. Emmanuel Brempong became the church's catechist and Edmund A. Atiase from Avetile, who had until then been the EPC minister at Klefe, became the pastor. During my fieldwork in 1992 the relations between the two churches, whose members often belonged to the same families or were husband and wife, were tense, with both sides insisting that they were right. Members of the old EPC maintained that synod decisions had to be accepted, while members of the new EPC insisted that the decision to prolong the Moderator's term for another four years had been unlawful. The conflict was thus mainly cast in terms of obedience to church authorities, not in terms of matters of faith, though it would have been difficult for members of the two EPCs to fight about such things in any case, as they shared the same cosmology. Most communicant members of the old EPC were also against *Meleagbe* theology because they considered Ewe religion the realm of Satan.

After the split, the old EPC had in a sense come full circle. Both the Africanisation of content and the establishment of a prayer group had proved ineffective in preventing an exodus to rival churches. During my fieldwork in 1992, the EPC authorities and members were rather at a loss as to how they might deal with the situation. Some were satisfied that with the secession of the dissidents order had returned. Others, wondering how to incorporate more spiritual forms of worship without once again undermining order, tried to revitalise the Wednesday evening prayer service. By and large, the congregations were licking their wounds and trying to reorganise church life. Nevertheless, members of the old and new EPC do not seem to have split at the level of ideas. Therefore, the quest continued for a Christian praxis capable of helping people cope with their troubles. As described in the next chapters, this stance unites the bulk of the members at the grassroots level of the old EPC with those of the EPC 'of Ghana' and Agbelengor. Before discussing the clash of Africanisation and Pentecostalisation it will be useful to examine the membership structure of the three churches.

## MEMBERSHIP OF THE EPC, AGBELENGOR AND THE EPC 'OF GHANA'

Significant differences between the three churches' membership structure, based on statistical information assembled by their leaders, is summarised in Tables 2–6. In all churches, a person counts as an adult member if he or she has been baptised and pays the church dues – at least 2,000 cedis a year (in 1992) for the EPC, and the tithe for the EPC 'of Ghana' and Agbelengor. Children also count as members, but do not have to pay any contribution. The EPC and the EPC 'of Ghana' practise child baptism and confirmation. Agbelengor favours adult baptism; newborn children are merely blessed but nevertheless counted as members. In all churches full members are those entitled to receive Holy Communion. In the old and new EPC this right is achieved as a result of confirmation, which is preceded by lessons in church doctrine and usually takes place between the ages of fifteen and seventeen. Agbelengor also organises introductory lessons for its adult baptism candidates. After a person has been baptised by immersion in the Amimli or any other stream in the area, he or she is entitled to receive the Lord's Supper. In all three churches, members failing to live up to the church rules may, albeit temporarily, lose the right to take communion. Thus, all churches differentiate between infant and adult members and separate the latter category into communicants and non-communicants.

Table 2 indicates the membership of all branches of the EPC (in the seven Peki villages and the Agbateh settlement), Agbelengor (in Blengo and Dzake) and the EPC 'of Ghana' (one branch for the whole of Peki). The EPC is by far the largest church because it is the oldest church in Peki, and it has a much higher percentage of infant members than the other two. It is clearly a church into which people are born. By contrast, Agbelengor and the EPC 'of Ghana' are churches which are chosen at a certain point in time. Nevertheless, members of these two churches also bring their children to church and in the course of time infant membership will increase.

A striking feature is the very large number of female members in all three churches. In Agbelengor and the EPC 'of Ghana' women far outnumber men. Whereas in the early mission church men formed the majority, the current situation is the complete reverse. Christianity has thus been transformed from a male into a female affair – in short, it has been 'feminised'. This also reflects the current population structure of Peki. As a

Table 2: Membership of EPC, Agbelengor, and EPC 'of Ghana', in Peki, June 1992

| Church | Adult Male No./% | Adult Female No./% | Children No./% | Total No |
|---|---|---|---|---|
| EPC | 944/20.7 | 1614/35.5 | 1993/43.8 | 4551 |
| Agbelengor | 36/13.9 | 143/55.2 | 80/30.9 | 259 |
| EPC 'of' Ghana | 40/14.9 | 166/62 | 62/23.1 | 268 |

result of male emigration, women form the majority in Peki as well as in Peki churches. This raises the question as to how the prevalence of women in the area, and thus in church, has contributed to changes within and outside the EPC. Is there a relationship between the 'feminisation' of Christianity and the Pentecostalisation noted above? The reasons for the popularity of the Pentecostal Agbelengor and the pentecostally oriented EPC 'of Ghana' among women are examined in the next two chapters.

That the EPC is a church into which people are born is also revealed by Table 3 which depicts the distribution of communicant to non-communicant members. Since only those entitled to take the Lord's Supper are seen as full members, the percentage of communicants indicates the extent to which church members live up to church rules. In the EPC those unable to do so are in the majority. Both in Agbelengor and the EPC 'of Ghana' communicants exceed non-communicants. In Agbelengor the ratio of male and female

Table 3: Non-communicants and communicants in EPC-Blengo, Agbelengor, and EPC 'of Ghana', in Peki, June 1992

| Church | Male | Female | Total |
|---|---|---|---|
| EPC | | | |
| non-communicants | 616 | 933 | 1549 |
| communicants | 328 | 681 | 1009 |
| total adult members | 944 | 1614 | 2558 |
| % non-communicants | 65.3 | 57.8 | 60.6 |
| % communicants | 34.7 | 42.2 | 39.4 |
| Agbelengor | | | |
| non-communicants | 7 | 30 | 37 |
| communicants | 29 | 113 | 142 |
| total adult members | 36 | 143 | 179 |
| % non-communicants | 19.5 | 21 | 20.7 |
| % communicants | 80.5 | 79 | 79.3 |
| EPC 'of Ghana' | | | |
| non-communicants | 5 | 66 | 71 |
| communicants | 35 | 100 | 135 |
| total adult members | 40 | 166 | 206 |
| % non-communicants | 12.5 | 39.8 | 34.5 |
| % communicants | 87.5 | 60.2 | 65.5 |

communicants to non-communicants is about four to one, while in the EPC
'of Ghana' the percentage of male communicants is considerably higher
than that of females, evidence that the relatively few active men behave
according to church rules, whereas some women fail to do so.

A similar picture arises from Table 4, which indicates the active and non-
active members in the three churches, [14] the criterion for active membership
being participation in one or more church groups for adult members. The
EPC organises a 'Women's Bible Class', a 'Church Choir', a youth choir
called 'Melody Choir', an elderly people's choir called 'Great Choir' or
Hadzihagã and male and female presbyters. [15] Agbelengor has a 'Women's
Fellowship', a 'Men's Fellowship', a 'Youth Fellowship' and official
prophets and deacons. The EPC 'of Ghana' offers its members 'Women
Ministries', a 'Church Choir', a 'Youth Fellowship', the BSPF, a 'Prayer
Force and Deliverance Team' and male and female presbyters. Table 5.4
reveals that in the old EPC the non-active members largely outnumber the
active. The reverse applies to Agbelengor where most members play an
active role. Interestingly, in the EPC 'of Ghana' most male members are
active, but the ratio of active to non-active women is even less than in the old
EPC. This may be largely due to the fact that some women are considerably
older and no longer feel inclined to participate in meetings of the various
groups, which take place some distance away on the outskirts of Avetile
(about 30–45 minutes walk from Blengo, Afeviwofe and Tsame, and even
further from the other Peki villages).

Table 4: Non-active and active members in EPC-Blengo, Agbelengor and EPC 'of
Ghana', in Peki, June 1992

| Church | Male | Female | Total |
|---|---|---|---|
| EPC | | | |
| non-active members | 90 | 146 | 236 |
| active members | 35 | 94 | 129 |
| total | 125 | 240 | 365 |
| % non-active | 72 | 60.8 | 64.7 |
| % active | 28 | 39.2 | 35.3 |
| Agbelengor | | | |
| non-active members | 5 | 59 | 64 |
| active members | 31 | 84 | 115 |
| total | 36 | 143 | 179 |
| % non-active | 13.9 | 41.3 | 35.8 |
| % active | 86.1 | 58.7 | 64.2 |
| EPC 'of Ghana' | | | |
| non-active members | 6 | 105 | 111 |
| active members | 34 | 61 | 95 |
| total | 40 | 166 | 206 |
| % non-active | 15 | 63.3 | 53.9 |
| % active | 85 | 36.7 | 46.1 |

Table 5 gives the active members' professions. In the EPC, most active members earn their living by farming, but other professions are also relevant. As far as Agbelengor is concerned, a large number of members is involved in farming and other professions are of minor importance. This church clearly has fewer members earning their living through salaried jobs such as teachers, nurses or clerks, than the old EPC and the EPC 'of Ghana'. Female members of Agbelengor have a considerably lower level of education, and its members in general have a lower social position, than those of the two EPCs.

Table 5: Occupations of active members in EPC-Blengo, Agbelengor, and EPC 'of Ghana', in Peki, June 1992

| Occupation<br>% | EPC<br>% | Agbelengor<br>% | EPC 'of Ghana' |
|---|---|---|---|
| Farming | 25.6 | 42.6 | 11.6 |
| Trading | 18.6 | 5.2 | 14.7 |
| Salaried work | 16.3 | 8.7 | 17.9 |
| Crafts | 13.9 | 5.2 | 17.9 |
| Student | 7 | 17.4 | 24.2 |
| None/retired/unemployed | 18.6 | 20.9 | 13.7 |

Particularly striking in the case of the new EPC is the high number of students among its members. That it is very much a young people's association is also confirmed by Table 6, which gives the age of active members. In the case of the EPC 'of Ghana', young people between twenty and twenty-nine are in the majority. By contrast, in the two other churches members tend to be older. If members under and above the age of fifty are grouped together,[16] it becomes clear that in both the EPC and Agbelengor these groups are about equal, while in the EPC 'of Ghana' younger people account for almost two-thirds of all members.

Table 6: Ages of active members in EPC-Blengo, Agbelengor, and EPC 'of Ghana', in Peki, June 1992

| Age<br>% | EPC<br>% | Agbelengor<br>% | EPC 'of Ghana' |
|---|---|---|---|
| under 20 | 6.2 | 13 | 6.3 |
| 20–29 | 12.4 | 7 | 39 |
| 30–39 | 17 | 18.3 | 17.9 |
| 40–49 | 11.6 | 16.5 | 6.3 |
| 50–59 | 19.4 | 20.9 | 9.5 |
| 60–69 | 23.3 | 7.8 | 14.7 |
| 70+ | 10.1 | 16.5 | 6.3 |
| under 50 | 47.2 | 54.8 | 69.5 |
| 50+ | 52.8 | 45.2 | 30.5 |

Comparison of the three churches' membership structure throws an interesting light on the two secessions discussed in this chapter. Though no statistical information is available on the membership of Agbelengor at the time it became independent, it is possible to get a general picture from interviews and current statistical information. In the case of Agbelengor's secession, those dissatisfied with the EPC were mainly less educated women who earned their living through farming and, as we saw, a handful of men low in the church hierarchy. By and large, the elite remained in the EPC.

In the case of the subsequent secession, matters were different. Those dissatisfied with the EPC were evidently educated women of all ages and educated young men. In contrast to the first secession, the second involved a representative part of the church. Looking at this secession from a social point of view, the conclusion is that people joining the new EPC did not differ significantly from those remaining in the old EPC. In contrast to the first secession, educated as well as less educated, poor as well as more wealthy, and low as well as high-standing people all left the old EPC.

Significantly, a disproportionately large number of young people, both male and female, left the old EPC for the new one. This reflects young people's dissatisfaction with the old EPC's gerontocratic hierarchy which attributes authority to older men. In the new EPC, by contrast, young people – provided they are considered to be filled with the Holy Spirit – have much more say.

## 'AFRICANISATION' VERSUS 'PENTECOSTALISATION'

Since the 1960s the question of 'how to be Africans and Christians at the same time' has been crucial for African intellectuals and theologians. Arising from discontent with the way the Christian message took shape in Africa,[17] this question originates from the following complex of ideas. Catholic and Protestant missionaries are criticised because they held their own interpretations to be the only true ones and rigorously disapproved of African concepts and practices which they described as 'heathen' or 'diabolic'. African critics of the missions, for example Baëta (1968), Mbiti (1979) and the authors contributing articles to Dickson and Ellingworth (1970) and Fasholé-Luke et al. (1978), counter this by claiming that the universality of Christianity can produce different local expressions. At the same time, African Christians' interpretation of the Christian message is a problem for these critics: members of the mission churches, many of whom secretly participate in non-Christian rituals, are seen as the missionaries' victims, bereft of their African identity, while the followers of the new movements, who are mainly recruited from the mission churches, are not considered true Christians. Whereas the former are thought to have a 'split consciousness', the latter's ideas are seen as 'syncretistic'.[18] According to the perspective of critical African theologians and intellectuals, both are in a position betwixt and between Christianity and African religion. They therefore find it necessary to replace split and conflict on the one hand, and 'syncre-tism' on the other, with a more appropriate synthesis, a synthesis based on a dualist conception of African, or 'traditional', versus Christian. Under the banner of 'Africanisation' or 'Indigenisation' a successful combination of both elements is advocated in order to provide an authentic African expression of Christianity. Through Africanisation members of the mission churches are expected to refrain from joining 'syncretistic' movements.

The descriptions 'syncretistic' and 'split consciousness' both deny that members at the grassroots level of independent as well as of mission churches have developed an appropriate understanding of Christianity. By making use of these terms, theologians contest local interpretations rather than merely describe them (see Droogers 1989: 20). At the same time, the two descriptions suggest a difference between the ideas of members of the two types of churches. Also, by employing these two descriptions, a conceptual gap is constructed between independent and mission churches, which prevents scholars from investigating why and how people actually move from one church to another.

This gap has been confirmed in anthropological study of Christianity in Africa. Like missiologists, anthropologists have shown a remarkable lack of interest in the actual study of mission churches at grassroots level. They seem to assume that members of these churches simply share the missionaries' ideas, and they have preferred to study religious movements which they find more truly African (see Introduction, note 2). In the vast literature on African independent churches and movements, only a few studies have examined how people move from mission into independent churches and how actual secessions from the former, leading to foundation of the latter, take place. One of the main objectives of this study is to overcome the artificial conceptual separation of the two types of churches and investigate historically and ethnographically what unites and separates them.

To compare the first and second secession occurring in the EPC establishes significant differences and common features. One important difference is that the second secession occurred on a national, rather than a merely local scale, and that the dissidents kept the name of the church, testifying to the BSPF's strong feeling of righteousness and self-assuredness. While the Agbe-lengor people merely left the EPC to start a new church, the BSPF claimed to be the true guardian of the missionary heritage. This strong self-confidence is based both on education and the claim to be filled with the Holy Spirit. In contrast to Amedzro and his co-leaders, the local and national leaders of the BSPF were educated people of good standing in the EPC congregations and administration. It is significant that, as the name BSPF reveals, they empha-sise Bible study as well as prayer. Contrary to Agbelengor when it focused on prayer healing before its turn to Pentecostalism, the BSPF took knowledge of the Bible, and thus literacy, to be a prerequisite for effective healing.

In this sense, the second secession has much in common with those occurring within the framework of Western Protestantism, for instance in the Netherlands – a country known for the frequency of splits in its Protestant Calvinist Churches. Secessions there were usually carried out by active, knowledgeable church members opposing church leaders. Indeed, Protestantism, by emphasising that all members should have a good knowledge of the Bible, actually encourages lay members to revolt against leaders and to found new churches, and contains the seeds for the continuing multiplication of churches. Thus, secession of the BSPF indicates that the EPC had reached a point where its members were increasingly educated and emancipated and hence able to threaten old gerontocratic obedience structures.

The BSPF's emphasis on biblical knowledge has to be seen against the background of the shift from Spiritual to Pentecostal churches which has been occurring all over Ghana since the mid-1980s. Indeed, as Gifford recently noted, '[a]mong the most striking characteristics of African Christianity in the last decade has been the proliferation of new autonomous Pentecostal churches' (1994: 241).[19] Rather than placing confidence in objects such as candles and incense, the Pentecostals trust the power of the Bible alone; they are convinced that the Spirit works through the Scriptures rather than through objects, which might easily be appropriated by devilish forces. Thus, whereas in its early beginnings as a Spiritual church Agbelengor relied on the Holy Spirit and did not give much emphasis to reading the Bible, the BSPF (and Agbelengor after its Pentecostal turn) understand the latter as a condition for making the former effective. Contrary to what one might expect on the basis of Goody's theory on the transformative power of literacy (1977, 1987), the reading and writing ability of church leaders and members is shown not necessarily to entail the fixation of doctrine and orthodoxy. By emphasising the Holy Spirit, believers can claim to experience God in their lives, thereby reaching beyond the biblical text as a source for divine revelation. The 'letter' (the emphasis on written texts) and the 'spirit' (the emphasis on works of, and revelations through, the Holy Spirit) may therefore coexist (see Probst 1989).

Despite differences between the first and second secession there are also crucial common features. While, from the beginning, the first prayer group's challenge of the EPC's understanding of Christianity was unacceptable to the EPC authorities, thirty years later they realised that change was necessary and institutionalised the BSPF as part of the church. Despite having successfully eliminated the typical characteristics of Spiritual churches initially adopted by the prayer group, the EPC faced a new problem in the BSPF: they were now disturbed by the BSPF's proximity to Pentecostalism. As in the case of the first secession, they emphasised that the prayer group's practices were incompatible with Presbyterian tradition. In turn, the BSPF loudly accused the mother church of not guarding the boundary between 'heathendom' and Christianity, thereby opening itself up to the Devil. The BSPF claimed that only its own, pentecostally oriented way of worship would be able to keep this boundary intact and Satan out of the church. In this sense, the secessions of Agbelengor and the BSPF resemble each other.

In both cases dissidents formed purificatory movements aimed to keep Christianity and Ewe religion apart, and at the same time, eliminate believers' need for the ambivalent *Yesu viɖe, dzo viɖe* stance. Both Agbelengor (in the early days as well as currently) and the new EPC are united in a reliance on the Holy Spirit and in categorical condemnation of African religion which, in good missionary tradition, they represent as the domain of Satan. At the same time, through prayer healing, they offer protective and curative practices comparable to those provided by Ewe priests and *dzotɔwo* (for an elaboration of this point see chapters 6 and 7). Here lies the main difference between the EPC authorities and the dissidents. The prayer groups' paradoxical opposition and proximity to Ewe religion is the actual source of conflicts between them and the EPC establishment.

Opposition to the Africanisation of the Christian content in the EPC raises the question of why people who hold 'traditional' ideas about the existence of witches and evil spirits reject the integration of 'traditional' elements into Christian theology. Do the adversaries of *Meleagbe* theology, who not only encompassed the BSPF but also a wide range of local EPC members, have no need for Africanisation? Do they themselves understand their situation in terms of split and conflict, as African theologians such as Dzobo assume? Had they perhaps already developed a synthesis on their own, unnoticed by theological reformers?

The fact that both supporters and opponents hold concepts pertaining to Ewe religious traditions does not result in similar ideas about it: they construct Ewe religion in different ways. So it is clear that Africanisation is not just a question of incorporating 'tradition' into African Christianity. Neither can understanding the concept of 'tradition' solve this conflict. How then can the struggle between supporters and opponents of *Meleagbe* theology be approached? It is striking that belief in the Devil is the watershed between the two parties. Supporters of the new theology understand him as an outdated figment of the imagination, but for opponents he is a threatening and terrifying reality. Undoubtedly, the image of the Devil is the key to answering this question and this can shed light upon the question of Africanisation.

On the basis of this complex situation studied here, mission church members' presumed 'split consciousness' and lack of synthesis has no empirical foundation. Assumption of the necessity of Indigenisation of the Christian message is founded on a fundamental misunderstanding that the ideas of church members are not understood as an 'African' product of the contact between the missionaries' Christianity and the pre-Christian Ewe religion, but as a result of Western imposition. However, Indigenisation has in fact been operative since the beginning: conversion did not mean mindless acceptance of the missionary teachings, but rather, as discussed earlier, their appropriation on the basis of existing ideas and concepts. Ewe interpretation of the missionary message was, and still is, a product of the interaction between both parties concerned, which differs from the missionaries' as well as the pre-Christian Ewe ideas. The Ewe imagination of the translated Devil is a convincing illustration of this interaction process.

Ever since the beginning of Christianisation, ideas held by most Ewe Christians differed considerably from those of the missionaries. The former continued to believe in the existence of the old gods and spirits which they saw as agents of *Abosam*. They measured the success of Christianity by its capacity to counteract evil at least as successfully as Ewe religion. The missionaries saw this divergence as an indicator of 'heathen' remnants and 'superstitions' on the part of the newly converted, and thought it was just a question of time before these childish and naive ideas would disappear. But almost 150 years after the arrival of the first missionary, most church members still conceptualise non-Christian spiritual beings in the same way as the first converts. Now it is church intellectuals who see their linking of pre-Christian and Christian entities as a faulty mixture of tradition and Christianity and feel called to present a more adequate synthesis to prevent believers from 'sliding back' into Ewe religion. At the same time, they wish to restore the self-esteem which Africans have lost in the course of Christianisation and colonisation.

Thus, church intellectuals do not take the ideas of the majority of church members seriously. People's adoption of a *Yesu viɖe, dzo viɖe* stance, and 'back-sliding' resulting from it, should not be mistaken as a sign of 'split consciousness' and a loss of self-esteem, but rather as an indication of a critical stance towards Protestant Christianity. Comparing missionary Pietism with Ewe religion, it was clear to any Ewe Christian that the former failed to provide them with prophylactic and, above all, curative rituals with which to counteract evil (for a similar view see Isichei 1995: 6ff). For this reason, once they were in trouble, Christians virtually *had* to turn to non-Christian remedies. The rise of independent churches outside, and prayer groups within the EPC and other mission churches, shows that this really is the crux of the matter. These new churches and prayer groups attacked the mission churches' neglect of ritual and filled this gap with practices able to help their members cope with troubles. Due to their difficult life conditions, this, rather than their identity as Africans, is the main concern of these people. Instead of assuming that mission church members simply had a 'split consciousness', one should rather state that through conversion to

Christianity they adopted a religion that *split them away* from the possibility of undertaking ritual action against evil powers. The rise of Spiritual and Pentecostal churches is an attempt to provide for a ritual praxis *within* Christianity and thereby abolish this split. That not all mission church members joined one of the new churches does not mean that the stance described here only applies to those actually making the decisive step. Most communicant EPC members at grassroots level share with members of the EPC 'of Ghana' and Agbelengor a Christian discourse based on belief that Ewe religion is the realm of Satan, and the idea that missionary Pietism lacks a clear ritual dimension (see also chapters 6 and 7).

Thus, members of these three churches are not separated on the level of concepts, but rather with regard to the actual establishment of a ritual praxis. It follows that the new churches did not bring something completely new, but rather provided a solution to the basic contradiction inherent in missionary Pietism. On the conceptual level, Africanisation is a process inherent in Christianisation since its beginnings. Only recently has it manifested itself more visibly in a Spiritual or Pentecostal praxis.

The perspectives of *Meleagbe* theology and Pentecostalism on Africanisation are opposed to each other just as much as the missionaries' contradictory statements about the ancestors' godly as well as devilish orientation (see Chapter 3). Those willing to incorporate African traditions into Christianity accuse those believing in the existence of demons to be superstitious, whereas the latter vehemently oppose this incorporation as diabolical. Pre-Christian religion is thus approached from two perspectives: from one, it contains something godly, from the other it is purely devilish. From such different perspectives, two different forms of Africanisation result. While the former strives to indigenise Christianity, that is, to express its message in an African idiom, the latter understands Christianity as a religion which has nothing in common with 'heathendom' and which separates its adherents from their past. Indeed, for Pentecostals, the attraction of Christianity lies in the fact that it is a new and strange religion opposed to African religion and culture. The existence of these two contradictory perspectives on pre-Christian religion is evidence that it is possible to make the past meaningful in the context of Christianity in different ways. Thus, there is not just one possible Africanisation of Christianity, as some African theologians would seem to suggest.

It is important to distinguish between Africanisation 'from below' and 'from above'; the transformation of missionary Pietistic ideas and practices by church members at grassroots level being Africanisation 'from below' and, for example, Dzobo's theology being Africanisation 'from above'. While the Devil is the basis of the former's conceptualisation of Christianity, Dzobo considers belief in his existence to be theologically unfounded, and the fear of witches and evil spirits superstitious. His Indigenisation is an academic philosophical construct that approaches correspondences between Ewe 'tradition' and Christian doctrine on a metaphysical level, and turns Ewe religion, to quote Peel, 'into harmless "culture"' (1994: 163). This synthesis is therefore closer to Western theologians than to church members in the villages who still fear local gods and ghosts as dangerous powers. Between Dzobo and them stands *Abosam*, without whom Christianity would not make sense to the latter and with whom it would be 'super-stitious' to the former.

# 6

# DOCTRINES AND RITUALS

To consider the three churches – the EPC, Agbelengor and the EPC 'of Ghana' – in more detail, and examine the doctrines and rituals which they offer their members, is to realise that the distinction between what churches offer and what their members expect and do is artificial. The relationship between church organisation and members' actions is actually dialectical: members give form and contribute to church organisation while the latter shapes the actions and ideas of the former. They are distinguished here for practical reasons only in order to give a narrative structure to this account of various facets of the three churches.

In what ways do the Pentecostal churches' doctrines and practices differ from those of mission churches such as the EPC? How do the former define the boundary between 'heathendom' and Christianity and relate to Ewe religious ideas and practices? In what ways do the new churches' doctrines and ritual practices take up concerns of nineteenth-century missionary Pietism? In the previous chapter some clues indicated answers to these questions: the main difference between the EPC on the one hand, and Agbelengor and the EPC 'of Ghana' on the other, lay in their different ideas about the Devil, which in turn gave rise to considerably different practices.

## DIFFERENCES IN WORSHIP

The Sunday church bell is among the last reminders of the EPC's former monopoly on Christianity in Peki. All other churches follow the EPC bell and begin their worship at about the same time. The bell is rung for the first time around 8 a.m. and again one hour later. This second bell means that it is time for the morning bath – nobody would enter the house of God unclean. The third bell around 9.15 a.m. signals that people should leave the house. Churchgoers then depart for their respective services in their best clothes. Women avoid wearing the same clothes as the Sunday before and borrow dresses from friends if necessary. While some wear Western fashions, most adorn themselves with African-style clothes: a long skirt, a top and a cover cloth. Almost all conceal their hair, except younger girls in Western dresses. Most men cover themselves with a large colourful cloth (a *Kente*) hanging loosely from the left shoulder; underneath they wear shorts. Only a few older men wear Western suits, while schoolboys wear trousers and shirts.

For members of all churches, Sunday is clearly a day on which to dress up. Members of the EPC worship in a chapel built at the beginning of the century and situated in *Kpodzi*, those of Agbelengor in a newly constructed building on top of the hill in Afeviwofe, and those of the EPC 'of Ghana' in a shed on the outskirts of Avetile. Sunday services last for about three hours, and even longer on particular occasions. In each of the churches, people sit in fixed order – the space in which worship takes place mirrors and reproduces the congregational structure. High-ranking members are usually seated in front, and women and men usually sit separately.

Liturgical order is also fixed in the three churches. Liturgies offer participants the possibility of travelling along a sequence of steps which will transform them. First there is a confession of sin (varying in elaborateness), an invocation of God and his Holy Spirit and a restatement of the basic tenets of Christian faith. Other parts of the service include announcements which provide important news; the offertory, which asks people to give away part of their property; the sermon, which teaches people how to understand the Bible and how to behave; and, at the end, the 'Lord's Prayer' and blessing, which unite people in faith and promise protection in the future. Attendance at Sunday service marks the transition from the old to the new week. People should leave the service free of the sins they had committed in the past and be strengthened intellectually (through the sermon) and spiritually (through prayers and songs) to undergo the new week.

Similarity between the three liturgies is due to the mission church initially providing the model for Sunday worship. However, both Agbelengor and the EPC 'of Ghana' have adapted this liturgical sequence, thus implying a critique of the organisation of worship in the mission church. Examining three important aspects of this critique, namely the emphasis on worship (*subɔsubɔ*), prayer (*gbedodoɖa*) and spirit (*gbɔgbɔ*), provides a better understanding of Ewe Christianity at grassroots level.

To focus first on *worship*; as noted in Chapter 3, there is no Ewe term for religion as such. All practices related to the service of a *trɔ̃* (god) were, and are, designated as *subɔsubɔ* (service). *Subɔ* is also used in secular contexts: a person serving another person is called *subɔla* (servant). Consequently, Christians refer to the worshippers of *trɔwo* as *trɔ̃subɔlawo*. The Ewe expression for the Sunday service as a whole is *Mawusubɔsubɔ* ('God's service') and Christians used to call themselves *Mawusubɔlawo* ('servants of God'). The use of this same expression suggests a link between Ewe and Christian worship (though of course the former is represented as satanic and hence inferior).

However, in the old EPC, worship is not understood as a distinct set of actions. It is assumed that just by attending church service God is worshipped. By contrast, Agbelengor and the EPC 'of Ghana' have institutionalised worship as a separate complex of practices: for much of the time people praise

God with spoken words and songs. As in the context of Ewe religion, in these churches *subɔsubɔ* is thus held to consist of a set of actually performed practices. But whereas traditionally the service of a deity implies all sorts of rituals involving libations, sacrifices and the like, in line with Pentecostalism (and Pietism), Agbelengor and the EPC 'of Ghana' confine themselves to the practices of speaking and singing. Thus, God has to be served explicitly during the church service, and not merely by attending services and leading a good Christian life, as the old EPC maintains.

Agbelengor and the new EPC legitimate the need for actual worship with reference to the angels in heaven, who praise God all the time and whom human beings should take as their example. The aim of these praises is to establish a close relationship between God and human beings, involving not only their spirits but also their bodies. During the worshipping and praising session, people temporarily transform the chapel into heaven and themselves into angels, and in doing this they realise a short-lived 'pleasure dome' (Fernandez 1982) which contrasts sharply with the insecurities and fears evoked in the course of the sermon that follows. In the old EPC, of course, hymns of praise are sung as well, but only singers with a lot of imagination would be able to experience a temporary heaven on earth in these hymns. Worship in the two other churches involves all participants. No one undergoes the Sunday service passively; all participate fully in body and spirit.

Second, the emphasis on more elaborate practices also comes to the fore in the way in which *prayer* is understood in the two dissident churches. The worshippers of *trɔ̃wo*, the old EPC, Agbelengor and the new EPC are all united in the conviction that prayer is a powerful means by which to connect people with the divine, and as a result, achieve certain ends. Leaders and members of the three churches would certainly agree with Brempong's description in 1989 of how he experienced prayer:

> When you are praying or when you are reading the Scriptures you go into deep thought ... And you come to a stage, you will see that you are not within yourself and your mind. You'll see that you are conversing with a supernatural power, that is God. You are conversing with him spiritually. He will speak to you and you also speak within the Spirit.

In the old EPC the congregation listens to the preacher's prayers and is only entitled to pray aloud once (during the 'Lord's Prayer'), while in the two other churches prayer involves the whole congregation for a considerable time. In these two churches the differentiation of prayer into sequences with particular themes suggests that great importance is attributed to individual communication with God. Here, confession of sin and invocation of the Holy Spirit cannot be achieved by one representative speaking on behalf of the group, but only individually. Through a sequence of mass prayers on particular themes, people have time to meditate on their lives, to relate themselves personally to God and, occasionally, to speak in tongues, thought to be the most intimate connection anyone can have with God.

Prayer does not only connect human beings with the divine; it is also considered a powerful practice capable of achieving particular ends. Devotion of prayer sessions to particular topics again shows how much power Agbelengor and the EPC 'of Ghana' attribute to the praxis of speaking. Once contact between a person and God is made, he can be implored to do certain things. The power of prayer is thus understood as a product of intense communication with God, whose Spirit, as a result, merges with the person praying. Therefore, these two churches insist that their members always pray – at home, in the market, on journeys, etc. People are encouraged to seek contact with the divine virtually all the time and to pray over all things received from others or bought in the market. In this way, potentially evil, destructive influences inherent in such objects are said to be rendered ineffective (Meyer 1999). Through prayer, good Christians are to attempt to situate themselves permanently on the boundary between the world and the divine realm. Those filled with God's Spirit are supposed to be able to ward off danger, to escape temptations and even to bring about healing and exorcise evil spirits for others in need.

Emphasis on individual experience of the divine, and contact with it, is a characteristic feature of Pentecostal churches to which Agbelengor and the EPC 'of Ghana' (at least to some extent) belong. By encouraging members to pray for themselves, these churches have individualised access to the divine. This is also expressed by the fact that there is room for people testifying to their miraculous experiences. At the same time, members are thereby held responsible for their lives; they themselves have to make sure they are in contact with God and lead decent lives. Only if things go wrong and a person is in trouble, i.e. if he or she is assumed to be filled by an evil spirit rather than the Holy Spirit, does the preacher intervene. By contrast, in the framework of Ewe religion and the mission church, access to the divine is mediated through a priest who is consulted in order to bring about or restore a person's relationship with a spiritual being. Although the old EPC does not deny the importance of personal prayer, it has never gone so far as to institutionalise an elaborate prayer practice. And during Sunday service at least, it is the task of the preacher to mediate between human beings and God in the same way as an Ewe priest makes the contact between gods and people. When people find themselves in trouble, the EPC does not provide special treatment. This is why many people leaving the old EPC complained that in this church people 'do not know how to pray'.

The third and final critique of the old EPC's organisation of worship concerns the domain of *spirit* – the relationship between God's Holy Spirit (*Gbɔgbɔ Kɔkɔe*), Satan's evil spirits (*gbɔgbɔ vɔ̃wo*) and a person's spirit (*gbɔgbɔ*). In the EPC the invocation of the Holy Spirit at the beginning of the service occurs through the preacher's prayer and a hymn sung by the congregation. In the two other churches this process is much more elaborate. Once again, the decisive difference between the EPC and the other two is not on the level of doctrine, but rather on the level of practice. In the EPC, God is also asked to send down his Holy Spirit and drive away all evil spirits that are eager to distract people's attention. And in line with Pietism, the dualism of *Mawu* and *Abosam* lies at the heart of the EPC's doctrine. But while in the EPC the preacher merely alludes to the spiritual domain in a short prayer, the two other churches deal with it in a more practical way which involves the whole congregation. They thus 'unpack' and make explicit what remains compressed and implicit in the EPC.

The semantics of '*gbɔgbɔ*' (see also Chapter 3) is important in relation to the complex of 'spirit'. The term *gbɔgbɔ* was not only used to translate the 'Holy Spirit', and 'evil spirits' who were thereby represented as oppositions, but also to designate an individual's spirit. Thus it came to replace the pre-Christian *aklama*, a term discarded by the missionaries who systematically avoided making use of terms which originally entailed a ritual praxis. For Ewe Christians, *gbɔgbɔ*, instead of *aklama*, became responsible for a person's fate. Like *aklama*, *gbɔgbɔ* is considered to have a decisive influence on one's life. But unlike *aklama*, one's *gbɔgbɔ* is not conceived as a separate, independent entity, but rather as an open space in the mind which can either be filled by *Mawu*'s spirit or an evil one. The same term is used to express possession by the Holy Spirit or an evil spirit; it is said that the spirit 'is upon a person' (*gbɔgbɔ le ame dzi*) or enters a person (*gbɔgbɔ ɖe ame dzi*).[1] This is how possession by an evil spirit is imagined:

> There are some people who are being possessed or who are possessing these evil spirits. But they don't know that these evil spirits are within them. So evil spirits have made them something like a rented room: they are staying there. And they go out to do bad things and then come back to stay. (Kofi Akoto, EPC-candidate catechist, in 1989)

Members of all churches share the understanding that individuals are connected with a higher spiritual entity, either good or bad, which governs their lives through the possession of their personal *gbɔgbɔ*:

> Those who are bad Christians are dominated by evil spirits. They are bad. Without the spirit of God you are bad. You are baptised with the Holy Ghost, but it must get within you. (Alice Mallet, EPC, in 1989)

Christian baptism is to ensure that one's *gbɔgbɔ* will be possessed by the *Gbɔgbɔ Kɔkɔe* rather than evil spirits. According to Agbelengor and the EPC 'of Ghana', an individual's connection with the Holy Spirit through baptism is not permanent, but has to be realised again and again through prayer.

This is what happens during the prayer session at the beginning of these churches' services. If people do not make sure that the Holy Spirit enters them, they can easily be possessed by evil spirits which will cause bodily sickness and material ruin. These evil spirits are considered agents of the Devil, who is represented as the head of all the *trɔwo* and other non-Christian entities.

The use of *gbɔgbɔ* is a very interesting phenomenon: through translation, a secular word was vested with a new meaning which expresses an idea that did not previously exist in that form (see Chapter 3). At the same time the importance of the term in its new meaning was supported by its original meaning. 'Spirit', by implying 'breath', became a matter of vital importance. Through introduction of the term *gbɔgbɔ* in a suprasensory sense the linguistic base was laid for a theory of spirit possession which integrated both non-Christian spiritual beings and the Spirit of the Christian *Mawu* as comparable, though conflicting, entities, thereby opposing them on a single, spiritual battlefield. And from possession by either the Holy Spirit or satanic spirits, it is just one logical step to the praxis of exorcism, although this had never been official policy in the old EPC. It is only institutionalised in Agbelengor and in the EPC 'of Ghana'.

In sum, there is no fundamental difference in terms of doctrine between the three churches – a statement emphasised over and over again by the leaders of the three churches and their members during interviews. They all share the same cosmology, but differ with regard to the extent to which they are ready to thematise the satanic. The main difference lies in the space reserved for the practice of worship and prayer, where both Agbelengor and the EPC 'of Ghana' aim to let the Holy Spirit enter a person's spirit so that it cannot be possessed by an evil spirit, and have developed special services devoted to these practices.

## EVIL SPIRITS AND THE BOUNDARY BETWEEN CHRISTIANITY AND 'HEATHENDOM'

### EPC

After the split, leading to the exodus of the BSPF, the old EPC once again faced the same problem as before the institutionalisation of the prayer group: how to deal with the spiritual and physical problems its members attributed to evil spirits, without diverging too much from the Presbyterian heritage? After the BSPF had left, the traditional prayer service on Wednesday evening had to be reshaped. During 1992, local EPC leaders started experimenting with new forms. The old Wednesday evening liturgy, which consisted of songs, a brief sermon and some prayers of intercession for the sick, was adapted. In Tsame, the Reverend Edmund Y. Tawia began organising prayer sessions for the confession and forgiveness of sins, for thanksgiving and for all those in need. Then he called the sick forward for the laying on of hands and prayed for them individually. In Avetile, the Reverend S. K. S. Agyagbo organised a prayer service on the same lines. In many respects it resembled the prayer services previously held by the BSPF, but in contrast to these, there was no mass prayer, no ecstatic dancing and no exorcism. The prayer for the sick occurred in a calm atmosphere devoid of the dramatic behaviour characteristic of possessed people, so common in Pentecostal and Spiritual churches. In Blengo, the Reverend S. S. Agidi did not pray for sick individuals in public. Rather, he organised silent prayer sessions devoted to thanksgiving, asking for things needed and for healing of the sick. He also used the prayer service to teach people about matters distinguishing the EPC from the Spiritual and Pentecostal churches.

Despite the new form of the prayer service, EPC members by and large continued to consult the pastors individually in order to demand special prayers, as had always been the case. Pastors explained that many members have troubles they attribute to powers such as *adze* (witchcraft), *dzo* (magic), *trɔ̃* and *ŋɔli* (a dead person's spirit). While some clandestinely consult Ewe religious specialists in order to get rid of these powers or even to obtain protective *dzo*, others demand healing and deliverance prayers from the EPC pastors. Although not all pastors were convinced of the existence of these spiritual entities, they responded similarly: they would take people's ideas as a point of departure and pray that these powers would leave the afflicted person alone. But they all stressed that one should not talk about these powers too much. While not denying the existence of Satan, they emphasised that he was not mentioned in the Creed (which after all defined what a Christian should believe) and that the EPC Church Order (*Nyanyui Hame le Ghana kple Togo fe Hamedodo*, 1980) explicitly rejected belief in witchcraft and other 'superstitions' – these were 'unimportant things' and belief in them was a sign of fear and unfaithfulness (ibid.: 42). As Agidi explained:

> Actually I try to drive them (the EPC congregation) to facts, to the real, the hard fact that Christ is always sufficient. ... What I have been telling them is, the more they talk about the Devil, the more fears drive into them when they think about him. But when you concentrate on God and his power, I think this will solve our problem. The power that is within us is greater than the power that comes.

Far from denying the existence of the Devil and evil spirits, local EPC policy was to emphasise that it was wrong to dwell on the powers of darkness for too long, as happened in Pentecostal and Spiritual churches. According to local EPC leaders, anybody praying to God regularly and really believing in his powers would be filled with his Spirit and not fall victim to evil powers.

In their view, being filled with the Holy Spirit is not a matter of church affiliation, but of the strength of one's personal faith, a true Christian being

considered to be separated from the realm of the Devil. According to local
EPC leaders, conversion to Christianity calls for a decisive turn away from
'heathendom' (the realm of Satan), which need not be repeated over and
over again. In this vein, Agidi complained that the so-called 'born-again'
Christians in the Pentecostal churches always remain stuck at the beginning, constantly reiterating their separation from satanic powers; Christians,
however, are more mature and no longer involve themselves with 'the other
side' which they long ago chose to leave behind. Therefore the conceptual
boundary separating the divine from the satanic should not be thematised to
any great extent.

By signing the *burial rites declaration* on the EPC membership certificate,
members simply declare that they abstain from any involvement with
'heathendom':

> i. I (...) having accepted Jesus Christ as my personal Lord and Saviour
> hereby vow to abstain from all heathen practices and rites in my life
> time; and that no person or persons shall in any way undertake any of
> these on my behalf during sickness.
> ii. At my death I want my body to be buried according to the rules and
> regulations of the E.P. Church. [...]
> iii. After my burial, no person or persons shall perform any heathen
> practices. [...]

The submission by personal signature to the EPC church order is thus
considered an appropriate way by which to separate oneself from
'heathendom'. Those having done so are considered more or less safe
(though in practice the chance of 'back-sliding' always exists). This again
illustrates the extent to which the EPC defines Christian faith in terms of the
observance of rules and regulations.

In the case of an active member's death, pastors and presbyters always try
to make sure that the family respects the burial rites declaration. Occasionally this leads to serious problems. For instance, when the Blengo
presbyter R. Y. Botwoe, a member of the royal Nyangamangu clan, was
buried on 21 March 1992, members of his clan tried to stop the people
carrying the coffin to the cemetery in order to perform some customary
rites after the burial service. Agidi was furious with the interruption and
ordered the cortege to march on. This resulted in a chaotic situation in the
course of which members of the congregation and the family of the deceased
came to blows. In the end, the family allowed Botwoe's body to pass without
performing any rites. This incident made it clear that local pastors (as
well as Agidi, those from other Peki districts were also present) are not in
favour of a more positive valuation of customs as propagated by Dzobo, but
rather represent Christianity and traditional rites as completely incompatible.

To sum up, in Agbelengor and the EPC 'of Ghana', and also in the EPC, the concept of the Devil is employed to define the boundary between Christianity and 'heathendom'. All three churches ultimately base their doctrines on the dualism of God and the Devil. But whereas the dissident churches deal extensively with the dark side of this dualism in discourse and ritual, the EPC propagates its neglect and asks its members to renounce the satanic once and for all with their signature. As a result, despite performance of prayer services, the EPC offers no public discursive space or ritual practices dealing explicitly with evil spirits.

## Agbelengor

Agbelengor organises short prayer meetings during the week[2] and each month there is a period of three days of fasting during which services are held from 6 a.m. until 1 or 2 p.m. each day. I witnessed two such fasting periods. The liturgy is not completely fixed, but usually contains prayer sessions devoted to the same topics as covered on Sundays; testimony and prophecy; songs and dances; a long sermon and some teaching regarding the dangers of Ewe religion; and prayers for the improvement of health and wealth and for deliverance. The fasting sessions abound with people's reports on their experiences of divine interference in their lives. Prophetesses may claim they saw Jesus coming down to be with the congregation or may confirm that the Holy Spirit really dwells in the pastor. Others are eager to testify to great deeds God has done for them. Praying, singing and dancing are all more ecstatic than during ordinary Sunday services, often including speaking in tongues and whirling round to the rhythm of the drums. It is especially the women who seem to experience the Holy Spirit within them.

While fasting, more emphasis is given to evil spirits than during regular Sunday services and weekly prayer meetings. The assumption is that denial of bodily needs such as food and drink brings people closer to God and makes the Holy Spirit more accessible than ordinarily. Through fasting, people are to leave behind bodily desires and become more spiritual, a state of being considered the most appropriate in which to fight evil forces.

For the purpose of investigating how Agbelengor defines and deals with the boundary between 'heathendom' and Christianity, a sermon and some prayer sessions devoted to the improvement of health and wealth and to the deliverance from evil spirits will be examined. The chronological order of the liturgy will be followed and essentials of Agbelengor's doctrinal and ritual attitudes towards traditional worship will be highlighted.

A sermon delivered by Amedzro on 1 March 1992, the third day of the February fasting session[3] contains elementary parts of Agbelengor's doctrine regarding 'heathendom'. Since much remains implicit in this terse text, my comments in rectangular brackets will serve to provide a context for what is said.

I want to talk about the worship our ancestors had before the worship of God came. [He reads Genesis 1, 3: 8–10, part of the account of the Fall]. The Bible lets us know that in the beginning God created Adam and Eve. And God's Spirit came to them. And when they fell into sin, the human beings were looking for a safe place. Thus, when the human beings ran away [to hide from God], they hid under a tree and thought that the tree [which became a locus of worship for them] should help them. The human beings ran and hid under a tree. And God had seen them already and asked them: 'What is better for you, being with me or being with a tree?' And they were afraid because they had sinned. And they started looking for a saviour. [Repeats this]

Formerly this was our ancestors' worship. If we would go deeper into this matter, we would see that in the beginning, before the worship of Jesus Christ came, our ancestors were worshipping the living God in heaven. And look, how the human beings ran away from the garden and were looking for God. In the same way our ancestors were also struggling to find something to take refuge in him.

These people knew that without God they would not be completely whole; they knew this in their heart. Therefore they wanted something to mediate between them and God. When they needed something, they were to take it to God through a tree [who acted as mediator between them and God]. But God said that a tree could not understand his language and tell them [what he meant]. This, in short, is how our ancestors' search for God went. That is, they knew that his power in heaven is stronger than the power of human beings. And the human beings were afraid of God and wished to receive something from him. Therefore they looked for something to be between them and God. Therefore the human beings looked around, carved a tree in the bush and called it God. Therefore the Akan call God *Nyame Srodza*. And the Ewe call him Great *Mawu*. This shows that we had a God.

They gathered all those things [such as trees, stones, pots] and worshipped them. We all worshipped in this way. When you pour palm oil on it [i.e., on any object representing a *trɔ̃*] to pray to it today and regard it as God or as something between you and God, when you poured red palm oil on it today and yesterday and forget to pour it on it later, it catches [and punishes] you. Because you called a spirit into it.

There are two spirits. The first is God's spirit. Since you were not invoking that one, the Devil's spirit, which is in the world, would come to occupy it [i.e. the *trɔ̃* worshipped by the ancestors] and you would be worshipping it. But this god takes you along and keeps on finding faults with you. There is no pardon for the least thing you do.

... If this spirit [that of the Devil] is in a house and an ancestor stool [*tɔgbekpukpo*] is in the house, its power covers the entire house. The spirit of the ancestor stool covers everybody staying in the house. And when you wake up and are about to go to farm, even the smallest child can come to tell the ancestor stool: 'When I return I will offer you a sacrifice.' When he or she returns and does not offer the sacrifice, it will become another matter. This is how all these things we worship work.

As long as an ancestor stool, a *trɔ*'s spirit, a *ŋɔli*'s spirit has got power over you, it becomes a thing within you, right from our childhood! Thus, when a child [upon whom these powers were invoked] grows up, it grows up with a stool's spirit, a snake's spirit, a witchbird's [*adzexe*, owl] spirit. And these spirits will be leading a person. Since there was no Christianity then, we merely lived on. And when you live on for a while, you fall ill. Then your belly will swell and they [the priests] say that *Mami Water*'s spirit [mermaid – a spirit either male or female who can provide people with children and money, see Chapter 7] is responsible for this and that your body will only be healed if they come to perform certain rites.

When our ancestors were celebrating, early in the morning they led a person to the stool. They called his/her name saying that God had had mercy on them and that the stool had looked after that person and that they were entrusting that person's remaining days to the spirit and that it should receive the person and stay with him/her. Such a person has been given to the spirit! An evil spirit has entered him/her, but he or she him/herself does not know. As the person grows, his/her whole behaviour will not be proper; he or she will be confused because an evil spirit is leading him/her.

When a child has been born, we take schnapps [alcohol] and pour it on the ground to call the great grandfathers because they have made a good great thing for us: 'We call all of you of different types and put Akosua's [a girl born on Sunday] spirit, body and whole life into your hand. If anybody plans evil against her, turn your face against him/her. Here is drink, take it and drink.' When you just call the girl's name and pray for her, the dead people's spirits [*ŋɔliwo*] receive her and she becomes theirs. Thus, the spirit of an ancestor who misbehaved in the past will come and enter the child. The spirit of a grandmother who was formerly a witch will come and enter the child. [In this way], an evil spirit has already entered that small child! Because you handed it over to a *ŋɔli*, *ŋɔli* becomes the guardian of the child's life. The child will do what the spirit wants the child to do for him. This is one way in which an evil spirit enters a person. Our ancestors have been behaving in this way. This is why spirits have been worrying us since our childhood.

Another source from which we can also receive an evil spirit is this: you are going to build a house and you buy drink and pray: 'Oh, *ŋɔliwo* of all ancestors, I call you!' You call all to the place. 'I entrust the house and the land to your hand, watch over it night and day. If anyone wants to use force on the land, take it away from him.' And you call the name of the person building the house and say that he struggled to work and get money to build the house. Therefore the spirit should stay with him. And you pour libation and leave. My friend, you call the *ŋɔli* to come into the house. A person staying in that house will wake up in the night and run off.

They are going to marry and invite evils [*busuwo*]. They call [in a libation prayer] an old woman, whose marriage was a failure, to the marriage. Do you want your marriage to be successful? [Meaning: if you want your marriage to be successful, don't do such a thing.] Our ancestors were doing these things and they brought evil onto us.

Another way to receive an evil spirit is that it is put into people when they are in the [mother's] womb. Pardon me [before alluding to sexual matters, people always apologise], you are unable to bring forth and consult *Mami Water*. If *Mami Water* lets me give birth, the child becomes his/hers. The child will trouble you all the time [and you may think it is disturbed by an evil spirit]. But the evil spirit did not come from any place and enter the person, unless you yourself buy it into yourself.

[Another way to receive an evil spirit is this:] You are keeping an ancestral thing given to you. You think it is an inheritance. Yet it is an evil thing in your hand.

And later on we shall see how Jesus Christ came to deliver us. Amen.

This sermon, fairly representative of Agbelengor's stance towards non-Christian worship, is interesting for several reasons. First, it reveals that the Agbelengor pastor closely follows the missionaries' explanation of the origins of 'heathendom' (see Chapter 3). Having been banned from the garden of Eden, the ancestors failed to find the true God and began to worship trees, thereby unknowingly serving the Devil. This was the condition of the Peki people until the Christian religion was (re)introduced to lead them back to God. By representing the past in this way, Amedzro sympathises with pre-Christian ancestors who were on the wrong track without being aware of it. Indeed, before the Fall, they too had been close to God. However, despite this sympathy there is no reason for him to be positive about ancestors' worship. By stating that they unknowingly invoked the Devil's spirit when they were worshipping the *trɔwo*, he makes clear that he considers this worship satanic, and thus totally wrong. He thus draws a strict boundary between 'heathendom' and Christianity.

Second, the preacher represents non-Christian worship as the source of much evil befalling people. He expands on the fact that participation in traditional rites, such as outdooring babies, marriage or the consecration of a new home, is dangerous. By pouring libation, the ancestors are called upon to interfere in the lives of people. Since many of the ancestors may have been bad people in addition to the fact that they were unknowingly linked with the Devil, praying to them often brings about a connection between them and the living that is disastrous for the latter. Mere pouring of libation – a practice regarded as harmless by many mission-church Christians – can thus confer evil on a person. This happens beyond a person's consciousness: a spirit may dwell in a person for a long time before it reveals itself through dreams or serious afflictions. Like the missionaries, Amedzro thus advocates an uncompromising attitude towards non-Christian worship. Far from representing it as a complex of more or less harmless customs making up 'Ewe culture', he takes this worship seriously and considers it to be effective: the old powers are still at work even if one is not aware of this. Therefore, the congregation is asked not to engage in any traditional custom involving the pouring of libation.[4]

This emphasis on the bad nature and danger of tradition and its continued effects on people's unconscious is a characteristic feature of Pentecostal churches. In contrast to mission churches such as the EPC, they claim that being a Christian does not mean merely crossing the boundary between 'heathendom' and Christianity once and for all, dwelling happily on 'the other side' and considering satanic powers to be 'unimportant things'. They maintain that, against the background of experience that Satan is indeed active in the world, there is a need to talk about and decisively fight against the realm of darkness.

The third point concerns the range of evil spirits mentioned. In this sermon, Amedzro refers to the ancestor's stool, dead people's spirits, the old gods, witchcraft and *Mami Water*. The fact that dwarfs and *dzo* are absent does not mean that these powers do not play a role in Agbelengor's discourse; they, too, are referred to in other contexts. But whereas in the EPC particular agents of Satan are hardly ever mentioned, in Agbelengor reference is made to particular spiritual entities. Apart from sermons and prayers, this occurs in songs:

1. Jesus lives, he will do it for you. Hallelujah.
   Hallelujah, Jesus reigns.
   *Bokɔnɔwo* [diviners] fail in their attempts
   *ŋɔli vɔwo* fail in their attempts
   *Gbɔgbɔ vɔwo* fail in their attempts
   Indian spirits fail in their attempts
   [other insertions possible]
   Jesus lives, he will do it for us. Hallelujah.

The semantic domain of *Abosam*, in which the missionaries and early Ewe Christians 'stored' different powers, is thus opened up and supplemented with new powers such as *Mami Water* or 'Indian spirits', powers mainly invoked by young people who hope to achieve powerful magic through them (see Chapter 7). In other words, Agbelengor provides an elaborate discourse on particular agents of evil.

To turn to the 'prayers for the afflicted', as already noted Agbelengor considers the fasting period to be the most appropriate time in which to fight evils because members are then in a more spiritual state – this is the time for the decisive strike in the spiritual war taking place in a person's spirit between God and the Devil, over the control of his or her life. After confession of sins, and prayers and songs expressing confidence in the work of the Holy Spirit, prayers for those in trouble begin. The pastor usually mentions particular afflictions, calls forward those in trouble, lays his right hand on them and asks the Holy Spirit to enter them and take away their problems. These sessions are devoted to improvement of members' health and wealth. At the same time, they provide the listening anthropologist with a long and sad catalogue of sorrows.

The aim of such sessions can be inferred from the following quotation from an exposé on the power of Jesus. It was given by Amedzro on the occasion of a fasting service on 29 February 1992, after having prayed and laid on hands:

> Therefore, if we receive Jesus, no *ŋɔli gbɔgbɔ* will have power over us. As soon as somebody who plans evil against you will see your face, he will start running away. Because the one [i.e., the power] within us is stronger than the one in the world. If *ti* [a destructive *dzo* in the form of black powder] is sprinkled on the way, you will walk across it in the name of Jesus [without being harmed]. God gives power to all Christians over all spirits. If you put Jesus first, you will be above any spirit. Regarding the spirits that trouble us, today I want to say: we have been cut [*tso ka*] from every spirit. If you profess that Jesus is the son of the living God, you shall have the Holy Spirit and you, too, will stand up and tell an evil spirit to leave a person, and it will leave. You will recognise the Devil's ways at once, you will just realise it. [Then follows a brief account on how the Holy Spirit worked on St Paul]. There is a power in you. Because God's strong hand is on us, nothing can harm us. (original in Ewe)

This text confirms the gist of the Agbelengor sermon discussed above and supplements it in important respects. It shows how the three divine powers, God, Jesus and the Holy Spirit, work against their satanic counterpart. God is referred to as the almighty father and Jesus is represented as the one who has power over evil spirits. In an earlier part of the exposé, Amedzro stated that Jesus managed to overcome Satan and made him bow down. Jesus is considered the exemplary exorcist and is almost always referred to in this way. In Agbelengor, as in similar churches, Christology thus boils down to an image of Jesus driving away demons. The Holy Spirit is considered to have come in Jesus's place at Pentecost, after Jesus had gone to heaven; therefore these churches call themselves Pentecostal, whether or not they are official members of the Christian Council of Ghana Pentecostal Churches. Pentecost is the source of the power with which people must be filled in order to perform once again the healing and deliverance brought about by Jesus 2,000 years ago.

Moreover, the text explains how the Holy Spirit works. Once it is inside people – and this is supposed to have happened in the previous prayer session – they are protected against all evil coming from outside. Amedzro's expression that people have been *cut* from the spirit is significant because it throws light on how people's bonds with evil spirits is conceptualised. The impact of this image can only be fully understood if one considers that possession by evil spirits is imagined as a state of being tied (*nɔ bablame*, 'stay in a rope') to them or the Devil himself. In another context, an Agbelengor pastor explained what is meant by 'bondage' (an extensively used English term) to Satan:

> Excuse me, the way a rope is used to bind a person physically [*le ɲutilãme*] is not what is meant, but rather everyone who is under the Devil's yoke, who cannot use his or her will and thus continues to do the Devil's will. That is what the Bible is saying: Jesus has been anointed to deliver [*ɖe*] you from that prison. (original in Ewe)

It is the purpose of the prayer session to cut this bond and free the person. Another expression used in this context also emphasises this separation: *tɔ kpɔ fo xla ame* ('to make a fence around somebody'). Once a person has been freed from the grip of an evil spirit, the latter has in turn to be tied up. To express this, the preacher would say: *miebla gbɔgbɔ sia* ('we tie this spirit') or *miebla Abosam* ('we tie Satan' – see song 7 below). Prayers for the improvement of a person's condition are thus understood as the means for isolating them from powers they are consciously or unconsciously involved with, and filling them with the Holy Spirit. In this way satanic powers are deprived of their influence and can no longer harm people. People then gain power over them and are eventually able to drive away evil spirits themselves. The link with God's Holy Spirit is not expressed by the terms *bla* ([to] tie) or *ka* (string), but rather as *ɖe adzɔgbe na Mawu*, 'to make a covenant with God'. The use of this expression shows that although the image of the link is maintained in the definition of an individual's relationship with God, it is imagined as different from connection with the Devil.

During the prayer session, the congregation continues singing songs. Some of these examples can be classified as songs of praise emphasising the almightiness of the Christian God and the power of Jesus, who acts in the name of the Holy Spirit:

2. Begin with Jesus
and end with him
Place all your hopes
on Jehovah
Place all your hope
into the hand of Jehovah.

3. A spiritual power exists
That is Jesus' power
Hallelujah
A power exists
That is Jesus' power.

4. He speaks to winds
Who, at all, is this?
He speaks to winds
Who, at all, is this?
He speaks to winds
They obey him.

5. He is a miracle performer
He delivered Daniel from the lion's mouth
He delivered Jonah from the whale's belly
He is a miracle performer.

6. He is greater than all of them
Jesus is greater than all of them
Whom at all shall I compare Jesus with?
He is greater than all of them

Apart from these and similar songs, there are aggressive war songs focusing on the spiritual fight between the Holy Spirit and Satan:

7. Tie, tie the Devil with a rope
yes, tie the Devil with a rope.

8. God will make the matter come to an end
as it will be good for you
Don't be frightened
if only you are with Jesus.

9. The great Babylon has been pushed down
It has been pushed down, broken and scattered.

10. Even when the Devil becomes violent
Children of God, don't be afraid
Jesus is in our (war-)camps.

11. Christian do not rest
    Your war captain says
    you are in the midst of enemies
    Be watchful.

12. Prayer is a weapon
    That alone we shall carry
    to overcome the enemies.

These short songs are learned by heart and sung with much enthusiasm, accompanied by drums and clapping hands. People stand up and repeat the text over and over again until the liturgist or pastor begins a new one. A song of praise is usually followed by a war song and vice versa. War songs especially are performed triumphantly. By singing these songs, people transpose themselves into the realm of the spiritual. The war metaphor provides the master trope for their conceptualisation of what happens during healing. By using it, they move themselves away from the visible into the invisible realm, which is thought to have a decisive influence on people's actual lives. Real problem solving has to be achieved in the spiritual realm (*le gbɔgbɔme*), by defeating Satan and his agents, and this is expected to have consequences in the physical realm (*le ŋutilãme*). Thus, like Pietist missionaries, Agbelengor members use metaphors in order to come into contact with the transcendental. Moreover, by singing, people try to reassure themselves that they are beyond the powers of darkness and have full confidence in *Mawu*'s omnipotence. Through singing they protect themselves against the evil spirits expected to leave the afflicted during prayer. Every time I witnessed a prayer session like this I was encouraged to sing, and not merely to look round or talk to people.

The prominence of healing prayers suggests that health is a problem to many members. Indeed, many people, especially women and children, suffer from physical weakness, headaches, back aches, etc. Many women also face problems related to pregnancy and childbirth. In contrast to its early beginnings, Agbelengor currently distinguishes between natural sicknesses that can be cured with medicine, and spiritually caused sicknesses which can only be healed by the Holy Spirit. This difference, however, has no actual influence on the prayers as such, but rather provides a reason for when prayers may fail. In any case, the cause of a sickness can only be known in retrospect, when a person is healed. If prayers do not help, sickness may be attributed to natural causes. On the other hand, if medical treatment fails to improve health, sickness may be considered to have been caused by spirits. Therefore, all those feeling ill usually come forward to be prayed for anyway.

During a fasting service on 1 March 1992, Amedzro recounted a healing dream he had once had when he was sick. He dreamt that he was treated in hospital and the next morning he woke up healthy. He concluded that God had operated on him spiritually using 'heavenly spare-parts'. Amedzro then asked sick people to come forward to pray for these spare-parts. Almost all women and children present came forward, as well as many men (altogether around seventy people) and he laid his hands on them. What happens in dreams is considered real; a dream can give a believer insight into the spiritual realm and the power of the Holy Spirit or the machinations of evil spirits. Dreams are a fully accepted means of receiving revelations concerning the invisible.[5]

Another point of concern during the fasting prayers is members' financial situation. Clearly, many people have money problems. During the same prayer session on 1 March 1992, Amedzro prayed for government workers to receive higher salaries, for farmers to receive rain and not be troubled by bushfires, for traders to receive capital and for all those in debt to be able to repay it. He called forward the last two categories (twenty-five women and eleven women and men respectively) to lay his hands upon them, but before doing so, he urged them to send a spiritual cheque to heaven: they should close their eyes, fill in a certain amount and let it go up to have it signed by God. According to Amedzro, sooner or later God would cash this cheque with real money. Yet the church's stance towards wealth is not solely positive. People are warned not to make money through evil sources, such as *dzo* employed to enhance one's trade, or *adzegã* and *Nzima bayi*, modern forms of witchcraft in which riches are achieved at the expense of one's own fertility or the life of a close relative (see Meyer 1995a).

These prayers are usually followed by testimony from members recounting how, after the last fasting session, their condition improved. Such testimony often deals with wonderful healings or miraculous financial gifts, but those who testify may also merely rejoice in the fact that, despite all setbacks, their situation has not deteriorated further. These statements confirm the efficacy of previous prayers and enhance people's belief that Christianity has practical results for their lives.

The laying on of hands in prayers for the improvement of health and wealth is usually a calm affair. It is believed that the pastor and his assistants are not only containers of the Holy Spirit, but can also function as his brokers. At the moment when the pastor and his assistants place their hands on the heads of those standing before them, the Holy Spirit residing in the former enters the latter. In this way, people are 'loaded' with heavenly power. However, the laying on of hands may also result in uncontrolled reactions. Once this happens, it is taken as a sign of severe spirit possession, because it is also believed that once a possessed person is connected to the Holy Spirit, the power controlling him or her feels offended and aggressively tries to keep hold of its host. In such a case, exorcism is necessary and often those affected will be sent to the healing station at Tokokoe.

I visited this healing station twice for several days in February and April

1992.[6] There I witnessed 'deliverance prayers' that diverged considerably from those conducted in the congregation at home. Tokokoe is a place where many possessed people are assembled from different places in the Volta Region and Togo and there are many strong reactions during the prayers. Each Thursday morning from 6 a.m. until about 2 p.m. there is an open-air fasting service devoted to healing and deliverance which is attended by approximately 150 (mainly female) patients staying at the healing station for long-term treatment, as well as by people living nearby. Residents are often accompanied by relatives taking care of them. Since all these people are unable to earn cash, but rather spend whenever they have it, long-term deliverance is often a costly matter. If a person's mental or physical condition is very bad, it is considered necessary to isolate her or him from the relatives and spiritual powers at home. Patients are not treated every day, but usually just attend the daily devotions and occasionally talk about their sickness with the pastors present at the station. They may also do some agricultural work to grow food to eat. The Thursday deliverance service is the main occasion they attend.

In the service itself, prayers and songs devoted to thanksgiving, to the forgiveness of sin and to praises and worship are followed by the sermon and the offertory. Then comes the time for deliverance. This session takes place in an empty field next to the sheds in which the first phase of the service is organised. Those in need of healing (about two-thirds of the people attending the service) group themselves in three long columns. Three to six pastors stand facing the patients. While the congregation sings songs such as those quoted above, one after another each patient approaches one of the pastors who enquires about her or his problem. He then places his right hand on the patient's head. Some people begin to tremble, but others remain calm, a calmness that is taken as a sign that no evil spirit dwells in the person. Indeed many attend deliverance sessions in order to make sure they are not possessed by an evil force. The laying on of hands therefore functions as a sort of Christianised oracle.

Many of those present, however, begin to move once they have been touched by the pastor, lose consciousness and thus self-control, and his or her body becomes a marionette as if operated by the possessor. These patients fall down on the plastic mats in front of the pastors or throw themselves into the dust. Some even run off into the bush, others start groaning and crying, and some remain silent. Sometimes people are not aware that an evil force has got hold of them, but once told that they lost their self-control, they are shocked and decide to seek further help in order to get rid of the force that has been controlling their lives without them having been aware of it. However, many realise they are going to lose control and that their body will be moved by forces possessing them, and prepare themselves by dressing in old clothes. Many women wear long trousers under their skirts.

Once the patient loses consciousness, the pastor regards her or him as a vessel of Satan, approaches the person in an unfriendly manner, and in a harsh voice commands the spirit to come out. Again and again, the deliverer shouts: *ɖo go, ɖo go! Le Yesu Kristo fe ŋkɔme!* (Come out, come out! In the name of Jesus!) *ŋkɔ wo ɖe?* (What's your name?) The treatment is understood in terms of a war between God's Holy Spirit and the Devil. If a deliverer is attacked violently or even beaten by the person possessed, or rather, by the evil spirit incorporated in the person, he calls for assistance from his colleagues. Deliverance is considered a spiritually and bodily difficult task and only those firm in faith and health are supposed to perform it. In Agbelengor, I saw no women involved in performing deliverance prayers. When I asked why this was so, I was told that women are usually 'too weak in body and spirit' to perform such a difficult task; they are rather prone to possession by evil spirits. Thus, in Agbelengor deliverance is gendered: the victims of evil spirits are (mainly) women, the exorcists are all men.

It may take a long time before the spirit possessing a person and controlling his or her body during the session actually confesses its name. It may refuse to come out, and moves its host until the person is completely exhausted. It may not leave a person until after several exorcisms and fasting periods. In the end, the spirit is sent back to where it came from or into the sea. Sometimes, a person is possessed by several spirits who have to be exorcised one after the other. Though a spirit may refuse to give its name, its identity can be determined through other means, such as visions and dreams. While not involved in the actual work of exorcism, prophetesses present closely follow the course of the deliverance. Accustomed as they are to looking into the invisible realm of *le gbɔgbɔme*, they often happen to 'see' which spirit is in a person. But this is not the only way to find out a spirit's identity. Occasionally spirits may also reveal themselves to a deliverer or the afflicted person through a dream. In any case, once they have had a vision, the prophetesses and deliverers inform the head of the healing station, an elderly Reverend by the name of E. K. Wuaku (one of the founders of Agbelengor), who notes the information in a file kept for each patient attending the station.

Though therapy is not confined to the deliverance session, by enticing the agents possessing a person to reveal themselves, clues are provided to the case history of the sickness. What, then, do the prophetesses and deliverers see? How do they discover a spirit's identity? Who are the spirits possessing the people that attend the deliverance sessions? To begin with the last question, the spirits possessing patients at Tokokoe may be *gbetsi vɔ, ŋɔli, trɔ̃, ametsiava, adziakpe, adze*, various types of *dzo, Mami Water* or, occasionally, a snake (*ɖa*) spirit. Thus, the deliverance session brings to life the old non-Christian spiritual entities, which obviously continue to play an important role even in the lives of Christians. People are possessed by and want to get rid of either old objects of collective worship such as 'black' and 'white' *trɔwo, ametsiavawo, adziakpewo* and snake spirits (worshipped in the south); or potentially or purely destructive powers such as *gbetsi, dzo* and *adze*; or they wish to be liberated from new seductive powers, such as *Mami Water*. In the deliverance session we are thus confronted with a perform-ance of (neo-)traditional practices in a Christian context.

Possession by spiritual entities follows particular patterns ascribed to particular spiritual agents. By taking hold of a person's body, a spirit partly reveals his identity by the way he allows his host to move or by his or her behaviour: a 'black' *trɔ* spirit steps forward majestically; a 'white' *trɔ* spirit, such as the god of thunder, behaves violently and throws the person on the ground; an *ametsiava* spirit, which represents the spirit of a person who has died a violent death, continuously re-enacts the terrible moment of dying; *adziakpe* makes its host bow down, becoming small and dwarf-like and bending his or her feet outwards; while snake spirits make the person writhe on the ground. These entities are the easiest to discern. Others can be easily recognised on the basis of observation: *gbetsi* does not have a particular movement pattern, but makes its host sit down silently and weep; *adze* makes people stand on their head or continuously turn around; *Mami Water* spirits make their hosts smile and call for cigarettes, soft drinks and sweets, but may also make them move like a fish or a snake. How *dzo* spirits take possession of their hosts depends on their nature; these are therefore more difficult to discern by mere observation. For instance, the much feared *dzo Tukpui* ('short gun'), which is thought to project spiritually glass, nails and similar hard objects into a person's body, is only revealed by the person vomiting these things. Often, the vomiting is said to occur spiritually and can therefore only be seen by the deliverers and prophetesses.

But a spirit is not identified on the basis of direct observation alone. Its identification requires that prophetesses (or exorcists) 'see' its characteristic image in a vision or dream: a 'black' *trɔ* spirit wears a black gown and carries a knife in his hand; a 'white' *trɔ* spirit is dressed in white (often northern attire) and carries some typical paraphernalia such as a fly-whisk; an *ametsiava* spirit or a *ŋɔli* takes the shape of the deceased person it represents; *adziakpewo* come as three-foot high creatures with their feet turned backwards and covered with bushy brown hair; *gbetsi*, too, shows up as a small creature with bushy hair wearing many amulets; *adze* appears as a cow, cat or dog, and someone possessed by *adze* may be seen flying or feasting with others and eating meat; *Mami Water* is represented as a beautiful (often white) man or woman whose upper half is human and whose lower half a fishtail. Only *dzo*, of which there are many types, does not have a clear iconography.

These movement patterns and iconographies revealed through dreams are congruent with these spiritual beings' manifestations in the framework of Ewe religion. During traditional possession dances, the priestesses of trɔwo, ametsiavawo, adziakpewo and Mami Water move in exactly the same way as the women possessed by these spirits in the deliverance sessions. And, through interviews, priestesses revealed that they dreamed about the beings possessing them in exactly the same way as described above. Thus, deliverance sessions allow people to behave in the very same way as they would during traditional worshipping ceremonies.

Once a spirit has revealed itself through movement and dreams, a patient is informed about the possessor. In this way, patients and pastors gradually work out an anamnesis and are able to diagnose the cause of the sickness. In this process symptoms come to be regarded as effects from a hitherto unknown origin and healing is thus achieved by constructing a case in terms of 'linear determinism' (see Zizek 1994: 2). Therapy is not limited to the deliverance session as such, but also involves private discussion and prayers. Gradually, people become aware of the powers dwelling within them and which expose themselves so violently during the deliverance sessions. By becoming conscious of these powers and designing a case history, patients eventually (re)gain control over their lives. Usually, this ensures that they separate themselves conceptually from their family and become conscious of themselves as individuals.

## EPC 'of Ghana'

The stance of the EPC 'of Ghana' towards Ewe religion is aptly condensed in Brempong's statement: 'When the knowledge about Jesus increases, then the knowledge about demons also increases.' Thus, the more people grow in faith, the more they are able to know, and subsequently face, the satanic. This stance lies at the basis of the church's healing and deliverance meetings during which the fight against evil spirits reigns supreme.

Meetings of the Bible Study and Prayer Fellowship are held on Tuesday evenings, and a fasting and healing service on Thursday mornings.[7] There are also occasional 'Crusades' in various Peki villages. These open-air services, which also involve prayer sessions, serve to attract more people to the new EPC. I attended several of the Tuesday and Thursday prayer meetings, a 'Crusade' in Wudome and a national 'Crusade' organised in Accra. The meetings of the BSPF, which take place between 7 p.m. and 10 p.m., are organised by Emmanuel Brempong. He institutionalised a so-called 'Deliverance Team' consisting of young men and women with a hardcore of members forming part of the 'Prayer Force' which lays on hands during the healing and deliverance prayers. Here, deliverance can also be undertaken by women, although in practice most exorcists are men. The opportunity to organise deliverance rituals and thus assume power irrespective of age and gender makes the new EPC attractive to younger people.

The Thursday morning fasting services, which regularly contain healing and deliverance prayers, are headed by two elderly men, the Reverend Edmund A. Atiase and Mr Victor Akudeka. Akudeka specialises in the exorcism of evil spirits, and people also consult him privately. In his deliverance sessions he usually calls upon those young men and women whom he considers spiritually strong, and asks them to assist him. There seemed to be a certain competition between the leaders of the Tuesday and Thursday meetings, but little actual difference between the meetings, which consisted of prayers devoted to the usual topics; songs and dance; testimony; sermons and short teachings; and above all, prayers for healing, deliverance and success with business. In addition, people dance energetically and occasionally speak in tongues. Since it is only the Thursday service which requires general fasting, it is regarded as superior to the Tuesday evening prayers. The young organisers of the latter meetings compensate for this with long preparatory prayers and some do not eat before involving themselves with deliverance.

The EPC 'of Ghana' dwells on the boundary between 'heathendom' and Christianity in the same way as Agbelengor. The following fragment of a sermon delivered by Brempong on the war between God and the Devil was recorded on the occasion of a 'Crusade' to Wudome on 15 January 1992:

> The kingdom of heaven is God's power which stands against the kingdom of the Devil. The kingdom of heaven is God's power that comes from heaven and that stands against the Devil's kingdom. And the kingdom of heaven which came was Jesus Christ who came from heaven. [Expands about the kingdom of heaven.]
>
> What is striking is that many times when a person falls ill and is said to have been shot with *Tukpui*, they will go to the diviners to remove the *Tukpui* for him/her. The Devil is killing the Devil. Have we ever heard this!?! But this is what happens among us every day.
>
> When the Devil had come to steal what God had given to man [*amegbetɔ*, 'living person'] and said that God had put all things on earth into his hand, Jesus Christ came from heaven. Yet the Devil was telling a lie. God did not put anything into the Devil's hand. God put all things into the hands of man.
>
> *He came down to invade the kingdom of Satan. It is a spiritual war, not a physical war. Praise the Lord!* It was a spiritual war [*gbɔgbɔme va*] Jesus came to set up. The world in which we are is a battlefield. The first war began in heaven and it is spoiling things on this earth. And if you do not have a share in the war, then there is nothing left for you. And the kingdom of heaven which descended and came and which is God's reign stays in human beings. It does not stay in large houses. The kingdom of heaven stays in human beings' hearts. God's reign stays in human beings. God's power stays in human beings. God's peace lives

in people. God's love stays in people. Hallelujah! Thus, if God's power and reign is in human beings and those people meet at one place, then God's power is in the town. (original in Ewe)

The recurring emphasis on the dualism of God and the Devil is a characteristic feature of sermons and prayers in the new EPC. Like Amedzro's sermon, this text explains how the Devil came to rule on earth, as a result of a palace revolt – 'the first war began in heaven' – which culminated in Satan's ejection from heaven (see Chapter 2). This story is well known among Christians since the days of the missionaries and therefore a small reference in Brempong's sermon is sufficient to evoke it. Though he does not expand further on this topic, to his listeners it is clear that the gods worshipped traditionally are the fallen angels dragged down by Satan in his fall. Here, too, non-Christian worship is diabolised.

Like Amedzro, Brempong depicts this worship as the source of evil. For him, Satan is the power behind local priests, such as the explicitly mentioned diviners. He makes it very clear to his listeners that it is impossible to counteract evil by recourse to traditional priests, because they all belong to the satanic complex and it is impossible to drive out Satan with Beelzebub. The correct way to get rid of problems is to rely on Jesus, who came down to earth to fight Satan. Not only Ewe spiritual beings but also non-Christian remedies against evil are disqualified as bad.

Differentiation of the satanic domain into various spirits is also adopted by the new EPC. We have already seen that special reference was made to the greatly feared dzo, Tukpui. Earlier on in the service, Brempong had prayed for all witches to leave town and, in other contexts, more spirits are mentioned by name. In this respect, the new EPC resembles Agbelengor and differs completely from the old EPC's policy.

The old EPC's taboo on referring to adze in public was reason enough for one pastor from Peki to leave this church where he had served for many decades. After a morning devotion at Klefe (a place near Ho), he related to his congregation that during the night he had seen a witch in front of his house who was trying to harm him. By disclosing this experience to the congregation he went further than merely violating the old EPC's taboo on mentioning particular agents of the Devil in public. He exposed the witch by calling a certain woman's name, for which he was reprimanded by the EPC authorities. However, to the new EPC, to which he turned as a BSPF member once the split came, a public discourse on witchcraft was not a problem, but rather a necessity. Thus, in contrast to the old EPC, but in line with Agbelengor, the new EPC openly discusses evil forces in full detail.

This is worked out in the new EPC's 'prayer practice'. The continuation of Brempong's sermon quoted above shows how healing is understood in this church:

Jesus worked with his apostles with the power that descended. And he gave that power to them that they should also go and that everybody in the Devil's kingdom should be delivered from him [the Devil]. [Reads Matthew 10: 1, 8, about Jesus giving the apostles the authority to cast out evil spirits.] And Jesus Christ called his disciples one by one – twelve people – to come to him and he gave them power to drive out all unclean spirits. He put the kingdom of heaven into them. He put God's reign into the apostles' mouth and told them to go and enter the Devil's kingdom and take out of his hand whoever they saw to be his [the Devil's] captive. They should remove all types of sicknesses and bodily weaknesses.

The other day, when we were worshipping in Avetile, an old lady came. She was not in our church and we told her to go to her church so that they could pray for her. One arm was paralysed. She had a stroke in her right arm. And we sent her to a presbyter and that presbyter told her that when one of their members is sick they do not pray for him/her. Have we ever heard this? But Jesus Christ said that he has entrusted all power that is in heaven and on earth into our hand. We should remove sicknesses. We should remove all types of bodily weaknesses. Jesus Christ said we should heal sicknesses, bring dead people back to life, cleanse the skin of those who have fallen, drive out evil spirits. Freely you receive. Freely you give …

Expanding upon the statement that the coming to earth of Jesus triggered the war against Satan, Brempong makes clear that Christians received the power to face Satan and drive away evil spirits from Jesus. This spiritual warfare is the main thing Christians should be involved in. Thus, here too, salvation is conceptualised as the exorcism of evil spirits. This understanding is confirmed by the fact that the terms xɔxɔ (from xɔ, to receive, to get, to save) and ɖeɖe (from ɖe, to take away) are both used to translate 'salvation'. Since ɖeɖe is also used to translate 'deliverance (from evil spirits)', it is no great surprise that salvation is conceptualised as the act of being taken away from the realm of Satan.

In the EPC 'of Ghana', even more time is devoted to healing and deliverance prayers than in Agbelengor. It seems the new EPC needs to emphasise how different it is from the mother church and to demonstrate the superiority of its own power. This is clearly expressed in the passage of the sermon where Brempong recounts the case of the old lady suffering from a stroke. Though he does not mention the name of the woman's church, it is clear he is referring to the old EPC. Brempong uses this case to clarify once again that 'over there' Christians would not take Jesus's spiritual gift seriously and use it to drive away evil; therefore, the old EPC is powerless vis-à-vis Satan's guile. Clearly, for Brempong, as for other members of the new

EPC, a truly Christian church must face and exorcise satanic spirits and thereby cut people's bonds with the Devil.

During the EPC 'of Ghana' sessions of 'prayers for the afflicted', the congregation continues to sing songs. Many of these praise and war songs are the same as those sung in Agbelengor. And as in Agbelengor, through song, participants transpose themselves into the spiritual realm which is considered the appropriate place to solve real-life problems. Here, too, the war metaphor serves as a master trope.[8]

While the congregation is singing, the leader calls forward those in need of personal prayers. The BSPF meetings on Tuesday evenings are usually attended by about thirty people. Four male members of the 'Deliverance Team' and the 'Prayer Force' receive the afflicted. Their colleagues sink into prayer behind them. Although the Deliverance Team has female members, deliverance proper is done by men as in Agbelengor. Usually those with problems related to health and wealth are called forward first. These people, three-quarters of them women, inform the Prayer Force member about their problems and he then places his hand on each afflicted person's head. Most problems are related to troubles in business, lack of money, familial troubles, bodily pains, infertility, or fear of miscarriage. After this prayer session, all those with spiritual troubles are asked to come forward. Troubles of this kind include the experience of frightening dreams, sicknesses whose cause could not yet be identified and the fear of familial spirits. While most who come for prayers remain calm and are thus considered free of evil spirits, there is usually one serious case in each session. Such a person would start trembling or fall over; for example, a middle-aged woman from Blengo became very aggressive and crossed her hands behind her head. The Prayer Force tried to prevent her from doing this, because it would hinder the evil spirits possessing her from coming out. Later, it was revealed that this woman was the sister of the newly installed Amimli priestess (see Chapter 7) and that the river spirit had also tried to bring her under his control. When such a serious case occurred, Brempong would close the meeting and stay behind with his Deliverance Team to perform the exorcism. The team acts in the same way as the deliverers in Tokokoe and other Pentecostal churches. Brempong and his colleagues also conduct private prayers at home.

Not all Thursday morning services are devoted to healing and deliverance, but if they are this is often organised by Victor Akudeka, a retired accountant aged about sixty who specialises in exorcism. Akudeka considers exorcism his special gift and uses it whenever he has the opportunity. This spiritual gift of being able to drive away agents of the Devil means he occupies a high position in the new EPC.[9] Though some members found him all too eager to use his talent, the new EPC gave him the chance to organise deliverances both at his home in Tsame and in the framework of the fasting on Thursday. Akudeka believed there were many witches both outside and within the new church. In considering himself able to expose and exorcise them (and thus cleanse the church), he had much in common with the 'witch doctors' operating in the framework of regional cults. He knew that church members were afraid of his 'spirit of discernment' and that some avoided attending his deliverance services for fear of being exposed.

During one deliverance service organised by him on 12 March 1992, he explained that Christians had been given the authority to cast out demons. If they could not succeed in doing so then this was due either to fear and doubt, sin, or God's unwillingness to cure a person. Since Peki Christians had been enmeshed in sin for generations, it was difficult to get rid of the curse (fifode) on their families.[10] And since God was not only a loving but also a punishing God, it was possible that he killed severe sinners – there was no general forgiveness for everybody. By arguing in this way, Akudeka made sure that failure to cure people was not attributed to his lack of power but to the afflicted themselves. Nevertheless, the meeting as such was almost wholly devoted to healing and deliverance. Having assembled a prayer team consisting of three women and one young man, he called forward all those who had had strange dreams, such as experiences of flying, feasting and eating meat. By doing so, he clearly wanted to sort out potential witches, who reveal themselves through such dream experiences. Nobody came forward. He therefore called all those who felt sick. Eighteen people, mainly women and children, stepped forward. To show how Akudeka organises healing and deliverance prayers, an account of his methods and some of the cases he treated follows.

First, Akudeka prays by the laying on of hands. Some people are merely attacked by demons and thus considered passive victims to be delivered more or less easily. Others, more serious cases, are really possessed and true agents of the Devil. Once he suspects demonic possession, he puts a finger of his left hand into the patient's right ear, thereby 'locking up' the demons so that they are unable to communicate with their allies outside. His finger also functions as a 'spirit detector' (his expression) which, according to his explanation, works in a similar way to the metal detectors one finds at airports. He considers himself to be an instrument in God's hands, and able to detect those evil forces which control a person. Once he has an idea about the possessor he commands it to come out. If he suspects that the spirit works through material objects such as jewellery, he asks the person to take them off. When he commands a spirit to come out, he often uses short sentences spoken 'in tongue' (his expression), such as *Yehova Usa perusa tabu kaba*. He explained: 'This tongue of mine, nobody understands it, except God. It means: "God, I am begging you to send marcher angels, fight angels, which can defeat satanic forces to destroy Satan. Immediately to kill Satan, immediately!"' He said that this 'tongue' was derived from 2 Samuel

6: 6, where a certain Usa touched Noah's ark and was immediately punished by God with death. Another 'tongue' is *Jesus Messiah Satana tabu kaba*. Akudeka explained: 'That one, the meaning is: "Satan, whatever I am doing, the person should bow down to Jesus Christ."' These 'tongues' should not be confused with the glossolalia usually referred to by the expression 'speaking in tongues'. Akudeka's tongues consist of the names of the main protagonists of the Christian religion, and biblical personalities; Ewe terms such as *tabu*, which means 'to bow down', and *kaba*, which means 'quickly'; and loanwords probably taken from English, such as *perusa* (probably from 'perish'). These formulae, which Akudeka allegedly received from God, contain the power of the whole Bible. At the same time, the Devil, unable to understand and thus appropriate them, is forced by the Holy Spirit to leave his host. Besides the gift of these 'tongues', Akudeka claims to be able to see demons leaving a person by looking at the spot at the base of the neck and between the collar bones. The spirits' identity is revealed to him by observation of possessed people's movement patterns and through visions and dreams, and he refers to the same images as those described above in the context of Agbelengor's deliverance practices.

For cases treated during the Thursday fasting service, Akudeka publicly announced what he had discerned. Later I received additional information from him and the patients themselves. One case he treated was that of a six-year-old girl suffering from asthma. He shouted 'Asthma out! Asthma out!' When the child put her hands on her head, he took off her beads, held her upside down and threw the beads away. The mother told me later that the girl had received the beads from relatives when she was born. Akudeka considered these beads responsible for the child's sickness and by throwing them away, he symbolically separated the little girl from her family. Other children were also treated by cutting their family ties. In one case he even told a little boy that there was no connection between him and his mother and father.

Akudeka also prayed for a young woman who felt sick and suffered from pain in her heart. He attributed this disease to her family and announced that she had a hole in her heart which had been made by *Mami Water*. And the fact that she bent down and pressed her knees together was a sign that she was possessed by *adziakpewo* which he also commanded to come out. Finally he prayed for her old heart to burn and for the Holy Spirit to give her a new one. Later, Akudeka explained to me that this woman had been consulting him for a long time because during her pregnancy she had experienced frightening dreams and occasionally wriggled like a snake. He attributed her sickness to a curse on her family and to the fact that her mother was a witch. He had already delivered her in the past, but a short time ago she had felt the hole in her heart open up again. Akudeka attributed the recurrence of her sickness to the fact that, despite his advice, she had continued to live in her family house. In other sickness cases I again witnessed Akudeka explicitly separate adult patients from family ties and cast out 'the unclean spirits of the family'.

Another intriguing case was that of a seventeen-year-old girl who wore a Western-style dress with a flower design, a belt with a lock in the form of a butterfly, a necklace with a coloured heart, and earrings in the shape of strawberries. She did not come forward on her own, but on Akudeka's command. He said that through her jewellery she was related with a *Mami Water* spirit, and that the necklace meant her heart was possessed by this spirit. He also enquired as to whether she had a boyfriend and, when the answer was affirmative, commanded the 'spirit of flirting' to leave. He put his finger into her ear and shouted for the spirit of *adze* to leave her as well. She smiled – according to Akudeka, a 'demonic smile' – and went back to her seat. Later, Akudeka called her up again, put his finger into her ear and said that except for the 'spirit of pride' all other spirits were gone. He handed her jewellery to an old woman, but when the girl staunchly requested their return, he eventually returned them to her. When asked about this case, he said that when he was touching her, he had experienced a fierce fight between the Holy Spirit and that of *Mami Water*. In his view, by adorning themselves, young women risk devoting themselves to this dangerous spirit which would later prevent them from finding a husband and giving birth. The fact that he returned the jewellery to the girl indicates that he did not consider her to be successfully delivered. He thought she would continue to behave as before and thus be called forward for treatment for some time to come.

Among other patients there was a nurse, whom Akudeka was treating, and for this reason he did not say much about her affliction in public. He directed her to lie down and ordered the 'unclean family spirits' to go to hell, and the Holy Spirit to enter her. Later the woman told me that she often dreamed of having sexual intercourse with a good-looking man and that, since giving birth to her little daughter, she had suffered from pains in her belly which prevented her from becoming pregnant again. Akudeka said he suspected that the man she had sex with in her dreams was a fallen angel (an *incubus*, one might say). These creatures would sleep with human beings either spiritually or in reality. In order to achieve the latter they would often take the shape of good-looking strangers and entice village women to have sex with them, thereby binding these women to the Devil.

The last case described is that of an old lady suffering general sickness. In contrast to other patients, she was immediately asked by Akudeka to name her demon. Since the old lady did not know what to say, he sent her outside to look at the sky and meditate. She seemed worried and went back to her friends on the bench. Her face expressed fear and even panic: did Akudeka see her as a witch, even though she had only come forward because she suffered bodily pains?[11] Angrily, Akudeka told her that she was to go outside rather than return to the congregation. Minutes later he called her again and commanded her evil spirits to come out. He claimed that he saw three of them leaving her, but not more. When he dismissed her he was still unsatisfied, and made crosses in the air in front and behind her. Later he said that dreams had revealed to him that this old lady was a witch and that she was responsible for the sickness of her daughter, one of his patients. However, the old lady had not yet confessed and he had not been able to drive out the witch spirit.

Akudeka performed this type of deliverance both in public, and privately in his own house. As well as the cases mentioned here he also treated possession by *gbetsi*, *dzo*, *ŋɔli* and *ametsiava*, and tended to represent particular bad attitudes, such as pride, avarice or talkativeness, as demons (he himself allegedly suffered from the latter). By delivering people from evil spirits, he assumes a position similar to that of Ewe priests who also free people from evil spirits or offer protection against them. At the same time, however, Akudeka distances himself decisively from non-Christian worship, which, not surprisingly, he considers to be dominated by the Devil. As in Tokokoe, treatment of patients is not confined to public deliverances but may stretch over a long period of various prayer sessions and reflections upon the cause of the sickness.

Thus, as in Agbelengor, in the EPC 'of Ghana' there is also room for a discourse on evil spirits and ritual practices related to them. Here, too, the boundary between 'heathendom' and Christianity is located in people's body and spirit, and this is most clearly revealed during the deliverance prayers in which people may act out their relationship with 'heathen' spirits and finally be brought back to Christianity. A remarkable feature of this procedure is that it mirrors Ewe religion by allowing people to perform their possession by old and new non-Christian gods and spirits in church. At the same time, by symbolically cutting people's family ties, the procedure subverts the bonds created and protected by the collective worship of particular *trɔwo*, as well as the bonds between parents and children: Satan is tied up through the untying of social relations between people. In doing this, a great deal of emphasis is placed upon the destructive effects of witchcraft which may cause a mother to destroy her children. All family ties are considered potentially dangerous. Whereas traditionally, the fight against evil is to a large extent focused on the restoration of bonds between people (see Chapter 4), Christian deliverance basically unties them. The aim of the deliverance sessions is to turn people into individuals who are independent of and unaffected by family relations. Unlike Ewe gods, the Spirit of God does not bind together families but rather turns their members into separate individuals.

## PENTECOSTALISM AND DEMONOLOGY

The main difference between Agbelengor and the EPC 'of Ghana' on the one hand, and the old EPC on the other, lies in the dissident churches' emphasis on worship and prayer, which are both understood as distinct sets of practices, causing the Holy Spirit to enter a person and evil spirits to leave. By recurrent use of images, both churches construct (and reconfirm) the realm of *le gbɔgbɔme* ('the spiritual') which they contrast with that of *le ŋutilame* ('the physical'). Highly metaphorical sermons, prayers, songs and testified dreams and visions visualise what is going on in the unseen. Temporarily, members are transposed into this otherwise inaccessible, invisible realm, thereby enabling them to experience personal contact with the divine. But the experience of the spiritual realm is not confined to this contact; it also entails revealing and confronting satanic forces.

Through the image of the war between God and the Devil, the spiritual realm is conceptualised as a battlefield. The outcome of this spiritual war has consequences for both a person's spirit and eventually the world as a whole. Since it is considered almost impossible to change the world – the domain of Satan – as such, all energy is devoted to the salvation of people's own spirits through protective and curative prayers and deliverance. Thus, rather than changing the macrocosm, Agbelengor and the EPC 'of Ghana' focus on the microcosmic level of the individual body and spirit. Sickness and weakness are understood to be the result of evil spirits intruding into a person's spirit and body. Consequently, deliverance is to ensure that an individual is severed from all previous ties with old and new spiritual entities, as well as from the social relations they imply. In the end, prayers create individuals whose spirits are fully possessed by the Holy Spirit and separated from the Devil. But, it must be pointed out that this individualism is not a completely new phenomenon. As noted earlier, the increasing fear of witchcraft occurred together with integration into the colonial economy, resulting in an increased need for individual protection through *dzo* and new anti-witchcraft cults. Thus, neither the early mission church nor the Pentecostal churches can be held responsible for the introduction of individualism. Rather, in providing rituals through which a person's relations with others can be severed, the Pentecostal churches are responding to an already existing need which in the framework of Ewe religion has been met by *dzɔtɔwo* and new cults (see also Thoden van Velzen 1988).[12]

However, this separation remains an ideal, not yet reached. During deliverance sessions, people (re-)enact their possession by non-Christian powers, thereby integrating these entities into Christian worship, albeit in a subordinate sense. With this in mind, we can expand upon Hagan's suggestion that the experience of divinity in Ghanaian Spiritual and Pentecostal churches echoes traditional ways of contacting the gods through trance states (Hagan 1988). Though he is right, it should be added that, above all, these trances are experienced in terms of possession by evil spirits, and to a much lesser extent as an experience of divinity. The important point to be made is that these churches offer their members the opportunity to experience the satanic, i.e. the chance to experience possession which is simultaneously denounced as 'heathen'.

In the context of the hegemonic integration of spiritual entities, particular evil agents are thematised in prayers, songs and sermons. The leaders of the old EPC subsumed all these beings under the category of *Abosam* and represented it as closed and no longer worthy of attention. By contrast, Pentecostal preachers and deliverers unpack this category. In short, the old EPC's practice of integrating gods and ghosts into the category of *Abosam* can be seen as 'centripetal' strategy, resulting in diabolisation; the strategy of the two other churches has been to redifferentiate the satanic into a range of demons and is 'centrifugal', bringing about demonisation. Consequently, rather than talking about the Devil in general terms, the latter churches provide an elaborate discourse on particular demons and ritual practices related to them. Evidently, this demonisation embellishes the grassroots understanding of Christianity discussed in Chapter 4.

Thus by constructing a strict boundary between 'heathendom' and Christianity, a boundary thought to exist within the body and spirit of all converts, Agbelengor and the EPC 'of Ghana' take Ewe religion quite seriously. They detest it because they are convinced of its power, and for this reason they reject Ewe priests as personal agents of the Devil. Yet despite their dissociation from these priests, Pentecostal preachers and deliverers resemble them. Through the conceptualisation of religion as a set of practices which are actually performed they closely follow Ewe ideas about the relationships between people and gods (see also Assimeng 1986: 158). They also conceptualise the source of evil as social and offer assistance against the same evils as do Ewe priests; that is, *adze, ŋɔli* and destructive *dzo*, as well as ailments caused by them. However, while Ewe priests attempt to remove evil by restoring distorted relationships, Pentecostal preachers and exorcists see familial links as the prime cause of evil and seek to separate their clients from them. This individualisation also comes to the fore in the Pentecostal understanding of human beings' contact with the divine. While Ewe priests operate as intermediaries between ordinary people and spirits, in the framework of Pentecostalism access to the divine is (to be) achieved by individual believers themselves.

This confirms Mullings's conclusions derived from her comparison of Ga traditional and Spiritual healers (1984: 53–160). Whereas for the former, the unit of therapy was the lineage or the extended family,[13] the latter dissociated themselves from Ga religion, concentrated on the sick individual and often advised patients to keep away from their families. This suggests that these Spiritual churches also professed individualism.

However, an important difference between these churches and the cases described in this chapter is that Pentecostal churches provide much more elaborate separation rituals than the Spiritual churches and thus profess individualism in a stronger and more overt fashion.

In representing Ewe religion as powerful and real, Agbelengor and the EPC 'of Ghana' offer believers the opportunity to be a Christian without giving up the concerns of Ewe religion which they are required to leave behind. By depicting Ewe religion as the realm of Satan and by referring to it continuously, it is still possible for people to deal actively with this fascinating complex. This situation is similar to that of the first Ewe Christians: by separating Christians spatially and symbolically from their families, missionary Pietism stimulated an individualism which gave rise to contradictions within and between people. The image of the Devil enabled converts to address their ambivalent stance towards the complex of ideas and social relations which they wished to leave behind, and yet were still involved in (see Chapter 4). In the framework of Pentecostalism, the image of the Devil serves the same purpose: people are enabled to reflect upon their existing social, economic and spiritual links with their families, while simultaneously being spiritually released from them. Furthermore – and here early mission-based Christianity is surpassed – Agbelengor and the EPC 'of Ghana' sever people's relationships with modern spirits such as *Mami Water* (representing the temptations of full indulgence in riches). During the first decades of Christianity among the Ewe, converts, to the dismay of the missionaries, did not problematise the pursuit of worldly riches. Today, this situation has changed: the image of the Devil is used to address converts' ambivalent stance towards money.

Pentecostal churches therefore mediate between Ewe religion and mission-church Christianity. On the one hand, they profess individualisation and separation in the same way as the mission church. On the other, by providing believers with an explicit and elaborate ritual praxis, they make up for the shortcomings of the mission church, which have existed ever since the introduction of Christianity to the Ewe. In this sense, they eventually have realised the Ewe understanding of religion as praxis within the framework of Christianity. Interestingly, the Pentecostal stance towards the satanic has much in common with that of missionary Pietism at home (see Chapter 2). Pietism also provided a highly dualistic doctrine and, through the use of allegory, produced an imaginary space allowing for continuous imaginations of the Devil or, from the believers' point of view, revelations about him. Furthermore, at home in Germany the work of Blumhardt stimulated the development of an elaborate Pietist praxis of exorcism. Striking parallels emerge if we compare the deliverance of Gottliebin Dittus with that of members of Agbelengor or the EPC 'of Ghana': the connection with the satanic was thought to have been brought about unconsciously (and often through the instigation of relatives); healing was achieved through a long period of exorcisms conceptualised as a confrontation of the Holy Spirit with the Devil; and deliverance was understood as a revelation of what happens in the satanic realm. In short, in both cases non-Christian religion was integrated into Christianity through the image of the Devil, and then fought in the framework of an imagined spiritual war between the divine and the satanic. The point here is not that Ewe converts repeat what missionaries did in the nineteenth century, but that churches such as Agbelengor and the EPC 'of Ghana' eventually realised a part of the Pietist heritage which the missionaries, and later the EPC leaders, had denied Ewe converts. As this heritage is much cherished by the current Pentecostal movement it is no surprise that dissatisfied mission church members feel attracted to churches in this spectrum.

If one compares Pentecostalist churches such as Agbelengor and the EPC 'of Ghana' with African independent Churches which provided central research data for students of Christianity in Africa in the 1960s and 1970s, the former appear to maintain a much more critical stance towards so-called 'tradition' than the latter. Several authors have noted Pentecostalism's harsh stance towards non-Christian religions in Africa (for example, Gifford 1994; Marshall 1993; Schoffeleers 1985: 21, 1994b: 110; Van Dijk 1992). Gifford (ibid.), who noted the importance of the image of Satan and his agents, explicitly called for further research on the demonology of these churches. However, it is possible that demonology also played a role in independent Spiritual churches and that they drew a much stricter boundary between non-Christian religion and Christianity than earlier studies of such churches might suggest. In Ghanaian independent churches demonisation of spiritual beings certainly occurred: Baëta's study of Spiritual churches and prayer groups (1962), Mullings's (1984) study of Ga Spiritualist healers, and my own study of the early beginnings of Agbelengor before its turn to Pentecostalism (see Chapter 5) reveal an aggressive refutation of non-Christian religion. Therefore, in the analysis of religious movements, whether they be independent 'syncretistic' movements of the 1960s and 1970s or Pentecostal churches of the 1980s and 1990s, it would be fruitful to examine carefully the ways in which the boundary between 'heathendom' and Christianity is defined and exactly what people are supposed and willing to dissociate themselves from once they become members. In this way, it may be possible to develop a fuller understanding of the creative ways in which colonised peoples deal with contradictions arising from their encounter with modernity.

# PEOPLE AND SPIRITS

So-called 'traditional' religion is not something of the past (although Christian rhetoric locates it there), but is still practised and, as it seems, on the increase. While *dzo* has been purchased secretly since colonial times, and chiefs and family elders have continued worshipping their stools and ancestors, public worship of indigenous deities has reappeared only recently. Significantly, the Reverend Edmund Y. Tawia complained to me that while *trɔ̃* worship in Peki had been on the decline in the first half of this century,[1] today there is a considerable revival of this practice. Indeed, during my fieldwork in 1992, the installation of a new priestess – a woman baptised into the EPC as a child – for the river *trɔ̃* Amimli was a spectacular event. During a previous visit I had hardly witnessed any traditional drumming sessions and possession dances – at that time the worship of the deities Wuve and Amimli (not to mention others) had virtually disappeared because these gods lacked priestesses through whom they could speak[2] – but in 1992 I attended many such meetings. At Blengo in particular, the newly installed Amimli priestess was especially eager to present herself in public.

Her élan also had repercussions on other priests. There was not only a revival of *trɔ̃* worship, but also of the worship of *ametsiavawo*, especially among women. Moreover, a *Mami Water* priestess – the first and only priestess of this spirit in Peki – was preparing to install her shrine in Avetile.[3] During my stay there were quite a few celebrations, such as initiations of priestesses, yam festivals and, once, the performance of *busuyiyi* (by and large these performances followed the patterns described in Chapter 3). But unlike in the past, when priests and priestesses of the native 'black' *trɔ̃wo* and those dressed in white (i.e. priests of foreign *trɔ̃wo*, *adziakpewo*, *ametsiavawo*, *Mami Water* and the *dzotɔwo*) did not attend each others' festivals, today all priests (except those worshipping chiefs' stools) have joined forces and celebrate together.[4] Apparently they now do this because, with the increase of Christianity, non-Christians became a small minority who preferred to emphasise what they had in common rather than maintain traditional divisions. Formerly, all deities had their own drumming groups, while today one and the same group under the leadership of the *dzotɔ* Anim Komla plays at all ceremonial occasions. These drummers know the rhythms and songs of all the spirits that are to be called and play them one after the other. The spirits then enter their respective priestesses. Usually, these priestesses come from the clan to which the *trɔ̃* belongs, but occasionally a woman may also be possessed by a *trɔ̃* from her husband's side. Possession – especially in the more pronounced forms referred to as '*ele trɔ̃ fom*' and '*egli*' – is still a female affair in Peki.[5] Male priests never become possessed during dances and thus never embody the spirit they serve; at best a spirit may 'catch' a man (*gbɔgbɔ lé ame*) and 'be upon' him (*gbɔgbɔ le ame dzı*), indicating that he wants the man to serve him as his priest (see Chapter 3). With the exception of some young men who were moved by a 'white' *trɔ̃* (*wole trɔ̃ fom*) or a powerful *dzo* during a song, I never saw any man possessed in this way in Peki.

In dance (*ɣeɖuɖu*), each priestess embodies her god and gives voice to his wishes. The priestesses of the 'black' *trɔ̃wo* are dressed in black gowns and carry a knife and a fly-whisk in their hand. As they slowly move around, they express the *trɔ̃wo*'s wishes, and when they sit down, the spirit calmly leaves them. The *trɔ̃wo* mainly complain about violation of their taboos and explain every misfortune occurring in Peki along these lines. The *adziakpewo*, who make their priestesses bend down and turn their feet outwards, put forward similar arguments. The *ametsiava* priestesses re-enact the violent death of the deceased person possessing them. When exhausted from dancing and wanting to get rid of the spirit, they have to wash their faces with herbs. They have few messages directed to the community as a whole. Similarly, the *Mami Water* priestess, whose body movements are gentle and who likes smoking cigarettes, does not have much to say. The dancing ceremonies I attended mainly took place at night and were witnessed by many curious spectators, among them many Christians. Even for those staying at home it was impossible to ignore these ceremonies, because the drums could be heard all over the Peki valley.

Like the Spiritual and Pentecostal churches, priests of local deities and *dzotɔwo* offer remedies against evil powers such as *adze*, evil *dzo*, a bad *gbetsi* and *ŋɔli*, as well as improvement of people's material conditions. As in the 'olden days', the *trɔ̃wo* and *adziakpewo* have to be approached on their special day of worship. The person requesting support brings a bottle of drink and informs the priest and priestesses of his or her problem. They try to find its cause – usually the priest prays to the god and then a priestess becomes possessed and states the deity's verdict – and then determine the treatment and its costs. Then the healing procedure begins, a process which may imply a ritual bath or the observation of certain taboos. Usually, members of the afflicted person's family are called upon in order to restore disrupted relations. If the person approaching the spirit is satisfied, his priest and priestesses have to be thanked and presented with gifts. By contrast, *dzo* can be received individually from the *dzotɔwo* at any time and in secret.

Members of Agbelengor and the EPC 'of Ghana' see this conspicuous presence of priests as proof that Satan's demons really exist and are active, and that the Devil is trying to win souls through this new popularity of (neo)-traditional cults. Many grassroots EPC members also fully share this view, despite their leaders' discursive and ritual neglect of demons. This view, of course, further develops existing ideas stemming from the missionary heritage. In 1989, Victor Ntem, a member of the EPC, explained to me: 'For a Christian, all the fetishes and *trɔwo* are evil spirits. But no heathen will think of fetishes as an evil spirit.' Around the same time Pearl Mensah-Kaklaku, another EPC member, stated: 'In the book they told us that when God sent that Lucifer from heaven, he became Satan. He accompanied some angels with him. They are staying with us here. They are the evil spirits. Some are under the sea.' Although talk about particular demonic forces was and is taboo in the EPC, members at the grassroots level conceptualise African deities as fallen angels, thereby echoing the missionaries' point of view. These EPC members consider the *trɔ*, *adziakpe* and *ametsiava* priests, as well as the *dzotɔwo*, to be agents of the Devil. They fear evil powers such as *adze*, *dzo* and, to a lesser extent, *ŋɔli* and *gbetsi vɔ*, among which *adze* is seen as the greatest enemy. For EPC members witchcraft is Satan's main agency: 'If you are a Devil you are a witch, and if you are a witch you are a Devil,' Agnes Binder (EPC, 1989) pointedly formulated. Except for a handful of people who do not believe in the existence of witchcraft, local EPC church members – among them pastors – are convinced that it is a real power. Quite a few members have at one time in their lives experienced misfortune which they attributed to *adze*, and dealt with it through private prayers.

Expectations of EPC church members echo those of non-Christian worshippers: they want a long life, a good spouse and many children, to be and remain healthy, and to achieve some prosperity. In addition, people are proud of being able to show, through their membership of the EPC, that they are 'civilised' – after all, it is the church with the highest local prestige. But when they experience severe troubles and insecurities, many members forget about 'civilisation' and search for the kind of help that can restore their fortunes. When asked whether they feel sufficiently protected against evil forces in their church, some staunch EPC members told me that protection is not a matter of church affiliation but rather of personal faith. As long as they pray, God will not allow evil spirits to invade them. Other members, however, are not satisfied with the protection available in the EPC and consider magic to be more effective. As noted earlier on, the Blengo EPC pastor complained that quite a few members follow the *Yesu viɖe, dzo viɖe* stance ('a little bit of Jesus, and a little bit of magic') and secretly consult *dzotɔwo* for protection.

The following, much discussed event occurred in May 1992 and is illustrative in this respect: E. K. Adjima, the sixty-year-old official representative of the polygamous men in the EPC session, intended to protect his farm up in the mountains from theft by erecting a *dzo* directed against thieves. In order to produce the appropriate *dzo*, he approached the spokesman of the newly installed Amimli priestess for a piece of black cloth. When the priestess heard about this case, she – or rather her *trɔ̃* – became very angry and decided to expose this hypocritical Christian behaviour by disturbing the Sunday church service. However, she tried in vain, because people stopped her in the street outside. Nevertheless, by informing people about the case she had achieved her aim of exposing Adjima. Once his secret had been made public, Adjima asserted that he himself did not believe that anti-theft *dzo* was itself powerful, but that he thought it would keep away from his farm those who believe in its power. Clearly, in his view, Christians were less able than traditionalists to protect their property because they could not threaten others with immediate divine punishment. Many people shared this view. Hence EPC members frequently consult priests and *dzotɔwo* in secret.

Within the EPC, two divergent views exist on Christianity's capacity to provide protection. While some, like Adjima, consider it insufficient, others maintain that their individual faith in God alone is able to prevent mishaps. Protection against physical, material and spiritual troubles clearly was and is a problem in the EPC. Indeed, as noted in Chapter 5, most members of Agbelengor were initially EPC members who fell ill and could not obtain treatment in their own church. In the same way, many members of the new EPC could not get healed in the old EPC, or felt increasingly insecure. Thus, departure from the EPC results, above all, from an experience of helplessness vis-à-vis diabolical powers.

These powers are confronted in the Spiritual and Pentecostal churches. By having hands laid upon them, members can test whether a demonic force has entered them with the intention of causing harm. If so, such powers are explicitly mentioned and cast out. Both this continued provision of protection and people's deliverance from evil spirits make for the attraction of these churches. Those attending them feel in continuous need of prayers through which they may improve their personal condition and their business. Most members of Agbelengor and the new EPC are women, many of whom live on the edge of poverty and try hard to make ends meet through petty trade and other small-scale 'informal' economic activities. Others hold official jobs, yet fail to generate sufficient income to feed their children.[6] Young men especially lack the funds with which to marry properly and bring up children (and this, in turn, has consequences for the condition of young women who often have to take care of their [illegitimate] offspring alone). All these categories of people are attracted to pentecostally oriented churches and attribute the problems they encounter not to the economic situation as such, but to the machinations of evil spirits.

Protection against and deliverance from evil spirits are both understood in terms of the spiritual war between God and Satan. The difference between these practices is that the performance of deliverance is more dramatic, because evil spirits have already beset a person's spirit rather than merely threatening it from outside. To members of Agbelengor and the EPC 'of Ghana', protection is not merely a matter of individual faith, as some staunch EPC members maintain. Search for protection has to be reasserted regularly through particular prayers performed in both public and private prayer meetings. Members of these churches differ from those at the grassroots level of the old EPC, not with regard to the idea that evil spirits actually exist and can wield power over people, but with regard to the actual experience that the old EPC could neither protect them against nor cure them from the afflictions brought about by these forces.

## SPIRITS, FAMILY TIES AND THE INDIVIDUAL

Through the study of particular cases, relationships between people and evil spirits will be examined. The aim is to develop a better understanding of what causes people to turn away from the old EPC or similar churches in favour of Pentecostal congregations, by concentrating on the experiences of the members of Agbelengor and the EPC 'of Ghana', i.e. ex-EPC members turning to one of these churches. But in order to assess the peculiarity of the Pentecostal point of view, non-Christian ideas and practices regarding human–spirit relations will also be considered.

Spirits can be classified in the following way. First, all the deities known traditionally, i.e. the *trɔwo*, *adziakpewo*, *ametsiavawo* and *tɔgbekpukpowo* (ancestor's stools),[7] can be grouped together. They are worshipped in and by a particular family or clan and are thought to unite and protect its members. Though in some cases a god's protective power extends to a whole village or even the Peki state (for instance Wuve), he is still worshipped in one particular family on whose compound his shrine is erected and from where he draws his priests. The *adefiewo* (ancestor spirits), who are worshipped through the pouring of libation in the family house, also belong to this category of spiritual beings. However, it is the deities mentioned above, whose worship is much more explicit and public than libation prayers to the ancestors, who will be concentrated on here.

Second, as well as these entities expressing familial ties in a positive way (in terms of unity and identity), there are also *adze* and *ŋɔli*. *Ŋɔliwo* are ancestors troubling a living relative because they are unable to enter the place of the dead (*tsiefe*). They can be pacified by the performance of certain rites and thus only temporarily render familial ties negative by bringing about mishaps. *Adze* is a thoroughly and permanently destructive force held to operate among relatives. *Adze*, at least today, is feared much more than *ŋɔliwo*.

Third, apart from these older, established spirits there are new powers such as *Mami Water* and Indian Spirits, as well as modern forms of *dzo* (see below). These new powers have in common that they are called upon primarily by young people for the sake of individual progress.

## Old Gods and Blood Ties

All cases presented in this section pertain to Agbelengor. In fact, quite a few members of this church have a 'heathen' background – they come from families where the worship of *trɔwo* and other spirits was, or still is, practised. Since these people take the existence of these powers quite seriously, they feel at home in a church like Agbelengor which fully recognises the existence of demons and offers its members the possibility of facing them.

First, the case of Christian Sai Kwadzo (75) from the Dzama clan at Blengo,[8] whose decisiveness gave rise to the first burial conducted by the prayer group preceding Agbelengor. Like his parents, he had been a '*trɔ* worshipper' and never attended school. Since his youth he had been the priest of the dwarfs (four in number) worshipped in his family. They appeared to him in the house or called him to the bush and taught him how to use herbs (*amãwo*) and where to hunt game. They not only initiated him into the secrets of the wilderness (*gbeme*) but also taught him book knowledge, since, unlike him, they were able to read. Although as an *adziakpe* priest he received money from clients in return for curing them with herbs, he never became rich. The money earned through the *adziakpewo* disappeared easily; it could not be used in a constructive way. Sai Kwadzo spent a lot of money on drink and was a poor man, but things changed when one of his children fell ill. Failing to cure the child with his own herbs, he sought help from the newly established prayer group. The founder, Amedzro, and his people told him that they would only help him if he stopped drinking, serving the dwarfs and protecting himself with *dzo*. Sai Kwadzo agreed and converted. He abstained from serving dwarfs and other spiritual beings because he realised that 'all these things are the work of the Devil'. He was 'fed up' worshipping spirits because 'God's ways are more powerful than all of them'. When the child died nevertheless, he remained in the church. But after his conversion, he was still troubled by spirits roaming about unattended in the family. Though he no longer served them, he was convinced that they really existed and that, in contrast to human beings, they would never die.

After the death of the priest of Henema, a *trɔ* served in the Dzama clan, Henema approached Sai Kwadzo in his dreams. He appeared in the typical attire of local *trɔwo*, in a black gown with a knife (and even a gun) in his hand. Although the god threatened to kill one of his children if he failed to serve him, Sai Kwadzo remained firm. He and Amedzro prayed over the matter and the *trɔ* ceased appearing to him. After he had turned away from the dwarfs they left him alone, but tried to get his son Yao under their control. This began more than twenty years ago and has continued ever since. Except for Yao, all members of his family became members of Agbelengor. Though unable to read, Sai Kwadzo frequently had visions about Bible texts, for instance Psalm 91, which he would see in his mind's eye. When asked about the benefits of his turn to Christianity, he said that only after his conversion was he able to build a house for himself. This proved to him that money earned as a Christian – next to farming he made some money through herbalism – was more productive than money earned as a *trɔ* worshipper.

Another interesting case is that of an old woman (84) in Tsame who called herself Celestine Mawueyɔm ('God called me') after her conversion.[9] Her parents were *trɔ̃* worshippers and earned their living through (cocoa) farming. When she was still a young woman – though unmarried she already had one child – she once walked home from Avetile with her mother, accompanied by a stranger dressed in a white northern gown (*batakari*). When she asked her mother whether she had also seen the man, her mother replied that she had not. As they entered the house, she felt the man lean on her; his body was touching her as if he were a human being. Then he lay down on her bed and slept with her; he told her that he had been looking for her for a long time. Later, she learned that the stranger's name was Sowlui[10] and that he was an Akan spirit. Though she had never been to the Akan area (*Bli*) and did not know Twi, when Sowlui 'came upon' her (*ele edzi*) she communicated with him in that language. She told her mother about the incident and asked her to inform her father. The latter performed all the customs necessary to establish the worship of Sowlui, because his daughter was expected to die if he failed to do so. Sowlui was not unknown in this family; previously he had tried to control other daughters. The woman was to serve the *trɔ* on Saturdays and perform his yam festival once a year. If she did not observe the *trɔ*'s food taboos, she would die as well. Although in the beginning Sowlui was known for making his worshippers rich, she herself did not gain much from his service. Since she did not receive clients, his worship cost more than she earned from it. She attributed to her spiritual marriage with Sowlui the fact that she could not find a husband, kept having children by different men and remained in her father's house. She wanted something else for her children and therefore she sent them to the EPC school and had them baptised. But due to 'spiritual attacks', one of her daughters left the EPC for Agbelengor in the 1970s; and from then on, the daughter prayed for the mother. Celestine Mawueyɔm's own conversion occurred around 1982. When her daughter and the rest of the Agbelengor congregation were fasting on the prayer ground one day, she received a visitor in her house who told her to throw away her *trɔ̃* things. This man was Jesus, but she did not see him, she just heard his voice. Without telling anybody what had happened, she took the things and threw them away in the bush. Then she started singing the hymn '*Tsa tsa menya Yesu o*' ('Formerly I did not know Jesus'), which just came to her. On her way home from the bush, she lost her way, and this she interpreted as the revenge of Sowlui, who refused to be deserted. In order to clear her mind, the Reverend Annan (now deceased, formerly of Agbelengor) came to burn her last remaining *trɔ̃* objects that were still in the shrine. After this she started to attend the church services and became a full member. Due to her old age, in 1992 she received the Lord's Supper from the pastor at home after it had been shared by the congregation.

Both of these cases concern former Ewe priests. The next case involves an EPC member's switch to Agbelengor.

Edith Adzoa Makefe Ntem (born in 1942), a serious EPC member who even sang in the church choir, became one of the first members of Agbelengor.[11] She belongs to one of the royal families (Gu) of the Adivieyi clan. After marriage to a son of the old EPC catechist Theodor Karl Ntem, she soon gave birth to a daughter, on the day her uncle, Kwadzo De X, celebrated his yam festival. Some time afterwards, her newborn daughter fell ill and Edith travelled to various hospitals in order to get the girl cured, but all attempts failed. The baby would not take her breast and cried throughout the night. At Anfoega hospital she consulted a white female doctor who told her that the cause of the child's sickness was spiritual, and therefore physicians could do nothing for her. Upon the advice of her mother, Edith went to Amedzro, in whose house she stayed for three months. By this seclusion she was to be separated from the spiritual powers active in her family. Through visions, Amedzro discovered that the baby was attacked by the spirit of the *kpukpo* (stool) of the *fiagã* (paramount chief), who had died on exactly the same day Edith and her daughter were discharged from Anfoega hospital. The child, who was after all born during the yam festival, started to fall ill two weeks before the *fiagã*'s death. Amedzro found out that the child was to die with him for, as the elders said, 'when Tɔgbe [the chief] dies, he carries a messenger along'. Amedzro said that the child was also disturbed by witchcraft which 'always precedes the stool'. The spirit of the stool also possessed Edith's siblings during the yam festivals. But because of her staunch church membership, the stool's spirit and the other spirits attached to it could not 'come upon' her. This, however, did not apply to her baby daughter who was not yet 'under' the protection of any spirit. Through prayers, the spirit of the witch and of the stool were driven away, and the baby began suckling and stopped crying throughout the night. After this cure Edith realised that 'the EPC did not know how to pray' and that 'they had no provisions for healing'. Evil spirits were not discussed and there was no way to get rid of them once they attacked believers. The prayer group, by contrast, was able to drive evil spirits away and heal all bodily and spiritual diseases, even those which could not be cured by Western medicines. Since they 'knew how to pray', there was no need for Agbelengor members to consult the *dzotɔwo* in secret. After her daughter's healing, Edith therefore stayed in the prayer group and, once the group was excluded, became a member of Agbelengor. During the thirty years of her membership she received many benefits from this: she had visions telling her how to proceed in life (and how to make a living – she had once been a cook, but had switched to trading some years ago) and felt well protected by prayers. Her husband, who had died in 1978, never opposed her Agbelengor member-ship, though he himself was in the EPC.

The cases presented so far have all successfully resulted in the full separa-tion of the person from evil spirit(s). This separation, however, may take some time and in some cases, may never be finally resolved (for example, see Meyer 1998). Such is the case of Grace B., a seventeen-year-old girl from one of the royal families of the Adivieyi clan at Blengo.[12] Like her parents, she had been a member of the EPC. Her mother's first children had died, so her parents had become members of Borkuma's prayer group in Tekrom (to which Agbelengor initially belonged – see Chapter 5); but after some years they had returned to the EPC. Grace was staying in Kumasi with her elder sister when she was first approached by the spirit man who was eventually to possess her. When she saw him for the first time in 1987, she was selling provisions. He was dressed in a cloth sewn from flour sacks and was wearing chains of cowrie shells around his wrists and his neck; he began to talk to her (in Fante). Grace felt frightened and wanted to run away, but she did not dare to leave her goods unattended. While the man sat beside her some of her school mates came to ask for sweets, but they behaved as if there was nobody with her. Shortly after this experience she completed Form 4 and returned home to attend secondary school in Peki. But she was suddenly afraid to leave the house and go to school. She neglected her outward appearance, could no longer concentrate on anything, and often felt afraid and shy, but the man she encountered in Kumasi never showed up again. Because of her troubles she went to Tokokoe for deliverance. When hands were laid on her she became possessed ('*menɔ trɔ̃ fo*', 'I was beaten by the *trɔ̃*') and started rolling on the ground. By then, nobody knew (or would tell her) the reason for her troubles. However, since she felt somehow relieved, she returned home to attend school again against the advice of the Tokokoe station pastor. But all the old symptoms soon returned and even-tually she was unable to pursue her education. A second visit to Tokokoe failed to cure her. Though she was praying to the Christian God in her mind she felt that something had taken control of her head. The prayers of the EPC school pastor, S. Ofori, who was a member of the BSPF, could not deliver her either. When hands were laid on her she again started rolling on the ground and danced 'in the fetish way'.

Since Christian treatment had failed, she and her father consulted various local priests and priestesses. Gradually, it turned out that the spirit troubling her was in the family. A priestess became possessed by this spirit, and, speaking through her, the spirit directly addressed Grace's father Paul B. and said that Grace could no longer run away from him. When the spirit said that B. knew him well and that he should mention his name, B. finally admitted that the spirit might be the *ametsiava* Tata Kodzo-Kpo, Kwadzo Dei X's son who had been murdered with a gun after returning from Tsibu in 1925. Previously, this *ametsiava* had possessed other women in the family.[13] The spirit confirmed that this was his name and said that he did not do evil things and that there was no reason to fear him – he was protecting the town and could do anything for the B. family and the royal clans. Therefore, his shrine was to be established in the palace of the *fiagã*. Grace was then willing to become a priestess of this family god. *Ametsiava* priests and priestesses were invited to install her and she began to attend traditional dance ceremonies where she re-enacted her ancestor's violent death. But she could not find relief from her troubles, nor become properly possessed. For this reason, up until 1992, she had been unable to obtain customers and earn money as other priestesses do.

In all these cases, the spirit from whom each person wished to escape was 'in the family'. While Sai Kwadzo, the first case examined above, served *adziakpewo* which had been in his family for a long time, Celestine Mawueyɔm, the second case, served a foreign Akan god who had only arrived in her family in her generation. Thus, Celestine's case is one of possession by foreign rather than native spirits and is in this respect comparable to possession by new foreign spirits such as *Mami Water* (see below). The reason for discussing her case in this context is that her family played such an important role in her installation as a priestess. Like the priestesses of native *trɔwo* she thereby became tied to her family. Both Sai Kwadzo and Celestine Mawueyɔm were Christians who found that their condition did not improve through their worship and this was their main reason for turning away from the old god. Their conversions resemble those occurring in the early days of the Ewe mission, described in Chapter 4. They sought assistance from Agbelengor, and not from the EPC, because the former offered a more elaborate discourse and practices pertaining to evil spirits.

In the other cases presented, a spirit of the family attempted to bring the person concerned under his control. In the case of Grace B., the family *ametsiava* was thought to aim at turning her into a priestess, though the priestess failed to become properly possessed. In Edith Ntem's case the stool appeared to be angry about the fact that he could not wield power over her in the same way as he controlled her siblings; therefore, he tried to take her baby away to accompany the dead *fiagã*.

Interestingly, all but one of the cases involve women. This is representative of the fact that many more women seek deliverance than men. Various male and female members of the three churches were asked why this was so: many men maintained that women's continuing need for deliverance resulted from their 'spiritual weakness'; after all, had not their sister Eve also been tempted by the Devil? Women, of course, strongly opposed this view and said that they were more spiritual, that is, more alert to what was going on in *le gbɔgbɔme* (the spiritual realm). Therefore, in contrast to men who were mostly unattentive and closed-minded, they realised the destructive presence of evil spirits and could eventually be filled with the Holy Spirit. Some male preachers also held this view. Emmanuel Brempong, for instance, stated that women closed themselves off from the outside world much less than men. As a result of this openness they were more likely to be disturbed by spiritual forces. This spiritual openness reflects women's position in society: they are the ones who marry out into strange families and clans and must adapt themselves to their husbands' relatives.

It is important to note that the spirits' attempts to possess Christians followed the pattern of the possession of priestesses as it traditionally occurred, and still occurs today. Interviews with *trɔsiwo*, and also Celestine Mawueyɔm's account, reveal that these women did not at first choose to become priestesses; rather, they were approached by the deity against their own will and were afraid they might die if they failed to give in. Many had been (or were about to be) baptised as Christians. But suddenly they had suffered symptoms such as headache, general weakness, a failure to concentrate, confusion and weight loss which could not be counteracted by either Western or local medicine. Also, each woman had recognised the spirit wishing to possess her in her dreams; he had slept with her and told her to become his wife. Since symptoms and dream occurred together, family members consulted shrines outside Peki to inquire about the cause of the sickness. Finally, it was confirmed that a certain family or clan god wanted to possess the afflicted woman. Once the family or clan elders accepted this, the woman was installed as a *trɔsi*. Prior to possession, many of these priestesses had marriage problems; either having failed to find a husband and therefore remaining in their father's house, or having had troubles with their husbands which made them return to their paternal homes. Through their instalment, which turned them into wives of a *trɔ*, the link with their own family or clan was emphasised.

Therefore, within the framework of Ewe religion, spirit possession offered a possibility for women who were unable to integrate themselves into a strange family through marriage, to strengthen the ties they had with their own family. Once such a woman was installed as a priestess, she was respected and sometimes even feared by her own blood relatives as well as by other people in the town. This was especially important for women who failed to marry or who got divorced and thus had to remain with or return to their own family. Normally, a woman's brothers did not like their sister staying in her paternal home and preferred her to marry out, though she was always counted as a member of her patrilineage. But when a woman became the mouthpiece of a *trɔ* within her own family, she could assume a powerful position which restrained possible opposition against her identification with, and return to, her roots. She had to be consulted in family matters and could earn money by curing clients. In the same way, a woman possessed by a *trɔ* in her husband's family – a much less frequent occurrence – could assume a more powerful position than an ordinary wife.

Grace B.'s initial reluctance to give in to the spirit trying to possess her indicates that the confirmation of a woman's ties with her paternal family through spirit possession is not a satisfying option for everyone. Celestine Mawueyɔm, for example, experienced as purely negative the *trɔ*'s attempts to tie her to her kin and prevent her from a successful union with a man from another family, and from becoming rich. In the same way, Grace B. initially aspired to continue secondary school and thereby become a modern, well-educated woman. Thus, in contrast to the *trɔsiwo*, who agreed to confirm the blood ties connecting them with their paternal families, these women wanted to leave these ties behind. The strengthening of blood ties seems to be no solution for Christian women who would rather have separation. According to the Christian viewpoint, spirits roam about in families and seek to bring all members, Christians included, under their control. We saw this clearly in the case of Sai Kwadzo. Even after his conversion he himself was called upon by the Henema clan *trɔ* to become his priest, and his son was later approached by the dwarfs who remained unattended. The same pattern applies to all cases presented above. All these people (along with many not presented here) turned to Agbelengor because they considered this church – and not the EPC or any other mission church – the most appropriate to help them achieve their aim of being 'cut off' from their family.

A spirit is thought to be able to influence people (even if they are Christians) because he can work through the ties connecting blood relatives: old gods have control over blood (*vu*). Since, as a result of their conversion to Christianity, many people have refused to take an active part in *trɔ* ceremonies, it is nowadays thought that the old gods can no longer unite all paternal family members in worship as had been the case in pre-missionary days. Nevertheless, the gods are still considered capable of wielding power over any family member from the moment of his or her conception simply because each person is born into a particular family. As shown by the *kpukpo*'s alleged attempt to kill Edith Ntem's daughter, those trying to eschew the family spirit's control can be severely punished. The spirit can even try to ally himself with other destructive spirits such as *adze* in order to achieve his aim. The view and experience that spirits have control over and work through blood ties is not confined to members of Agbelengor, but held by Peki Christians in general. How faithful Christians view a spirit's power over blood ties was summarised pointedly by Emmanuel Brempong in an account of how he delivered a Krobo woman from a family god:

> As long as you belong to that clan, to that family, and you don't belong to Jesus Christ, the Devil has control though you may not serve the Devil. But he may have control over you indirectly. And he will cause you to serve him indirectly, but you may not know.

Brempong told me that, this being the case, exorcists always first ask an afflicted person about his or her family. Then they pray in order to 'break the link of communication which comes from the family. We break it first. We break that link. Then the Devil can never supply people to come and take away that person.' He compared this deliverance strategy to American military strategies in the Gulf War: the Americans blew up bridges and this made it impossible for Saddam Hussein's soldiers to reach certain areas. In the same way, deliverance destroys the links between family members.

Thus, by equating old gods and demons, blood ties are represented as channels through which the Devil can influence a person, even without him or her being aware of it. In short, the Devil operates through blood ties, the Christian God severs them. Though this holds true for both sexes in principle, in practice – both traditionally and within the framework of Christianity – more women than men are considered to be under the influence of family gods. Given that Ewe society is patrilineal and patrilocal, this is not surprising. In contrast to men who may stay in the safety and familiarity of their homes, women were and are expected to marry out into strange families and clans and adapt themselves to their husbands and in-laws. In many cases, this gives rise to problems between women and their in-laws, and as a result of men's migration these problems increased. While traditional spirit possession offers women the possibility to confirm their relationship with their paternal family (or occasionally to emphasise their relationship with their in-laws), the option provided by Christianity is separation from the family ties, symbolically expressed by the family *trɔ̃*. Transformation into an independent individual was the dearest wish of all the women and the one man discussed above.

## Witchcraft, or 'The Dark Side of Kinship'

Leaders of both Agbelengor and the EPC 'of Ghana' asserted that most cases they are asked to treat concern *adze*. Although, occasionally, people are afraid of being turned into witches themselves, the problem is more usually the experience of witchcraft attacks, i.e. the experience of falling victim to witchcraft, rather than becoming an active agent of it. Fear of such attacks is a current concern of both Christians and traditionalists.

Both Agbelengor and the EPC 'of Ghana' publicly acknowledge the existence of witchcraft and refer to this evil spirit in sermons. But most members of these churches (though there are always some exceptions) prefer to confine discussion of witchcraft experiences to private conversations with pastors, deliverers and close friends. Reason for the reluctance to speak openly about personal witchcraft experiences is that witchcraft cases lead straight into familial conflicts, which many people do not like to make public. Because most of the conversations about witchcraft experiences on which the following cases are based were confidential, the names of those concerned have been changed.

Patricia A.,[14] a woman of about sixty years of age from the Adivieyi Dome clan in Blengo, was married with six children when interviewed in 1992. All her life she had been farming, assisting her husband who had a cocoa farm in Kedjebi (up north). Her mother had been a church mother (*hameḍaḍa*) in the EPC and she herself was a member of the Great Choir. Until 1970, when she started suffering from severe headaches, she was a committed member of the EPC. EPC presbyters prayed for her health, but to no avail. After looking everywhere for cures, she was finally healed by Agbelengor, where she was treated both at the church's prayer site uphill at Blengo and in Tokokoe. At first she did not know what caused her sickness, but later this was revealed to her: she and her mother, who was a successful baker and trader in cloth and sweets, were very close. As well as the trade she herself was involved in, her husband had a good income through his cocoa farm. Her elder sister, however, had not prospered, and envied her; it was this sister who had tried to destroy Patricia with *adze*. Gradually Patricia became aware of this. At first, she dreamed about a dog biting her – a dream sign which indicates a witchcraft attack. But she did not yet know that her sister was making *adze* against her. This was realised only after her mother had heard that Patricia often spoke about the elder sister in her sleep. Later on, an Agbelengor pastor, the late Reverend Annan, confirmed this diagnosis which had also been revealed to him. Rather than exposing her sister publicly, Patricia was symbolically separated from her influence and filled with the Holy Spirit (in the way described in Chapter 6). After her treatment by Agbelengor, Patricia no longer suffered from headaches and since then she has been a full member of Agbelengor and has even been appointed a prophetess.

The next case shows that a witch thought to cause a person's troubles need not necessarily be identified. Margareth N.,[15] a thirty-six-year-old woman married with three children, had been born an EPC member. She came to Agbelengor around 1976, when her first-born baby fell sick: the girl suffered from symptoms such as convulsions and fever which could not be treated in hospital. As a last resort, the mother turned to Agbelengor (at Dzake, where she then lived), whose pastor prayed for the baby every evening. The pastor 'saw that a witch was worrying the baby'. Both he and Margareth had dreams indicative of witchcraft. For instance, they saw an old lady chasing the child. It was never discovered which person had attacked the baby, but after a period of intensive prayer and fasting, the child recovered. From then on, Margareth remained in Agbelengor. She and her children were never again attacked by witchcraft or any other evil spirit.

Whereas the previous two cases were resolved, others, such as the following, may remain open for some time. Elisabeth M. (45)[16] was another ex-EPC member who sang in the church choir and who joined Agbelengor because she was desperately concerned about her spiritual and physical state. She attended the prayer meetings after her divorce from her first husband. In her view, there was not enough prayer and Bible study in the EPC. In Agbelengor she had more opportunity to be prayed for: 'They help you when you are in trouble.' However, even at the time of writing her condition is not very good and she continues to seek further deliverance. Her second marriage with an elderly widower and EPC member is full of conflicts. She regrets not having children and suffers from severe asthma. At night she often dreams about women having sex with her and when she wakes up the next morning her nightdress is covered in blood. She feels that she does not breathe during the whole night (a sign that she has been 'truly possessed'). In the past she had had several miscarriages. One problem solved in the course of her membership of Agbelengor concerns the loss of trading capital. Formerly, she had often been unable to earn back the money she herself had invested in the purchase of goods and had made no profit. Though she alleged that in many cases such losses are due to the fact that husbands fail to give 'chop money' to their wives who cannot help but eat up their trading capital, she also believed that not all the losses can be explained in this way. In her own case the loss could not be attributed to human fault. She was sure that witches stole the money from her spiritually, but she did not know who it was in her family who directed witchcraft against her. However, ever since she had been giving ten per cent of her income to the church, as requested, her trade no longer suffered from *adze* attacks. If only she could be cured from asthma, her business would really improve.

Some cases of witchcraft attacks experienced by EPC members prior to or after turning to the EPC 'of Ghana' are now examined.

Gabriel T.[17] recalled a witchcraft attack in his family that had occurred at the beginning of the 1970s. His parents were members of the EPC and 'somehow well-to-do':

> And my mother's mother, that is, my maternal grandmother, became jealous about the efforts being made by my parents. ... And she opened an attack. And it began in the physical. She would come here and talk about our possessions in some sort of envious manner, using envious words.

This went on for some time before the matter 'went to the spiritual and it was a fight between the spirit of faith and the Devil. A battle between the blessed and the cursed.' In the course of this battle, two of his younger siblings died. At this dramatic point, his mother joined Agbelengor to obtain better protection. Gabriel himself fasted and went into the bush with some friends and prayed for God to avenge them. Eventually, the grandmother died and all the trouble came to an end. Gabriel's mother became a successful trader and Agbelengor member, while he and his father, who had been a presbyter in the EPC, turned to the EPC 'of Ghana'.

Grace N.[18] (born in 1956) was married with five children and living in Blengo *Kpodzi* in 1992. She was a ward assistant in the 'Maternal and Child Health Care Services' in Peki hospital. According to her, there was a great deal of witchcraft around in Peki. *Adze* was mainly directed against small children. When she was a child she had experienced two witchcraft attacks. One night in a dream she saw people piling blocks on her. When she woke up, her arms and legs were shorter than before and they have remained so ever since. When she attended Class 6, she saw a black bird pecking her in a dream. From then on her mind was blocked and she could no longer learn anything, and for this reason could not further her education. Also, just after she had joined the BSPF her little daughter fell ill and was in a coma for twelve days. At that time, Grace was not yet able to pray with power and thus protect herself and her children. In the end her child was cured through both medicine and prayers by BSPF members. She never tried to find out the identity of the witch who had attacked her child, but she believed that no evil would befall her if she acted according to God's word. She could now pray for her own children, and whenever owls – the most common animal shape *adze* is believed to take – approached her house at night, she could prevent the witches from disturbing her family. Since 1989 she had been offering healing prayers on behalf of others, and when the split came she joined the new EPC because the old EPC was not in favour of such prayers.

Yayria K. (39)[19] was a baker. Before she married her current husband and moved into his house, she had stayed in her father's house in Avetile. She had had four children from two earlier marriages. Born into the EPC, she had become a member of the BSPF and joined the EPC 'of Ghana' after the secession. Her third husband was a widower and EPC member, forty years her senior and already the father of many children. He owned a cocoa farm in the Asante area and a large house in Dzogbati. There were rumours that she had married him because he was relatively wealthy, but she assured me that she had done so because she had liked the idea of being with a calm, experienced man. However, the marriage was unhappy. Prior to the marriage, he had not only promised to build an oven for her and buy chickens, to enable her to trade with bread and eggs, but also to take care of her children. While he had indeed delivered the oven and the chickens, he was now unwilling to maintain the children. Though she stayed in his house, she did not feel happy. There were conflicts with his elder sons and these increased after she again became pregnant. The pregnancy was problematic. In the third month she dreamt of a person telling her to 'push the baby out'. In subsequent dreams she was beaten severely, and when she woke up in the morning she had pains in her womb. She called her friends from the prayer group, among them Akudeka and Brempong, who came to pray for her, and the problems disappeared. But when she was giving birth, other problems occurred: for example, the baby was lying transversely and her perineum was almost torn. Again prayers helped her to deliver the child safely, but she was sure these problems were brought about by witchcraft. Recently, she and her baby daughter were disturbed by giant red ants. Since she had heard that witches can take the shape of any animal, she was sure these ants also represented a witchcraft attack. Once, she had seen red ants eat up all the dough she had formed into loaves to be baked, and this had destroyed her business. But she was uncertain who wanted to destroy her with *adze*. In any case, she was sure that many people, both within and outside the family, were jealous of her because of her success. She did not feel safe in the house either. Sometimes she heard a voice calling '*agooo*' (the usual greeting of a stranger about to enter a house) without seeing anybody. She suspected that before he had built it, her husband had made a sacrifice to a pagan spirit which now controlled the house. For all these reasons she was in dire need of protection.

Both the old gods and witchcraft are thought to operate within the framework of the family. But while the attempts of *trɔwo* and other deities to possess a person are confined to people who have such gods in their family, *adze* attacks can occur in any family. Therefore, fear of witchcraft is more widespread than fear of being possessed by old spirits. Spirits get access to a person through blood ties, *adzetɔwo* ultimately destroy these ties by feeding on relatives' blood and flesh. A witch may invite other witches to participate in the cannibalistic meal. In order to get access to a person, a witch has to make use of family ties. Therefore, people suffering pains which they attribute to a witchcraft attack know that these pains are inflicted on them by a close relative, even though they may not be sure of the witch's identity. *Adze* is thus indicative of tensions within the family. Here, too, witchcraft is 'the dark side of kinship' (Geschiere 1994).

In all the cases presented above, the root of witchcraft has been identified as envy (*ŋuvavã*). Because of her comparative prosperity, Patricia A. was attacked by her own sister and in the same way, Gabriel T.'s well-to-do parents became the object of his maternal grandmother's jealousy. But people do not necessarily have to be rich in order to become the victims of witchcraft attacks. A poor person's inability to escape poverty can also be attributed to witchcraft. The cases of Elisabeth M., whose capital was spiritually stolen, and of Yayria K., whose bread dough was eaten up by red ants, show that witches may also destroy a person's trade to prevent future profits in it. Also, Grace N. attributed to witchcraft the fact that she was unable to attend secondary school, and thus unable to obtain an education that would lead to a well-paid job.

Witches do not only destroy a person's own health or (potential) material property. We saw that in many cases they also attack children. They either make them sick, or prevent a woman from having children, for instance, through causing miscarriages. Here, the cannibalist motive figures once again: witches are supposed to feed on children and unborn babies. By killing offspring, witches thwart people's strongest desires: to have children and thereby prolong blood ties.

In all the cases presented above people were victims of witchcraft attacks. Only rarely do people report that they have been actively engaged in witchcraft. Occasionally, people may report frightening dreams indicating someone is attempting to force them to become part of a group of witches, but even here people see themselves as victims rather than agents of evil. In Peki, many stories circulate surrounding how someone can be turned into a witch. For example, *adze* can be given to an unborn baby through the mother, to a new-born baby through a midwife, to a (grand)child through the (grand)mother's beads, to a non-suspecting person through the consumption of food – especially food containing red palm oil (*amidze*) – or to an ignorant customer through any goods purchased in the market or a store. In all these cases the person receiving *adze* is doing so actively but is represented as a passive recipient. However, during my fieldwork in Peki I did not meet anybody, not even in Tokokoe, who admitted being, or having been, a witch, save for one young woman afraid of being turned into a witch (her case is described below).[20] This resembles the situation at the beginning of the century, described in Chapter 4, when to a large extent both the offence and suspicion of witchcraft occurred in secret, and witchcraft confessions were extremely rare.[21]

Today, confessions about a person's active witchcraft activities are usually published in popular papers which are brought to Peki from Accra and circulated among many people, or they are made during the 'Crusades' (large open-air meetings in the course of which much time is devoted to public deliverance and confession) organised by Pentecostal churches. For instance, many people I talked to recalled that on a 'Crusade' organised by Agbelengor a certain Reverend Agbemodzi confessed that he had once been a witch, eaten babies, and even sold their meat on skewers. Such confessions are considered eye-witness accounts of the realm of darkness through which insight can be gained into the invisible, spiritual realm determining people's daily lives. Listening to confessions provides a glimpse into the realm of the 'powers of darkness' from a safe distance. The popularity of confession stories stems from the light they shed on the darkness and what happens there. They are, in other words, revelations serving to explain how and why things go wrong in the physical world. People draw their information about witches' actions from these kinds of sources and are well-informed about modern forms of witchcraft, involving the active purchase of occult powers in order to obtain wealth and power – usually in exchange for one's own fertility or the life of a close relative (Meyer 1995a).[22] As far as their own experiences regarding *adze* are concerned, however, people in Peki mainly express them in terms of affliction. This holds true in the context of Christian as well as indigenous views which both denounced witchcraft occurring in Peki as purely destructive and motivated by envy.[23]

Though victims may be both men and women, the cases presented above suggest that, at least in the context of Pentecostalism, women suffer from *adze* more frequently than men. Often, however, it is not the women themselves who suffer, but rather their (unborn) children or their business (through which they have to feed them). The burden of caring for the off-spring is mainly in the hands of women and, as a result of these responsibilities, women are more in need of protection against and deliverance from witchcraft attacks than men. By attributing mishaps such as miscarriages, sickness and money problems to *adze*, women can then free themselves from blame, attribute their troubles to others and appear as passive victims.

Any blood relative, usually a woman, in the maternal or paternal line may be suspected of performing *adze*. Though people I spoke to still see the paternal aunt (*tasi*) as a person who is most likely to perform witchcraft, they also think that any paternal or maternal relative, even a small child, may be a witch. Many of the cases show that people's main concern is not to detect who exactly is responsible for the witchcraft attack inflicted upon them; indeed they probably fear the trouble resulting from open witchcraft accusations. Rather, they seek effective personal protection. Relative lack of interest in the witch's identity, as well as the view that any envious relative may perform witchcraft, indicate general feelings of insecurity about one's family. Since the person afflicted need not actually be rich or have many children, this feeling of insecurity applies not only to the well-to-do but also to poor people who attribute their lack of progress in life to *adze*. Both rich and poor feel uneasy about the diffuse grip an envious relative may have on them, and therefore strive to become inaccessible to the potentially destructive spiritual powers of their kin.

But how is *adze* diagnosed? The tricky thing about witchcraft is that it cannot simply be reduced to what it is considered to express. Though the root of *adze* is envy, people do not launch their destructive attacks directly in the visible, material realm: they do not kill and steal openly. Rather, they operate through the detour of the spiritual: 'Witchcraft begins in the physical and then goes into the spiritual,' as Gabriel T. pointedly formulated. Witchcraft being a double-edged phenomenon operating both '*le ɲutilame*' (in the 'physical' realm) and '*le gbɔgbɔme*' (in the 'spiritual' realm), it is useful to reflect upon the relationship between dreams and everyday life represented in these cases.[24] Both victims and pastors use dreams as a window through which to see what is going on 'in the spiritual' and thereby understand why things go wrong 'in the physical'. For Peki people the former is as real as the latter. Dreams reveal what is going on in someone's life but may be hidden to his or her eyes when awake. In contrast to Western, Freudian ideas about dreams in terms of subjects' own constructions, here dreams are understood as actual encounters of the dreamer with others who may be held responsible for what happens to the dreamer in his or her dreams. A pregnant woman's dream experience of a baby being taken from her womb is considered indicative of the attack of a witch who is thought to feed on the child. In the same way, when a person dreams about participating in feasts or flying through the air this is held to expose witches' attempts to incorporate the dreamer into their group. Since witches are considered capable of taking the shape of various animals, such as owls, dogs, cows, pigs or ants, an encounter with such a creature in a dream is seen as a sign of witchcraft.[25]

The truthfulness of a dream is confirmed by correspondences between what is seen in a dream and what is experienced while awake. For example, Yayria K. not only dreamt of being told to abort her baby, she actually suffered pains in her womb when she woke up. To her this was not new: earlier, she dreamt she had beaten a woman thought to be a witch and the next day the woman had been unable to walk. All other cases presented also rely on correspondence between dream image and experience. Interestingly, it is not only possible to know what is going on in 'the physical' by looking into 'the spiritual', but also the other way round. Grace N. indicated that owls are often witches who can be sent away through prayer and Yayria K. diagnosed the visit of destructive red ants as a witchcraft attack. Many stories – for instance, the one about how a girl destroyed twelve cockroaches (i.e. witches) attacking her at night and how the next morning twelve people were dead – circulate about how 'the physical' and 'the spiritual' can merge at certain points. They are taken as proof of the truth of what was revealed within the spiritual realm.

In all the cases presented above people turned away from the EPC because they had not received adequate treatment there. Churches such as Agbelengor and the 'EPC of Ghana', however, take the spiritual realm seriously. Not only do they make use of dreams and visions in order to detect witchcraft, they also fight it through spiritual means. Interestingly, dream signs indicative of witchcraft are part of a stock of indigenous ideas about dream interpretation, and priests and *dzotɔwo* make use of them in order to diagnose *adze*. Earlier I stated that, because of secrecy traditionally surrounding *adze*, it was difficult to counter this evil force and the only thing to be done was to ensure personal prophylactic protection. As a result of the increase of *adze* together with the increase of envy instigated by a more and more unequal distribution of riches, there has been a rising need for protection through *dzo*. Many EPC members did not feel sufficiently safe in the EPC and secretly consulted *dzotɔwo*. Churches such as Agbelengor and the EPC 'of Ghana' have provided an alternative to this *Yesu viɖe, dzo viɖe* stance. Like the *dzotɔwo*, they provide individual protection against *adze*, but they go further than the *dzotɔwo* and local priests in that they offer members long periods of seclusion (for instance in Tokokoe) and explicit rites of separation from their families. When witchcraft has been diagnosed as the cause of someone's trouble, as in the case of possession by old gods, all the energy is devoted to cutting the victim's ties with his or her family. Individualisation is the main option in the fight against Satan.

## New Spirits and the Selfish Pursuit of Individual Interests

Emphasis on the severance of family ties does not mean that Pentecostalism endorses the selfish pursuit of individual interests. That this extreme form of individualism may be considered problematic will become clear from some examples that occurred shortly before or during my stay in 1992.

About four years ago, Felicia B. (32) from Peki Avetile[26] fell ill. Some members of her paternal family belonged to the EPC, but in her view they were not real Christians because they participated in the worship of a *trɔ* in the house. Her own mother, who belonged to the family in charge of Wuve, had turned to drink and was not affiliated to any church. Felicia herself was also 'a child of the world'. Having attended school until Form 4, she went to Accra to earn her living as a house girl. She worked for various European

families, among them those of the Bulgarian Ambassador and of a man
working at the Yugoslavian Embassy. Her salary in the Bulgarian family was
poor, but the man gave her additional money in exchange for sex. Since she
did not like this situation, she left his house for that of the Yugoslavian. Here
the pay was better, but the man also slept with her. While still working in his
house, she started having frightening dreams: she was eating together with
other people (a sign of *adze* possession), but was also chased by people with
knives (a sign of *adze* attack). She also saw many different spirits enter her,
one of which was Wuve, who appeared to her in a black gown with a knife in
his hand and wanted to sleep with her. Another frequent visitor was *Mami
Water*, a spirit who always talked about sex and riches. It said: 'I'll marry
you, I'll buy this thing for you, I am a white man [called] So-and-so [here
the spirit mentioned particular names], I'll buy a car for you, you'll be rich.'
Felicia often had dreams related to this spirit. For instance, together with
another woman and a man, all dressed in white knickers and white gloves,
she entered the sea or, in other words, *Mami Water*'s dwelling place. On
another occasion she dreamed that she had sex together with two white men
and one white woman. But the *Mami Water* spirit not only appeared in her
dreams, it also manifested itself when she was awake:

> When I was in the house, I would lock the door, I would be alone in
> the house. And I would put on my dress, the new dress, I would put on
> lipstick, eye-shadow and dress, and I would put a mirror down. I would
> be dancing on it. I would be looking at myself in the mirror and dance.

Moreover, when the spirit told her 'to spot herself' (i.e. to masturbate) she
did so. When I asked her why all this was so bad, she told me that it was bad
because she did it alone, solely for herself and in isolation.

Not only did Felicia experience spirits invading her, she also felt
increasingly shy towards people. Often in her dreams she saw evil befalling
people, and once this evil occurred in 'the physical', she felt guilty and
accused herself of being responsible for it. For instance she once dreamt of
herself offering sweets to the children of a Christian. When one of these
children later fell ill, she thought that she had caused the illness through her
sweets. Her condition became so bad that she had to stop working and
return home. Her relatives did not consider her to be sick at all but thought
that she was merely lazy and pretending. When she went to Agbelengor to
get delivered, her problems became worse. In her view this was because the
deliverance prayers sparked off the war between the Holy Spirit and the evil:
'Everything I do turns upside down.' She suffered from frightening dreams,
severe feelings of guilt, and often experienced satanic temptations.
Sometimes, she could not refrain from cursing people who annoyed her in
her mind and then she felt guilty about the difficulty she had in controlling
such thoughts. The *Mami Water* spirit still talked to her about the pleasures

of money (so that she could buy a car) and sex (for instance with a pastor). She heard drumming in her ears and was scared to witness ceremonies for fear that the evil spirits invoked there might enter her. For the same reason, she felt uneasy during deliverance sessions because there were so many cast-out evil spirits around. She felt permeable to any evil spirit around, though she often called on Jesus for help. To no avail, because she remained in the grip of Satan: her personal spirit was not yet filled with the Holy Spirit. She came to Tokokoe around December 1991 because in Peki she was troubled by too many evil spirits. While she sought full dissociation from her family, she wanted to be friends with other people. At the time when I met her, she felt excluded and thought that nobody liked her. Even though she was afraid of the big city, she wanted to continue working in Accra once the Holy Spirit had entered her.

Jacob K. (21)[27] lived in Peki Avetile in the home of his maternal grand-mother. His father was from Ada (the area where the river Volta enters the Atlantic) and both his parents and maternal grandparents were Jehovah's Witnesses; his paternal grandfather had been a *'juju* man' (that is, a *dzotɔ*). After the death of his grandfather, Jacob's family members wanted him to take charge of these powers. However, he refused and fled to Peki. The reason he did not wish to take over these powers from his grandfather was not that he was a Christian – though his family considered him to be one – but the fact that he already 'owned' a couple of spirits from India. Nobody in his family knew that he was in possession of these foreign occult forces, which were thought to be more powerful than his grandfather's *dzo* and should not be mixed with it. He had received the Indian spirits about four years earlier, when involved in a conflict with the principal of his school, the 'Ada Technical Institute', who had snatched the girlfriend of Jacob's best friend. His strong wish to fight this teacher was one of the reasons for becoming involved with Indian spirits. He had once helped a rasta-man repair an outboard motor and the man gave him an address in Bombay (India Spiritual Company, Struktu Center) to which he should write in order to obtain Indian spirits. Jacob was told that through these spirits he would be able to perform miracles. In contrast to native *dzo*, these powers were provided free of charge.

After a while, Jacob received various objects, such as a Bible, a book called 'The Secret Book of Psalms' (both books were employed to curse people), oil and incense, a 'magical handkerchief', a 'magical cloth', a 'magical mirror', a 'talisman', a cowrie to swallow and six magic rings. These objects enabled him to do wonderful things: he could overcome time and travel to other places, see what was going on and contact people all over the world, foretell the future, spiritually steal money from the bank that had been gained through corruption, overcome enemies in a fight, punish those insulting him, and free himself once he was imprisoned. The spirits behind these objects were called Adonai, Jasahata, Eloi, He Yehova and Vahodze. These spirits also made him come into contact with the spirit of *Mami Water* from whom he received a seventh ring which enabled him to fight large numbers of people at the same time. He himself had been under the sea among the *Mami Water* spirits and had seen houses made from gold. A friend of his was married to a *Mami Water* spirit, but he himself was not. Sexual intercourse with women, be it spiritual or physical, was incompatible with his Indian spirits, who required him to be 'clean'. Moreover, he some-how feared *Mami Water* spirits. While the males were nasty, the females were nice and sweet, albeit only at first sight. They could make their spiritual husbands immensely rich by transforming grains of sand into banknotes and were friendly as long as the men acted according to their wishes. As soon as they felt neglected they would make their partners crazy. He himself regularly invoked this spirit as well as the others mentioned above, either on the estuary in Ada or at the *ametsiava* cemetery in Peki. At first he did not realise that they all were servants of Satan, but later he became aware of this. Satan preached to him through stones and told him that He was better for mankind than God. Jacob used his evil powers for some years, making people sick and causing accidents, but never killed anybody.

At the beginning he was able to obtain some money with the help of the spirits. However, it was impossible to use this money for constructive purposes – it could only be squandered. Later, he was unable to obtain any money at all and he attributed this to the fact that the name of Jesus Christ, taboo for the spirits, was mentioned three times in his presence. He told me that in his view it was typical of Satan to 'give you joyful things first, and after that you'll pay him'. He failed his exams and was unable to get a job. Only recently he ordered another spirit from India to help him find work, but as a result of his recent conversion he decided to send it back. He attributed the mishaps he had encountered prior to his conversion to the fact that people started praying for him. In this way, the power of the satanic spirits declined and some of the magical objects flew away. Though at first Jacob was annoyed by the effects of people's prayers, he also felt very touched by the prayers of a young girl from Agbelengor who wanted him to escape from the grip of Satan.

I witnessed Jacob's deliverance in an Agbelengor fasting service on 29 February 1992. Whereas all other people remained calm when Amedzro or one of his assistants laid hands on them, Jacob began to move. After some time I saw him vomit a cowrie, which he later told me he had received from India and had swallowed four years ago. Thereafter Amedzro, to whom the young man had earlier confessed his involvement with evil spirits, sent him home to fetch his magical things. On his return, the pastor called a senior male and female deacon, a young man, Jacob and also myself to go uphill into the bush. In the meantime, the congregation was to study the Bible. The magical objects were assembled on the ground and then Amedzro started to pray aloud. He asked Jacob to say the names of all his spirits. Repeating their names, the pastor commanded them to leave and implored God to free Jacob from all evil. Afterwards, the objects were beaten with Amedzro's Bible, covered with dry sticks and set on fire. The people assembled recited Psalm 27 and sang deliverance songs. They laughed at the defeat of Satan which they were witnessing before their eyes and said: 'Go, fly where you came from!' Though the fire burnt well, it took a long time until the thick Bible was destroyed. Jacob watched the fire closely, and finally he said: 'Now I am free.' After a final prayer, the group went back to church. This was the first and only time I witnessed the burning of objects related to evil spirits.

A similar case occurred in the EPC 'of Ghana': Peter T. (22)[28] was an EPC member from the Adivieyi Dome clan of Blengo and was confirmed in 1988. He only had a basic education and did not learn a particular profession, but earned his living through farming. His mother was a member of the EPC church choir and joined the new EPC after the secession. His father, who had died several years earlier, had also belonged to the EPC, but had not been a serious Christian and had given *dzo* to his son. Peter told me that shortly after his confirmation he joined a group of men from different clans and villages, both young and old, who met in the cemetery on Wednesday evenings. He learned to draw a circle around himself and, once a light had appeared, to invoke spirits. They called on all sorts of demons, dead people, wild animals, and also some handsome giants. The leader of the spirits was a man with very bushy eyebrows which touched the grey hair on his head. Once the spirits were there, the men present danced the 'robot dance' – a dance resembling the movements of Michael Jackson on video-films. Peter was assigned to a spirit called *Hard* and was taught to close one eye and recite the sentence '*Dadi me no na kame o*' ('A cat does not stay in a rope'). Then he could see any place he wanted to. In any country appearing before his mind – he saw America and England – he saw shops filled with goods such as bicycles, watches and television sets. *Hard* taught him how 'to convert these goods into the demonic world' (that is, to bring them under the control of Satan) by sprinkling lavender water on the ground whenever he saw a shop. In this way, anybody who bought these objects would be tied to the Devil because the things would exert a destructive influence on their buyers. Subsequently, the goods could only be used to the glory of Satan. Nobody would ever know that Peter had spoiled these objects because he did his work 'in the spiritual', invisible to the naked eye. Only those who are in the Spirit of God are able to detect such misdeeds.

Peter and his colleagues also invoked spirits in the *ametsiava* cemetery where they met their spiritual wives (fallen angels) with whom they feasted to the sound of babies crying in the night. Peter had a spiritual wife as well, but he never slept with her. Here, he and his comrades received money to spread around town. Anyone picking up these coins would soon start losing money. This money would be spiritually stolen from purses and used to buy 'British Dry Gin' for the men feasting with the female demons. If children picked up such a coin, the Devil would be able to suck their blood (through the intermediation of *adze*) and this blood would be used to produce the demons' favourite drink: Johnny Walker. Some of Peter's older colleagues borrowed large amounts of money from people and only returned 10 per cent of the amount without the lender becoming aware of being cheated.

Once, when Peter saw an American shop in his mind's eye and was just about to sprinkle lavender water on the ground to spoil the goods, he suddenly noticed heavy smoke. When he asked his spirit master about this incident, *Hard* told him that they were unable to attack that shop because it was protected by another power. Peter's spiritual wife told him that such a fire could be seen in various places and that it indicated the power of the Christian God and his son 'small boy' (it was taboo to mention the name of Jesus). When Peter inquired further about this power, his wife arranged for him to be taken to a church service. He was taken there in a cage borrowed from the witches and carried by a hawk. The cage looked like the one in *The Head of Medusa*, a film revealing exactly what was going on in the demonic world. When he reached the church service – which he attended as an invisible spirit – he saw that there was a heavy fire burning when the Christians were singing. Although this fire did not hurt the Christians, he and the demons accompanying him could not approach it and had to retreat. This made him think.

Apart from the ability to 'convert' goods to Satan's realm, Peter could hurt and overcome any person he wished, could make someone fall off a bike or squeeze a person's soul between his toes – a practice usually employed in the context of sacrificing a chicken – thereby killing them. Once, he almost killed his mother in this way because he was annoyed with her for giving him too small a piece of meat. At the last moment, something (after conversion he thought it was God) told him not to do this. When involved in the demonic world, he regarded other human beings as chickens. He respected nobody. Once he made an old lady fall over just for fun. However, when he boasted about this in the demonic world, another demon claimed that he had been responsible for the woman's fall, contributing to Peter's confusion. The spirits became annoyed with him and he in turn refused to attend their meetings any longer.

Peter was converted by the Reverend Hope from the Great Commission Church who burned all the magical objects he possessed. Later, Peter realised that this Spiritual church was still making use of objects such as candles and incense, and since this could still link people to Satan, he preferred to attend another church that relied on the Bible alone. Finally, in December 1991 he joined the EPC 'of Ghana', and since becoming 'born-again', his life had changed: he had become apprenticed to a carpenter, was at peace with himself and no longer hated people, but instead helped them get rid of their links with the demonic world. Shortly after having testified about his involvement with demons during a healing and deliverance meeting, he even became part of the Prayer Force.

Of course, these three cases could be regarded as expressions of individual psychopathological disturbances. But like all those discussed in the two previous sections, these cases were constructed as testimonies and exposed in the framework of Pentecostalism, so it has to be assumed that they resonate with ideas shared by a significant group of people. Indeed, it seems that a growing number of young people (many still students) are involved in the practice of calling upon spirits in the cemetery and of dealing with occult forces from India, and *Mami Water* spirits.[29] Members of Agbelengor and the EPC 'of Ghana' state that these new occult forces have recently become a problem, comparable to or even worse than *adze*. While *adze* attacks are the chief problem of middle-aged women, among the young in Agbelengor, and above all among the EPC 'of Ghana', possession by these new forces is an important topic of conversation.

The testimonies of Jacob and Peter (and in fact many similar ones) were given in public and in this way, their personal experiences in the spiritual world were turned into revelations about what is going on in the realm of Satan. And Felicia, though not 'coming out' with her story, related her experiences to the pastors, who considered them to be revelations (in the same way as Blumhardt regarded Gottliebin Dittus's account to be a window on the satanic realm). In turn, such revelations have become a topic of conversation for many other people who have not personally been involved with these new spirits. Thus, by representing personal experiences as revelations of truth, these experiences are transformed into shared narratives which are part of a popular culture addressing existential concerns in people's lives. These narratives can be approached as 'collective fantasies', a term describing a complex of partly hidden, highly affective fantasy images which are usually developed 'in response to some urgent need, to widespread feelings of alienation, when older normative structures have broken down while alternative structures fail to command people's allegiance' (Thoden van Velzen and Van Wetering 1988: 8; see also Thoden van Velzen 1995). Collective fantasies usually expose ideas in the framework of an 'imaginary world' and often employ the 'realm of darkness' in order to express and clarify existential conflicts.

Significantly, in contrast to cases of people seeking separation from their families, in the cases treated in this section this separation was not the aim, but rather a point of departure. Felicia lived away from her family in Accra and was involved with European men, Jacob refused to take over his grandfather's *dzo* and sought individual powers without his family being aware of it, and Peter, though living with his mother, was so detached from human beings that he only wanted to harm them (including his mother). In short, these three young people were, at least to some extent, independent and individualised.

Pursuit of money and power is the main theme in all three cases. Felicia wanted to become rich and own a car like her European masters. She enjoyed dressing up and having a love affair with a white man. However, for whatever reason, she began to feel uncertain and even guilty about these pleasures. Her desires, and to some extent her actual lifestyle, appeared to her to be a manifestation of *Mami Water* possession. This spirit, which only became popular in Ghana in the twentieth century, represents the temptations of modern life. *Mami Water* has become a culturally accepted (and thus shared and meaningful) image allowing people to deal with the desire for money and sex, or, more precisely, money through sex. As also revealed in Jacob's account, these spirits are thought to sleep with human beings and make them rich in return. However, the condition for receiving wealth is the neglect of sexual relations with human beings and ultimately of marriage and procreation. Felicia appeared to struggle with this problem in her life: should she go on sleeping with Europeans and receive a comparatively large amount of money or should she follow the ideal of her society and obtain a husband and children? She was eventually forced to give up her involvement with Europeans because of psychological troubles. This made her turn to Agbelengor for help and realise that in the past her life had been dominated by Satan's evil spirits. But she was still trapped in a conflict between desire and guilt, oscillating, as it were, between Satan's temptations and the knowledge that it was wrong to follow him. She felt permeable to all sorts of spirits who could take control of her and cause her to harm others as if she were a witch. Turning back to her family was no realistic option: her relatives did not understand her and she did not want to be involved with the paternal family *trɔ* or to serve Wuve, to whom she was linked through her mother. Ultimately, she wished to go on from where she felt stuck and lead her own life in the big city, free from the powers of darkness; that is, able to control her desires so that there was no need for her to attribute other people's troubles to her own bad thoughts. This was what she expected from her treatment in Agbelengor.

Felicia's experience of desire for money and sex and her guilt feelings about it cannot be dismissed as merely an individual problem. Rather, her state signals a general problem with individualism which engages many others, especially young women. Indeed currently, *Mami Water* attacks are considered to have become a source of widespread trouble. For many girls and women – especially if they want to survive in the city, but to some extent also if they stay at home – sex with well-to-do and often elderly men is one of the very few ways of making money to pay for school fees and/or to buy beautiful, highly desired objects. The relationship between money, sexuality and the family is however not only a problem for young women but also for wider groups in society who would like to be rich and independent from their families and feel that they are tied to them at the same time. This ambivalence is crucial to the lives of many who turn to Pentecostal churches.

Unlike Felicia, disturbed by the *Mami Water* spirit *after* having given in to her desire for money, the two young men became actively involved with spirits *in order* to get money and other powers. They strove to overcome not only poverty, like Felicia, but also time and space. And they wanted powers to harm and control their peers as well as other people whom they were required to respect according to gerontocratic hierarchy; for instance superiors such as the principal of Jacob's school or old people like the woman Peter caused to fall over. In their efforts, neither relied on traditional *dzo*. While Jacob actually rejected it, Peter supplemented his father's *dzo* with other powers. Though in many respects the new spirits, which the two young men possessed, could achieve similar things to traditional *dzo*, enabling people to vanish and appear elsewhere, making money and controlling others, these new spirits were different in that their sphere of influence was the whole world. Jacob received his powers from India. Significantly, although the contact could also have been made through a local *Mami Water* priestess (there are many on the coast near Lomé), it was through his Indian spirits that Jacob became linked to *Mami Water*. This emphasises the global nature of *Mami Water* spirits, who are said to dispose of all sorts of Western luxury goods produced in their realm under the sea. Furthermore, Jacob was able to communicate with anyone anywhere in the world. In the same way Peter could travel to America and England in spirit form and gaze at Western luxury goods.

No doubt the two young men's active invitation of these spirits was an expression of their desire to go beyond the limitations of their local life and operate on a global scale. They wanted to be strong, rich, influential and see the world (ideals that had earlier enticed young men to become Christians). As in the case of Felicia, their desire to escape the limitations of local conditions is not merely idiosyncratic, but rather culturally significant. To escape obligations to obey elders, the poverty of everyday life and also the boredom of the familiar is the wish of many young people, especially men. It not only motivates some to seek their luck in large African cities or even in the West, but also occupies a great number unable to make the step. Rather than actually travelling to the West, they watch Western (horror) videos which are shown wherever electricity is available, and go there in spirit. These spiritual travels amount to more than mere mimesis of physical travel: back home 'in the physical' those who have travelled in spirit not only relate what they saw in the Western world, they also claim to have looked behind the surface of 'the physical'. Through their spiritual travels the true nature of things is revealed to them. After conversion, this knowledge enables them to present themselves as eye-witness reporters of the realm of Satan and gain the prestige of knowing what is really going on in the world. On the basis of this knowledge, Peter was able to become a member of the Prayer Force after his own deliverance. His accounts of how he and the demons 'converted' goods into devilish products even led the leaders to advise church members to pray over objects bought, in order to neutralise the destructive, satanic power dwelling within them (see Meyer 1997a).

Note that neither Jacob nor Peter called upon or wished to be freed from spirits because of sickness, as is the case when a trɔ seeks to possess someone or when adze attacks a relative. Their main reason for discarding the spirits was a feeling of loneliness and the growing realisation that the spirit of God was stronger than their own occult forces. Both said that they quickly became annoyed with people and irritated by them. Significantly, in contrast to Felicia, who made money through sex, Jacob and Peter made money at the expense of it. They abstained from sexual relationships with spiritual or physical women and this emphasises their detachment and individualisation. Prior to their deliverance, Jacob felt touched by the young girl praying for him, while Peter became worried about having wished to kill his own mother. Their dilemma was this: should they be rich, powerful and active on a global scale, but alone; or should they be in the company of friends and have contacts with girls, but be poor and more or less confined to the local world? In the course of their conversion, during which they had to burn all magical objects, they came to regard these options in terms of the dualism between the Devil and God. However, in my view, this does not mean that they dismissed all the desires that had driven them to engage with the new spirits. The fact that they both chose to attend a church which claimed to have the power of God, a power which they experienced as stronger than that of Satan, indicates that they still sought a sort of compromise: an acceptable moral individualism allowing them to be modern subjects open to the world and at the same time not lonely, extremely egoistic or harmful to their neighbours.

## HUMAN–SPIRIT RELATIONS IN THE CONTEXT OF PENTECOSTALISM

In the previous sections different forms of human–spirit relations – priesthood, witchcraft (experienced through attacks), and the involvement with new, foreign, occult forces – have been encountered. From a Pentecostal point of view, these three forms of human–spirit relations are all considered to be manifestations of satanic forces. Those experiencing these relationships (or fearing they might become involved in them) all eventually wished to be delivered from these 'evil spirits' invading their personal spirits. To understand the appeal of Pentecostalism, it is thus necessary not to limit oneself to the study of the positive side of human–spirit relations, i.e. possession, but also to consider its negation, i.e. exorcism. The term 'possession' is used here in a very broad sense, namely to refer to a person's active or passive, deliberate or unwilling, involvement with a spirit.[30] Through exorcism performed in the framework of deliverance prayers, possession by evil spirits is reversed and replaced by possession with the Holy Spirit. This sequence, in the course of which 'heathens', or more often mission-church Christians, are turned into Pentecostals, is discussed below.

The anthropological literature on 'spirit possession' in Africa is vast. While there are numerous studies of (neo-)traditional forms of 'spirit possession',[31] research on Christianity in Africa has resulted in comparatively few studies focusing on this phenomenon (but see Barrington-Ward 1978; Lee 1969: 152ff; Schoffeleers 1985; Sundkler 1961; Ter Haar 1992; Van Binsbergen 1979; Welbourne 1969). As outlined in the Introduction, an important objective of this study is to establish a link between the hitherto more or less separate fields of research on African 'traditional religion' on the one hand, and Christianity on the other. People's continuing concern with the boundary between 'heathendom' and Christianity and their involvement in the dialectics of possession and exorcism requires students of Christianity in Africa to examine these dialectics closely.

To begin with possession: the most fascinating aspect of this phenomenon appears to be its opposition to a modern concept of man as master of his own life, as a monad locked up within himself, for it represents an individual as open and susceptible to forces from outside. Taking this as a point of departure, Kramer (1987) has developed an intriguing perspective on spirit possession in Africa in which he attempts to 'translate' this phenomenon into Western discourse, rather than exoticising it. Inspired by Lienhardt's attempt to 'translate' Dinka cosmology into a modern Western language, he makes use of the Latin term *passiones*, which denotes the inverse aspect of action: a person's notion of being moved (*ergriffen*), filled (*erfüllt*) or possessed (*besessen*). This conceptualisation takes as a starting point the specific experience of the possessed as being dominated by external forces. Understood in this way, spirits are images of *passiones* and in turn these images are conceptualised as active sources of the *passiones* they illustrate. By experiencing themselves as passive recipients of active spirits who seek embodiment through their human hosts, the possessed acknowledge the existence of an Other within themselves. This Other, which often confounds established definitions of identity and accepted forms of thought and behaviour, articulates itself in the state of possession. Put differently, for Kramer, possession is mimesis, an expression of the realistic representation of the cultural Other dwelling within an individual.

Kramer sees spirit possession as a manifestation of the tension between society's power to make its members share values and norms and people's incapacity or unwillingness fully to identify with them. Spirit possession not only expresses, but also attempts to resolve, the tension between the social and the individual. Making use of various cases from all over the African continent, Kramer shows how possession allows for a person's internal differentiation and, at the same time, external mimetic representation of the Other. Possession by an Other enables an individual both to differentiate his or her identity and to represent publicly forces countering established social values and norms. This articulation of the Other may occur in contexts as diverse as healing, art or entertainment and include any statement ranging from mere play to social critique.

Kramer did not develop his views on spirit possession on the basis of intensive fieldwork, but mainly through consulting existing literature on the phenomenon. Though he has rightly been criticised for his 'structuralist distance' from spirit possession, which caused him to omit real people from his analysis (Lambek 1994), his approach appears extremely helpful in understanding particular cases of spirit possession.[32] Seeing possession as the presence of an Other within an individual, which allows for both the differentiation of identity and the external expression of difference, is illuminating and highly sensitising. It certainly pushes the anthropological discussion beyond any simplistic conceptualisation of spirit possession in terms of instrumental reason, a view which conceptualises possession as people's attempt to achieve certain goals (Lewis 1971); in terms of an individualist concept of the self, a view which fails to take into account the social context in which possession occurs (Bourguignon 1973, 1976); in terms of an individual biological need, a view which plays down culture (Goodman 1988); or in terms of an enactment of childhood traumas, a view which locates problems giving rise to possession in a distant (unconscious) past (Obeyesekere 1990).

What can this view contribute to a better understanding of phenomena of possession as presented in this chapter? Those discussed did not see themselves as masters of their own lives, but rather as dominated by satanic forces. The evil spirits from which they were eventually delivered were conceptualised as separate entities besetting their personal spirit. Put in terms of Kramer's view, to those concerned, these evil spirits were images of *passiones*, external forces taking hold of their personal spirit and representing an Other within themselves. Yet our cases are more complicated than forms of spirit possession occurring outside the Christian context. For there are two Others: the satanic and the divine. The satanic Other, incorporated in a person's spirit and, at certain times, embodied in the context of deliverance prayers or encountered in dreams, has to be chased away and replaced by a divine Other, the Holy Spirit, after a period of spiritual war. In order to take this complexity into account, we have to consider the differences between these two forms of possession and assess the specific tensions with social norms and values expressed through each of them. In this way we shall be able to discern the crucial ambivalences and conflicts with which people grapple in such circumstances.

It is significant that while EPC leaders maintain that Christians are to cross the boundary between 'heathendom' and Christianity once and for all through baptism and/or confirmation, Pentecostal churches allow for possession by evil spirits; i.e. for the presence of heathendom in their members' personal spirit. This evokes the question as to why the heathen Other is so prominent in these people. Why does this Other not simply disappear? What are the ideas, attitudes and desires that people express through the incorporation of this Other?

In the context of possession by old gods and witchcraft, in both cases the Other invading a person's spirit stood for the links with his or (more usually) her family. In the first case these links were characterised as integrative. Christians' continued experience of possession by family gods shows that they have not been able to dissociate themselves definitely from family ties. Despite the fact that, ever since its introduction among the Ewe, Christianity has stood for the emphasis on the nuclear family and the neglect of blood ties connecting people with their extended families, many Christian converts seem to find it difficult to endorse this. Possession by an old family god expresses the individually experienced incapacity to live up to the ideal Christian way of life. This sense of failure stems from the subjectively experienced tension between the demands of two worlds. By incorporating the spirit of the family as an Other into their personal spirit, Christians are able to express their doubts regarding the possibility of realising the ideal Christian way of life. This echoes the situation they live in: many Christians are still materially, socially and emotionally so much involved with and dependent upon their families that the step towards the Christian ideal cannot be made easily, though it is attractive. To them, the family is a highly ambivalent factor. Ambivalent, because incorporation into the modern capitalist world economy gives rise to a double-sided stance towards the family: 'while the individualization of the market economy promotes the rupture of reciprocal obligations, the hardships created by colonial capitalism often require the mobilization of reciprocal aid for survival' (Mullings 1984: 160). It is exactly this tension between the individual and the family that is addressed by Pentecostalism.

In the case of witchcraft attacks, family ties are depicted as potentially destructive. The witch invading a person's spirit is the hostile Other causing harm. This Other, however, is not expressed through mimesis, as in the case of old gods, but merely encountered in dreams. Those concerned do not identify with the spirit as such, but remain at a distance. They have internalised the enemy who continuously threatens their activities. I understand this specific possession experience as an expression of the tension between the social norm of sharing one's wealth with relatives – we noted earlier that this was one of the main imperatives of Ewe ethics sanctioned by the belief that envious relatives would attack more prosperous blood relatives with witchcraft – and the wish to keep things for oneself. All victims of witchcraft attributed the sickness and troubles which befell them or their children to envy on the part of a relative who begrudged them their progress in life. Here again, an ambivalent stance towards the family turns into a source of fear for egoistic individuals unwilling to share with others. From this perspective, the fear of witchcraft attacks expresses a feeling of uneasiness with the Christian imperative to focus solely on one's own nuclear family and the even more outspoken Pentecostal imperative to separate oneself from blood links, though this is appealing and, indeed, simultaneously longed for.

It is significant that the tension between the ideal of Christian nuclear family life and individualisation on the one hand, and the experience of being connected with, and vulnerable to, paternal and maternal kin on the other is, above all, experienced by Christian women (both prior to and after their turn towards a Pentecostal church). This reflects their position in society. In practice, many women have been obliged to assume a very independent position. Though the Christian nuclear family may be an ideal for many, matters of marriage and parenthood often do not match this ideal. Many husbands have migrated to faraway places and fail to send money home regularly for child maintenance. Other men stay at home, but are unable to muster sufficient funds to provide their wives with 'chop money' or to pay for school fees and other matters of importance to their children. In addition, many men have to cope with relatives' demands for financial support. Wives who live in the husband's family house therefore often experience conflicts between their own concerns and those of their in-laws, who prevent their sons from supporting wife and children. All this thwarts the realisation of nuclear family life propagated by the EPC, and even more so by churches such as Agbelengor and the EPC 'of Ghana'. In this situation, women are to a large extent obliged to maintain themselves and their offspring through their own agricultural work and trade. In order to make ends meet, many women have to rely on their own paternal families for shelter or assistance in times of need. Often, this situation results in physical and psychological problems which the women are inclined to attribute to evil familial spirits.

Through possession by a family god, a woman can confirm her ties to her own family. In the case of witchcraft attacks, women can thematise their negative feelings about their actual independence, in many cases forced upon them by the conditions sketched above. This independence arouses in them a sense of uneasiness about their own achievements (or their attempts in this direction) which in turn makes them attribute their experiences of misfortune to this very independence. Thus, possession by evil spirits allows women to articulate what they cannot easily express in daily life. Since these evil spirits are conceptualised as different from their personal spirits, women can maintain the ideal of Christian family life and, at the same time, expose its actual shortcomings in the possessive mode. I agree with Boddy's view (1989) that spirit possession may allow women to express a counter-discourse which creates a critical meta-statement on daily life, without having to assume the responsibility of individual authorship for its articulation. Like Boddy and others (for example, see Kapferer 1991: 128ff; Masquelier 1995; Van Binsbergen 1979: 101), I reject any simplistic view of spirit possession as an attempt by women to gain compensation through religion for what they are unable to gain in society, to realise psychologically what they cannot attain socially. This view, whose most famous representative is I. M. Lewis (1971), fails to take into account the most crucial feature of possession; namely the possessed's idea that there is an Other acting through their body. While the expression of critique is confined to this Other, the female hosts continue to oscillate between the ideal way of life and its actual shortcomings, thereby keeping apart social norms and values, and individual difficulties in fully endorsing them.

In cases of possession occurring in the framework of Pentecostalism this is even more evident than in cases of possession occurring outside this framework. Here there is no possession ritual which encourages women temporarily to merge with the spirit possessing them. Rather, the spirit expresses itself at the moment when it is being chased away, that is, in a situation of spiritual war between the Devil and God, resulting in possession by the Holy Spirit. This implies that the spirits possessing women are not only conceptualised as external forces, as is the case in possession cults, but also that the expression of spirits in ritual is extremely limited: women are only allowed to embody them at the cost of being denounced as vehicles of Satan. In this way, the boundary between Christian ideal and actual reality is reconfirmed and any openly and positively articulated critique of the ideal evoked by the reality is avoided. Before delving further into the issue of exorcism, let us turn to young people's involvement with the new spirits.

Involvement with *Mami Water*, as manifested in the case of Felicia (and to a lesser extent in that of Jacob), was experienced as a typical instance of possession in the sense of the experience of otherness present within oneself. In contrast to family gods, *Mami Water* spirits are of foreign origin. In his study on *Mami Water* possession in (West) Africa, Wendl (1991) has shown that these spirits became increasingly popular in the post-independence era. In his view (which owes much to Kramer), people possessed by this spirit articulate their own individuality in terms of their relationship to the beautiful, prosperous white lady living at the bottom of the sea. In this ritual of possession they expose aspects of themselves which they are unable to express in their daily lives. By embodying the spirit of *Mami Water*, the possessed ritually appropriate the Western world as they understand it. As Drewal (1988) has shown, *Mami Water* can be understood as an image mediating the African perception of contact between Africans and the foreigners they were and are involved with economically. It represents an attempt to make sense of these contacts. Thus *Mami Water* spirits, understood as part of global culture, act as mediators between the global and the local. Possession by these spirits allows their hosts to cope with tensions arising between local conditions of life which may entail poverty and the imposition of an identity experienced as too limited to allow for individual expression, and the vast range of possibilities suggested by observing Western people and objects in the real world or in a cinema.

This also holds true for the image of the mermaid held by Christians, a group Wendl and Drewal do not deal with explicitly. For Peki Christians, *Mami Water* mediates between the local and the global. However, by classifying these spirits – which as we saw were not only female but also male – as agents of the Devil, Christians approach them from a negative stance. In the case of Felicia, the Other represented by this spirit enabled the young woman to express her continuing desire for money and sex, which is at odds with both traditional and Christian ideals of life. Through the incorporation of this strange and foreign spirit, she could expose an aspect of herself which she was unable to reveal in her daily life as a maid in a European family and, later, as a member of Agbelengor. Thus, as in the case of possession by familial spirits, the boundary between ideal Christian life and actual desire is again maintained by associating the former with God and the latter with the Devil. Nevertheless, by admitting the possibility of *Mami Water* possession, Pentecostalism enables young people to express their longing for mundane pleasure without the necessity of taking responsibility for subscribing to it.

The acquisition of Indian spirits and new *dzo* differs from *Mami Water* possession, in that people actually ask for these new spirits rather than being overwhelmed by them. Nevertheless, these spirits are also perceived as external forces enabling their owner to do certain things which he is unable to do by himself. Moreover, these new spirits share with *Mami Water* the fact that they are foreign and that they link their owners with global culture. Indeed, through the acquisition of these spirits, young men are able to express their desire for power and pleasure beyond the limits of local life. In this case, too, this wish is allowed to be expressed in the framework of Pentecostalism under the condition that it is attributed to the Devil.

It is not surprising that new spirits are of special concern to young people. Many of them live in a situation that is a long way from their aspirations and, therefore, they try to bridge the gap between reality and ideal through personal efforts. To them, new foreign spirits provide access to the modern, global world; showing once again that modernity and spirits go hand in hand.

The final matter raised in this chapter is that of desire for possession by the Holy Spirit. Since Pentecostalism offers not only the possibility of experiencing possession by evil forces, but also delivers people from them through the Holy Spirit, we now have to ask which Other is represented by the Holy Spirit. Significantly, someone possessed by the Spirit – the ideal 'born-again' Christian – is also conceptualised as being overwhelmed by an external force, rather than as a self-conscious individual devoting herself or himself fully to God. Pentecostalism, often suspected of promoting Westernisation, does not however promote a Western concept which teaches people to understand spirits as aspects of themselves. Pentecostals regard not only evil spirits, but also the divine, as the presence of an Other. Yet this Other does not have an iconography and specificity of its own; rather, it enables the evil Other which besets a person's spirit to reveal itself. The divine Other is merely a mirror image of the old gods and witches as well as of *Mami Water*, Indian spirits, modern *dzo*, etc. But it is much less specific than these various personifications of evil. The Holy Spirit is a generalised antipode to the differentiated domain of Satan. It is a power separating an individual from any links, thereby isolating them. The Other represented by the Holy Spirit does not stand for itself, but is simply a negation of the satanic. Therefore, the experience of otherness through possession by the Holy Spirit leaves much less room for individual differentiation and external embodiment, that is, the expression of specific ideas, attitudes or desires, than possession by one evil spirit or another. Paradoxically, though the Holy Spirit individualises by severing links with the satanic, it does not allow for individual specificity. Possession by the Holy Spirit alone is comparatively dull and meaningless. It lacks the appeal of the possibility of articulating forbidden ideas, wishes and desires or to express facets of oneself evoking one's actual life conditions.

The appeal of Pentecostalism does not lie in people's definitive possession by the Holy Spirit and the individualisation brought about by God as such, but rather in the whole sequence of steps leading to this last stage.[33] By creating room for the expression of the satanic in the context of deliverance, Pentecostals are allowed to enact otherwise forbidden or muted aspects of themselves. While the old EPC propagates subsumption of all evil spirits under the category of the Devil and asks its followers to cross the boundary between 'heathendom' and Christianity once and for all, Pentecostals, though allegedly 'born again', are continuously brought back

into contact with what they have left behind. Put differently, while the old
EPC represents conversion as a linear process which comes to an end,
churches like Agbelengor and the EPC 'of Ghana' conceptualise conversion
in circular terms and allow their members to move back and forth through
the sequence of possession by evil spirits, exorcism and possession by the
Holy Spirit. In this way, members are enabled to mediate between indigenous attitudes towards spirits and Christianity and at the same time face
the contradiction that their daily lives actually fit with neither indigenous
nor modern nor Christian ideals. Pentecostalism, rather than representing a
safe haven of modern religion in which people permanently remain, enables
people to move back and forth between the way of life they (wish to) have
left behind and the one to which they aspire. Pentecostalism provides a
bridge between individualistic and family-centred concerns and allows
people to express and reflect upon the tensions between both. By offering a
discourse and ritual practices pertaining to demons, believers are enabled to
thematise continuously the 'old'.

# EPILOGUE: MODERNITY, TIME
# AND THE DEVIL

Throughout this study we have gained insights into the ways in which the Peki Ewe experience the modernising and globalising processes into which they became incorporated through the activities of the NMG. It has become clear that they can neither be described as alienated victims overwhelmed by Western impact, nor as clones of their colonial masters. By converting to Christianity, many Ewe expressed their wish to change. They felt attracted to missionary Pietism because it offered the material and conceptual means by which to dissociate themselves from what became represented as 'backward', 'traditional' society. Ewe Christians distinguished themselves through their dress, their houses and furniture. They understood themselves to be 'civilised' people far ahead of the rest; and this symbolic distance was expressed, for instance, by the Christian village called *Kpodzi* ('on the hill'). Though converts shared the same time and space with their non-Christian fellows, they separated themselves by adopting a temporalising device. In their view, 'traditional' society was a matter of the past. Christianity, by contrast, was a matter of the future. By employing this device, Christians transposed themselves into a different time from that for non-Christians, thereby denying they all actually shared the same time and space.

Striving for future progress through a rupture with 'traditional' society is not only the defining feature of the Pietist understanding of conversion, but at the same time the pre-eminent characteristic of modernity (e.g., Luig and Behrend 1994; Habermas 1986; Tourraine 1995). Indeed, as Weber has shown in his work on the Protestant ethic (1984 [1920]), in modern society essential ideas of Reformed Protestantism have become secularised. The wish to move on and on towards future pleasures, both in heaven and preferably in this world as well, and continuously to improve one's living conditions rather than remain part of 'traditional' society, entailed Ewe Christians' pursuit of individualism and independence from the family. This orientation has remained a defining feature of Ewe Christianity throughout the twentieth century: education, the Christian religion and 'civilisation' were conceptualised as synonyms. The Pentecostal churches, which oppose the routinisation of Christianity and instigated a wave of 'second christianisation' (Schoffeleers 1985), promote individualism with even greater emphasis than the mission churches. By emphasising salvation and individual spiritual and material progress in life, they clearly qualify as agents of modernisation. This stance is aptly captured in the popular Ghanian picture *Judgement Day* (see frontispiece), which depicts heaven as the ultimate fulfilment of modernity, and contrasts it with the Devil's hellfire.

But why then, to return to the central question posed in the Introduction, did demons have more influence on people's interests in their daily lives than the High God, and why do they continue to do so? What did and do they need the image of the Devil for? Clearly, orientation towards the future is only one side of the Christian project. The popularity of the image of the Devil and demons in past and present reveals the inability of Ewe Christians merely to look forward. While, in Christian Ewe discourse, God is associated with the future, the Devil is associated with the past. It is important to realise that Ewe Christians have recourse to 'time' as an epistemological category which enables them to draw a rift between 'us' and 'them', 'now' and 'then', 'modern' and 'traditional' and, of course, 'God' and the 'Devil'. The latter is considered Lord of all heathen gods and spirits, defined as matters of the 'past' and from which Christians should dissociate themselves. Though evidently this 'past' is the product of a temporalising device which denies Ewe religion's actual 'coevalness' (Fabian 1983) with Christianity, it is conceptualised as existing somewhere back in time, yet still threatening to manifest itself in Christian lives.

This use of time as a discursive strategy relates to actual experiences of conflicts in the present. Ewe Christians' actual life conditions are characterised by a simultaneous entanglement in 'old' and 'new' ways of life. Despite their wish to proceed, they were and still are linked to their families socially, economically and spatially. This relatedness can be expressed by possession through spirits believed to operate through blood ties. It appears that in the early days of Christianity among the Ewe, this link could only be re-experienced through 'backsliding'. Currently, it can also be experienced in the Pentecostal churches, which in contrast to mission churches, offer a discourse on evil spirits and allow for the occurrence of possession. In this way, albeit temporarily and in the confines of the framework of the deliverance ritual, converts can return to what they represent as their 'past' and from which they eventually want to dissociate themselves. This ritualised return to and subsequent rupture from the 'past' is a need evoked by people's wish to proceed, for, as we have seen, modernity for Ewe Christians is highly ambivalent because it entails a great number of conflicts both within and between people.

It is a commonplace that Pentecostalism is especially appealing to people involved in modernisation processes and longing for upward social mobility. Much less clear is where Pentecostal churches' ability to create a discursive and ritual space with which to address and enact converts' ambivalent experiences with modernity originates. Johannesen (1994) has shown that the God who is addressed and, as it were, constructed through Pentecostal prayer does not link his followers to any particular community, but only confirms their individuality. He argues that Pentecostalism can cross cultural boundaries and easily spread throughout the world because it has no cultural specificity. This argument is confirmed by the cases studied in this book. We saw that on the level of doctrine, there was virtually no difference between the EPC and the neutrally oriented churches that seceded from the former. Rather than offering new *content*, Pentecostalism offers converts above all a new, more adequate *form* through which to express their ideas. It is because this form as such is culturally unspecific that Pentecostalism could become a vehicle to express a grassroots Ewe appropriation of Pietist Protestantism. Yet – and here I wish to carry Johannesen's argument a step further – precisely because the most important thing Pentecostalism offers is a new form, it can easily become localised and thus express a highly culturally-specific version of Christianity. In the cases studied here, this cultural specificity is mainly produced through converts' emphasis on the image of the Devil, for it is Satan, not God, who provides a channel through which they may return to the local conditions that they (strive to) leave behind. Put differently, the evolution of a local, indigenised version of missionary Pietism depends a great deal on the image of the Devil, which enables converts to discursively and ritually return to what they conceive of as their 'past'. There is therefore some truth in Sundkler's statement that '[t]he syncretistic sect becomes the bridge over which Africans are brought back to heathendom' (1961: 297). Pentecostal churches do indeed provide a bridge between Ewe religion and Christianity. But it is not a one-way bridge leading people back to the 'old' ways so that they can, to use another metaphor employed by Sundkler, pour new wine into old wine skins. Rather, as we saw, Pentecostalism provides a bridge over which it is possible to move back and forth and thereby to thematise modernity's ambivalences.

These findings may throw some new light on the relationship between religion and modernity in general and the popularity of Pentecostalism in particular outside the confines of the cases studied here. There are clear indications that Pentecostalism is on the increase all over Africa (Gifford 1993; Marshall 1991, 1993; Marshall-Fratani 1998; Maxwell 1998; Schoffeleers 1985; Ter Haar 1992; Van Dijk 1992, 1997) and that, in contrast to groups trying to come to terms with African tradition and to reconcile new and old ideas in order to develop a genuinely African synthesis, Pentecostals' main cry is to 'Make a complete break with the past'. This cry should certainly not be mistaken as a plea to simply forget and proceed. After all, in the course of the deliverance ritual, people are held to realise that they are in the grip of 'the past', which is represented as fearful, out of control, and that they can only gain control over their individual lives – and, indeed, become modern individuals – by re-enacting in a ritual context all the links connecting them with that 'past' (i.e. their actual connections with, for instance, their extended family). In contrast to mission-church Christ-ianity, Pentecostalism does not only speak modernity's language of progress and development but, at the same time, offers the possibility of approaching in the safe context of deliverance what people seek to leave behind but which still disturbs them. Although here matters of immediate relevance to people's lives in the present are falsely recast as belonging to an occult 'past', for those striving to run away from this 'past', and from all the social ties and obligations entailed, it is at least possible to express the ambivalences which accompany their wish to progress and 'become modern'. It is therefore worthwhile to consider that Pentecostalism's popularity in Africa may to some extent be due to the fact that it offers a ritual space and an imaginary language to deal with the demons which are cast out in the process of modernity's constitution, but which continue to haunt people the more they try to progress.

Certainly people's concern with the demons of the 'past' urges us to move beyond a non-dialectical conceptualisation of modernity in terms of mere progress, involving a continuous rupture with the past which still informs much social science discourse. Rather than assuming that modernity goes hand in hand with disenchantment, it is important to realise that the images of the Devil and demons, and the discursive and experiential possi-bilities that ensue, are an immediate product of the encounter between Western missionaries and African converts, not a relict of 'traditional' society. Modernity and enchantment should certainly not be conceptualised in terms of an opposition in which the latter is represented as a sign of 'backwardness'. As both belong together, the emergence of occult images at particular times and places should alert us to the fact that their study may reveal crucial contradictions, about which dominant, 'progressive' discourses keep silent, but which are at the heart of modernity and teach us something about the ambiguity of progress.

# APPENDIX: POPULATION STATISTICS

Table 7: Population Peki (1901–84)

| Date | Population |
|------|------------|
| 1901 | 2889 |
| 1911 | 2991 |
| 1921 | 5686 |
| 1931 | 5726 |
| 1948 | 7700 |
| 1960 | 10414 |
| 1970 | 11850 |
| 1984 | 15488 |

NB: Peki here stands for the places Avetile (also called Abanase), Tsame (also written Chome or Tsamey) Blengo, Afeviwofe (also written Avefiave or Apevepe), Dzogbati (also written Jobati or Dzobati), Wudome, and Dzake (also written Jaka, Jakai, Dzakai). These statistics were computed on the basis of the following sources:

'Report on the Census of the Gold Coast Colony 1901', National Archives of Ghana, ADM 5/2/2
'Census of the Population 1911', National Archives of Ghana, ADM 5/2/3
'Returns of Native Population in Towns and Villages of the Colony and the Districts of Ashanti 1911', National Archives of Ghana, ADM 5/2/4
'Census Report 1921 for the Gold Coast Colony, Ashanti, the Northern Territories and the Mandated Area of Togoland' (1923), National Archives of Ghana, ADM 5/2/5
'Returns of the African Population in the Towns and Villages of the Colony, Ashanti, the Northern Territories and the Mandates of Togoland' (1925), National Archives of Ghana, ADM 5/2/6
'Appendices Containing Comparative Return and General Statistics of the 1931 Census' (1932), Ghana National Archives, ADM 5/2/8
'The Gold Coast Population Census 1948. Reports and Tables', National Archives of Ghana, ADM 5/2/9
'1960 Population Census of Ghana', Ghana National Archives, ADM 5/2/10 and 11
'1970 Population Census of Ghana. Vol. 1. The Gazetter. Alphabetical List of Localities with Population, Number of Houses and Main Source of Water Supply', Census Office Accra, 1973
'1984 Population Census of Ghana. The Gazetter 2. Alphabetical List of Localities with Statistics on Population, Number of Houses and Main Source of Water Supply', Statistical Service Accra, 1987

# NOTES

1. Within the last decade, Pentecostalism has become increasingly popular all over Ghana. Existing Pentecostal churches, such as the Church of Pentecost, the Apostolic Church and the Assemblies of God, grew. Recently also a newer type of Pentecostalism has developed, especially in urban areas. These churches, which are called 'charismatic' and imply organisations such as Dr Mensa Otabil's International Central Gospel Church, Bishop Duncan William's Christian Action Faith Ministries and Rev. Sam K. Ankrah's International Bible Worship Centre, have been founded by Ghanaians in the mid-1980s. These organisations are strongly internationally oriented and have branches in Europe and the USA (see Gifford 1994; Van Dijk 1997). In Peki, as in other rural areas, there were no 'charismatic' churches of the latter type. However, a clear distinction between these two types is problematic, because both have much in common and influence each other. The EPC 'of Ghana', in particular (see below), is clearly inspired by both.

2. While knowledge of the doctrine of the mission churches was assumed, the 'syncretistic' mixture of Christianity and African traditional religion that characterised African independent churches (Sundkler 1961) intrigued students of religion in Africa. From the 1960s onwards, the study of these churches became their main objective. Missiologists tried to understand why an increasing number of members of mission churches were attracted to the indigenous counterparts (for example, Baëta 1962, 1968; Barrett 1968; Hayward 1963; and Oosthuizen 1968). Anthropologists, who considered independent churches and movements as expressions of the ruptures caused by the transition from traditional to modern society, expected to gain insight into the phenomenon of social change (for concise overviews of this vast field of study in Africa see Fabian 1979, 1981; Fernandez 1964, 1978; Jules-Rosette 1994; Werbner 1977). From the mid-1970s onwards, independent churches gradually ceased to be considered as deviations from churchly and societal order and came to be regarded as representations of a more or less authentic African form of Christianity. A good example of an anthropological study in this vein is Fernandez (1982). For missiological works in this line see Baëta (1968), Mbiti (1979), Taylor (1963), the authors contributing to Dickson and Ellingworth (1970) and Fasholé-Luke et al. (1978).

   By contrast, mission churches were not regarded as interesting objects of study. They were held to be mere replicas of their Western models and to 'preserve essentially the same form and content in Africa that they have in Europe' (Bond et al. 1979: 2). However, this assumption lacks an empirical basis and often goes hand in hand with the notion of mission church members as passive victims of missionary domination (see Dzobo 1988a; Kapenzi 1979;

Opoku 1978; and Shorter 1973: 24). Only a few studies take into account the African contribution to the Africanisation of Christianity (Hastings 1994; Pirouet 1978; Rieber 1979; Sanneh 1983). For a discussion of Africanisation stimulated by missionaries see Kaplan (1986) and Oosthuizen (1972).

3. There are, of course, historical studies of mission churches, that is those African churches that resulted from the activities of nineteenth-century missionaries and became 'independent' in the course of the twentieth century. They are often written by clergymen and show how Christianity was implanted by particular societies in certain regions (for example, Ajayi 1965; Crampton 1979; Kalu 1980. For a bibliography see Clarke 1986: 250–5). For histories of Ghanaian mission churches see Bartels (1965) on the Methodist Church and Smith (1966) on the Presbyterian Church of Ghana.

4. For a reflection on a more appropriate anthropological conceptualisation of missionaries see the articles in Stipe (1980).

5. But see for instance Comaroff and Comoraff (1991), Huber (1988), Pels (1993) and Wright (1971).

6. In the German original text Weber wrote '*Praktisch* aber kam und kommt es darauf an' (1985 [1922]: 255, my emphasis). This was translated as 'The decisive consideration was and remains'. In my view, the elimination of the term 'praktisch' (that is, 'practically' or 'in practice') from the English translation is unfortunate, because in this way the contrast suggested by Weber between theological theory and the everyday praxis of believers is less evident.

7. In my view Appiah's suggestion is a more satisfactory attempt to deal with the problem of eurocentrism implied in the concept of modernity than talking about 'modernities' (e.g. Comaroff and Comaroff 1993). The latter option appears somewhat deceitful in that it particularises local apprehensions of modernity while still maintaining the concept as such. In this way the necessity of intercultural dialogue for a more adequate understanding of modernity as propagated by Appiah is not acknowledged.

8. For historical work on the NMG see, for example, Adick 1980; Buhler 1979; Grau 1964, 1968; Knoll 1982; Müller 1904; Schlunk 1936; and Ustorf 1986a.

9. A great deal has been written on the Ewe. For a bibliography which also lists short pieces in missionary and German colonial magazines, see Zielnica (1976). Of special interest to the present study is ethnographic work on Ewe religion (for example, De Surgy 1985, 1988a, 1988b, 1990; Fiawoo 1958; Pazzi 1980; Rivière 1980, 1981; and Spieth 1906, 1911), Ewe history (Amenumey 1964, 1986; Greene 1996a), and Ewe society and culture (for example, Agblemayon 1984; Asamoa 1971; Ellis 1970 [1890]; Manoukian 1952; Medeiros 1984a; Nukunya 1969; Verdon 1979, 1982, 1983; Ward 1949; and Westermann 1935). In other chapters I refer to more books and articles pertaining to the Ewe. To my knowledge there is no detailed study on how Ewe people in a local congregation experience Christianity. Debrunner (1965) wrote about the French-speaking counterpart of the EPC, the *Église Évangélique du Togo* (EET). His study examines the EET's position in colonial society and does not deal with local congregations.

## CHAPTER 1

1. They called themselves *Weme* [inhabitants of valleys]. To the missionary L. Wolf this name must have sounded as he transcribed, *Eibe*. Only the later missionaries, who standardised the language of the *Weme*, decided to write *Ewe*.The term *dukɔ* (pl. *dukɔwo*) has been translated as 'tribe' [*Stamm*] by the missionaries (Spieth 1906). However, 'tribe' is an inadequate translation because this term,

by somehow evoking the exotic, suggests a fundamental difference between European and African forms of nineteenth-century political organisation without actually comparing them. The term 'state', which designates a complex political organisation, is more appropriate.

2. The Ewe states were to pay their tributes to the Akwamu with men (Wilks 1975: 68). The European traders especially appreciated slaves from Krepe. They were sold at high prices and considered to be good plantation workers. For Akwamu control over Krepe see also Wilks (1975: 57, 74, 210–11).

3. The king, in turn, had to pay tribute to the Asante and guarantee them safe passage on the trade roads through Krepe and Asante. This, however, was not always undertaken and Asare notes that the Akwamu frequently tried to cheat Asante traders (1973: 45).

4. With the British abolition of the slave trade, Akwamu not only lost an important source of income, but also the foundation of its rule over Krepe: 'The slave trade was ... the area in which both Akwamu and Peki had vested interest and so had meaningful exploitation of other Krepe states' (ibid.: 63).

5. According to Asare, the paramount stool of Peki was founded somewhere in the second half of the eighteenth century; that is, during the Akwamu rule (1973: 142).

6. Spieth collected his material mainly in the 1880s and 1890s. He preferred to speak to older people from Ho and other *duwo* in that area who were not yet Christianised. Though his ethnographic work is evidently biased by his own ideas and values (see Chapter 3), his study is of great importance because as well as translations it contains many Ewe transcriptions of his informants' statements.

7. In Ghana, the English term used to refer to the spokesmen of royal persons is 'linguist' (the Ewe term *tsiame* derives from the Akan term *okyeame*).

8. Though the term *fome* is often used for the bilateral family, it can also designate the 'patrilineage'.

9. In the course of time, the presents that were to be given to the bride and the parents-in-law changed. An account of the marriage customs in Peki can be found in the MB of 1868 (ibid: 957-58). At that time, the groom had to present money (cowries), yam and palm wine. See also Spieth (1906: 738).

10. Between 1896 and 1903 Peki was part of the newly created Kwahu and Krepi District with its administrative headquarters at Anum. After 1903 this district was abolished and Peki was again administered through the DC at Akuse (Welman 1925: 22).

11. Ghana National Archives, file ADM 11/1/188, Report Balstone, 20.1.1910.

12. For cases documenting the troubles between Peki and Awudome, and Peki and Boso/Anum, see Ghana National Archives, files ADM 11/1/1127, ADM 11/1/1714, ADM 11/1/1757 respectively.

13. Stab 7, 1025–27/1, *Schulbericht der Station Peki von 1913*, C. Spiess 10.1.1914.

14. In her study on the economic position of women in Tsito, Bukh (1979) has shown that the introduction of cocoa farming increased the burden of subsistence production on women. Her study contains the results of her detailed research on the role of women in the changing economic situation of Awudome Tsito. Tsito is a small town very close to Peki where very similar economic developments had taken place. My own interviews confirm her findings.

15. Public Record Office, London, CO-98-23, 'Report on the Agricultural Department for the year 1913', p. 63.

16. The missionaries preferred to build their stations on a hill, because they considered the climate at that altitude healthier than down in the villages. In this

way, *Kpodzi* became the Ewe expression for Christian village. *Kpodzi* not only denotes the spatial, but also the symbolic difference between the 'heathen' and the Christian village. Even if there was no hill on which a Christian village could be built, it was called *Kpodzi*, thereby expressing its state of development. For a more detailed description of the semantics of *Kpodzi* see Meyer 1997. On Christian villages in Ghana see also Isichei (1995: 167ff) and Mobley (1970: 73ff).

17. Mallet had a European name because he was one of the 'slave children' bought freedom by the mission (on the NMG's policy of buying so-called 'slave children' see Ustorf 1986b). As usual, the required amount had been provided by a German donor – in Mallet's case a Pietist pastor from Bremen – whose name was subsequently given to the child. Slave traders had caught him when he was a little boy playing in the bush near his home on the Agu mountain. When he was offered for sale at the slave market at Keta, the NMG missionaries redeemed him. Mallet died in 1912. During his service in Peki he baptised more than 1,000 people, consecrated 120 marriages and conducted 300 burials (Stab 7, 1025–26/6, *Brief* Freyburger 8.2.1912).

18. In 1933 the first church order (*Kirchenordnung*) for the Protestant Ewe church in Togo and Gold Coast appeared. The difference between the church order (the German translation appeared in 1935) and previous congregational orders is that the former contains long passages about church organisation and hierarchical order. B. Gutmann, a missionary famous for his propagation of an authentic African Christianity with African forms of expression, criticised this church order because it imposed a European presbyterian form of organisation upon an African Church. Moreover, he found that it was too loosely based on the Gospel and that the hierarchical order was over-emphasised. The mission inspector Schreiber defended the church order against this critique. He made clear that the NMG understood the Christianisation of the Ewe as 'a sharp break with their previous religion and thus in many respects also with their customs (*'Volkstum'*)'. Making use of a war metaphor, he presented the church order as a 'fight' or 'field-service order' that was appropriate in the conditions prevailing at that time in that place (Schreiber 1937: 4; original in German, my translation). The congregational orders of 1876 and 1909 can be found in Stab 7, 1025–43/2 and 43/4.

19. Since, in this respect, the orders of 1876 and 1909 are virtually identical, in the following I refer to the earlier version. The translations from German are mine.

20. Firing guns, singing, drumming and dancing on the occasion of funerals was meant to please the deceased and let him depart smoothly to the place of the dead [*tsiefe*, see Chapter 3].

21. Stab 7, 1025, 5/31, *Aufsatz Nyalemegbe zur Lehrerkonferenz Agu-Palime*, 22.3.1916.

22. Originally, the NMG did not present itself as a national mission society. But when Togo became a German colony in 1884, the NMG accommodated to the new political and economic circumstances and cooperated as much as possible with the government officials.

23. Stab 7, 1025, 5/31, Essay Emmanuel Buama, 23.10.1909, original in English.

24. For a similar conclusion regarding the appeal of the Jehovah's Witnesses in the Serenje District (Zambia) see Long (1972). Through being able to neglect matrilineal kinship obligations, converts were able to accumulate wealth gained through cash-crop farming. See also Seur's re-study (1992).

25. However, against most diseases traditional medicines were more effective. Until the end of the nineteenth century, when Western tropical medicine made a big

step forward through the discovery of quinine as a prophylactic against malaria, the missionaries had unscientific medical ideas. They clung to 'humoral pathology' which explained sickness as resulting from an unbalanced relationship between bodily fluids, and demanded therapies such as blood-letting and purging (Fischer 1991). Their medical ideas thus were not necessarily superior to those of the Ewe, and were less well adapted to tropical circumstances.

26. In his account of the Peki congregation, Spieth stated that the largest group of Christians were children, followed by young and then old men (MB 1892: 12). He did not even mention women.

27. But compare the case of the north Cameroonian women converting to Islam, studied by Van Santen (1993), where this step improved their situation. For a similar observation with regard to women's attraction to the Basel Mission on the Gold Coast see Isichei 1995. 169. There is a need for more comparative studies on women and missions (see Bowie et al. 1993).

28. Ghana National Archives, file ADM 11/1/648, 'Petition by the Peki State Council for submission to his Excellency, the Governor, praying for the incorporation of the Peki State and the mandated sphere of British Togoland,' 13.9.1930.

29. One such case occurred in Peki in 1910 when people wanted to destool the *fiagã* Kwadzo Dei VII. Initially, the DC, who was called to investigate the case, interfered to support the *fiagã*, because he supposed that the real source of people's disagreement lay in the *fiagã*'s implementation of the British ordinance to bring trade goods to the British ports (Ghana National Archives, file ADM 11/1/188, letter of Philipps 26.5.1910). Later the administration agreed to the installation of a new chief, but opposed the fact that he, being a Christian, refused to perform the required rituals (ibid., file ADM 11/1/188, Report DC, 20.9.1911).

30. Usually, farmers spent much of the money gained on the purchase of British products. Nimako stated that between 1900 and 1950 50 per cent of the cocoa revenues in the Gold Coast were spent on consumer goods of European origin (1991: 33).

31. Apart from houses, people invested their money in the education of their children. Though Peki was noted for a relatively high interest in girls' education, parents put much more of their funds into the education of boys. Whereas girls usually left school after Standard 3 (six school years), many boys went on until Standard 7 (ten school years). This was in line with the situation on the labour market which reserved most white collar jobs for men. Women could only become teachers and nurses but, once married, were supposed to become housewives.

32. In many respects, the economic development of Peki was similar to that of Tsito described by Kaufert (1976) and Bukh (1979). One important difference is that in the 1940s cocoa production declined in Peki, while it continued to develop in Tsito. For that reason, massive migration occurred earlier in Peki than in Tsito. For statistics on migration from Tsito see Kaufert (ibid.: 82) and Bukh (ibid.: 33). To my knowledge, apart from these studies, there is no general study of socioeconomic developments among the Ghanaian inland Ewe. For a study of rural economic growth in the Lower Volta area (between Akuse and Ada) from 1954 until 1967 see Lawson (1972).

33. Well into the 1940s, an educated married woman was not expected to work outside the house, which was reason enough for many of them to delay marriage. In Peki, a teacher by the name of Josephine A. Mensah was the first woman to be allowed to return to work after the birth of her children, in 1947. This illustrates that (as in the West) until then it was virtually impossible for educated women to remain financially independent once they were married.

34. Among them were Paul Wiegräbe whom I have met several times since 1989 and Frieda Schindelin whom I met once in 1991.

35. I was told in Peki that if a girl became pregnant before her confirmation, she and her family became subject to the same public contempt as girls who were pregnant before having undergone the puberty rites. This contempt also involved throwing stones at the girl's family home.

36. For a very short description of this church see Barrett (1968: 88). There are also two texts written by the Yota mission leader in 1926 and 1930 in Stab 7, 1025–44/1. In these texts he explained the tenets of his church's doctrine to the NMG by reference to numerous biblical passages.

37. They were only welcome from the 1960s when the NMG was sufficiently transformed to allow for a true partnership with the EPC.

38. Funerals organised in Peki have much in common with modern Akan funerals described by Arhin (1994). On Ewe funeral customs see also Fiawoo et al. (1978) who explored the hardships and advantages involved in the performance of traditional funeral customs in modern times.

## CHAPTER 2

1. The society was also active in India (until around 1850) and among the Maori in New Zealand. But after 1850 the Ewe mission became more or less its only target.

2. For a description of the missionary training in Basel see Eiselen (1986) and Vogelsanger (1977); for the BM's Pietist premises see Dah (1983: 7–25).

3. When the missionaries in Africa were shown to be in good health, they were allowed to get married. In the first decades, the committee chose wives for these missionaries and sent them to Africa. These women did not receive a special training. Gradually, more missionaries chose their wives when on leave in Germany. In Pietist discourse, a wife was called *Gehülfin* (helper) of the husband who was considered the head of the family. From 1884 onwards, the mission also recruited women – often teachers – to work in Africa as 'sisters'. They ran the Kindergarten for the small children. It would be interesting to study this group of missionary's wives and sisters and find out what motivated them to go to Africa. For a pioneering collection of articles about women missionaries and the effects of missions on women see Bowie et al. (1993).

4. The Pietist Awakening, however, was not limited to this area. For a study of how this movement coped with the economic, social, political and religious changes in Westfalen see Mooser (1989), and among mine-workers in the Ruhrgebiet see Greschat (1985).

5. For an overview of the political, social and economic changes occurring in nineteenth-century Germany, see for example Kulischer (1929: 417–541), Nipperdey (1983, 1991) and Stearns (1967).

6. What made working for wages attractive was the practice of *Realteilung* that was common in Württemberg: land would be inherited in equal parts by all children, thereby dividing it up into smaller and smaller pieces of land which could not then feed a whole family. This peculiar practice of inheritance, which provided all family members with a piece of land, enhanced people's attachment to the land, though at the same time depriving them of full subsistence farming.

7. For an overview see Andresen (1988: 97ff) and Wallmann (1990). On Württemberg Pietism's political quietism see Fulbrook (1983: 100–52).

8. In Württemberg, the established church was more in favour of the Pietists than in other German states. Due to the influence of the eighteenth century theologian J. A. Bengel, many Württemberg church leaders propagated a Pietist theology,

but there were still tensions between Pietists and church officials. In the nineteenth century Pietism clearly was a minority movement as only 7–8 per cent of the adult population of Württemberg belonged to them (Trautwein, quoted in Scharfe 1980: 132).

9. For the history of the theme of the broad and narrow path in Christian iconography, see Knippenberg (1981), Rooijakkers (1993: 18–26) and Scharfe (1990).

10. Literary critics have judged *The Pilgrim's Progress* one of the highlights of English literature, and there are innumerable literary, psychological and theological analyses of the work. In the context of this study, however, we shall refer to *The Pilgrim's Progress* only in order to develop a clearer idea of the relationship between the Bible, images, and their relationship to the world, crucial in the production of the worldview of the Pietist missionaries. Comaroff and Comaroff occasionally refer to *The Pilgrim's Progress* and state that missionaries active among the Tswana conceptualised the spiritual journey through the wilderness to the celestial city and their imperial overland travels in analogous terms (1991: 173).

11. In the framework of this study it is impossible to give an exhaustive overview of the development of Christian diabology. It has been worked out in detail in an impressive work by Russell on images and concepts of the Devil from antiquity until primitive Christianity (1988a), in the early Christian tradition (1987), in the Middle Ages (1988b) and in the modern world (1986); a summary is presented elsewhere (1989). Other important overviews have been provided by, for example, Roskoff (1987 [1869]), Carus (1991 [1900]), di Nola (1990), Messadié (1993: 349ff), O'Grady (1989), Rooijakkers et al. (1994).

12. Calvin, though he believed in the existence of the Devil and demons as personal beings and considered them as powerful as Luther did, paid much less attention to diabology – a theoretical stance that did not, however, prevent him from personally convicting witches in Geneva (Russell 1986: 47ff; Tavard 1981: 297).

13. The Dutch theologian Balthazar Bekker was the first to refute the traditional image of the Devil on the basis of his exegetical analysis of the New Testament. According to Bekker, belief in the Devil and demons was a 'pagan' and Jewish 'superstition' that had mistakenly been emphasised and brought into Christianity by Catholicism and was bad for Christian faith; therefore good, rational Protestants had to read the Bible without being influenced by 'superstitions' of their time and the traditional diabology (Bekker 1691: 4, 290; Carus 1991 [1900]: 318ff; Vogt 1913: 1156). This position, though generally attacked by both Protestant and Catholic churches, was shared and developed further by certain enlightened thinkers. On the 'abolition' of the Devil in the eighteenth century see Kittsteiner (1993).

14. For a discussion of the use of the term and its association with popular religion see Bächtold-Stäubli (1927: 64ff).

15. See Nipperdey (1983: 423–49, 1991: 468–507) on the various factions within the Protestant field.

16. Schleiermacher found that 'the representation of the devil, as it developed among us, is so unmaintainable that one cannot expect anybody to be convinced of its truth' (1861: 209; original in German, my translation).

17. Whereas formerly, Pietists had not openly propagated their ideas – and had been called 'Die Stillen im Lande' ('the silent ones in the country') – the Awakened ideas were now actively spread through numerous booklets. This nineteenth-century Awakened literature has been described and analysed by Müller-Salget (1984); see also the more descriptive articles by Bischoff-Luithlen (1965/69), Brecht (1985), Schäferjohann-Bursian (1989). It is striking that none of these

authors discussed the image of *The Broad and the Narrow Path* (to be found in many homes), and Bunyan's classic (so widely read in Awakened circles up to the present).

18. This sketch is based on Zündel's (1979) biography of his friend Blumhardt which appeared for the first time shortly after his death in 1880 and has been reprinted many times.

19. A booklet called *Die Heilung von Kranken durch Glaubensgebet* (Blumhardt n.d.) also provides the names of six other Awakened healers.

20. Moreover, in nineteenth-century Württemberg many customs and *rites de passage* were still performed by peasants (ibid.). For a description of nineteenth-century popular religion in the neighbouring Schwaben, see Pfister (1924), and for Germany in general see Buschan (n.d.). From these sources it is clear that popular religion and culture was very much alive in rural areas in nineteenth-century Germany.

21. Lehmann (1980) has shown that segregation from the 'sinful world', and the community of born-again believers were characteristic features of Pietism from its beginnings. This stance also applied to nineteenth-century Awakened Pietism (Scharfe 1980).

## CHAPTER 3

1. Some Catholic mission societies also adhered to the notion of untranslatability. Although they translated the message into the vernacular they retained certain Hebrew or Latin biblical terms, especially for God (see Rafael 1988: 28-9; Ranger 1989: 134-7).

2. As early as 1658 a Spanish Capucin priest had translated some common prayers, the creed, and a catechism into the language of Allada ('Slave Coast', later part of Dahomey), an area culturally and linguistically related to the Ewe (Law 1991: 48). I found no indication that the NMG missionaries knew or made use of this text. They learned the Ewe language from scratch and realised only in the course of their studies that the Ewe dialects they encountered were part of a greater complex (see Schlegel's *Schlüssel zur Ewe-Sprache*, MB 1892: 107). The Spanish Capucins not only worked on a language similar to Ewe, they also adopted similar mission strategies, such as propagating worship of the supreme God *Mawu* and denouncing the local dominant snake cult as satanic (Law 1991: 65-9).

3. These missionaries were Steinemann (he developed a list with 4,600 words); Reindorf (a native of the West Indies working for the Basler Mission who in 1885 drew up a word list containing 5,700 terms); and Knüsli, with a word list of 11,000 (after his death the work was completed by his wife and Däuble) (MB 1906: 13-14). For a list of linguistic works by NMG missionaries, see Schreiber (1936: 263ff).

4. For a list of Christian literature produced by the mission, see Schreiber (1936: 261ff).

5. The fact that the first ethnographies of the Ewe were written by missionaries forms a problem for current research: 'Les travaux des ethnologues de la génération de Westermann pèsent sur la recherche ultérieure ...' (Medeiros 1984c: 9). On the other hand, researchers cannot do without these works because they are the only written source of Ewe tradition. The works of Spieth and Westermann are cited in virtually all ethnographic work on the Ewe. In order to assess the value and validity of these sources, it would be necessary to undertake a detailed study of the missionary bias and their way of selecting the data presented. To my knowledge no such study exists.

6. In his ethnographic work Spieth abstained from religious statements, though his missionary bias is evident. Though in the framework of ethnography, he did not depict non-Christian Ewe as servants of the Devil who had to be reconciled with God, he and his colleagues did just this in the MB.

7. There are two terms for god: *trɔ̃* and *vodu*. The latter seems to be used more frequently by eastern Ewe people (in Togo), the former is preferred by western Ewe people (among whom the missionaries of the Norddeutsche Mission began their work and among whom I conducted my own research). For a discussion of the historical origins of both terms, see Rivière (1981: 26ff).

8. According to Spieth it was not clear whether *aklama* and *dzɔgbe* designated the same spiritual entity. It seems that many people used the terms interchangeably (1906: 511).

9. The Ewe acquire one of their names from the name of the weekday on which they were born.

10. Up until now, the ethnography of Ewe religion suffers from this bias. Rivière (1980), Pazzi (1980), and De Surgy (for example, 1988a) attempt to systematise the 'traditional' ideas of the Ewe (as if they were not yet influenced by the presence of Christianity), in order to discover the laws guiding Ewe religious representations. They confine themselves to producing blueprints of 'traditional' religion, rather than delving into people's actual religious praxis.

11. The etymology of the term is not certain. Motte (quoted in Tossou 1988: 152), Rivière (1981: 16) and Dzobo (1976: 5ff) gave different possible etymologies, while Parrinder stated that the etymology of *Mawu* is 'dubious': 'it is lost in the mists of time' (1950: 231).

12. It is an important characteristic of missionary ethnography that it tended to neglect the female dimension in indigenous notions of *Mawu*, which the Ewe expressed with *Sodza*, and also mentioned a general *Mawu*.

13. *Sogble Sodza* is the equivalent of the Fon's notion of the dual male-female *Lesa-Mawu* (De Surgy 1988a: 95).

14. Spieth presented a transcription and translation of an informant's account of the yam festival celebrated at Ho. From my own research I found that it was celebrated in the same way in Peki.

15. Goody (1975) has rightly stressed that it is wrong to conceptualise African religions as a static phenomenon. He therefore criticised the (Durkheimian) view of religion as a preserving, reactionary element in social structure. He argued that new cults spread as a result of internal contradictions of religious activities. Ewe cults were certainly as dynamic as those of the Asante and LoDogaa mentioned by him.

16. A man could become a *dzotɔ* by choice. If he had enough money he could consult a *dzotɔ* and buy some of his *dzo*. This involved swearing an oath of silence about how the *dzo* was made. For a detailed description of how *dzo* was bought see Spieth (1906: 526–8, 1911: 276ff).

17. According to some of Spieth's informants there was friction between the *dzotɔwo* and the *trɔ̃* priests, but others described their relationship as cooperative. Many *trɔ̃* priests owned *dzo*. It seems that rivalry gradually developed between these two groups of religious specialists (see Chapter 4).

18. Also, outside the confines of Christianity, notions about *Mawu* changed (Greene 1996b).

19. *Vasede fifia la wobada Mawunyala kple trɔ̃* (Until now they mess up Mawu's word with the *trɔ̃*). The evangelist made this remark after having described the case of a priestess who claimed that the Christian *Mawu* was the brother of the *trɔ̃wo* (Stab 7, 1025–56/8, Taviefe 1905, p. 126).

20. I did not find any description of the Lord's Supper in the missionaries' accounts. My information about it comes from interviews with old people in Peki.
21. As early as 1857, the missionaries translated the Devil as *abosam* (then written *abosã*) (Schlegel 1857: 163). It is interesting that the NMG missionaries translated 'Devil' as *Abosam* and not as *Legba*. The latter term designates a statue representing a guardian god and was used for 'Devil' in Anexo (a south-eastern Ewe group in Togo) where Catholic missions were active. That the NMG chose the term *Abosam* mirrors its close connection with western Ewe groups who had been heavily influenced by the Akan language and culture.
22. *Bayi* is another Akan term for witchcraft and is used to refer to female witches that do harm in their own families. This concept is the equivalent to the Ewe term *adze*.
23. For instance, the native teacher Schlegel had the following idea about the Hereafter: 'Like the Israelites, he (Schlegel) assumed the existence of two underworlds, Hades and Gehenna or hell. The good and bad were in Hades and waited for the last day, Judgement day. On that day the separation would take place: the good would then go to heaven, the bad to hell' (MB 1890: 7). Many Christians still hold this view today. Others, however, believe that each person is judged individually after death and sent to either heaven or hell.
24. At the same time, however, he avoided using Ewe terms associated with ritual because he feared that this might confirm 'heathen' ideas and 'overgrow' the Christian content. He thought that by avoiding those loaded terms Christian contents could be transferred into Ewe word forms.

## CHAPTER 4

1. This concern with life is pointedly expressed in the standard morning exchange of greetings: '*Wole agbea?*' (Are you alive?). '*E, mele agbe*' (Yes, I am alive). Dzobo, an Ewe philosopher and the moderator of the EPC, based his new African theology on this affirmation of life. He called it *Meleagbe* theology (see Chapter 5).
2. Though references to *aklama vɔ̃* and *dzɔgbe vɔ̃* can be found in several places in Spieth (1906, for instance: 486–7), it remains unclear how these entities affected a person. For this reason I am unable to deal further with these entities.
3. If a dead person confessed to have been a *dzoƒuametɔ* while being interrogated by a *dzevusi* (a priest communicating with the dead), the body was exhumed and burned or buried in the bush. Such a case is documented in an Ewe evangelist's report, who was against burning the body because, according to him, the man would be punished by God anyway (Stab 7, 1025–56/8: 539, Aname 1903).
4. Some of my non-Christian informants told me that witchcraft was a miraculous power able to bring about great things such as Western technological inventions, but that it was also sometimes used destructively. In their view, Africans mainly used it in the latter way. I would not be surprised if, even prior to direct contacts with European technology, *adze* also had this positive dimension. Hallen and Sodipo (1986) have shown that the Yoruba concept *aje*, which had much in common with the Ewe's *adze*, did have this positive aspect.
5. In his handbook Spieth presented a report about *adze* among the Ho people (1906: 544–5) and short statements about *adze* by other informants (ibid.: 682, 724, 832, 850, 906). In his book on the Ewe religion he devoted three pages to this phenomenon (1911: 299ff). According to him, the Ewe's concept and practice of witchcraft originated from the Yoruba.
6. The suffix *tɔ* expresses a possessive relationship between the noun preceding it and the object or person referred to. The term *adzetɔ*, which is usually translated

as 'witch', thus literally describes a person as 'owner of *adze*'. Another expression employed by my own informants was 'he or she *has* witchcraft'. The Ewe expression was *adze le asi*, witchcraft is in his/her hand (the Ewe express active ownership by saying that something is in somebody's hand).

7. Crick (1982) rightly pointed out that the incorporation of different concepts into the category 'witchcraft' reduces particular cultures' conceptual structures into a Western definition of the phenomenon. He therefore advocated dropping the use of the term 'witchcraft' and employing the local terms instead. I agree that it is indeed misleading to translate different phenomena with the same European term and that in order to gain insight into the phenomenon it is important to investigate local concepts carefully. On the other hand, it does not seem to me fruitful to deal with culture in a particularistic way. For cultural translation is not only the praxis of Western anthropologists; Africans themselves actually translate terms from one African language into another or into a European one, thereby establishing the similarity of phenomena occurring in different cultures. It seems to me that many of the concepts from different cultures brought together under the umbrella of 'witchcraft' do indeed have something in common. In one way or another, they are part of a discourse on power and wealth in inter-familial or inter-human relationships. Therefore, it is important to compare how people in different cultures deal with this problem. As a first step this project demands a careful analysis of the local terms translated as 'witchcraft'. On this basis they can then be compared with other local terms employed in another culture. For a discussion of terminology see also Geschiere (1997).

With regard to the question of how the Ewe define 'witchcraft', it can be said that in contrast to other African peoples, they attribute *adze* to envious people who want to bring down their luckier, prosperous, relatives. It is not that, as in the cases of many other African peoples, the wealthier fail to distribute their gains and are accused of witchcraft (e.g. Geschiere 1994, 1997 and Rowlands and Warnier 1988 with regard to Cameroon; and Ekholm Friedman 1993 with regard to Kongo). The Ewe thus thought of *adze* as a power motivated by envy, not greed. It was not the achievement of wealth that was considered problematic, but the jealousy it might trigger in poorer people if the rich failed to share with them. Thus, the Ewe and many other peoples associated 'witchcraft' with the well-to-do's failure to distribute riches.

8. The fact that it was difficult to restore human relationships distorted by *adze* and *dzo* does not imply that it was impossible to restore bonds among human beings *per se*. There was another form of *busu* or *nuvɔ̃*, *gu*, which could be counteracted by restoring the social relationships whose breakdown it had caused. Westermann described *do gu* (to commit *gu*) as violating accepted laws of mutual respect (1905a: 203). These rules, which people internalised in the course of their socialisation, regulated the behaviour of husbands and wives, and parents and children towards each other. Any violation of these rules would result in sickness which could only be cured by the performance of certain rites (*guɖeɖe*) in the course of which family relations were restored.

9. According to many reports the *dzotɔwo* were the most respected in town. The *trɔ̃* priests and even the chiefs 'by-and-by almost became their subordinates' (Stab 7, 1025–58/8: 126). For references, see for example Stab 7, 1025–56/8: 56, 106, 124, 127.

10. See Stab 7, 1025–56/8: 230, 256–57, 321.

11. I have found lists of new Peki converts who confessed with whom they had had sexual intercourse, which *trɔ̃* they had served and which *dzo* they had owned (Stab 7, 1025–56/8: 452–502). Among the *dzo* owned, the war *dzo* (*dzrapa*) and

protective *dzo* (*nuke*) were the most common. Such a *dzo* was owned by men in particular.

12. According to Spieth, the Ewe's desire for atonement was still more or less indirect and revealed itself through a dissatisfaction with Ewe religious practices (Spieth 1903b).

13. For example, see Stab 7, 1025–56/8: 209, 256, 507, 533, 534 for more indications.

14. Stab 7, 1025–56/3, letter of Mallet 14.2.1901. For another similar case see Stab 7, 1025–56/8: 137–38.

15. This council was founded in 1929, and it comprised the African Methodist Episcopal Zion Church, the English Church Mission, the Ewe Presbyterian Church, the Presbyterian Church of the Gold Coast and the Wesleyan Methodist Church. In 1934 the Salvation Army also became a member.

16. In the Ghana National Archives there is a file containing British administrators' discussions (during the 1930s) of how to deal with witchcraft. They debated the question as to whether witchcraft should be considered a crime, as Section 46 (23) of the Native Administration Ordinance stated. Whereas some found that witchcraft was non-existent and suggested prosecution of the accusers rather than the presumed offenders, others maintained that, since witchcraft was a reality to most inhabitants of the colony, it had to be considered a criminal offence (Ghana National Archives, ADM 11/1/886, 'Witchcraft'). The Provincial Council of Chiefs of the Central Province strongly opposed the suggestion that witchcraft should cease to be considered a crime (ADM 11/1/886, 'The Provincial Council of Chiefs, Western Province, 19.2.1931').

17. Tawia (1947) deals with the history of the church up to 1947 and does not give special emphasis to the war years. As far as school attendance during the war is concerned, Tawia states that it increased slightly in Peki against all expectations (ibid.: 15). This may be explained through the fact that, along with land becoming scarce and unsuitable for cocoa cultivation, young people had no valid alternative to education.

18. This also applies to missions active in Oceania (e.g. Howard 1996; Jolly 1996; Keane 1996).

19. It is not my intention here to discuss fully Horton's conversion thesis and its critics (e.g. Fisher 1973; Hefner 1993: 20ff; Ifeka-Moller 1974; Ikenga-Metuh 1987: 13–16; Ranger 1993); I will simply comment on certain points relevant in this context.

20. There is a great deal of literature on 'African ideas about God' (e.g. Booth 1979; Dickson and Ellingworth 1970; Dzobo 1976, 1981; Kibicho 1978; Parrinder 1950; Ryan 1980; Schoenaker and Trouwborst 1983; Smith 1950) and almost none regarding African ideas about the Devil.

21. In his reflections on what happens to the old religion once the Christian world religion becomes a social framework, Peel (1978: 451) mentioned the denunciation of deities as devils and the incorporation of elements of the old religion as two different possibilities. The case of the Ewe makes clear that these two possibilities do not exclude each other, but can occur simultaneously.

## CHAPTER 5

1. I discussed this conflict with several people, including the Reverend B. A. Y. Menka, one of the founders of Agbelengor; the late Reverend Annan, who was its pastor at Blengo during my first fieldwork in Peki in 1989; the Reverend Stanley Amedzro, son of Amedzro, the founder, and pastor of Agbelengor

during my second fieldwork; several church members; and the Reverend E. Y. Tawia, who was posted at Blengo when the split occurred. I also made use of the Blengo congregation diary (in which Tawia reported on the course of the conflict), a written history of Agbelengor (n.d.) and the draft of a constitution.

2. The term 'prayer group' (in Ewe, *gbedodoḍa hame*) was thus used to refer to spiritually oriented groups within Ghanaian Protestant mission churches long before it became a standing term to designate local manifestations of the international (neo-Pentecostal) Charismatic movement in the 1970s.

3. Almost all branches in the Buem District, which is inhabited by Akan speaking people, split away from Agbelengor and formed their own church in 1963 (*Brief History of the Lord's Pentecostal Church*, n.d.: 5).

4. People of this category were known as people with '*xɔsegbadza*', that is, people with 'a broad belief'. If such a person died, the family could pay the deceased's arrears and thereby obtain a Christian burial.

5. It was only possible to collect the material for this overview because of the generous assistance of G. F. Atiase, EPC catechist and secretary of the All Churches Prayer.

6. By virtue of their numerical importance alone these churches certainly became a factor which the mission churches had to take into consideration. Leferink (1985), a Catholic missionary, estimated that there were 400–500 independent churches in Ghana in 1985.

7. Unfortunately I have only been able to find a few scattered issues of this journal in the library of the Peki Seminary. Since the EPC does not keep archives it was impossible to consult the whole journal.

8. On the history of this hymn book see Wiegräbe (1989).

9. Yet even very strict pastors would have no objection against the Christian adaptation of the traditional Asante and Ewe chieftaincy stools, in which the traditional carved symbol in between the seat and the ground would be replaced with a Christian one. The image on the cover depicts an example of such a stool, which is on display in Reverend Tawia's living room.

10. Dzobo's interpretation of this sign is: 'Except if God dies I am not going to die.'

11. This way of dealing with prayer groups is typical of mission churches. In Ghana, the same occurred in the Presbyterian Church of Ghana. In the same way, the Catholic Church attempts to keep prayer groups under control by institution-alising the Charismatic Renewal.

12. In the Synod reports I found cases which clearly documented this. For instance, in 1985 in one congregation thirty-one members of the BSPF were baptised by immersion. The 'local session' obliged the dissenters 'to undergo six months course of study about the teaching and the faith of E.P. Church' (Synod Report 1985: 7).

13. The BSPF even printed a 'souvenir programme' (including the group's history) of this meeting which took place from 31 August to 4 September 1998. (Bible Study and Prayer Fellowship E.P. Church, Ghana. Ebenezer, 10th Anniversary Souvenir Programme and History).

14. As indicated, the statistical information concerning the EPC in Tables 3–5 refers to the Blengo congregation. I asked the leaders of the three churches to write down the names of those persons participating in each group, as well as their age, educational background and occupation. I established tables 3–5 on the basis of this information. Quite a few members participated in more than one group, but were counted only once.

15. The EPC also has a youth association, the CYB (Christian Youth Builders). In Peki this group still existed in 1989, but had broken up when I returned in 1992.

16. This age is not an arbitrary dividing line. In Peki, people below fifty are considered 'young' people who do not have much to say. People over fifty, however, can claim much more authority.

17. See for example, Baëta (1968), Mobley (1970: 110ff), Oosthuizen (1972: 308ff), Shorter (1973) and Fasholé-Luke et al. (1978). On African theologians' interest in Africanisation from the 1950s onwards see also Mudimbe (1988: 56ff).

18. For the concept of 'syncretism' see Sundkler (1961: 297). In his sense 'syncretistic' means 'not purely Christian'. For a similar view see also Barrett (1968), who applied the concept to all initiatives deviating from mission church Christianity, or Hastings' characterisation of 'village Christianity' (1979: 274). The term 'syncretism' has mainly been used in the framework of theories on 'acculturation' or 'culture contact' which aim to classify religious expressions along a continuum whose poles are 'traditional' and 'Western'. Used in this way, the term describes local versions of Christianity by reference to the origins of their elements. However, this 'mechanical assignation of cultural traits' (Peel 1968: 140) is of no help in understanding how the mixture termed 'syncretism' actually comes about and is conceived by African Christians themselves. Recently I have argued that rather than dismissing processes of religious mixture as 'syncretism', it is more appropriate to study how this mixture actually comes about (Meyer 1994).

19. This shift is confirmed by a recent survey by the 'Ghana Evangelism Committee' (1993). In the Volta Region, between 1982 and 1986, African independent churches (that is, so-called Spiritual churches) increased by 71%, whereas between 1987 and 1992 they increased by only 2%. By contrast, Pentecostal churches (represented in the Pentecostal Council) rose by 54% in the first and 43% in the second period (ibid.: 59). For Ghana as a whole these figures were 36% and 7% respectively for African independent churches, and 59% and 26% for Pentecostal churches (ibid.: 24). It should be noted that the category of African independent churches may also contain Pentecostal churches, because like Agbelengor, many hitherto African independent churches transformed themselves into Pentecostal ones (see also Gifford 1994: 241). Nationally, between 1987 and 1992, the number of Pentecostal churches grew by as much as 43% and that of African independent churches by only 16%. Growth rates of other types of churches also remain much less than the growth rate of Pentecostal churches (Christian Council churches: 16%; mission-related churches, such as Baptists and New Apostolic Churches: 16%; Seventh Day Adventists: 5%; and the Catholic Church: 4%) (ibid.: 21). I am most grateful to John Peel for sending me a copy of this survey.

## CHAPTER 6

1. Thus, in contrast to Western Christian doctrine (see Ter Haar 1992: 117–18), no linguistic distinction is made between a positive state of being 'filled with the Holy Spirit' and a negative state of being 'possessed by evil spirits'.

2. Small groups of people, the so-called prayer-cells, also meet every day for short prayers.

3. Since 1992 was a leap year, a year considered more dangerous than ordinary years, fasting was organised around 29 February.

4. In order to avoid the pouring of libation the church itself organises ceremonies such as 'outdooring'. Thus, it accepts that there is a need for rites of passage, but it gives them form in its own way.

5. However, members are warned that a dream that is thought to be sent by God

may also derive from Satan who is seeking to confuse them. In cases of doubt, people are to ask the advice of the pastor or a prophetess. Thus, though in principle dreams are considered true revelations of the divine, the possibility that they can mislead exists. In this way, pastor and prophetesses have authority to determine the truth of dreams.

6. The second deliverance I attended there was organised on a national level from 2–4 April 1992. It was announced on radio and television and attracted many buses from Accra and other faraway places with people feeling the need for prayers. This deliverance was very much a mass affair and it was hoped that the event would raise funds for the church. The preachers hardly touched anyone, but rather passed through the rows of people saying that the Holy Spirit was at work. The whole organisation was modelled on the 'Crusades' of the American preacher M. Cerullo in Nigeria which a delegation of Agbelengor leaders had attended. Later, some of the local pastors complained to me that such a mass occasion could not replace the more individual treatment provided during regular deliverance sessions taking place each Thursday.

7. Like Agbelengor, the new EPC also encourages members to group themselves into prayer cells.

8. War songs are also sung in the old EPC, but here these hymns do not form part of a particular ritual. Several hymns in the *Hadzigbale* evoke this trope (for example, 156: *Mienye dzifoasrafowo*, 'We are heavenly soldiers'; 157: *Miheyi ava dzidefotoe faa*, 'Go to war with courage'; 173: *Kristo f'asrafowo mido ta ŋgogbe*, 'Christ's soldiers, march ahead'). However, in contrast to the war songs of Agbelengor and the EPC 'of Ghana', in these hymns *Abosam* is not mentioned as such (though he is in many other hymns).

9. While he was still leader of the BSPF in the old EPC in Tsame he often had problems with the church leaders. In a speech during a deliverance service on 12 March 1992, Akudeka recalled that a pastor of the old EPC had told him not to behave like Jesus Christ himself. Akudeka, however, maintained that human beings should seek to resemble him and thus also to deliver people from demons.

10. In explaining why many families are cursed, Akudeka referred to Exodus 20: 5. According to this verse (a part of the Second Commandment) Jehovah is a jealous God who does not want his people to bow down before idols and will punish even the great grandchildren of those who do so. Since the ancestors of the Peki – and even older people still living – indulge(d) in idol worship, Akudeka argued that it is no surprise that there is a curse on many families. Some women did not agree with this argument and maintained that Jesus would be able to take away curses on families.

11. While possession by evil spirits as such is not considered shameful, possession by *adze* is.

12. Thoden van Velzen (1988, see also Thoden van Velzen and Van Wetering 1988) has shown that neo-traditional Puritan movements may emerge as a response to modernisation processes. The similarities between the Tanzanian Mazimu cult (Thoden van Velzen 1988: 228ff) and the churches described here are striking. It follows from Thoden van Velzen's description that Christianity is not the sole idiom able to express Puritan concerns. This topic would warrant further elaboration in the debate surrounding the relationship between globalisation and the rise of so-called religious fundamentalism. Up until now, the epithet 'fundamentalist' is used with regard to 'world religions'; neo-traditional fundamentalist movements have hardly been taken into account.

13. This also applies to 'traditional' healing among the Akan (see Twumasi 1979: 349-50; Appiah-Kubi 1981: 32-3).

## CHAPTER 7

1. Tawia told me that most of the Peki *trɔwo* had come to be neglected in the course of time. In some cases, the priests and priestesses had converted to Christianity, while in others, family elders had decided to bury or burn the family *trɔ* and the objects related to its worship. Tawia himself was responsible for the destruction of his family's *trɔ*, Dintri.

2. The Wuve priest had been dead a long time and nobody had been appointed in his place. The brother of the deceased priest performed a minimal number of rituals (such as cleaning Wuve's house on Fridays), but did not fulfil any further tasks. Moreover, there was no priestess through whom Wuve could speak. The situation had been the same for Amimli at Blengo. There was no priest and the last priestess had converted to the Church of Pentecost. However, since a number of deaths in the Adivieyi Dome clan (the clan in charge of Amimli in Blengo) were attributed to Amimli, who was supposed to be angry about being neglected, the clan elders installed a young boy as his priest. The boy's family compound contained the Amimli shrine. After some time they also recognised the new priestess and installed her as well. Amimli was also represented at Avetile, where there was no priest, but where the daughter of the late priest had been installed as priestess.

3. In Peki the *Mami Water* priestess was born of Christian parents (who had both been born into the EPC and later switched to the Apostolic Church). Since her childhood, the priestess had had dreams about living at the bottom of the sea. Once she dreamt she was approached by a white man who kissed her. At first she sought deliverance in a Spiritual church, but gradually she realised that she herself belonged to these spirits and became initiated as a priestess. She told me that she had travelled to the bottom of the sea several times, where she saw many shops and riches. The people living there were all white and among them there was no death, sickness or poverty. According to her, *Mami Water* spirits can help people to get healing, children and money through their earthly priests and priestesses. When I interviewed her on 22 May 1992, the priestess had not yet been able to assemble sufficient funds with which to establish her shrine, but she intended to do so in the near future.

4. The following 'black' *trɔwo* were represented on such occasions: Amimli (with priestesses from Blengo and Avetile), Abia (Avetile), and Sega (Dzake). Dente (Dzake) was a prominent 'white' *trɔ* represented.

5. Among the Ga and Adangme, too, local priests are never themselves possessed (Field 1969: 11).

6. As I found out on the basis of inscription forms, most attendants of Agbelengor's National Deliverance at Tokokoe were women with business problems which they attributed to evil spirits. Many reported having encountered these spirits in their dreams. Like Agbelengor, the EPC 'of Ghana' also offered special prayers for traders during healing and deliverance services.

7. The frequently made distinction between the 'forces of society' and the 'forces of nature', which associates ancestors with the former and all gods located in nature with the latter (Horton 1983, as well as Middleton 1983: 3 and Kramer 1987: 60ff, who both employ it to describe the Akan pantheon), is problematic in our case. There are three main problems regarding the application of this distinction to Ewe cosmology. One concerns the fact that it lumps together too many different deities in the second category for, as we saw, local priests themselves distinguish between 'black' and 'white' *trɔwo*; and dwarfs, though associated with the bush, belong to the latter group while river gods such as

Amimli belong to the former. The second problem concerns the association of 'black' *trɔwo* with the forces of nature as opposed to the forces of society. In my view, the 'black' *trɔwo*, since they have a long tradition of being worshipped in particular clans or families, should also be considered as forces of society, at least to some extent. The third problem concerns the *ametsiavawo*. The spirits of ancestors who die a violent death also fall between the two categories, since although they are ancestors, they are laid in state in the bush and thus associated with nature.

8. I interviewed him on 5 February 1992 together with G. K. Ananga, who translated from English into Ewe and vice versa. The interview was recorded and transcribed. All statements were originally formulated in Ewe.

9. I interviewed her on 6 February 1992 together with the Reverend Stanley Amedzro, who translated from English into Ewe and vice versa. The interview was recorded and transcribed. All quotations are translated from Ewe. The old lady's daughter also took part in the conversation, which started and ended with prayers because otherwise the two women would have found it too dangerous to raise 'heathen' matters.

10. This is my transcription of her deity. *Sɔwlui* is the name of an Ewe god responsible for cowries (Spieth 1911: 17). I asked the old woman several times whether her 'Sowlui' was the same Ewe god, but she insisted that it was a foreign Twi-speaking deity.

11. I interviewed her on 9 June 1992 together with her late husband's cousin, Victor Ntem, who translated from English into Ewe and vice versa. I also frequently spoke to her alone. The interview was recorded and transcribed. All quotations are translations from Ewe.

12. I have changed her name. Two interviews with her and her parents (one in Ewe, 23 March 1992) and one in English (25 March 1992) were recorded and transcribed. Gilbert K. Ananga translated whenever necessary.

13. This is the story of the man's death which was told in Peki: When the Prince of Wales visited the Gold Coast in 1925, Kwadzo Dei X (from Nyangamangu family) and some people accompanying him went to Accra. One of these people, a man from Tsibu (a village close to Peki from where the *fiagã* had married a woman), was hit by a lorry and died. Back home, the *fiagã* sent one of his sons and a policeman to Tsibu to report the death. On their way home, the son was attacked and shot dead out of revenge. He was buried as an *ametsiava*. The family had wished to avenge his death and wage war against Tsibu, but this was prevented by the pastors Albert Binder and Christian Gati. About twenty-five years later the spirit started to possess women in the family and demanded that they serve him. According to Paul B., the fact that the family could never avenge the man's death may be the reason for the manifestation of his spirit.

14. I interviewed Patricia A. on 14 March 1992, together with Mary Akrobetu who translated from English into Ewe and vice versa.

15. I interviewed Margareth N. in English on 26 May 1992. Quotations are taken from the transcription.

16. I spoke to Elisabeth M. at Tokokoe on 3 April 1992 and at several times at home in Peki. We conversed in English.

17. Our conversation took place on 18 May 1992 (in English). The quotations are taken from the transcript.

18. I interviewed Grace N. in English on 28 March 1992.

19. Yayria K. related this case to me on 12 January 1992. I also had more conversations with her later (all in English).

20. There were rumours that a certain old lady in Tsame had confessed that she had

killed her son through witchcraft. Whereas some believed this to be true, others blamed Akudeka for pressing her to tell such stories. Later on, she denied participation and the matter was not pursued any further. I did not dare to interview this woman about the matter because one's personal involvement in witchcraft is a shameful matter about which people do not like to talk (except perhaps in the relatively safe context of deliverance). Another woman in Blengo, too, was said to be a witch. I visited her several times but never dared to raise the matter.

21. This is different among the Effutu (southern Ghana), where self-accusations seem to be more frequent (see Wyllie 1973). The same holds true for the Akan (see Rattray 1927: 31; Schönhuth 1992: 4, 131).

22. It would be an important line of investigation to conduct research into the question of when and why witchcraft became associated with the achievement of wealth. It would also be worthwhile if anthropologists examined such shifts in African witchcraft idioms and analysed how they represent the problems and opportunities of global capitalism. Up until now, such studies have been scarce (but see Bastian 1993; Fisiy and Geschiere 1991; Geschiere 1994, 1997; Rowlands and Warnier 1988; Shaw 1996), for anthropologists have concentrated mainly on formal witchcraft accusations (see the critique by Austen 1993, Thoden van Velzen and Van Wetering 1989: 155).

23. The literature on witchcraft in Ghana suggests that this form of witchcraft was traditionally more common than the other (Bleek 1975: 319ff; Debrunner 1961: 182; Field 1960: 35–9, 108–10, 121; Jahoda 1966). Interestingly, Jahoda even suggested that in the future, with the increase in education, rich people in Ghana would have 'less reason to fear the hostility of those they have left behind' (ibid.: 211). This chapter clearly shows that this has not been the case. See also Assimeng's study of witchcraft beliefs and practices in contemporary Ghana (1989: 166–94).

24. The critical study of dreams and dreaming has been comparatively neglected by Africanist anthropology (but see Fabian 1966, 1971a: 189ff). For a long time students of religion in Africa confined themselves to mere documentation. For a stimulating investigation of this phenomenon see *Dreaming, Religion & Society in Africa* edited by Jedrej and Shaw (1992). In this volume there are two articles dealing with dreams in African Churches (Charsley 1992; Curley 1992; in these contributions earlier work on dreams – Charsley 1987; Curley 1983 – is further developed). Neither of these authors reports dream experiences that are comparable to those described in this section but rather focuses on dreams as a means of revealing a person's conversion and relationship with the Christian God. Charsley emphasises that it is difficult to determine the relationship between dreaming in indigenous culture and in Christian churches (ibid.: 172). Against the background of the material presented in this section I would suggest that, at least in the case of dreams pertaining to agents of affliction (a category of dreams neither author deals with), Christian dream interpretation is fully in line with indigenous dream interpretation. Again, it becomes clear that through the image of the Devil elements of indigenous thought are incorporated into Christian discourse.

25. Rather than conceptualising dreams as a complex series of events, there is a strong emphasis on dream images which are supposed to convey certain messages. For a similar conceptualisation of dreaming among the Peruvian Quechua see Mannheim (1991).

26. I spoke to Felicia B. in Tokokoe on 3 April 1992 during Agbelengor's National Deliverance. I transcribed the interview, which was conducted in English. I have

changed her name because she was afraid that people might gossip about her if they heard of the experiences she related.

27. I talked to Jacob K. on the day of his deliverance (29 February 1992). Our conversation, which we conducted in English, was recorded and transcribed. Although he presented his testimony in public I have changed his name.

28. I heard and recorded Peter T.'s testimony of his demonic past during the Healing and Deliverance Service of the EPC 'of Ghana' on 14 January 1992. Unfortunately the quality of the recording was so bad that it could not be transcribed. Therefore, I interviewed him again on 18 March 1992. Emmanuel Brempong translated our conversation from Ewe into English and vice versa. I have changed Peter's name.

29. It would be worthwhile to study this phenomenon further. Until now it has received little attention because it falls outside the established fields of the study of Christianity or 'traditional religion'. Unfortunately I have never talked to anyone actively involved in such practices. I have only spoken to people like Jacob and Peter, who had left these things behind, and people who knew about these matters from hearsay. It would also be useful to study further the position of young people in Ghanaian society and investigate how they relate to their families. What I find especially intriguing is why many young people – the three cases presented here are no exception – seem to have separated themselves psychologically from their families and whether this is confined to a certain phase in their life (until marriage) or holds for a much longer period.

30. Note that I do not refer to 'possession' in the more limited sense of a spirit's particular manifestation in or through a person. 'Possession' in this narrow sense is a rather inaccurate, misleading term that does not have an equivalent in the Ewe language. As we noted in Chapter 4, the Ewe distinguish four ways in which spirits act upon their hosts: spirits 'catch' people in order to turn them into their priests; spirits 'come upon' or 'are upon' people and speak through them; spirits 'beat' people and cause them to embody them in dance; and spirits cause people to be 'out of their minds'. These possessive actions occur within the framework of Ewe priesthood.

31. Even in the first substantial collection dedicated to spirit possession in Africa (Beattie and Middleton 1969) such studies prevailed (exceptions are the chapters by Lee and Welbourne).

32. That Kramer's approach is not too distanced to make sense of particular cases is proven by Boddy's (1989) interpretation of the Sudanese Zar cult which has much in common with Kramer's (at that time his work was not yet available in English). She also understands possession as an 'experience of otherness' which the possessed are unable to express in their daily lives. See also Masquelier 1995.

33. In her examination of Pentecostalism, Goodman (1988: 52–63) argues that this variant of Christianity provides a remedy against 'ecstasy deprivation'; that is, it rebels 'against a divine service that does not include the trance' (ibid.: 62). Note the similarity of this argument to that of Hagan (1988) discussed in the last chapter, who stated that the main appeal of the new African Churches was that they offer members the possibility of experiencing trance states. In a similar vein, Ter Haar argues that the attraction of Archbishop Milingo's charismatic movement lay in the possibility of exchanging possession by 'evil spirits' for a state of being filled with the Holy Spirit (1992: 129). She places this development in the context of the 'erosion of the belief in distinctive local spirits, and their incorporation into a nationwide or worldwide phenomenon of possession' (ibid.: 113). Of course, I would not deny that there is some truth in these arguments. However, the point I wish to make on the basis of my study is that the attraction

of Pentecostalism lies not in enabling people to be possessed by the Holy Spirit as such, but rather in enabling people to re-approach the circumstances they seek to leave behind through possession by agents of the Devil. In this way, they can mediate the tensions arising from the incorporation of the local into the global.

# GLOSSARY

*adefîe* (pl. *adefîewo*)  (evil) spirit of a dead person
*Abosam*  the Devil
*Adonten*  (Akan) centre in military organisation of Akan states
*adze*  witchcraft
*adzetɔ* (pl. *adzetɔwo*)  witch
*adziakpewo*  'little people' (inland Ewe)
*afakala* (pl. *afakalawo*)  diviner
*agbe*  life
*aka*  ordeal
*akatɔ* (pl. *akatɔwo*)  person in charge of an ordeal
*aklama*  entity held to determine a person's character
*akple*  corn porridge
*amãtsi*  water mixed with herbs
*ame* (pl. *amewo*)  human being
*amegã*  (pl. *amegãwo*) great person
*ametsiava* (pl. *ametsiavawo*)  spirit of a person killed accidentally
*atike*  medicine
*azizawo*  'little people' (Anlo)

*bayi*  (Akan) witchcraft
*Benkum*  (Akan) left wing in military organisation of Akan states
*Benkumhene*  (Akan) chief of Benkum
*bokɔ* (pl. *bokɔwo*)  diviner
*bokɔnɔ* (pl. *bokɔnɔwo*)  diviner
*busu*  evil matter
*busuyiyi*  ritual to drive away *busu*

*ɖasedidi*  testimony
*ɖeɖe*  salvation, deliverance
*drõekuku*  dreaming
*drõefe*  the land of dreams
*du* (pl. *duwo*)  town
*dukɔ* (pl. *dukɔwo*)  state
*dziŋgbe*  sky, heaven
*dzo*  fire, magic, medicine
*dzoɖuame*  'black magic'
*dzoɖuameto* (pl. *dzoɖuametɔwo*)  (destructive) sorcerer
*dzoka* (pl. *dzokawo*)  *dzo* string
*dzomavɔ*  hell ('everlasting fire')
*dzosala* (pl. *dzosalawo*)  synonymous with *dzotɔ*

*dzotɔ* (pl. *dzotɔwo*)   healer, magician

*ele ame dzi* or *eɖe ame dzi*   possession ('it is or comes upon a person')
*egli*   possession (out of mind, in a rage)
*ele trɔ̃ fom*   possession (a person is moved by the *trɔ̃* and dances)
*eva lé ame*   possession ('it comes to catch a person')

*fia* (pl. *fiawo*)   chief
*fiagã*   king, 'head chief', paramount chief
*fome* (pl. *fomewo*)   families or lineages
*fufu*   pounded yams

*gbetsi*   promise about one's return to the spirit world
*gbetsi vɔ̃* (pl. *gbetsi vɔ̃wo*)   'evil fate'
*gbedodoɖa*   prayer
*gbɔgbɔ* (pl. *gbɔgbɔwo*)   breath, spirit
*gbɔgbɔ makɔmakɔ* (pl. *gbɔgbɔ makɔmakɔwo*)   unclean spirit
*Gbɔgbɔ Kɔkɔe*   Holy Spirit
*gbɔgbɔ vɔ̃* (pl. *gbɔgbɔ vɔ̃wo*)   evil spirit
*gu*   evil resulting from violating accepted laws of mutual respect
*guɖeɖe*   driving away gu

*hamedada* (pl. *hamedadawo*)   presbytress
*hamemegã* (pl. *hamemegãwo*)   presbyter
*xlɔme* (pl. *xlɔmewo*)   patrilineal and patrilocal clans
*hɔnusi*   priestess

*kodzogbe*   visible, material world
*Kpodzi*   Christian village (on the hill)
*Kristotɔ* (pl. *Kristotɔwo*)   Christian

*le gbɔgbɔme*   spiritual realm
*le ŋutilame*   physical realm
*luvɔ*   shadow, soul

*Mawu*   God
*Mawukafukafu*   praises to God
*Mawusubɔsubɔ*   Sunday service

*Nifa*   (Akan) right wing in military organisation of Akan states
*Nifahene*   (Akan) chief of Nifa
*ŋɔli* (pl. *ŋɔliwo*)   bad ancestor's spirit
*ŋɔliyɔyɔ*   'calling a *ŋɔli*'
*ŋku vu*   'open eyes', civilisation
*ŋusẽ*   power
*nutegã*   vision
*ŋutilã*   body
*ŋutifafa*   peace
*nuvɔ̃*   evil matter, sin
*nuvɔ̃ɖeɖe*   ritual to drive away nuvɔ̃
*nyuie*   good
*subɔsubɔ*   service

*sukutɔwo*   'school people', Christians

*tasi*   the paternal aunt
*tɔgbekpukpo* (pl. *tɔgbekpukpowo*) ancestor stool
*tɔgbui* (pl. *tɔgbuiwo*)   ancestor
*tɔgbuizikpui* (pl. *tɔgbuizikpuiwo*)   clan god
*trɔ̃* (pl. *trɔ̃wo*)   traditional god
*trɔ̃si* (pl. *trɔ̃siwo*)   priestess
*trɔ̃nua*   priest
*tsiame*   spokesman
*tsiefe*   place of the dead, hell

*viɖe*   a little bit
*vɔ̃*   evil
*vɔsasa*   sacrifice
*vu*   blood

*xɔse*   faith, belief
*xɔxɔ*   salvation

*yɔ trɔ̃*   to call a *trɔ̃* upon somebody

# REFERENCES

Adick, Christel. 1980. *Bildung und Kolonialismus in Togo: eine Studie zu den Entstehungs-zusammenhängen eines europäisch geprägten Bildungswesens in Afrika am Beispiel Togos (1850–1914)*. Frankfurt am Main: Deutsches Institut für Internationale Pädagogische Forschung.

Agawu, Kofi. 1995. *African Rhythm: a northern Ewe perspective*. Cambridge: Cambridge University Press.

Agblemayon, F. N'Sougan. 1984. *Sociologie des sociétés orales d'Afrique Noire: les Ewes du Sud-Togo*. Paris: Éditions silex.

Agyemang, Fred. 1988. *Amu the African: a study in vision and courage*. Accra: Asempa Publishers, Christian Council of Ghana.

Ajayi, J. F. 1965. *Christian Missions in Nigeria 1841–1891: the making of a new elite*. London: Longmans.

Amenumey, D. E. K. 1964. 'The Ewe People and the Coming of European Rule, 1850–1914'. University of London: unpublished MA thesis.

——1986. *The Ewe in Pre-Colonial Times: a political history with special emphasis on the Anlo, Ge and Krepi*. Ho: E. P. Church Press.

Ananga, Gilbert K. n.d. 'Gbidukɔ'. Unpublished manuscript.

Andresen, Carl (Hg.). 1988. *Handbuch der Dogmen- und Theologiegeschichte*, vol. 3: *Die Lehrentwicklung im Rahmen der Oekumenizität*. Göttingen: Vandenhoeck & Ruprecht.

Ansre, Gilbert. 1971. 'Language Standardization in Sub-Saharan Africa', in T. A. Sebeok (ed.), *Current Trends in Linguistics*, vol. 7: *Linguistics in Sub-Saharan Africa*, pp. 680–98. The Hague: Mouton.

Appiah, Kwame Anthony. 1992. *In My Father's House: Africa in the philosophy of culture*. New York and Oxford: Oxford University Press.

Appiah-Kubi, Kofi. 1981. *Man Cures, God Heals: religion and medical practice among the Akans of Ghana*. Totowa, New Jersey: Allanheld, Osmun & Co.

Arhin, Kwame. 1994. 'The economic implications of transformations in Akan funeral rites', *Africa* 64 (3), 307–22.

Asad, Talal. 1986. 'The concept of cultural translation in British social anthropology', in J. Clifford and G. E. Marcus (eds), *Writing Culture: the poetics and politics of ethnography*, pp. 141–64. Berkeley: University of California Press.

——1993. *Genealogies of Religion: discipline and reasons of power in Christianity and Islam*. Baltimore and London: The John Hopkins University Press.

Asamoa, Ansa. 1971. *Die gesellschaftlichen Verhältnisse der Ewe-Bevölkerung in Südost-Ghana*. Berlin: Akademie Verlag.

Asare, E. B. 1973. 'Akwamu–Peki Relations in the Eighteenth and Nineteenth Centuries'. University of Ghana: unpublished MA Thesis.

Assimeng, Max. 1986. *Saints and Social Structures*. Tema: Ghana Publishing Corporation.

——1989. *Religion and Social Change in West Africa: an introduction to the sociology of religion*. Accra: Ghana Universities Press.

Austen, Ralph A. 1993. 'The moral economy of witchcraft: an essay in comparative history', in J. Comaroff and J. Comaroff (eds), *Modernity and its Malcontents: ritual and power in postcolonial Africa*, pp. 89–110. Chicago: The University of Chicago Press.

Bächtold-Stäubli, Hanns. 1927. *Handwörterbuch des deutschen Aberglaubens*, vol. 1. Berlin: Walter de Gruyter.

Baeta, Robert and Theodor Sedode. 1911. *Reste heidnischer Anschauungen in den Christengemeinden Togos: zwei Aufsätze von Lehrern der Norddeutschen Mission*. Bremen: Verlag der Norddeutschen Missionsgesellschaft.

Baëta, C. G. 1962. *Prophetism in Ghana: a study of some 'Spiritual' churches*. London: SCM-Press Ltd.

Baëta, C.G. (ed.). 1968. *Christianity in Tropical Africa: studies presented and discussed at the seventh international African seminar, University of Ghana, April 1965*. London: Oxford University Press for the International Africa Institute.

Barrett, D. B. 1968. *Schism and Renewal in Africa: an analysis of six thousand contemporary religious movements*. Nairobi: Oxford University Press.

Barrington-Ward, Simon. 1978. '"The centre cannot hold ...": spirit possession as redefinition', in E. Fasholé-Luke et al. (eds), *Christianity in Independent Africa*, pp. 455–70. London: Rex Collings.

Bartels, F. L. 1965. *The Roots of Ghana Methodism*. Cambridge: Cambridge University Press.

Barth, Karl. 1947. *Die protestantische Theologie im 19. Jahrhundert: ihre Vorgeschichte und ihre Geschichte*. Zürich: Evangelischer Verlag.

Bastian, Misty. 1993. '"Bloodhounds who have no friends": witchcraft and locality in the Nigerian popular press', in J. Comaroff and J. Comaroff (eds), *Modernity and its Malcontents: ritual and power in postcolonial Africa*, pp. 129–66. Chicago: The University of Chicago Press.

Beattie, John and John Middleton, John (eds). 1969. *Spirit Mediumship and Society in Africa*. London: Routledge & Kegan Paul.

Behrend, Heike. 1993. *Alice und die Geister: Krieg im Norden Ugandas*. München: Trickster.

Beidelman, T. O. 1974. 'Social theory and the study of Christian missions in Africa', *Africa* 44 (3), 235–49.

——1982. *Colonial Evangelism: a socio-historical study of an East African mission at the grassroots*. Bloomington: Indiana University Press.

Bekker, Balthasar. 1691. *De betoverde weereld. Synde een grondig Onderzoek van 't gemeen Gevoelen aangaande de GEESTEN, deselver Aart en Vermogen, Bewind en Bedrijf: als ook 't gene de Menschen door derselver Kragt en Gemeenschap doen*. Amsterdam: Daniel van den Dalen.

Bischoff-Luithlen, Angelika. 1965/69. 'Andachtsliteratur im Bauernhaus – ihre Bedeutung heute und einst', in *Württembergisches Jahrbuch für Volkskunde*, 99–106.

Bleek, Wolf. 1975. *Marriage, Inheritance and Witchcraft: a case study of a rural Ghanaian family*. Leiden: Afrika-Studiecentrum.

Blumhardt, Christoph. 1972. *Worte des evangelischen Pfarrers und Landtags-abgeordneten Christoph Blumhardt*. Wuppertal: Jugenddienst Verlag.

Blumhardt, Johann Christoph. 1978 [1850]. *Die Krankheitsgeschichte der Gottliebin Dittus*. Herausgegeben und eingeleitet von Gerhard Schäfer. Mit einer Interpretation der Krankenheilung von Theodor Bovet. Göttingen: Vandenhoek & Ruprecht.

——n.d.. *Die Heilung von Kranken durch Glaubensgebet*. Mit einem Geleitwort von Pfarrer L. Wittekind. Leipzig: Volksdienst Verlag.

Boddy, Janice. 1989. *Wombs and Alien Spirits: women, men, and the Zar cult in northern Sudan*. Madison: University of Wisconsin Press.

Bohnenberger, Karl. 1961. *Volkstümliche Überlieferungen in Württemberg*. Unter Mitwirkung von A. Eberhardt, H. Höhm und R. Kapff. Photomechanischer Nachdruck aus den Württembergischen Jahrbüchern für Statistik und Landeskunde 1904ff. Stuttgart: Silberburg Verlag.

Bond, G., W. Walton and S. Walker (eds). 1979. *African Christianity: patterns of religious continuity*. New York: Academic Press.

Booth, N. S. 1979. 'God and the gods in West Africa', in N. S. Booth (ed.), *African Religions*, pp. 159–81. New York: NOK Publishers International.

Bourguignon, Erika. 1976. *Possession*. San Francisco: Chandler & Sharp.

Bourguignon, Erika (ed.). 1973. *Religion: altered states of consciousness and social change*. Columbus: Ohio State University Press.

Bovet, Theodor. 1978. 'Zur Heilungsgeschichte der Gottliebin Dittus', in J. C. Blumhardt, *Die Krankheitsgeschichte der Gottliebin Dittus*. Herausgegeben und eingeleitet von Gerhard Schäfer. Mit einer Interpretation der Krankenheilung von Theodor Bovet, pp. 1–31. Göttingen: Vandenhoek & Ruprecht.

Bowie, Fiona. 1993. 'Anthropology and missionaries: comment', *JASO* 24 (1), 64–6.

Bowie, Fiona, Deborah Kirkwood and Shirley Ardener (eds). 1993. *Women and Missions: anthropological and historical perceptions*. Oxford: Berg.

Brecht, Martin. 1985. 'Christian Gottlob Barths "Zweimal zweiundfünfzig biblische Geschichten" – Ein weltberühmter Bestseller unter den Schulbüchern der Erweckungsbewegung', *Pietismus und Neuzeit: ein Jahrbuch zur Geschichte des neueren Protestantismus*, vol. 11, 127–38.

Brückner, Wolfgang and Rainer Alsheimer. 1974. 'Das Wirken des Teufels: Theologie und Sage im 16. Jahrhundert', in W. Brückner (ed.), *Volks-erzählung und Reformation: ein Handbuch zur Tradierung von Erzählstoffen und Erzählliteratur im Protestantismus*, pp. 394–418. Berlin: Erich Schmidt Verlag.

Buhler, P. 1979. 'The North German Missionaries in Eweland: religion and economics; 1847–1884'. Paper presented at the twenty-second annual meeting of the African Studies Association, Los Angeles, California, 31 October–3 November 1979.

Bukh, Jette. 1979. *The Village Woman in Ghana*. Uppsala: Scandinavian Institute of African Studies.

Bunyan, John. 1902 [1678]. *The Pilgrim's Progress from this World to that which is to Come, Delivered under the Similitude of a Dream*. London: Grant Richards.

——1906. *John Bunyan ƒe agbale, si woyɔna be Kristotɔ ƒe mɔzɔzɔ tso heheme yi dzifo. Akpa gbato kple evelia* [John Bunyan's Book, which is Called the Christian's Journey from the World to Heaven. Part One and Two], translated by Andreas Aku. Bremen: Norddeutsche Mission.

Burt, Ben. 1994. *Tradition and Christianity: the colonial transformation of a Solomon Islands society*. Chur: Harwood Publishers.

Buschan, Georg. n.d. *Das deutsche Volk in Sitte und Brauch: Geburt, Liebe, Hochzeit, Familienleben, Tod, Tracht, Wohnweise, Volkskunst, Lied, Tanz und Spiel, Handwerk und Zünfte, Aberglaube*. Unter Mitwirkung von M. Bauer, R. Julien, R. Mielke, H. -J. Moser, O. Schwindrazheim. Stuttgart: Union Deutsche Verlagsgesellschaft.

Capo, Hounkpati. 1984. 'Elements of Ewe-Gen-Aja-Fon dialectology', in F. De Medeiros, *Peuples du Golfe du Bénin (Aja-Ewé)*, pp. 167–78. Paris: Éditions Karthala.

Carmody, Brendan. 1988. 'Conversion and school at Chikuni, 1905–39', *Africa* 58 (2), 193–209.

Carus, Paul. 1991 [1900]. *The History of the Devil and the Idea of Evil: from the earliest times to the present day*. [reproduction of the 1900 edition]. La Salle, Illinois: Open Court Publishing Company.

Cervantes, Fernando. 1994. *The Devil in the New World: the impact of diabolism in New Spain*. New Haven and London: Yale University Press.

Charsley, Simon. 1987. 'Dreams and purposes: an analysis of dream narratives in an independent African church', *Africa* 57 (3), 281–96

——1992. 'Dreams in African churches', in M. C. Jedrej and Rosalind Shaw (eds), *Dreaming, Religion & Society in Africa*, pp. 153–76. Leiden: Brill.

Christaller, J. G. 1933. *Dictionary of the Asante and Fante Language called Tshi (Twi)* [2nd edn, revised and enlarged]. Basel: Basel Evangelical Missionary Society.

Christian Council of the Gold Coast. 1932. *Report on Common Beliefs with Regard to Witchcraft*. Accra: Scottish Mission Depot.

Clark, Stuart. 1990. 'Protestant demonology: sin, superstition, and society (c.1520–c.1630)', in B. Ankarloo and G. Henningsen (eds), *Early Modern European Witchcraft: centres and peripheries*, pp. 45–81. Oxford: Clarendon Press.

Clarke, Peter B. 1986. *West Africa and Christianity: a study of religious development from the 15th to the 20th century*. London: Edward Arnold.

Clifford, James. 1982. *Person and Myth: Maurice Leenhardt in the Melanesian world*. Berkeley: University of California Press.

Clifford, James and George E. Marcus (eds). 1986. *Writing Culture: the poetics and politics of ethnography*. Berkeley: University of California Press.

Comaroff, Jean. 1994. 'Epilogue. defying disenchantment: reflections on ritual, power, and history', in H. Hardacre et al. (eds), *Asian Visions of Authority: religion and the modern states of east and southeast Asia*, pp. 301–17. Honolulu: University of Hawaii Press.

Comaroff, Jean and John Comaroff. 1991. *Of Revelation and Revolution: Christianity, colonialism, and consciousness in South Africa*, vol. 1. Chicago: University of Chicago Press.

——1997. *Revelation and Revolution: the dialectics of modernity on a South African frontier*, vol. 2. Chicago: Chicago University Press.

Comaroff, Jean and John Comaroff (eds). 1993. *Modernity and Its Malcontents: ritual and power in postcolonial Africa*. Chicago: The University of Chicago Press.

Crain, Mary M. 1991. 'Poetics and politics in the Ecuadorean Andes: women's narratives of death and Devil possession', *American Ethnologist* 18 (1), 67–89.

Crampton, E. D. T. 1979. *Christianity in Northern Nigeria*. London: Geoffry Chapman.

Crick, Malcolm. 1982. 'Recasting witchcraft', in M. Marwick (ed.), *Witchcraft and Sorcery*, pp. 343–64. Harmondsworth: Penguin.

Curley, Richard T. 1983. 'Dreams of power: social process in a West African religious movement', *Africa* 53 (3), 20–37.

——1992. 'Private dreams and public knowledge in a Camerounian independent church', in M. C. Jedrej and Rosalind Shaw (eds), *Dreaming, Religion & Society in Africa*, pp. 135–52. Leiden: Brill.

Dah, Jonas N. 1983. *Missionary Motivations and Methods: a critical examination of the Basel Mission in Cameroon 1886–1914*. University of Basel: Ph.D. thesis.

Damman, E. 1977. 'Some problems of the translation of the Bible into African languages', *Kiswahili* 47, 88–95.

Debrunner, Hans W. 1961. *Witchcraft in Ghana: a study of the belief in destructive witches and its effect on the Akan tribe*. Kumasi: Presbyterian Book Depot.

——1965. *A Church between Colonial Powers: a study of the church in Togo*. London: Luttersworth Press.

De Surgy, Albert de. 1985. 'Examen critique de la notion de fétiche à partir du cas Évhé', *Systèmes de pensée en Afrique Noire* 8, 263–303.

——1988a. *Le système religieux des Évhé*. Paris: Éditions L'Harmattan.

——1988b. *De l'universalité d'une forme africaine de sacrifice*. Paris: Éditions du CNRS.

——1990. 'Bo et vodu protecteurs du sud-Togo', *Nouvelle Revue d'Ethnopsychiatrie* 16, 77–100.

Dickson, K. and P. Ellingworth (eds). 1970. *Biblical Revelation and African Beliefs*. London: Lutersworth Press/United Society for Christian Literature.

Doke, C.M. 1958. 'Scripture translations into Bantu languages', *African Studies* 17, 82–99.

Drewal, Henry John. 1988. 'Performing the Other. Mami Wata worship in Africa', *The Drama Review* 32 (2), 160–85.

Droogers, André. 1989. 'Syncretism: the problem of definition, the definition of the problem', in J. Gort et al. (eds), *Dialogue and Syncretism: an interdisciplinary approach*, pp. 7–25. Grand Rapids: William B. Eerdmans Publishing Company.

Dzobo, Noah K. 1971. *Modes of Traditional Moral Education Among Anfoega-Ewes: research report*. Cape Coast: University of Cape Coast.

——1976. 'The Idea of God Among the Ewe of West Africa'. Unpublished manuscript.

——1981. 'The indigenous African theory of knowledge and truth: examples of the Ewe and Akan of Ghana', *Conch* 13, 85–102.

——1988a. 'Life: central ideas as found in biblical and indigenous African traditions'. Paper presented at the Second Theological Consultation, Bremen.

——1988b. 'The Gospel and African Culture: contemporary issues related to...' Paper presented at The Consultation on the Gospel and African Culture, Gaborone, Botswana 25–30 April 1988.

——1992. 'The Gospel and the Life Affirming Religious Culture of the Third World of Africa'. Paper Presented at the International Consultation on Bilateral Dialogue, Princeton Theological Seminary, April 21–5 1992.

——n.d. 'Introduction to Meleagbe Theology'. Unpublished manuscript.

Edelman, Marc. 1994. 'Landlords and the Devil: class, ethnic, and gender dimensions of Central American peasant narratives', *Current Anthropology* 91 (1), 58–93.

Eiselen, Tobias. 1986. '"Zur Erziehung einer zuverlässigen wohldisziplinierten Streiterschar für den Missionskrieg": Basler Missionarsausbildung im 19. Jahrhundert', in W. Ustorf (ed.), *Mission im Kontext: Beiträge zur Sozialgeschichte der Norddeutschen Missionsgesellschaft im 19. Jahrhundert*, pp. 47–120. Bremen: Übersee-Museum.

Ekholm Friedman, K. 1993. *Catastrophe and Creation: the transformation of an African culture*. Chur: Harwood Academic Publishers.

Ellis, A. B. 1970 [1890]. *The Ewe-speaking Peoples of the Slave Coast of West Africa: their religion, manners, customs, laws, languages, &c*. Photomechanic reprint after the edition of 1890. Oosterhout N. B.: Anthropological Publications.

Fabian, Johannes. 1966. 'Dream and charisma: "Theories of Dreams" in the Jamaa Movement (Congo)', *Anthropos* 61, 544–60.

——1971a. *Jamaa: a religious movement in Katanga*. Evanston: Northwestern University Press.

——1971b. 'Language, history and anthropology', *Philosophy of the Social Sciences* 1, 19–47.

——1977. 'Lore and doctrine: some observations on storytelling in the Jamaa Movement in Shaba (Zaire)', *Cahiers d'Études Africaines* 66/67, 27 (2/3), 307–29.

——1979. Introduction, in J. Fabian (ed.), 'Beyond Charisma: religious movements as discourse', special issue of *Social Research*, 4–35.

——1981. 'Six theses regarding the anthropology of African religious movements', *Religion* 11, 109–26.

——1983. *Time and the Other: how anthropology makes its object*. New York: Columbia University Press.

——1986. *Language and Colonial Power: the appropriation of Swahili in the former Belgian Kongo. 1880–1938*. Cambridge: Cambridge University Press.

——1991. *Time and the Work of Anthropology: critical essays (1971–1991)*. Chur: Harwood Academic Publishers.

Fabri, F. 1859. *Die Entstehung des Heidenthums und die Aufgabe der Heidenmission*. Barmen: Langewiesche.

Fasholé-Luke, E., Richard Gray, Adrian Hastings and Godwin Tasie (eds). 1978. *Christianity in Independent Africa*. London: Rex Collings.

Fernandez, James. W. 1964. 'African religious movements – types and dynamics', *The Journal of Modern African Studies* 2 (4), 531–49.

——1974. 'The mission of metaphor in expressive culture', *Current Anthropology* 15 (2), 119–45.

——1978. 'African religious movements', *Annual Review of Anthropology* 7, 195–234.

——1982. *Bwiti: an ethnography of the religious imagination in Africa*. Princeton: Princeton University Press.

——1986. *Persuasions and Performances: the play of tropes in culture*. Bloomington: Indiana University Press.

Fernandez, James W. (ed.). 1991. *Beyond Metaphor: the theory of tropes in anthropology*. Stanford, California: Stanford University Press.

Fiawoo, D. K. 1958. 'The Influence of Contemporary Social Changes on the Magico-religious Concepts and Organisation of the Southern Ewe-Speaking Peoples of Ghana'. Edinburgh: unpublished Ph.D. thesis.

Fiawoo, D. K. et al. (eds). 1978. 'Funeral Customs in Ghana: a preliminary report'. Legon: Department of Sociology.

Field, M. J. 1960. *Search for Security: an ethno-psychiatric study of rural Ghana*. London: Faber and Faber.

——1969. 'Spirit possession in Ghana', in J. Beattie and J. Middleton (eds), *Spirit Mediumship and Society in Africa*, pp. 3–13. London: Routledge & Kegan Paul.

Fischer, Friedrich Hermann. 1991. *Der Missionsarzt Rudolf Fisch und die Anfänge medizinischer Arbeit der Basler Mission an der Goldküste (Ghana)*, Herzogenrath: Verlag Murken-Altrogge.

Fisher, Humphrey J. 1973. 'Conversion reconsidered: some historical aspects of religious conversion in black Africa', *Africa* 43 (1), 27–40.

Fisiy, Cyprian F. and Peter Geschiere. 1991. 'Sorcery, witchcraft and accumulation: regional variations in South and West Cameroon', *Critique of Anthropology* 11 (3), 251–78.

Forde, Daryll. 1956. 'Diedrich Westermann, 24 June 1875–31 May 1956', *Africa* 26 (2), 329–31.

Frimpong-Ansah, Jonathan H. 1992. *The Vampire State in Africa: the political economy of decline in Ghana*. Trenton: Africa World Press.

Fulbrook, Mary. 1983. *Piety and Politics: religion and the rise of absolutism in England, Württemberg and Prussia*. Cambridge: Cambridge University Press.

Gayibor, Nicoué L. 1984. 'Agɔkɔli et la dispersion de Nɔtsé', in F. de Medeiros (ed.), *Peuples du Golfe du Bénin (Aja-Ewé)*, pp. 21–34. Paris: Editions Karthala.

Geschiere, Peter. 1997. *The Modernity of Witchcraft: politics and the occult in post-colonial Africa*. Charlottesville and London: University Press of Virginia.

Geschiere, Peter (with Cyprian Fisiy). 1994. 'Domesticating Personal Violence: witchcraft, courts and confessions in Cameroon', *Africa* 64 (3), 321–41.

Ghana Evangelism Committee. 1993. *National Church Survey. 1993 Update: facing the unfinished task of the church in Ghana*. Accra: Assemblies of God Literature Centre.

Gifford, Paul (ed.). 1993. *New Dimensions in African Christianity*. Ibadan: Sefer Books.

Gifford, Paul. 1994. 'Ghana's charismatic churches', *Journal of Religion in Africa* 64 (3), 241–65.

Goodman, Felicitas D. 1988. *How about Demons? Possession and exorcism in the modern world*. Bloomington: Indiana University Press.

Goody, Jack. 1957. 'Anomie in Ashanti?' *Africa* 27 (1), 356–63.

—— 1975. 'Religion, Social Change and the Sociology of Conversion', in J. Goody (ed.), *Changing Social Structure in Ghana: essays in the comparative sociology of a new state and an old tradition*, pp. 91–106. London: International African Institute.

—— 1977. *The Domestication of the Savage Mind*. Cambridge: Cambridge University Press.

—— 1987. *The Interface between the Written and the Oral*. Cambridge: Cambridge University Press.

Grau, Eugene Emile. 1964. 'The Evangelical Presbyterian Church (Ghana and Togo) 1914–1946: a study in European mission relations affecting the beginning of an Indigenous Church [Peki]. Unpublished Ph.D. thesis (Faculty of The Hartford Seminary Foundation).

—— 1968. 'Missionary policies as seen in the work of missions with the Evangelical Presbyterian Church, Ghana', in C. G. Baëta (ed.), *Christianity in Tropical Africa: studies presented and discussed at the seventh international African seminar, University of Ghana, April 1965*, pp. 61–80. Oxford: Oxford University Press.

Gray, Richard. 1981. 'The origins and the organization of the nineteenth-century missionary movement', in O. U. Kalu (ed.), *The History of Christianity in West-Africa*, pp. 14–21. London: Longman.

—— 1990. *Black Christians and White Missionaries*. New Haven: Yale University Press.

Greene, Sandra. 1996a. *Gender, Ethnicity, and Social Change on the Upper Slave Coast*. Portsmouth, London: Heinemann and James Currey.

—— 1996b. 'Religion, history and the supreme gods of Africa: a contribution to the debate', *Journal of Religion in Africa* 26 (2), 122–38.

Greschat, Martin. 1985. 'Industrialisierung, Bergarbeiterschaft und "Pietismus": Anmerkungen zur Wirkungsgeschichte eines Frömmigkeitstyps in der Moderne', *Pietismus und Neuzeit: ein Jahrbuch zur Geschichte des neueren Protestantismus*, vol. 11, pp. 173–92. Göttingen: Vandenhoek & Ruprecht.

Groth, Friedhelm. 1983. 'Chiliasmus und Apokatastasishoffnung in der Reich-Gottes-Verkündigung der beiden Blumhardts', *Pietismus und Neuzeit: ein Jahrbuch zur Geschichte des neueren Protestantismus*, vol. 9, pp. 56–116. Göttingen: Vandenhoek & Ruprecht.

Habermas, Jürgen. 1986. *Der philosophische Diskurs der Moderne*. Frankfurt am Main: Suhrkamp Verlag.

Hagan, George P. 1988. 'Divinity and experience: the trance and Christianity in southern Ghana', in W. James and D. H. Johnson (eds), *Vernacular Christianity: essays in the social anthropology of religion presented to Godfrey Lienhardt*, pp. 149–56. New York: Lilian Barber Press.

Hallen, Barry and J. O. Sodipo. 1986. *Knowledge, Belief & Witchcraft: analytic experiments in African philosophy*. London: Ethnographica.

Hannerz, Ulf. 1987. 'The world in creolization', *Africa* 57 (4), 547–59.
Harries, Patrick.1989. 'Exclusion, classification and internal colonialism: the emergence of ethnicity among the Tsonga-speakers of South Africa', in L. Vail (ed.), *The Creation of Tribalism in Southern Africa*, pp. 82–119. London: James Currey, Berkeley: University of California Press.
Hastings, Adrian. 1979. *A History of African Christianity 1950–1975*. Cambridge: Cambridge University Press.
——1994. *The Church in Africa 1450–1950*. Oxford: Clarendon Press.
Hayward, Victor E. W. (ed.). 1963. *African Independent Church Movements*. London: Edinburgh House Press.
Hefner, Robert W. 1993. 'World building and the rationality of conversion', in R. W. Hefner (ed.), *Conversion to Christianity: historical and anthropological perspectives on a great transformation*, pp. 3–46. Berkeley: University of California Press.
Hill, Christopher. 1989. *A Turbulent Seditious and Factious People: John Bunyan and his Church*. Oxford: Oxford University Press.
Hill, Polly. 1963. *The Migrant Cocoa-Farmers of Southern Ghana: a study in rural capitalism*. Cambridge: Cambridge University Press [reprinted 1997, LIT].
Hobart, Mark. 1987. 'Summer's days and salad days: the coming of age of anthropology?' in L. Holy (ed.), *Comparative Anthropology*, pp. 22–51. Oxford: Basil Blackwell.
Horton, R. 1971. 'African conversion', *Africa* 41 (2), 86–108.
——1975. 'On the rationality of conversion: Part I & II', *Africa* 45 (3), 219–35, 373–99.
——1983. 'Social psychologies: African and Western', in Meyer Fortes, *Oedipus and Job in West African Religion*, pp. 41–82. Cambridge: Cambridge University Press.
Howard, Alan. 1996. 'Speak of the devils: discourse and belief in spirits on Rotuma', in J. M. Mageo and A. Howard (eds), *Spirits in Culture, History, and Mind*, pp. 121–45. New York and London: Routledge.
Huber, Mary T. 1988. *The Bishop's Progress: a historical ethnography of Catholic missionary experience on the Sepik frontier*. Washington and London: Smithsonian Institution Press.
Hvalkof, S. and P. Aaby (eds). 1981. *Is God an American? An anthropological perspective on the missionary work of the Summer Institute of Linguistics*. Copenhagen/London: IWGIA and Survival International.
Ifeka-Moller, Caroline. 1974. 'White power: social-structural factors in conversion to Christianity, Eastern Nigeria, 1921–1966', *Canadian Journal of African Studies* 8 (1), 55–72.
Ikenga-Metuh, Emefie. 1987. 'The shattered microcosm: a critical survey of explanations of conversion in Africa', in K. Holst Petersen (ed.), *Religion, Development and African Identity*, pp. 11–27. Uppsala: Scandinavian Institute of African Studies.
Ingham, J. M. 1986. *Mary, Michael, and Lucifer: folk Catholicism in central Mexico*. Austin: University of Texas Press.
Isichei, Elisabeth. 1995. *A History of Christianity in Africa: from antiquity to present*. Grand Rapids: W. B. Eerdmans Publishing Company, Lawrenceville: Africa World Press Inc.
Jahoda, Gustav. 1966. 'Social aspirations, magic and witchcraft in Ghana: a social psychological interpretation', in P. C. Lloyd (ed.), *The New Elites of Tropical Africa: studies presented and discussed at the sixth international African seminar at the University of Ibadan, Nigeria, July 1964*, pp. 199–215. London: Oxford University Press for the International Africa Institute.

Jedrej, M. C. and Rosalind Shaw (eds). 1992. *Dreaming, Religion & Society in Africa.* Leiden: E. J. Brill.

Jenkins, Paul. 1978. 'Towards a Definition of the Pietism of Wurtemberg as a Missionary Movement', African Studies Association of the United Kingdom. Oxford Conference 1978: Whites in Africa – Whites as Missionaries.

——1986. 'Wenn zwei Welten sich berühren: Kontextuelle Gedanken über die Basler Missionare in Südghana im neunzehnten Jahrhundert', *Reformation*, 551–9.

Johannesen, Stanley. 1994. 'Third generation Pentecostal language: continuity and change in collective perceptions', in K. Poewe (ed.), *Charismatic Christianity as a Global Culture*, pp. 176–99. Columbia (S. C.): University of South Carolina Press.

Jolly, Margaret. 1996. 'Devils, Holy Spirits and the Swollen God: translation, conversion and colonial power in the Marist mission, Vanuatu, 1887–1934', in P. van der Veer (ed.), *Conversion to Modernities: the globalization of Christianity*, pp. 231–62. London & New York: Routledge.

Jules-Rosette, Bennetta. 1994. 'The future of African theologies – situating new religious movements in an epistemological setting', *Social Compass* 41 (1), 49–65.

Kalu, O. U. (ed.), 1980. *The History of Christianity in West-Africa.* London: Longman.

Kapenzi, G. F. 1979. *The Clash of Cultures: Christian missionaries and the Shona of Rhodesia.* Washington: University Press of America.

Kapferer, Bruce. 1991. *A Celebration of Demons: exorcism and the aesthetics of healing in Sri Lanka.* Oxford/Washington: Berg and Smithsonian Institution Press.

Kaplan, S. 1986. 'The Africanization of missionary Christianity: history and typology', *Journal of Religion in Africa* 16 (3), 166–86.

Kassühlke, R. 1969. 'Bibelübersetzung in Ful', *Africana Marburgensia* 2, 9–13.

Kaufert, Patricia Alice Leyland. 1976. 'Migration and Communication: a study of migrant-villager relationships in a rural Ghanaian community'. University of Birmingham: unpublished Ph.D. thesis.

Keane, Webb. 1996. 'Materialism, missionaries, and modern subjects in colonial Indonesia', in P. van der Veer (ed.), *Conversion to Modernities: the globalization of Christianity*, pp. 137–70. London & New York: Routledge.

Kelly, Henry Ansgar. 1985. *The Devil at Baptism: ritual, theology, and drama.* Ithaca and London: Cornell University Press.

Kepel, Gilles. 1994. *The Revenge of God: the resurgence of Islam, Christianity and Judaism in the modern world*, trans. Alan Braley. Cambridge: Polity Press.

Kibicho, S. G. 1978. 'The continuity of the African conception of God into and through Christianity: a Kikuyu case-study', in E. Fasholé-Luke et al. (eds), *Christianity in Independent Africa*, pp. 370–88. London: Rex Collings.

Kirwen, M. C. 1987. *The Missionary and the Diviner: contending theologies of Christian and African religions.* New York: Orbis Books.

Kittsteiner, Heinz Dieter. 1993. 'Die Abschaffung des Teufels im 18. Jahrhundert: ein kulturhistorisches Ereignis und seine Folgen', in A. Schuller & W. von Rahden (ed.), *Die andere Kraft: zur Renaissance des Bösen*, pp. 55–92. Berlin: Akademie Verlag.

Knippenberg, W. H. Th. 1981. '"De brede en de smalle weg"', *Brabants Heem* 33 (2/3), 106–11.

Knoll, Arthur J. 1982. 'Die Norddeutsche Missionsgesellschaft in Togo 1890–1914', in K. Bade (ed.), *Imperialismus und Kolonialmission: Kaiserliches Deutschland und koloniales Imperium*, pp. 165–88. Wiesbaden: Steiner.

Kottje, Raymund and Bernd Moeller (eds). 1974. *Ökumenische Kirchengeschichte, vol. 3: Neuzeit.* Mainz/München: Matthias Gruenewald.

Kramer, Fritz W. 1987. *Der rote Fes: über Besessenheit und Kunst in Afrika.* Frankfurt am Main: Athenäum.

Kulischer, Josef. 1929. *Allgemeine Wirtschaftsgeschichte des Mittelalters und der Neuzeit, vol. 2: die Neuzeit*. München/Berlin: R. Oldenbourg.

Kumbirai, J. C. 1979. 'Shona Bible Translation: the work of the Revd. Michael Hannan', *Zambezia* 7, 61–74.

Kuper, Hilda. 1947. *The Uniform of Colour*. Johannesburg: Witwatersrand University Press.

Lakoff, George and Mark Johnson. 1980. *Metaphors We Live By*. Chicago: The University of Chicago Press.

Lambek, Michael. 1994. Review of F. Kramer *The Red Fez: art and spirit possession in Africa*, trans. M. R. Green. London/New York: Verso. *Man* (N. S.) 29 (3), 722–23.

Lan, David. 1985. *Guns and Rain: guerrillas & spirit mediums in Zimbabwe*. London: James Currey.

Lange, Dieter. 1979. *Eine Bewegung bricht sich Bahn: die deutschen Gemeinschaften im ausgehenden 19. und beginnenden 20. Jahrhundert und ihre Stellung zu Kirche, Theologie und Pfingstbewegung*. Giessen: Brunnen Verlag, Dillenburg: Gnadenauer Verlag.

Lattas, Andrew. 1993. 'Sorcery and colonialism: illness, dreams and death as political languages in west new Britain', *Man* (N. S.) 28 (1), 51–77.

Law, Robin. 1991. 'Religion, trade and politics on the "Slave Coast": Roman Catholic missions in Allada and Whydah in the seventeenth century', *Journal of Religion in Africa* 21 (1), 42–77.

Lawson, Rowena M. 1972. *The Changing Economy of the Lower Volta 1954–67: a study in the dynamics of rural economic growth*. London: Oxford University Press for the International African Institute.

Lee, S. G. 1969. 'Spirit possession among the Zulu', in J. Beattie and J. Middleton (eds), *Spirit Mediumship and Society in Africa*, pp. 128–56. London: Routledge & Kegan Paul.

Leferink, J. R. 1985. 'Independent Churches in Ghana', *Pro Mundi Vita: Dossiers* (1). *Africa Dossier* No. 32.

Lehmann, Hartmut. 1980. '"Absonderung" und "Gemeinschaft" im frühen Pietismus: Allgemeinhistorische und sozialgeschichtliche Überlegungen zur Entstehung und Entwicklung des Pietismus', *Pietismus und Neuzeit: ein Jahrbuch zur Geschichte des neueren Protestantismus*, vol. 4, pp. 54–82. Göttingen: Vandenhoek & Ruprecht.

——1989. 'Neupietismus und Säkularisierung: Beobachtungen zum sozialen Umfeld und politischen Hintergrund von Erweckungsbewegung und Gemeinschafts-bewegung', *Pietismus und Neuzeit: ein Jahrbuch zur Geschichte des neueren Protestantismus*, vol. 15, pp. 40–58. Göttingen: Vandenhoek & Ruprecht.

Lentz, Carola. 1994. 'Home, death and leadership: discourses of an educated elite from north-western Ghana', *Social Anthropology* 2 (2), 149–69.

Lewis, I. M. 1971. *Ecstatic Religion: an anthropological study of spirit possession and shamanism*. Harmondsworth: Penguin Books.

Lienhardt, G. 1982. 'The Dinka and Catholicism', in J. Davis (ed.), *Religious Organization and Religious Experience*. ASA Monograph 21, pp. 81–95. London: Academic Press.

Long, Norman. 1972. *Social Change and the Individual: a study of the social and religious responses to innovation in a Zambian rural community*. Manchester: Manchester University Press.

Luig, Ute. 1993. 'Besessenheitskulte als historische Charta: die Verarbeitung europäischer Einflüsse in sambianischen Besessenheitskulten', *Paideuma* 39, 343–54.

——1994. 'Constructing Local Worlds: spirit possession in the Gwembe Valley, Zambia'. Paper for the Tenth Satterthwaite Colloquium on African Ritual and Religion, 16–19 April 1994.

Luig, Ute and Heike Behrend. 1994. 'One or many modernities?' Unpublished manuscript.

Maccia, Frank. 1989. 'Spirituality and Social Liberation: the message of the Blumhardts in the light of Wuerttemberg Pietism, with implications for Pentecostal theology', Unpublished manuscript.

Maier, D. J. E. 1983. *Priests and Power: the case of the Dente shrine in nineteenth-century Ghana.* Bloomington: Indiana University Press.

Mamattah, Charles M. K. 1976. *History of the Eves. The Eves of West Africa. [Oral Traditions vol. 1). The Aŋlɔ-Eves and Their Immediate Neighbours.* Accra: Volta Research Publications, printed for publication by the Advent Press.

Mannheim, Bruce. 1991. 'After dreaming: image and interpretation in southern Peruvian Quechua', *Etnofoor* 4 (2), 43–79.

Manoukian, Madeline. 1952. *The Ewe-Speaking People of Togoland and the Gold Coast.* London: International Africa Institute.

Marshall, Ruth. 1991. 'Power in the name of Jesus', *Review of African Political Economy* 52, 21–38.

——1993. '"Power in the name of Jesus": social transformation and Pentecostalism in western Nigeria "revisited"', in T. Ranger and O. Vaughan (eds), *Legitimacy and the State in Twentieth Century Africa*, pp. 213–46. Basingstoke: Macmillan.

Marshall-Fratani, Ruth. 1998. 'Mediating the global and the local in Nigerian Pentecostalism', *Journal of Religion in Africa* 28 (3), 278–315.

Masquelier, Adeline. 1995. 'Consumption, prostitution, and reproduction: the poetics of sweetness in *Bori*', *American Ethnologist* 22 (4), 883–906.

Mauss, Marcel. 1990 [1925]. *The Gift: the form and reason for exchange in archaic societies*, trans. W. D. Halls. London: Routledge.

Maxwell, David. 1998. '"Delivered from the spirit of poverty?" Pentecostalism, prosperity and modernity in Zimbabwe', *Journal of Religion in Africa* 28 (3), 350–73.

Mbembe, Achille. 1992. 'Provisional notes on the postcolony', *Africa* 62 (1), 3–37.

Mbiti, John. 1979. 'The biblical basis for present trends in African theology', in K. Appiah-Kubi and S. Torres (eds), *African Theology en Route: papers from the Pan-African Conference of Third World Theologies, Dec 17–23, 1977, Accra, Ghana*, pp. 83–93. Maryknoll: Orbis Books.

McCaskie, T. C. 1981. 'Anti-witchcraft cults in Asante: an essay in the social history of an African people', *History in Africa* 8, 125–54.

Medeiros, Francois de (ed.). 1984a. *Peuples du Golfe du Bénin (Aja-Ewé).* Paris: Karthala.

Medeiros, Francois de. 1984b. 'Le couple aja-éwé en question, note sur l'historiographie contemporaine en Afrique de l'Ouest', in F. de Medeiros (ed.), *Peuples du Golfe du Bénin (Aja-Ewé)*, pp. 35–46. Paris: Karthala.

——1984c. 'Liminaire', in F. de Medeiros (ed.), *Peuples du Golfe du Bénin (Aja-Ewé)*, pp. 7–10. Paris: Karthala.

Medick, Hans. 1992. 'Buchkultur und lutherischer Pietismus. Buchbesitz, erbauliche Lektüre und religiöse Mentalität in einer ländlichen Gemeinde Württembergs am Ende der frühen Neuzeit: Laichingen 1748–1820', in R. Vierhaus und Mitarbeitern des Max-Planck-Instituts für Geschichte, *Frühe Neuzeit – Frühe Moderne? Forschungen zur Vielschichtigkeit von Übergangs-prozessen*, pp. 297–326. Göttingen.

Messadié, Gerald. 1993. *Histoire générale du Diable*. Paris: Éditions Robert Laffont.

Meyer, Birgit. 1989. '"Komm herüber und hilf uns" of hoe zendelingen de Ewe met andere ogen gingen bekijken (1847–1914)', *Etnofoor* 2 (2), 91–111.

——1992. '"If you are a devil you are a witch and, if you are a witch you are a devil." The integration of "pagan" ideas into the conceptual universe of Ewe Christians in southeastern Ghana', *The Journal of Religion in Africa* 22 (2), 98–132.

——1994. 'Beyond syncretism: translation and diabolization in the appropriation of Protestantism in Africa', in Ch. Stewart and R. Shaw (eds), *Syncretism/Anti-syncretism: the politics of religious synthesis*, pp. 45–67. London: Routledge.

——1995a. '"Delivered from the powers of darkness." Confessions about satanic riches in Christian Ghana', *Africa* 65 (2), 236–55.

——1995b. 'Magic, mermaids and modernity: the attraction of Pentecostalism in Africa', *Etnofoor* 8 (2), 47–67.

——1995c. 'Christianity and the rise of the Ewe nation: on the encounter between German Pietist missionaries and Ewe mission workers'. Paper presented at the International Conference 'Religion and Nationalism in Europe and Asia' at the Research Centre Religion and Society, Amsterdam 27–29 November 1995.

——1996. 'Modernity and enchantment: the image of the Devil in popular African Christianity', in P. van der Veer (ed.), *Conversion to Modernities: the globalization of Christianity*, pp. 199–230. London & New York: Routledge.

——1997. 'Christian mind and worldly matters: religion and materiality in nineteenth-century Gold Coast', *Journal of Material Culture* vol. 2 (3), 311–37.

——1998. '"Make a complete break with the past": memory and postcolonial modernity in Ghanaian Pentecostalist discourse', *Journal of Religion in Africa* 28 (3): 316–49.

——1999. 'Commodities and the Power of Prayer: Pentecostalist attitudes towards consumption in contemporary Ghana' in B. Meyer and P. Geschiere (eds) *Globalization and Identity: dialectics of flow and closure*, pp. 151–76. Oxford: Blackwell.

Michaëlis, Edgar. 1949. *Geisterreich und Geistesmacht: der Heilungs- und Dämonenkampf J. Chr. Blumhardts*. Bern: Verlag Paul Haupt.

Middleton, John. 1983. 'One hundred and fifty years of Christianity in a Ghanaian town', *Africa* 53 (3), 2–19.

Mobley, Harris W. 1970. *The Ghanaian's Image of the Missionary: an analysis of the published critiques of Christian missionaries by Ghanaians 1897–1965*. Leiden: E. J. Brill.

Mooser, Josef. 1989. 'Konventikel, Unterschichten und Pastoren', in J. Mooser et al. (eds), *Frommes Volk und Patrioten: Erweckungsbewegung & soziale Frage im östlichen Westfalen. 1800 bis 1900*, pp. 15–52. Bielefeld: Verlag für Regionalgeschichte.

Mudimbe, V. Y. 1988. *The Invention of Africa: gnosis, philosophy, and the order of knowledge*. Bloomington: Indiana University Press.

Müller, Gustav. 1904. *Geschichte der Ewe-Mission*. Bremen: Verlag der Norddeutschen Missions-Gesellschaft.

Müller-Salget, Klaus. 1984. *Erzählungen für das Volk: Evangelische Pfarrer als Volkschriftsteller im Deutschland des 19. Jahrhunderts*. Berlin: Erich Schmidt Verlag.

Mullings, Leith. 1984. *Therapy, Ideology, and Social Change: mental healing in urban Ghana*. Berkeley: University of California Press.

Murphree, Marshall. 1969. *Christianity and the Shona*. London: Athlone Press.

Narr, Dieter. 1957/58. 'Zur Stellung des Pietismus in der Volkskultur Württembergs', *Württembergisches Jahrbuch für Volkskunde*, 9–33.

Neill, Stephen. 1975. *A History of Christian Missions*. Harmondsworth: Penguin Books.

Nida, Eugene A. 1961. *Bible Translating: an analysis of principles and procedures, with special reference to aboriginal languages*. London: United Bible Societies.

Nida, Eugene A. and Charles R. Tabler. 1982. *The Theory and Practice of Translation*. Second photomechanical reprint. Leiden: E. J. Brill for the United Bible Societies.

Nimako, Kwame. 1991. *Economic Change and Political Conflict in Ghana 1600–1990*. Amsterdam: Thesis Publishers.

Nipperdey, Thomas. 1983. *Deutsche Geschichte 1800–1866: Bürgerwelt und starker Staat*. München: Beck.

—1991. *Deutsche Geschichte 1866–1918: Arbeitswelt und Bürgergeist*, vol. 1. München: Beck.

Nola, Alfonso di. 1990. *Der Teufel: Wesen, Wirkung, Geschichte*. Aus dem Italienischen von D. Türck-Wagner. München: Diederichs.

Norddeutsche Mission. 1935. *Kirchenordnung der Evangelischen Ewe-Kirche in Togo, West-Afrika*. Bremen: Verlag der Norddeutschen Missions-Gesellschaft.

Nugent, Paul. 1996. *Big Men, Small Boys and Politics in Ghana: power, ideology and the burden of history, 1982–1994*. Accra: Asempa Publishers.

Nukunya, G. K. 1969. *Kinship and Marriage Among the Anlo Ewe*. London: Athlone Press.

—1994. 'Insider anthropology: the case of the Anlo Ewe', *Etnofoor* 7 (1), 24–40.

Obeyesekere, Gananath. 1990. *The Work of Culture: symbolic transformation in psychoanalysis and anthropology*. Chicago: University of Chicago Press.

O'Grady, Joan. 1989. *The Prince of Darkness: the Devil in history, religion and the human psyche*. Longmead, Shafsbury, Dorset: Element Books.

Oman, D. J. 1927. *Report on the Direction of the former Bremen Mission of the Government of the Gold Coast from June, 1916 to March, 1926*. Ordered by his Excellency the Governor to be printed. Gold Coast, Accra: Government Printer.

Oosthuizen, G. C.1968. *Post-Christianity in Africa: a theological and anthropological study*. London: C. Hurst & Company.

—1972. *Theological Battleground in Asia and Africa: the issues facing the churches and the efforts to overcome western divisions*. London: C. Hurst & Company.

Opoku, Kofi A. 1978. 'Changes Within Christianity: the case of the Musama Disco Kristo Church', in E. Fasholé-Luke et al. (eds), *Christianity in Independent Africa*, pp. 110–21. London: Rex Collings.

Overing, Joanna. 1987. 'Translation as a creative process: the power of the name', in L. Holy (ed.), *Comparative Anthropology*, pp. 70–87. Oxford: Basil Blackwell.

Parkin, David (ed.). 1989. *The Anthropology of Evil*. Oxford: Basil Blackwell.

Parrinder, E. G. 1950. 'Theistic beliefs of the Yoruba and Ewe peoples of West Africa', in E. W. Smith (ed.), *African Ideas about God: a symposium*, pp. 224–40. London: Edinburgh House Press.

Parsons, R. T. 1963. *The Churches and Ghana Society, 1918–1955: a survey of the work of three Protestant mission societies and the African churches which they established in their assistance to society development*. Leiden: E. J. Brill.

Pazzi, Roberto. 1980. 'L'homme et son univers Evé, Aja, Gɛn, Fɔn: Dictionnaire'. Lomé: unpublished manuscript.

Peel, J. D. Y. 1968. 'Syncretism and religious change', *Comparative Studies in Society and History* 10, 121–41.

—1978. 'The Christianization of African Society: some possible models', in E. Fasholé-Luke et al. (eds), *Christianity in Independent Africa*, pp. 443–54. London: Rex Collings.

——1990. 'The Pastor and the *Babalawo*: the interaction of religions in nineteenth-century Yorubaland', *Africa* 60 (3), 338–69.

——1994. 'Historicity and pluralism in some recent studies of Yoruba religion', review article, *Africa* 64 (1), 150–66.

Pels, Peter. 1992. 'Mumiani: the White Vampire. A neo-diffusionist analysis of rumour', *Etnofoor* 5 (1/2), 165–87.

——1993. *Critical Matters: interactions between missionaries and Waluguru in colonial Tanganyika, 1930–1961*. Amsterdam: Amsterdam School of Social Research.

Pfister, Friedrich. 1924. *Schwäbische Volksbräuche*. Augsburg: Dr. Benno Filser Verlag.

Pina-Cabral, João de. 1992. 'The gods of the gentiles are demons: the problem of pagan survivals in European culture', in K. Hastrup (ed.), *Other Histories*, pp. 45–61. London: Routledge.

Pirouet, M. Louise. 1978. *Black Evangelists: the spread of Christianity in Uganda, 1891–1914*. London: Rex Collings.

Pool, Robert. 1994. *Dialogue and the Interpretation of Illness: conversations in a Cameroon village*. Oxford: Berg.

Probst, Peter. 1989. 'The letter and the spirit: literacy and religious authority in the history of the Aladura Movement in western Nigeria', *Africa* 59 (4), 478–95.

Quilligan, Maureen. 1979. *The Language of Allegory: defining the genre*. Ithaca and London: Cornell University Press.

Rafael, V. L. 1988. *Contracting Colonialism: translation and Christian conversion in Tagalog society under early Spanish rule*. Ithaca: Cornell University Press.

Ranger, Terence. 1978. 'The churches, the nationalist state and African religion', in E. Fasholé-Luke et al. (eds), *Christianity in Independent Africa*, pp. 479–502. London: Rex Collings.

——1987. 'An Africanist comment', *American Ethnologist* 14, 182–5.

——1989. 'Missionaries, migrants and the Manyika: the invention of ethnicity in Zimbabwe', in L. Vail (ed.), *The Creation of Tribalism in Africa*, pp. 118–50. London: James Currey, Berkeley and Los Angeles: University of California Press.

——1993. 'The local and the global in Southern African religious history', in R. W. Hefner (ed.), *Conversion to Christianity: historical and anthropological perspectives on a great transformation*, pp. 65–98. Berkeley and Los Angeles: University of California Press.

Rattray, R. S. 1927. *Religion and Art in Ashanti*. Oxford: Clarendon Press.

Rieber, Calvin. 1979. 'Christianity as an African religion', in N. S. Booth (ed.), *African Religions*, pp. 255–74. New York: NOK Publishers International.

Rivière, Claude. 1980. 'Les réprésentations de l'homme chez les Evé du Togo', *Anthropos* 75, 8–24.

——1981. *Anthropologie religieuse des Evé du Togo*. Lomé: Les Nouvelles Éditions Africaines.

Robertson, Robert. 1992. *Globalization: social theory and global culture*. London: Sage.

Roelofs, Gerard. 1994. 'Charismatic Christian thought: experience, metonomy, and routinization', in K. Poewe (ed.), *Charismatic Christianity as a Global Culture*, pp. 217–33. Columbia (S. C.): University of South Carolina Press.

Röhrich, Lutz. 1970. 'German devil tales and devil legends', *Journal of the Folklore Institute* 7, 21–35.

Rooijakkers, Gerard. 1993. 'De brede en de smalle weg. Vermaak en zaligheid in Noord-Brabant: een problematisch duo', in J. A. F. M. van Oudsheusden et al. (eds), *Ziel en zaligheid in Noord-Brabant*, pp. 18–39. Delft: Eburon.

Rooijakkers, Gerard, Lène Dresen-Coenders and Margreet Geerdes (eds). 1994. *Duivelsbeelden: een cultuurhistorische speurtocht door de Lage Landen*. Baarn: Ambo.

Roskoff, Gustav. 1987 [1869]. *Die Geschichte des Teufels: eine kulturhistorische Satanologie von den Anfängen bis ins 18. Jahrhundert.* Unveränderter Wiederabdruck der Erstausgabe von 1869. Nördlingen: Greno.

Rowlands, M., and J. -P. Warnier. 1988. 'Sorcery, power and the modern state in Cameroon', *Man* 23, 118–32.

Ruhbach, Gerhard. 1989. 'Der Erweckung von 1905 und die Anfänge der Pfingstbewegung', *Pietismus und Neuzeit: ein Jahrbuch zur Geschichte des neueren Protestantismus, vol. 15: Die Gemeinschaftsbewegung,* pp. 84–94. Göttingen: Vandenhoek & Ruprecht.

Russell, Jeffrey Burton. 1986. *Mephistophele: the Devil in the modern world.* Ithaca: Cornell University Press.

——1987. *Satan: the early Christian tradition.* Ithaca: Cornell University Press.

——1988a. *The Devil: perceptions of evil from antiquity to primitive Christianity.* Ithaca: Cornell University Press.

——1988b. *Lucifer: the Devil in the Middle Ages.* Ithaca: Cornell University Press.

——1989. *The Prince of Darkness: radical evil and the power of good in history.* London: Thames and Hudson.

Ryan, P. J. 1980. '"Arise, o God!" The problem of "gods" in West Africa', *Journal of Religion in Africa* 11 (3), 161–71.

Sanneh, Lamin. 1983. *West African Christianity: the religious impact.* London: C. Hurst & Company.

——1991. *Translating the Message: the missionary impact on culture.* Maryknoll: Orbis Books.

Schäferjohann-Bursian, Iris. 1989. 'Bibeln, Gesangbücher und Traktate: die Produktion und Verbreitung von Erbauungsliteratur im Rahmen der Erweckungsbewegung', in J. Mooser et al. (eds), *Frommes Volk und Patrioten: Erweckungsbewegung & soziale Frage im östlichen Westfalen. 1800 bis 1900,* pp. 259–85. Bielefeld: Verlag für Regionalgeschichte.

Scharfe, Martin. 1980. *Die Religion des Volkes: kleine Kultur- und Sozialgeschichte des Pietismus.* Gütersloh: Gütersloher Verlag.

——1990. 'Zwei-Wege-Bilder: Volkskundliche Aspekte evangelischer Bilderfrömmigkeit', *Blätter für württembergische Kirchengeschichte* 90, 123–44.

Schlegel, J. B. 1857. *Schlüssel zur Ewe-Sprache. Dargeboten in den grammatischen Grundzügen des Anlo-Dialekts derselben, mit Wörtersammlung, nebst einer Sammlung von Sprichwörtern und einigen Fabeln der Eingeborenen.* Bremen: W. Valett Co.

Schleiermacher, Friedrich. 1861. *Der christliche Glaube nach den Grundsätzen der evangelischen Kirche.* Fünfte unveränderte Ausgabe, vol. 1. Berlin: Georg Reimer.

Schlunk, D. Martin. 1936. *Die Geschichte der Norddeutschen Mission im Lichte der Bibel.* Bremen: Verlag der Norddeutschen Missions-Gesellschaft.

Schneider, Jane. 1990. 'Spirits and the spirit of capitalism', in E. Badone (ed.), *Religious Orthodoxy and Popular Faith in European Society,* pp. 24–53. Princeton: Princeton University Press.

Schoenaker, H. and A. Trouwborst. 1983. 'Het godsbegrip in de etnografische berichtgeving van de missie en zending in Oost-Afrika', in J. M. Schoffeleers et al. (eds), *Missie en ontwikkeling in Oost-Afrika: een ontmoeting van culturen,* pp. 24–39. Nijmegen: Ambo.

Schoffeleers, Matthew. 1985. *Pentecostalism and Neo-Traditionalism: the religious polarization of a rural district in southern Malawi.* Amsterdam: Free University Press.

——1991. 'Ritual healing and political acquiescence: the case of Zionist churches in Southern Africa', *Africa* 61 (1), 1–25.

——1994a. 'The Theological Construction and Deconstruction of Africa in Mainstream Christian Churches, 1850–1990'. Paper presented at the International Symposium on Conversion, University of Amsterdam, 13–15 June 1994.

——1994b. *River of Blood: the genesis of a martyr cult in southern Malawi, c. A.D. 1600.* Madison: University of Wisconsin Press.

Schönhuth, Michael. 1992. *Das Einsetzen der Nacht in die Rechte des Tages. Hexerei im symbolischen Kontext afrikanischer und europäischer Weltbilder.* Ethnologische Studien, vol. 20. Münster/Hamburg: LIT Verlag.

Schreiber, D. A. W. (ed.). 1936. *Bausteine zur Geschichte der Norddeutschen Missionsgesellschaft: Gesammelt zur Hundertjahrfeier.* Bremen: Verlag der Norddeutschen Mission.

——1937. *Ein Wort zur Kritik Missionar Dr. Dr. jur. Gutmanns an der Kirchenordnung der Evangelischen Ewe-Kirche in Togo (West-Afrika).* Bremen: Verlag der Norddeutschen Missions-Gesellschaft.

Schulz, Michael T. 1984. *Johann Christoph Blumhardt: Leben-Theologie-Verkündigung.* Göttingen: Vandenhoek & Ruprecht.

Selge, Kurt Victor. 1993 . 'Luther und die Macht des Bösen', in C. Colpe & W. Schmidt-Biggemann (eds), *Das Böse: eine historische Phänomenologie des Unerklärlichen,* pp. 165–86. Frankfurt am Main: Suhrkamp.

Seur, Han. 1992. 'Sowing the Good Seed: the interweaving of agricultural change, gender relations and religion in Serenje District, Zambia'. Landbouwuniversiteit Wageningen: Ph.D. thesis.

Shaw, Rosalind. 1996. 'The politician and the diviner: divination and the consumption of power in Sierra Leone', *Journal of Religion in Africa* 26 (1), 30–55.

Shorter, A. 1973. *African Culture and the Christian Church.* London: G. Chapman.

Smith, E. W. (ed.). 1950. *African Ideas about God: a symposium.* London: Edinburgh House Press.

Smith, Noel. 1966. *The Presbyterian Church of Ghana. 1835–1960.* Accra: Ghana Universities Press.

Spieth, Jacob. 1903a. *Die Entwicklung der evangelischen Christengemeinde im Ewe-Lande.* Bremen: Verlag der Norddeutschen Missions-Gesellschaft.

——1903b. *Das Sühnebedürfnis der Heiden im Ewelande.* Bremen: Verlag der Norddeutschen Missionsgesellschaft.

——1906. *Die Ewe-Stämme: Material zur Kunde des Ewe-Volkes in Deutsch-Togo.* Berlin: Dietrich Reimer.

——1907. *Die Übersetzung der Bibel in die Sprache eines westafrikanischen Naturvolkes.* Bremen: Norddeutsche Missions-Gesellschaft.

——1908. *Wie kommt die Bekehrung eines Heiden zustande?* Bremen: Verlag der Norddeutschen Missionsgesellschaft.

——1911. *Die Religion der Eweer in Süd-Togo.* Leipzig: Dietersche Verlagsbuchhandlung.

Stearns, Peter N. 1967. *European Society in Upheaval: social history since 1800.* London: The Macmillan Company.

Stewart, Charles. 1991. *Demons and the Devil: moral imagination in modern Greek culture.* Princeton: Princeton University Press.

Stine, P. C. (ed.). 1990. *Bible Translation and the Spread of the Church: the last 200 years.* Leiden: E. J. Brill.

Stipe, C. E. 1980. 'Anthropologists versus missionaries: the influence of presuppositions', *Current Anthropology* 21, 165–79.

Strümpfel, Emil. 1902. *Was jedermann heute von der Mission wissen muss.* Berlin: Verlag von Martin Warneck.

Sundkler, B. 1961. *Bantu Prophets in South Africa* [2nd edn]. London: Oxford University Press for the International African Institute.

Tanner, R. E. S. 1978. 'Word and spirit in contemporary African religious practice and thought: some issues raised by translation into Swahili', *Journal of Religion in Africa* 9 (2), 123–35.

Taussig, Michael T. 1980. *The Devil and Commodity Fetishism in South America*. Chapel Hill: The University of North Carolina Press.

Tavard, Georges. 1981. 'Dämonen: Kirchengeschichtlich', in G. Krause and G. Müller (eds), *Theologische Realenzyklopedie*, vol. 7, pp. 286–300. Berlin, New York: Walter de Gruyter.

Tawia, Edmund Y. 1947. *The Growth of the Ewe Presbyterian Church in Peki: the Peki centenary booklet, 1847–1947*. Accra: Lona Printing Works.

Taylor, J. V. 1963. *The Primal Vision: Christian presence amid African religion*. London: SCM Press.

Tell, Birgit and Uwe Heinrich. 1986. 'Mission und Handel im missionarischen Selbstverständnis und in der konkreten Praxis', in W. Ustorf (ed.), *Mission im Kontext: Beiträge zur Sozialgeschichte der Norddeutschen Missionsgesellschaft im 19. Jahrhundert*, pp. 257–92. Bremen: Übersee-Museum.

Ter Haar, Gerrie. 1992. *Spirit of Africa: the healing ministry of Archbishop Milingo of Zambia*. Trenton: Africa World Press.

Thoden van Velzen, H. U. E. 1988. 'Puritan movements in Suriname and Tanzania', in W. E. A. van Beek (ed.), *The Quest for Purity: dynamics of Puritan Movements*, pp. 217–44. Berlin, New York, Amsterdam: Mouton de Gruyter.

——1990. 'Social fetishism among the Surinamese Maroons', *Etnofoor* 3 (1), 77–95.

——1995. 'Revenants that cannot be shaken: collective fantasies in a Maroon Society', *American Anthropologist* 97 (4), 722–32.

Thoden van Velzen, H. U. E. and W. Van Wetering. 1988. *The Great Father and the Danger: religious cults, material forces, and collective fantasies in the world of the Surinamese Maroons*. Dordrecht: Foris Publications.

——1989. Demonologie en de betovering van het moderne leven', *Sociologische Gids* 36, 155–86.

Tourraine, Alain. 1995. *Critique of Modernity*, trans. D. Macey. Oxford (UK), Cambridge (USA): Blackwell.

Tossou, Kossi J. 1988. *Vom Geist der Sprache. Bewahrung und Umwandlung bei Übersetzungen. Griechisch-Ewe Metamorphosen am Beispiel der Ewe-Bibelübersetzung*. Münster: Nodus Publikationen.

Twumasi, Patrick. 1979. 'A social history of the Ghanaian pluralistic medical system', *Social Science and Medicine* 13B (4), 349–56.

Ustorf, Werner (ed.). 1986a. 'Einleitung', in W. Ustorf (ed.), *Mission im Kontext: Beiträge zur Sozialgeschichte der Norddeutschen Missionsgesellschaft im 19. Jahrhundert*, pp. 2–16. Bremen: Übersee-Museum.

Ustorf, Werner. 1986b. 'Norddeutsche Mission und Wirklichkeitsbewältigung: Bremen, Afrika und der "Sclavenfreikauf"', in W. Ustorf (ed.), *Mission im Kontex: Beiträge zur Sozialgeschichte der Norddeutschen Missionsgesellschaft im 19. Jahrhundert*, pp. 121–236. Bremen: Übersee-Museum.

Van Binsbergen, Wim. 1979. *Religious Change in Zambia: exploratory studies*. Haarlem: In de Knipscheer.

——1993. 'African Independent Churches and the State in Botswana', in M. Bax and A. Koster (eds), *Power and Prayer: religious and political processes in past and present*, pp. 24–56. Amsterdam: VU University Press.

Van der Veer, Peter. 1996. 'Introduction', in P. van der Veer (ed.), *Conversion to Modernities: the globalization of Christianity*, pp. 1–21. Routledge: New York & London.

Van Dijk, Rijk. 1992. *Young Malawian Puritans: young Puritan preachers in a present-day African urban environment.* Utrecht: ISOR.

——1997. 'From camp to encompassment: discourses of transsubjectivity in the Ghanaian Pentecostal diaspora', *Journal of Religion in Africa* 27 (2), 135–60.

Van Rooden, Peter. 1990. 'The concept of an International Revival Movement around 1800', *Pietismus und Neuzeit: ein Jahrbuch zur Geschichte des neueren Protestantismus,* vol. 16, pp. 155–72.

——1996. 'Nineteenth-century representations of missionary conversion and the transformation of Western Christianity', in P. van der Veer (ed.), *Conversion to Modernities: the globalization of Christianity,* pp. 65–87. Routledge: New York & London.

Van Santen, Jose C. M. 1993. *They Leave Their Jars Behind: the conversion of Mafa women to Islam (North Cameroon).* Leiden: VENA.

Van Wetering, Wilhelmina. 1992. 'A demon in every transistor', *Etnofoor* 5 (1/2), 109–27.

Venuti, Lawrence (ed.). 1992. *Rethinking Translation*: Discourse. Subjectivity. Ideology. London and New York: Routledge.

Verdon, Michel. 1979. 'The structure of titled offices among the Abutia Ewe', *Africa* 49 (2), 159–171.

——1982. 'Divorce in Abutia', *Africa* 52 (4), 48–65.

——1983. *The Abutia Ewe of West Africa.* Berlin: Mouton.

Verrips, Jojada. 1992. 'Over Vampiers en Virussen: Enige reflecties over de antropomorfisering van Kwaad', *Etnofoor* 5 (1/2), 21–43.

——1993. 'Op weg naar een antropologie van het wilde westen', *Etnofoor* 6 (2), 5–19.

Vogelsanger, Renate. 1977. *Pietismus und afrikanische Kultur an der Goldküste: die Einstellung der Basler Mission zur Haussklaverei.* Zürich: A. Wohlgemut.

Vogt, Carl. 1913. 'Teufel', in F. M. Schiele & L. Zscharnack (eds), *Die Religion in Geschichte und Gegenwart: Handwörterbuch für Theologie und Religions-wissenschaft,* vol. 5, pp. 1,151–57. Tübingen: J. C. B. Mohr.

Wagner, Werner-Harald. 1930. *Teufel und Gott in der deutschen Volkssage: ein Beitrag zur strukturellen Erforschung der primitiven Gemeinschaftsreligion.* Greifswald: Hans Adler.

Waldman, Marilyn Robinson, Olabiyi Rabalola Yai and Lamin Sanneh. 1992. 'Translatability: a discussion', *Journal of Religion in Africa* 22 (2), 159–72.

Wallace, Anthony F. C. 1956. 'Revitalization movements', *American Anthropologist* 58 (2), 264–82.

Wallmann, Johannes. 1990. *Der Pietismus. [Die Kirche in ihrer Geschichte. Ein Handbuch.* vol. 4]. Göttingen: Vandenhoek & Ruprecht.

Ward, Barbara. 1949. 'The Social Organisation of the Ewe-speaking People'. University of London: unpublished MA thesis.

——1956. 'Some observations on religious cults in Ashanti', *Africa* 26 (1), 41–61.

Warneck, Joh. 1913. *Die Lebenskräfte des Evangeliums: Missionserfahrungen innerhalb des animistischen Heidentums.* Berlin: Verlag von Martin Warneck.

Weber, Max. 1978 [1922]. *Economy and Society: an outline of interpretive sociology,* vol. 1. Edited by G. Roth and C. Wittich. Berkeley: University of California Press.

——1984 [1920]. *Die protestantische Ethik 1: eine Aufsatzsammlung.* Herausgegeben von Johannes Winckelmann. Gütersloh: Gütersloher Verlagshaus.

——1985 [1922]. *Wirtschaft und Gesellschaft: Grundriss der verstehenden Soziologie.* Fünfte revidierte Auflage, besorgt von Johannes Winckelmann. Studien-ausgabe. Tübingen: J. C. B. Mohr.

Weich, F. 1977. 'De Vertaling van Markus in !XU', in A. Traill (ed.), *Khoisan*

*Linguistic Studies* 3, pp. 63–74. Johannesburg: African Studies Institute, University of Witwatersrand.

Welbourne, F. B. 1969. 'Spirit inspiration in Ankole and a Christian spirit movement in Western Kenya', in J. Beattie and J. Middleton (eds), *Spirit Mediumship and Society in Africa*, pp. 290–306. London: Routledge & Kegan Paul.

Welman, C. W. 1925. *The Native States of the Gold Coast: history and constitution. I. Peki.* (Compiled from Materials in the Native Affairs Department at Accra.) Accra: Scottish Mission Book Depot, Printing Department.

Wendl, Tobias. 1991. *Mami Wata oder ein Kult zwischen den Kulturen.* Münster: Lit Verlag.

Werbner, Richard P. 1977. *Regional Cults.* London: Academic Press.

Westermann, Diedrich. 1905a . *Wörterbuch der Ewe-Sprache. I. Teil. Ewe-Deutsches Wörterbuch.* Berlin: Dietrich Reimer.

——1905b . 'Über die Begriffe Seele, Geist, Schicksal bei dem Ewe und Tschivolk', *Archiv für Religionswissenschaft* 8', 104–13.

——1906. *Wörterbuch der Ewe-Sprache. II. Deutsch-Ewe.* Berlin: Dietrich Reimer.

——1907. *Grammatik der Ewe-Sprache.* Berlin: Dietrich Reimer.

——1935. *Die Glidyi Ewe in Togo.* Berlin: De Gruyter.

——1936. *Volkwerdung und Evangelium unter den Ewe.* Bremen: Verlag der Norddeutschen Missionsgesellschaft.

——1952. *Afrikaner erzählen ihr Leben.* Berlin: Evangelische Verlagsanstalt.

White, Luise. 1993. 'Cars out of place: vampires, technology, and labour in East and Central Africa', *Representations* 43 (Summer), 27–50.

Wiarda, Diddo. 1936. 'Mission und Konfession: die konfessionelle Frage in der Anfangszeit der Norddeutschen Missionsgesellschaft', in A. W. Schreiber (ed.), *Bausteine zur Geschichte der Norddeutschen Missionsgesellschaft*, pp. 135–52. Bremen: Verlag der Norddeutschen Mission.

Wiegräbe, Paul. 1989. 'Zur Geschichte des Ewe-Gesangbuches'. Unpublished manuscript.

Wilks, Ivor. 1975. *Asante in the Nineteenth Century: the structure and evolution of a political order.* London: Cambridge University Press.

Wright, Marcia. 1971. *German Missions in Tanganyika 1891–1941: Lutherans and Moravians in the southern Highlands.* Oxford: Clarendon Press.

Wyllie, R. W. 1973. 'Introspective witchcraft among the Effutu of southern Ghana', *Man* 8 (1), 74–9.

Zahn, Franz Michael. 1895. 'Die Muttersprache in der Mission', *Allgemeine Missionszeitschrift*, 337–60.

Zielnica, Krzysztof. 1976. *Bibliographie der Ewe in Westafrika. Bibliographie Evhé (Ewé) en Afrique Occidentale. Bibliography of the Ewe in West Africa.* Acta Ethnologica et Linguistica 38, Series Africana 11. Wien: Institut für Völkerkunde der Universität Wien.

Zizek, Slavoj. 1994. *The Metastases of Enjoyment: six essays on woman and causality.* London: Verso.

Zündel, Friedrich. 1979. *Johann Christoph Blumhardt: Siegesmacht Jesu über Krankheit und Dämonie.* Bearbeitet von H. Schneider. 19. Auflage. Giessen und Basel: Brunnen Verlag.

## ARCHIVAL SOURCES

### Norddeutsche Missionsgesellschaft

Archiv der Norddeutschen Mission, Depositum des Staatsarchivs Bremen, Stab 7, 1025

Mittheilungen (MB) and Monatsblatt (MT) der Norddeutschen Mission, respectively
   Hamburg 1840ff/Bremen 1851ff

**Public Record Office, London**
Colonial Yearbooks on Ghana (CO–98–1ff)

**National Archives of Ghana**
ADM 11/1 files (Eastern Region)
ADM 5/2 files (Population)

**Evangelical Presbyterian Church**
Synod reports. Ho: E. P. Church Press (sporadically present in the EPC headquarters
   at Ho since the 1970s)
Evangelical Presbyterian Church: membership certificate. Ho: E. P. Church Press
Konfirmatiogbale na Kristohame le Evenyigba dzi. Tata Wuiedekelia. Ho: E. P.
   Church Book Depot, 1966
Hadzigbale na Eve-Kristo-Hame. Agbaletata Wuievelia. Ho: E. P. Church Press,
   1985
*Nyanyuie Hame le Ghana kple Togo fe Hamedodo.* Ho: E. P. Church Press, 1980
Blengo Evangelical Church Station Chronicle (Blengo congregation)

**The Lord's Pentecostal Church – Agbelengor**
Brief History of the Lord's Pentecostal Church. n.d.
Constitution, Concept

# INDEX